Shanghai University

上海大学

本书编委会 编

上海大学出版社

·上海·

Shanghai University Press

Shanghai

主　　　编　　成旦红　刘昌胜

执 行 主 编　　段　勇

执行副主编　　曾文彪　卢志国

执 行 编 辑　　纪慧梅　洪佳惠

英 文 翻 译　　曾桂娥　朱音尔　张　颖

封面上的"上海大学"是江泽民题写的校名，封底上的"上海大学"是钱伟长题写的校名，书脊上的"上海大学"是于右任题写的校名

"上海大学" on the cover is calligraphed by Jiang Zemin, that on the back cover calligraphed by Qian Weichang, and that on the spine calligraphed by Yu Youren.

本书编委会

主　　　任　　成旦红　刘昌胜

常务副主任　　段　勇

副　主　任　　周建军　胡大伟　聂　清　王从春　于雪梅
　　　　　　　张建华　苟燕楠　罗宏杰　忻　平

委　　　员　　（按姓氏笔画为序）

　　　　　　　王远弟　王国建　卢志国　朱明原　刘长林　刘绍学
　　　　　　　刘旭光　许华虎　孙伟平　李　坚　李明斌　杨　铿
　　　　　　　吴英俊　吴　铭　余　洋　沈　艺　张元隆　张勇安
　　　　　　　张基涛　陆　瑾　陆甦颖　陈志宏　陈　然　竺　剑
　　　　　　　金　波　孟祥栋　胡申生　秦凯丰　顾　莹　徐有威
　　　　　　　徐国明　陶飞亚　曹为民　彭章友　傅玉芳　曾文彪
　　　　　　　曾　军　褚贵忠　谢为群　潘守永　戴骏豪　魏　宏

Shanghai University

序　言

　　上海大学是由中国共产党主导创办并实际领导的第一所正规大学。

　　学校自20世纪20年代初露峥嵘，历经百年风雨，始终与国家和民族的命运紧密相连，如今是教育部与上海市人民政府共建高校、国家"双一流"建设高校。

　　建校时期，青云发轫。1922年，上海大学在国共两党的携手共创下应时而生。学校以"养成建国人才，促进文化事业"为宗旨，得到了孙中山、陈独秀、毛泽东等国共两党领导人的悉心关怀。于右任执掌校印，李大钊、瞿秋白、邓中夏、蔡和森、张太雷等名师汇聚于此，王稼祥、秦邦宪、杨尚昆、李硕勋等英才求学于此。彼时的上海大学，有着"文有上大，武有黄埔""北有五四时期的北大，南有五卅时期的上大"之盛誉。

　　奠基时期，育才造士。新中国成立后，上海科学技术大学、上海科技高等专科学校、上海工业大学三校继起，自力更生，艰苦奋斗，为国家和上海培养了大批适应"高精尖"工业发展需要的科学研究和工程技术人才。

　　再造时期，弦歌不辍。1983年，上海市人民政府复办上海大学，学校励志继承20世纪20年代上海大学的光荣传统。杨尚昆、俞平伯、阳翰笙、匡亚明等校友们纷纷致贺，祝贺母校"复校""重光"。巍巍学府焕发新颜，华章再起。

　　复兴时期，跨越发展。1994年，上海工业大学、上海科学技术大学、上海大学和上海科技高等专科学校合并组建为上海大学。时任中共中央总书记、国家主席、中央军委主席江泽民同志题写校名，著名科学家、教育家、社会活动家钱伟长院士担任校长。钱伟长独树一帜的教育理念和治校方略开创了学校思想解放和学术繁荣的新局面，推进了学校各项事业的新发展。学校植根上海，发挥综合优势，综合实力和核心竞争力显著提升，进入国家"211工程"重点建设高校，迈入研究型大学行列。

赶超时期，争创一流。步入 21 世纪，上海大学秉承传统，开拓创新。学校获批上海市首批高水平地方大学建设高校，入选国家"双一流"建设高校。学校扎实推进高等教育综合改革，积极打造学科高峰和创新高地；积极实施人才强校战略，初步形成了层次更为清晰、结构更趋合理、具有国际化程度、适应学校发展需要的师资队伍，并已形成了若干有特色、有影响、有潜力的学科团队。在传承以学生为中心的"学分制、选课制、三学期制"人才培养模式基础上，学校推进全程导师制、书院制协同育人模式，推动价值塑造、能力培养、知识传授"三位一体"的育人理念走深走实。学校服务国家战略，布局国家与省部级基地，学术研究成果丰硕。学校矢志科技自立自强，加强科技成果转化，助力长三角一体化发展；在哲学社会科学领域实现跨越式发展，社会影响力显著。在"五五战略"的引领下，微电子、人工智能、生物医药、新能源、量子科技等"五朵金花"竞相绽放，城市社会治理、考古与文保、新海派文化、艺术技术、数字经济与管理等"五大高地"陆续崛起。学校深入推进国际化战略，赋能世界一流大学建设，始终走在我国高等教育对外开放的前列。当前，学校正以高等教育综合改革试点为契机，奋力争当上海高等教育的"领头羊"。

百年上大，薪火相传。上海大学秉持"自强不息，道济天下"的校训，践行"先天下之忧而忧，后天下之乐而乐"的价值追求，弘扬"上善若水，海纳百川，大道明德，学用济世"的大学精神。以"养成强国济世人才，促进社会文明进步"为使命，上海大学将在世界大学之林中留下独特印记，彰显上大特质，为建成世界一流、特色鲜明的综合性研究型大学而奋斗。

Foreword

Shanghai University is the first formal university initiated and led by the Communist Party of China.

Since its founding in 1922, the university has remained closely tied to the growth of the nation. Supported by leaders such as Sun Yat-sen, Chen Duxiu and Mao Zedong, and shaped by revolutionary thinkers like Li Dazhao and Qu Qiubai, early Shanghai University became a cradle of progressive thoughts and revolutionary actions. Many of its faculty and students devoted themselves to national liberation, earning the university the reputation of being the cultural counterpart to Huangpu Military Academy.

Following the founding of the People's Republic of China, Shanghai's higher education landscape was restructured. Out of this transformation emerged Shanghai University of Science and Technology, Shanghai College of Science and Technology, and Shanghai University of Technology—institutions that laid the academic foundation for the city's rise in science and industry. In 1983, Shanghai University was reestablished with the municipal support, reviving its original spirit and launching a new chapter of innovation and reform.

A defining moment came in 1994, when today's Shanghai University was officially formed through the merger of the three aforementioned institutions with the reestablished Shanghai University. With its name inscribed by Jiang Zemin and guided by the visionary leadership of Qian Weichang, the university advanced rapidly under the "Project 211", optimizing its academic structure and achieving excellence in research and education.

Now a key player in China's "Double First-Class" initiative, Shanghai University continues to pursue both breadth and depth. Committed to reform and innovation, it has built dynamic faculty teams and developed distinctive disciplinary clusters with growing global influences. The university adopts a student-centered approach supported by comprehensive mentoring and residential college communities. This holistic model integrates values, competence and knowledge to foster well-rounded, forward-looking graduates. At the same time, the university is advancing its "Five-Five Strategy"—driving innovation in five strategic science and technology fields: microelectronics, artificial intelligence, biomedicine, new energyand quantum technology; while also deepening leadership in five key humanities and social science areas, namely urban governance, archaeology and cultural heritage, contemporary Shanghai-style culture, art and technology, and digital economics.

Looking ahead, Shanghai University enters its second century with renewed goals and missions. Guided by its motto, "strive for self-perfection, serve thecommunity", and driven by the core value of "being the first to share the world's woes and the last to rejoice in its weal", the university embraces a spirit of community, inclusion, integrityand service. With a mission to educate aspiring leaders to serve the nation and the world, Shanghai University is forging a distinctive global identity. Drawing strength from its cultural roots and historical legacy, it will continue to shape minds with vision and responsibility—striving toward its goal of becoming a world-class comprehensive research university with a unique identity.

上海大学精神谱系

使命：养成强国济世人才，促进社会文明进步

愿景：建成世界一流、特色鲜明的综合性研究型大学

人才培养目标：培养全面发展的卓越创新人才，造就担当民族复兴大任的时代栋梁

校训：自强不息，道济天下

校风：知行合一，追求卓越

学风：严谨、勤奋、求实、创新

价值追求：先天下之忧而忧，后天下之乐而乐

大学精神：上善若水，海纳百川，大道明德，学用济世

About Shanghai University

Mission: To educate aspiring leaders to serve the nation and the world

Vision: To become a world-class comprehensive research university with a unique identity

Talent Development Goals: To nurture outstanding talents with an innovative spirit and citizen responsibilities

Motto: Strive for self-perfection, serve the community

Ethos: Unity of knowledge and action, pursuit of excellence

Academic traditions: Rigorousness, diligence, practicality and creativity

Core Value: Being the first to share the world's woes and the last to rejoice in its weal

Spirit: Community, inclusion, integrity and service

Shanghai University

目 录
CONTENTS

上海大学精神谱系
About Shanghai University

第一部分　风云际会　青云发轫 / 1
Part I　Revolution and Foundation

一、国共精英　共建上大 / 3
　　Cooperation and Construction

二、教学演讲　名师云集 / 29
　　Outstanding Professors and Renowned Orators

三、人才培养　济济一堂 / 43
　　Excellent Talent Cultivation

四、革命堡垒　红色学府 / 47
　　Revolutionary Stronghold and Red Academy

五、文有上大　武有黄埔 / 85
　　SHU, as Prestigious as HMA

六、五四北大　五卅上大 / 93
　　SHU, as Revolutionary as PKU

七、追认学籍　筹划复校　/　102
Recognition of Student Status and Re-operation of SHU

八、知名校友　映照前路　/　107
Notable Alumni

第二部分　海纳百川　奠基再造　/　121
Part II　Integration and Reconstruction

一、上海工业大学（1960—1994）　/　123
Shanghai University of Technology (SUT) (1960—1994)

二、上海科学技术大学（1958—1994）　/　159
Shanghai University of Science and Technology (SUST) (1958—1994)

三、上海大学（1983—1994）　/　194
Shanghai University (SHU) (1983—1994)

四、上海科技高等专科学校（1959—1994）　/　224
Shanghai College of Science and Technology (SCST) (1959—1994)

第三部分　自强不息　复兴跨越 / 241
Part III　Pursuit of Excellence

一、上海大学新合并组建 / 246
　　Merger and Establishment

二、推行"三制"　建立创新性人才培养模式 / 249
　　"Three Systems" and Innovative Talent Cultivation

三、调整院系　建设新兴、交叉学科 / 250
　　Faculty Adjustment and Discipline Construction

四、"211工程"建设 / 253
　　"Project 211" Construction

五、新校区建设 / 257
　　Construction of New Campus

六、改革专业技术职务聘任制 / 263
　　Reform on Promotion System

七、接受本科教学工作水平评估 / 265
　　Assessment of Undergraduate Teaching Qualification

八、确立钱伟长教育思想 / 267
　　Establishment of Qian Weichang's Educational Thought

九、成立校董事会 / 271
　　Establishment of SHU Board of Trustees

十、实施"五五战略" / 273
　　Implementation of "Five-Five Strategy"

十一、人才培养 / 280
Talent Cultivation

十二、科学研究 / 311
Scientific Research

十三、社会服务 / 346
Social Services

十四、国际交流与合作 / 352
International Exchanges and Cooperations

十五、校园文化 / 364
Campus Culture

十六、师资队伍 / 374
Faculty

十七、党的建设 / 391
Party Construction

百年上大　薪火相传 / 409
A Century of SHU: Passing the Torch

一、百年奋进恰风华 / 411
A Century of Progress, A Flourishing Era

二、寻根溯源传薪火 / 422
Tracing the Roots, Igniting the Future

第一部分

风云际会　青云发轫

  1922年7月召开的中国共产党第二次全国代表大会明确提出反帝反封建的民主革命纲领，并主张建立民主的联合战线。当年10月23日，在中国共产党和中国国民党主要领导人的共同关注和支持下，上海大学成立。这是一所国共两党携手创办、由中国共产党实际领导的高等学府。在大革命时期，学校成为反帝反封建的一支有力的先锋队、五卅运动的一面旗帜，享有"文有上大，武有黄埔""北有五四时期的北大，南有五卅时期的上大"之盛誉。在中共中央的指导和上海区委的直接领导下，学校成为培养共产党干部的红色学府。1927年，蒋介石在上海发动四一二反革命政变，于5月3日强行封闭了学校。

Part I

Revolution and Foundation

The Second National Congress of the CPC held in July 1922, clearly put forward the democratic revolutionary program opposing imperialism and feudalism, and advocated the establishment of a democratic united front. On October 23 of that year, with the joint support of the main leaders of the CPC and the Kuomintang (KMT) of China, SHU was founded. It was a higher education institution jointly established by the CPC and the KMT, and actually led by the CPC. During the period of the Great Revolution, the university became a powerful vanguard against imperialism and feudalism and a banner of the May Thirtieth Movement, enjoying the prestigious reputation of "SHU for the literary, HMA (Huangpu Military Academy, also known as Whampoa Military Academy) for the military" and "Peking University (PKU) in the north during the May Fourth Movement, and SHU in the south during the May Thirtieth Movement". Under the guidance of the Central Committee of the CPC and the direct leadership of the Shanghai Regional Committee, SHU developed into a red institution for cultivating Communist Party cadres. In 1927, Chiang Kai-shek launched the April 12 Counter-Revolutionary Coup in Shanghai and forcibly closed the university on May 3.

第一部分 风云际会 青云发轫

一、国共精英　共建上大
Cooperation and Construction

1922年10月19日，位于上海青岛路（后改名青云路）的私立东南高等专科师范学校，因学生不满校长王理堂借学敛财、不理校政、携款私逃而引发学潮，学生强烈要求改组校务。在中国共产党和中国国民党主要领导人的关注与支持下，推举国民党元老于右任担任校长，锐意革新，改组学校，定校名为"上海大学"。

SHU was founded on Qingdao Road (later renamed Qingyun Road) on October 19, 1922. Yu Youren, a veteran KMT member, was appointed President.

（一）学潮风波　Student Movement

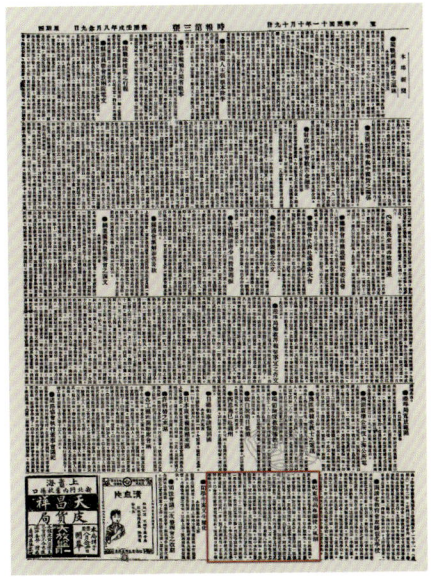

1922年10月19日，《时报》刊登《纪东南高专师校之风潮》
"Record of the Turmoil at Southeast Higher Normal School", reported by *Times*, October 19, 1922

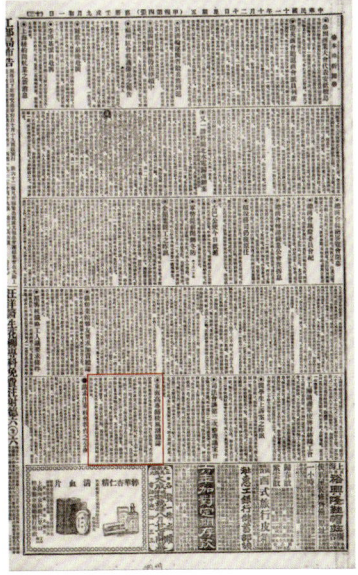

1922年10月20日，《申报》刊登《东南高专师校风潮续志》
"Continued Record of the Turmoil at Southeast Higher Normal School", reported by *Shun Pao*, October 20, 1922

（二）学校成立　Founding of SHU

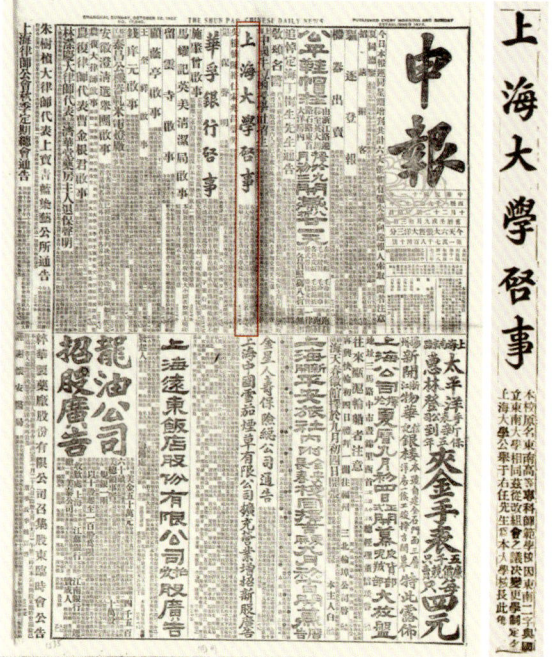
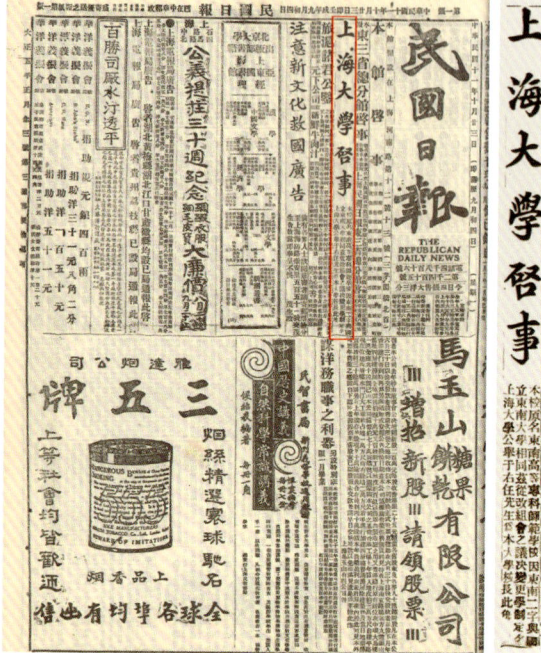

1922年10月22日、23日，《申报》《民国日报》刊登《上海大学启事》：本校原名东南高等专科师范学校，兹从改组会之议决，变更学制，定名上海大学

"Announcement of Shanghai University", reported by *Shun Pao* and *The Republican Daily*, October 22 and 23, 1922

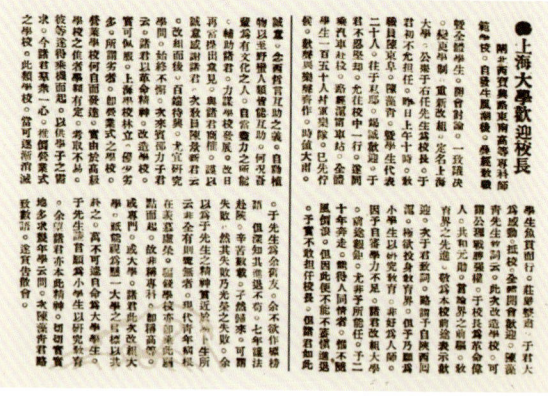

1922年10月24日，《民国日报》刊登上海大学师生欢迎于右任校长的消息。于右任在欢迎大会上致辞："自当尽力之所能，辅助诸君，力谋学校发展。"

The news on SHU teachers and students welcoming President Yu Youren, reported by *The Republican Daily*, October 24, 1922

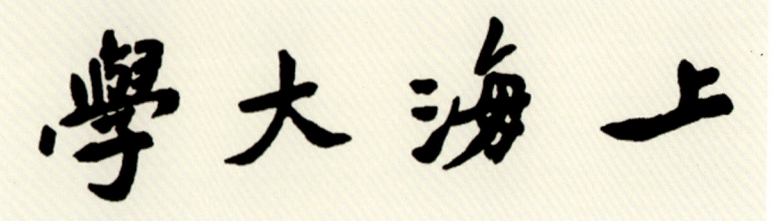

于右任校长题写的校牌
Shanghai University, inscribed by Yu Youren

第一部分　风云际会　青云发轫

（三）国共两党领导人与上海大学　CPC and KMT Leaders and SHU

1. 孙中山
Sun Yat-sen

孙中山（1866—1925），名文，广东香山（今中山）人。中国近代伟大的民主革命家，中华民国和中国国民党创始人。1923年2月，批准广州国民政府每月拨款1000元补助上海大学；同年9月，应上海大学评议会之邀，担任上海大学名誉校董。曾两次作出批示，指示上海大学接收遭到安徽当局通缉的爱国学生入校学习。

Sun Yat-sen (1866-1925) was a great democratic revolutionist in modernChina. In September 1923, Sun was invited to serve as Honorary Board Director of SHU.

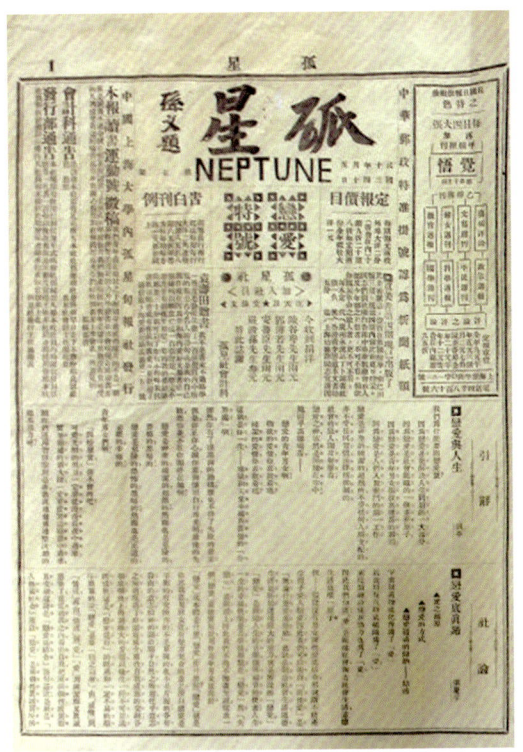

1924年3月3日，孙中山为上海大学学生社团"中国孤星社"主办的旬刊《孤星》题写刊名

On March 3, 1924, Sun Yat-sen inscribed the title for the journal *Neptune* started by Neptune, a student association of SHU

 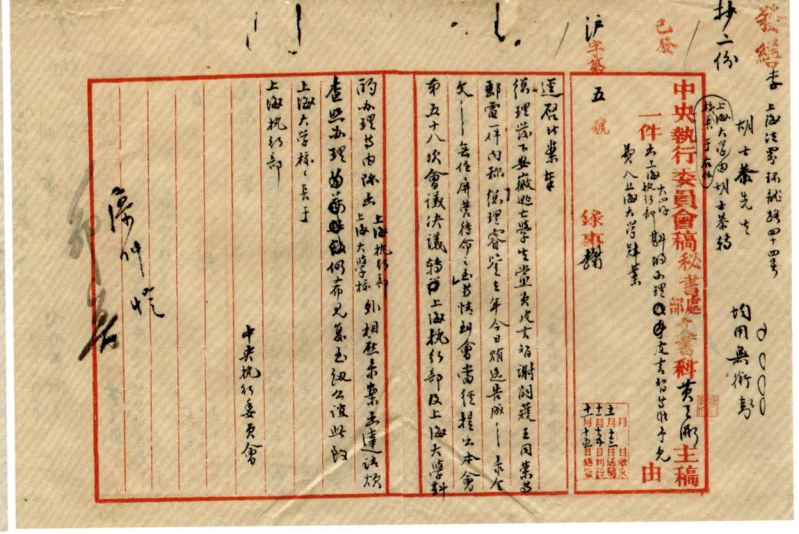

1924年11月，国民党中央执行委员会批文下发至上海执行部和于右任校长，转达孙中山关于酌情办理皮言智等入上海大学的指示

A document issued by the KMT delivering Sun Yat-sen's instruction on SHU, November 1924

2. 李大钊
Li Dazhao

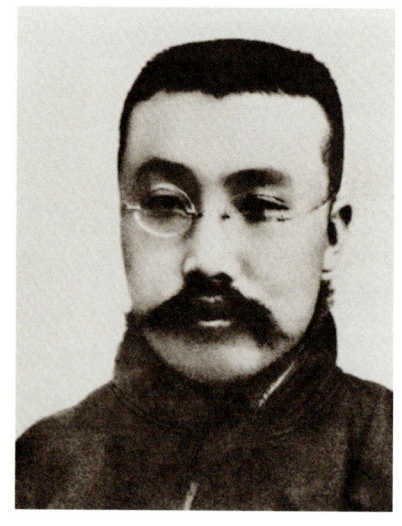

李大钊（1889—1927），字守常，河北乐亭人。中国无产阶级革命家，中国最早的马克思主义者，中国共产党的主要创始人和早期领导人。1923年，向于右任推荐邓中夏、瞿秋白等共产党人到上海大学任职任教；同年，五次到上海大学发表演讲。1924—1925年，被聘为上海大学经济学系主任、教授及特别讲师。

Li Dazhao (1889-1927) was a proletarian revolutionist, founder and early leader of the CPC. After the establishment of SHU, Li recommended Deng Zhongxia, Qu Qiubai and other communists to Yu Youren to teach at SHU, and delivered lectures at SHU five times. Between 1924 and 1925, he was appointed professor, special lecturer and Head of the Economics Department of SHU.

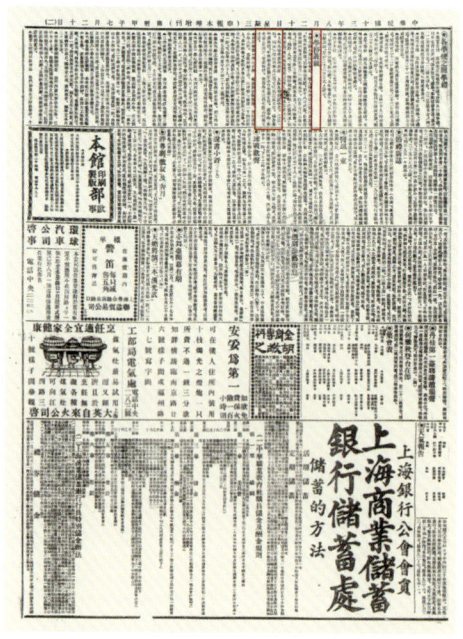 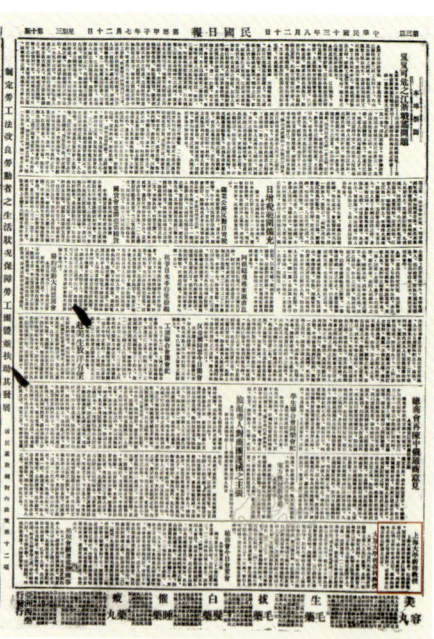

1924年8月20日，《申报》《民国日报》刊登李守常（李大钊）聘为上海大学经济学系主任的消息

The news that Li Shouchang (Li Dazhao) was appointed Head of the Economics Department of SHU, reported by *Shun Pao* and *The Republican Daily*, August 20, 1924

第一部分　风云际会　青云发轫

1923年4月15日，《申报》刊登李大钊在上海大学演说的消息，主题为"演化与进步"
The news "Lecture at SHU Today: Evolution and Progress by Li Dazhao", reported by *Shun Pao*, April 15, 1923

1923年7月13日，《申报》刊登李大钊在上海大学演说的消息，主题为"美术应将现代社会之困苦悲哀表现出来"
The news of Li Dazhao's lecture at SHU on "Function of Fine Arts", reported by *Shun Pao*, July 13, 1923

1923年11月13日，《民国日报》副刊《觉悟》刊登李守常在上海大学社会问题研究会所作的"社会主义释疑"演讲稿
The script of Li Shouchang's lecture at SHU on "Interpretation of Socialism", reported by *The Republican Daily*, November 13, 1923

1923年11月29日，《民国日报》副刊《觉悟》刊登李守常在上海大学所作的"史学概论"演讲稿
The script of Li Shouchang's lecture at SHU on "Introduction to Historiography", reported by *The Republican Daily*, November 29, 1923

1923年12月4日，《民国日报》副刊《觉悟》刊登李守常在上海大学所作的"劳动问题概论（二）"演讲稿
The script of Li Shouchang's lecture at SHU on "Introduction to Labor Issues (II)", reported by *The Republican Daily*, December 4, 1923

3. 陈独秀
Chen Duxiu

陈独秀（1879—1942），字仲甫，安徽怀宁（今安庆）人。中国共产党的主要创始人和早期领导人。上海大学成立后，以"知名"署名，写给陈望道一张条子："上大请你组织，你要什么同志请开出来，请你负责。"1924年10月，在瞿秋白离任后，指派施存统担任上海大学社会学系主任，并安排党内同志到上海大学学习。

Chen Duxiu (1879-1942) was a founder and early leader of the CPC. After the establishment of SHU, he wrote a note to Chen Wangdao, expressing his full support for the running of SHU.

1924年，在第87期《向导》周报"国民党右派惨杀黄仁案"专栏上，陈独秀以笔名"独秀"发表题为《这是右派的行动吗，还是反革命？》的文章

Chen Duxiu published an article entitled "Is This a Rightist Action or a Counter-Revolution?", criticizing the KMT for the Huang Ren Event on *The Guide Weekly*, 1924

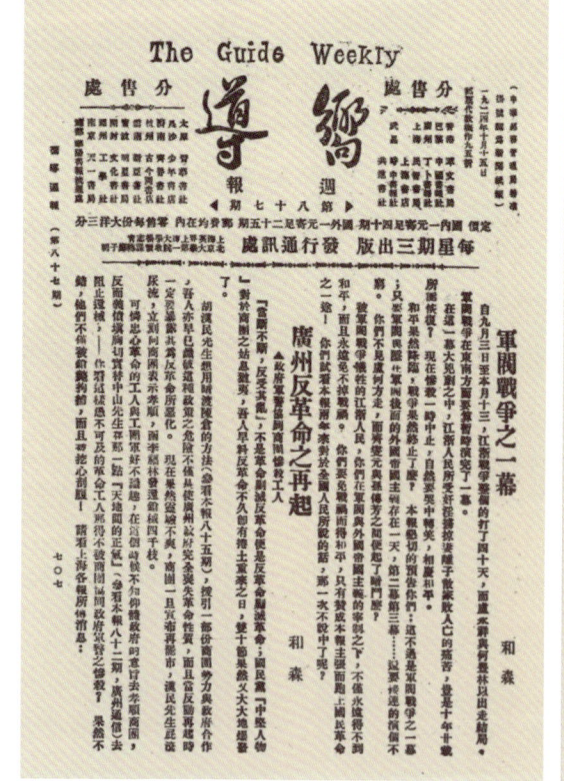
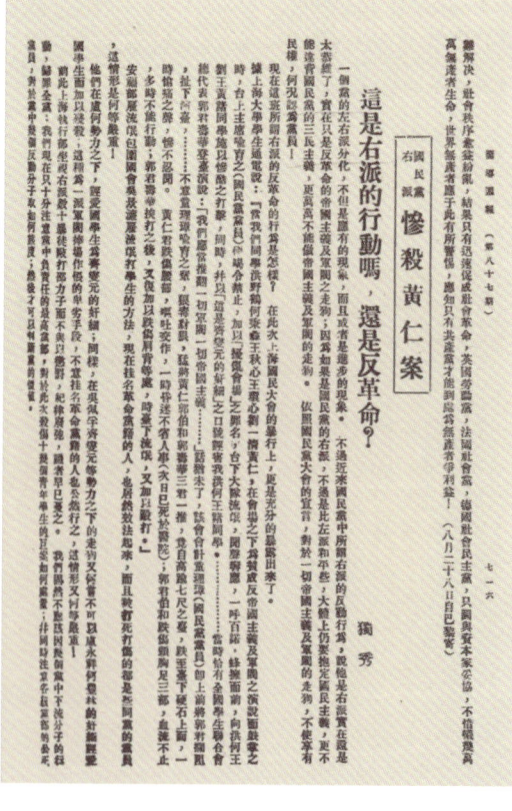

4. 毛泽东
Mao Zedong

毛泽东（1893—1976），字润之，湖南湘潭人。中国共产党、中华人民共和国和中国人民解放军的缔造者和领导人。1924年3月，以国民党上海执行部组织部秘书兼文书科主任的身份全面负责黄埔军校第一期上海地区考生复试工作，在西摩路上海大学考场负责招生；同年20日，出席国民党上海执行部第四次执行委员会会议并作记录，会议讨论在上海大学设立"现代政治班"问题。1926年5月7日，以国民党中央宣传部代理部长的身份出席国民党中央执行委员会常委会第二十六次会议，会议决定："命令财政部，关于上海大学补助费案，无论财政如何困难，务须依照第一次全国代表大会决议，每月津贴千元；在财政部未给领以前，暂由中央宣传费项下挪借。"1939年3月，出席中共中央书记处会议，在讨论陕北公学办学方针时指出："陕北公学是统一战线性质的学校，像过去的上海大学。"

Mao Zedong (1893-1976) was the founder and leader of the CPC, the PRC and the Chinese People's Liberation Army. On March 20, 1924, Mao attended the fourth Executive Committee Meeting of the KMT Executive Department in Shanghai, discussing the establishment of the "Modern Politics Class" at SHU. On May 7, 1926, Mao attended the 26th meeting of the Standing Committee of the Central Executive Committee of the KMT, where it was decided that the Central Publicity Department should pay the subsidy to SHU. At the meeting of Secretariat of the CPC Central Committee in March, 1939, when discussing about guidelines of Shaanbei Public School, Mao remarked: "Shaanbei Public School is a united-front type of college, just like SHU in the past."

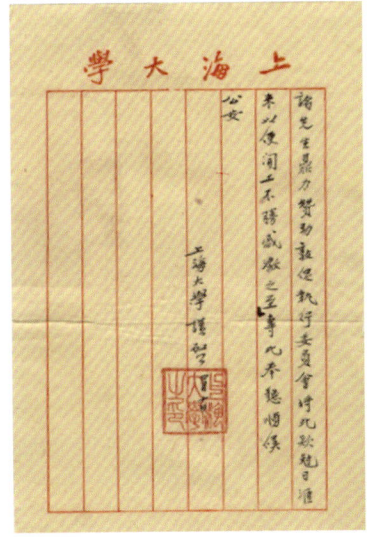
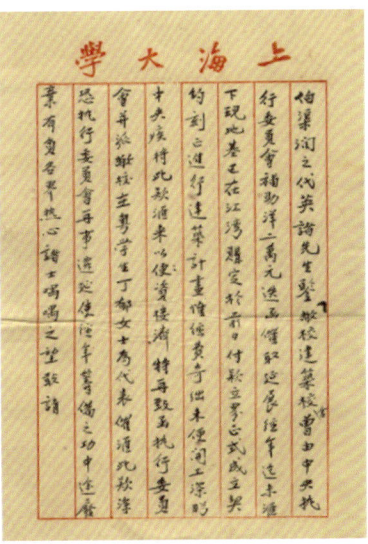
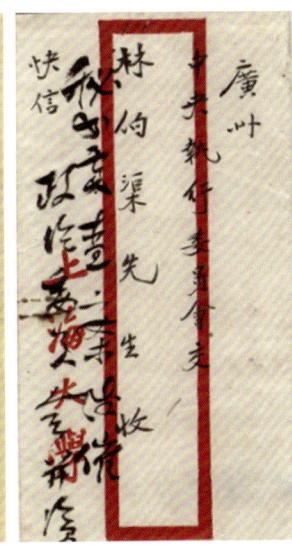

1926年4月10日，上海大学致函国民党中常委委员林伯渠、国民党中执委候补委员兼宣传部代理部长毛泽东、国民党上海执行部负责人之一恽代英，请求"鼎力赞助，敦促（国民党中央）执行委员会将此款（补助上海大学建筑款两万元）克日汇来，以便开工"

On April 10, 1926, SHU sent a letter to Lin Boqu, Mao Zedong and Yun Daiying, requesting them to "give full support and urge the Central Executive Committee of the KMT to remit the 20,000-yuan subsidy for the construction of SHU as soon as possible, so that the project can start."

（四）学校领导　SHU Leaders

1. 校领导
SHU Leaders

校领导一览
SHU Leaders

职　务	姓　名	任职时间
校长	于右任	1922年10月23日—1927年5月
代理校长	邵力子	1924年4月—1925年5月
总务长（校务长）	邓中夏	1923年4月—1924年9月
校务长	刘含初	1924年10月—1925年2月
总务主任（校务长）	韩觉民	1925年2月—1926年4月
教务长	叶楚伧	1922年10月23日—1923年7月
	瞿秋白	1923年7—12月
学务长	何世桢	1923年12月—1924年10月
学务主任（学务长）	陈望道	1925年2月—1927年5月

校长于右任先生

　　于右任（1879—1964），陕西三原人。早期同盟会会员，国民党元老。曾参与创办复旦公学（今复旦大学）、中国公学。1922年10月，任上海大学校长，后聘请共产党人邓中夏、瞿秋白任上海大学总务长和教务长。1934年，任国立西北农林专科学校（今西北农林科技大学）校长。1936年3月，推动国民党中央常务委员会通过追认上海大学学生学籍并与国立大学享有同等待遇的决定，积极准备复办上海大学。

　　Yu Youren (1879-1964) began to serve as President of SHU in October 1922. In March 1936, he promoted the KMT Central Standing Committee to pass a decision to posthumously recognize the status of SHU students, granting them the same treatment as that to the students of national universities, and actively prepared to reopen SHU.

第一部分　风云际会　青云发轫

邵力子（1882—1967），字仲辉，浙江绍兴人。早期同盟会会员，国民党元老。中国共产党发起组织成员。1922年10月，任上海大学教授。1923年8月，当选上海大学最高决策机构评议会评议员。1924年4月，任上海大学代理校长。新中国成立后，任政务院政务委员、全国人大常委会委员。

Shao Lizi (1882-1967) served as SHU professor in October 1922 and was appointed Acting President of SHU in April 1924. After the founding of the PRC, he served as a member of the Standing Committee of the National People's Congress.

邓中夏（1894—1933），又名安石，湖南宜章人。中国无产阶级革命家，中国早期工人运动领导人。1919年，参加领导五四运动。1920年，参加北京中国共产党早期组织。1922年5月，任中国劳动组合书记部主任。1923年4月，任上海大学总务长、教授；同年8月，当选上海大学最高决策机构评议会评议员。在上海大学任职期间，任中共中央职工运动委员会书记、共青团中央委员长、中共上海地方兼区执行委员会委员长。

Deng Zhongxia (1894-1933), a proletarian revolutionist and leader of the early workers' movements, served as Dean of General Affairs of SHU in April 1923.

叶楚伧（1887—1946），江苏苏州人。早期同盟会会员，国民党元老。1922年10月，任上海大学教务长兼中国文学系主任、教授。1923年8月，当选上海大学最高决策机构评议会评议员。

Ye Chucang (1887-1946) served as Provost and Chair of the Chinese Literature Department of SHU in October 1922.

瞿秋白（1899—1935），江苏常州人。中国无产阶级革命家、理论家，中国共产党早期领导人。1919年，参加领导五四运动。1922年，在苏联加入中国共产党。1923年7月，任上海大学教务长兼社会学系主任、教授；同年8月，当选上海大学最高决策机构评议会评议员。五卅运动期间，担任《热血日报》主编。1927年，主持召开八七会议，任中共中央政治局常委、主席。

Qu Qiubai (1899-1935), a proletarian revolutionist and early leader of the CPC, served as Provost and Chair of the Sociology Department of SHU in July 1923.

刘含初（1895—1927），陕西黄陵人。1923年，任上海大学教授。1924年春，加入中国共产党；同年10月，任上海大学校务长。1925年春，赴陕西从事统一战线工作。

Liu Hanchu (1895-1927) became a professor of SHU in 1923 and served as Dean of University Affairs in October 1924.

陈望道（1891—1977），浙江义乌人。中国共产党发起组织成员。《共产党宣言》首个中文全译本翻译者。1923年8月，任上海大学中国文学系主任；同月，当选上海大学最高决策机构评议会评议员。1925年2月，任上海大学学务主任。1927年4月，任上海大学行政委员会临时主席，主持学校工作。新中国成立后，任复旦大学校长。

Chen Wangdao (1891-1977), the first person to translate *The Communist Manifesto* into Chinese, served as Chair of the Chinese Literature Department in August 1923 and Director of University Affairs at SHU in February 1925.

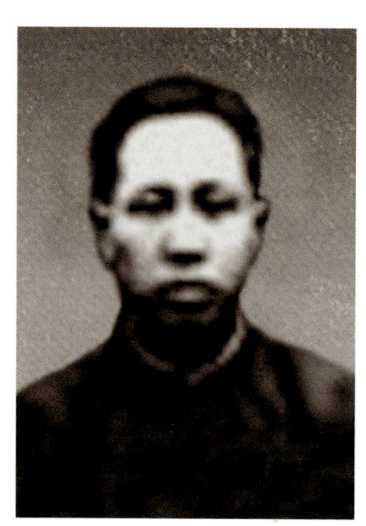

韩觉民（生卒年不详），湖北黄安人。1923年秋，任上海大学中学部教员。1925年2月，任上海大学总务主任；同年4月，任上海大学行政委员会委员。1927年，任北伐军总政治部秘书。

Han Juemin (dates of birth and death unknown) started to work at SHU in 1923 and served as Dean of University Affairs at SHU in February 1925.

何世桢（1895—1972），安徽望江人。何世枚胞兄。1923年秋，任上海大学英国文学系主任；同年12月，任上海大学学务长。1924年，与何世枚一起创办持志大学（校址为今上海外国语大学）并任校长。

He Shizhen (1895-1972) served as Chair of the English Department and later Dean of Student Affairs of SHU in 1923. In 1924 he co-founded Chi Zhi University (The campus is now Shanghai International Studies University) with He Shimei and served as its President.

2. 系、科领导
Department and Division Leaders

系、科领导一览
Department and Division Leaders

职　务	姓　名	任职时间
中国文学系主任（文学科主任）	叶楚伧	1922年10月23日—1923年3月
	张君谋	1923年3—8月
	陈望道	1923年8月—1927年5月
社会学系主任	瞿秋白	1923年6月—1924年10月
	施存统	1924年10月—1926年4月
	李　季	1926年4月—1927年5月
英国文学系主任	何世桢	1923年秋—1924年10月
	周越然	1924年12月—1926年8月
	周由廑	1926年8月—1927年5月
美术科主任	洪　野	1922年10月23日—1927年5月

张君谋（1894—1958），名乃燕，浙江吴兴（今湖州）人。国民党元老、上海大学校董张静江之侄。1923年3月，任上海大学文学科主任、教授。1928年，任国立中央大学首任校长。

Zhang Junmou (1894-1958) served as Chair of the Literature Department of SHU in March 1923 and the first President of National Central University in 1928.

Shi Cuntong (1899-1970) served as Chair of the Sociology Department of SHU in October 1924 and a member of the Administrative Committee of SHU in April 1925.

施存统（1899—1970），又名复亮，浙江金华人。中国共产党发起组织成员。1920年，创建旅日中国共产党早期组织。1921年回国，1922年当选第一届共青团中央书记。1923年秋，任上海大学社会学系教授。1924年10月，受陈独秀指派任上海大学社会学系主任。1925年4月，任上海大学行政委员会委员。新中国成立后，任劳动部副部长、全国人大常务委员会委员、全国政协常务委员会委员兼副秘书长。

李季（1892—1967），湖南平江人。中国共产党发起组织成员。1920年底，随陈独秀到广州参加中国共产党早期组织的创建工作。1925年，任上海大学社会学系教授。1926年3月，任上海大学行政委员会委员；同年4月，任上海大学社会学系主任。

Li Ji (1892-1967) became a professor of SHU in 1925 and a member of the Administrative Committee of SHU in March 1926. He served as Chair of the Sociology Department of SHU in April 1926.

周越然（1885—1962），浙江吴兴（今湖州）人。1924年12月，任上海大学英国文学系主任、教授。1925年4月，任上海大学行政委员会委员。

Zhou Yueran (1885-1962) served as Chair of the English Literature Department of SHU in December 1924 and a member of the Administrative Committee of SHU in April 1925.

周由厪（生卒年不详），浙江吴兴（今湖州）人。周越然兄长。1925年，任上海大学英国文学系教授。1926年8月，代理上海大学英国文学系主任。1927年3月，任上海大学行政委员会委员。

Zhou Youjin (dates of birth and death unknown), Zhou Yueran's elder brother, served as Chair of the English Literature Department of SHU in August 1926 and a member of the Administrative Committee of SHU in March 1927.

洪野（1886—1932），又名禹仇，安徽歙县人。1922年10月，任上海大学美术科主任。1923年8月，当选上海大学最高决策机构评议会评议员。

Hong Ye (1886-1932) served as Chair of the Fine Arts Section of SHU in October 1922 and a member of the Senate, the highest decision-making body of SHU in August 1923.

（五）完善组织机构　Organization Improvement

行政组织系统表
Administrative Organization System

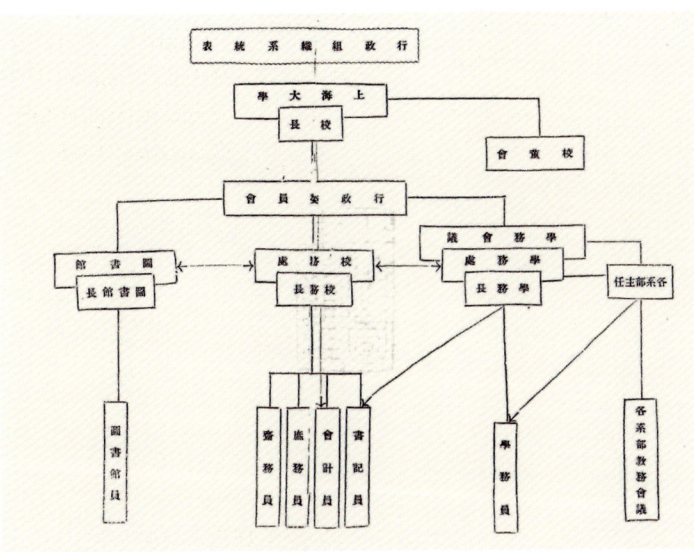

1923年4月24日，《民国日报》刊登《上海大学教职员会议》：（一）决议在宋园建新校舍事宜；（二）决议由邓安石（邓中夏）、陈德徵、洪禹仇（洪野）等起草学校章程；（三）议设俄国文学系、社会科学系、史学系

On April 24, 1923, *The Republic Daily* reported "The Faculty Meeting of SHU".

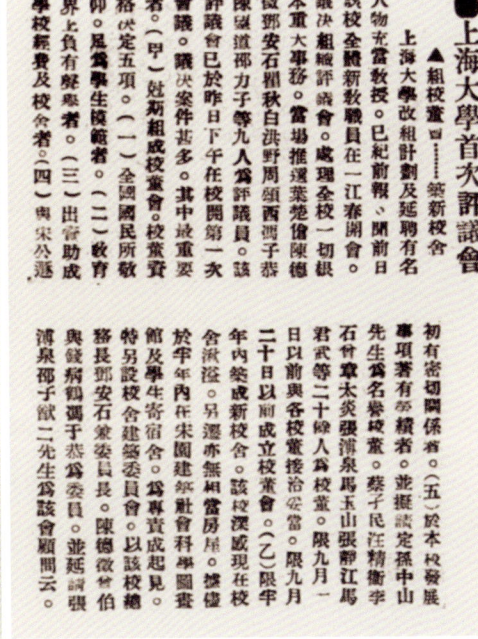

1923年8月13日，《民国日报》刊登《上海大学首次评议会》：决议组织评议会，并推选叶楚伧、陈德徵、邓安石（邓中夏）、瞿秋白、洪野（洪禹仇）、周颂西、冯子恭、陈望道、邵力子等九人为评议员

On August 13, 1923, *The Republican Daily reported* "The First Senate Meeting of SHU": Nine people were elected as senators.

上海大学聘孙中山为名誉校董，蔡元培（蔡子民）、张继（张溥泉）、章太炎（章炳麟）、柏文蔚、王一亭、简照南、李石曾、马君武、张静江、马素、马玉山、孙科、汪精卫、邹鲁等人为校董。

SHU appointed Sun Yat-sen as Honorary Board Director and Cai Yuanpei (Cai Jiemin), Zhang Taiyan (Zhang Binglin), etc. as board members.

1922年11月13日，著名物理学家、诺贝尔奖获得者爱因斯坦造访日本时，途经上海。上海大学校长于右任（前排右1）与校董王一亭（前排右2）在上海梓园（王一亭寓所）宴请爱因斯坦（前排右4）

On November 13, 1922, Yu Youren (first from right in the front row), President of SHU, hosted a banquet for Einstein (fourth from right in the front row) at the residence of SHU board member Wang Yiting in Shanghai.

（六）制定学校章程　Constitution Formulation

1923年12月5日，由邓中夏撰写的《上海大学章程》经学校评议会通过，明确提出上海大学办学宗旨为"养成建国人才 促进文化事业"。章程封面由校长于右任题签。

Constitution of Shanghai University was approved on December 5, 1923.

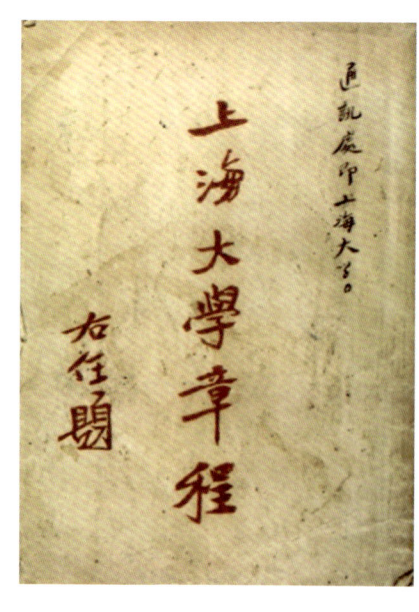
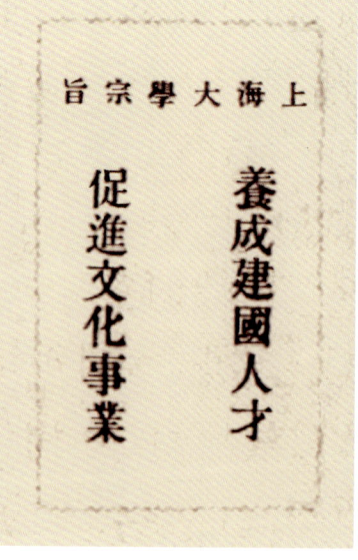
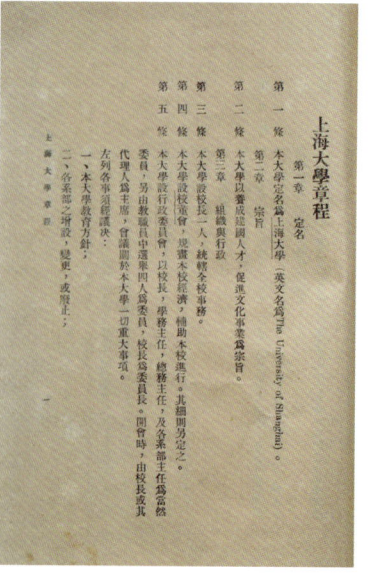

《上海大学一览》于1924年4月发行,由陈望道、杨明轩、邓中夏三人编辑,封面由张继题签,弁言由校长于右任亲撰。

Survey of Shanghai University was published in April 1924. The title was inscribed by Zhang Ji and the preface was composed by President Yu Youren.

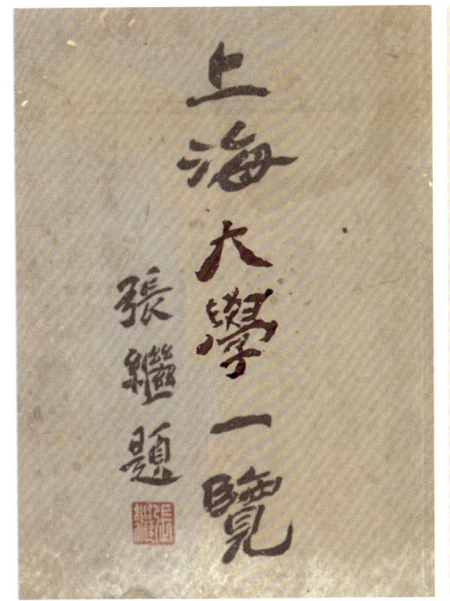

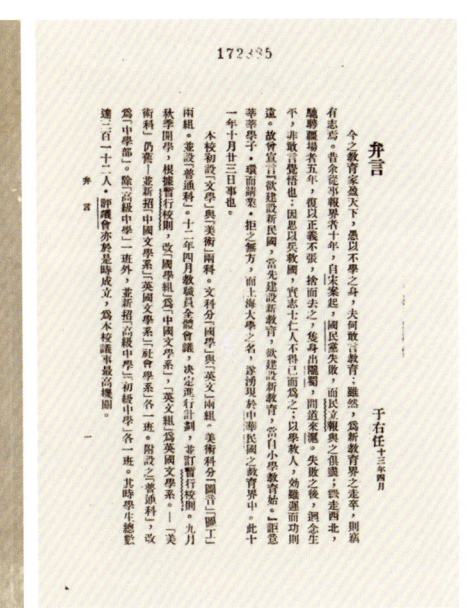

学制系统表

Diagram of Academic Department Structure

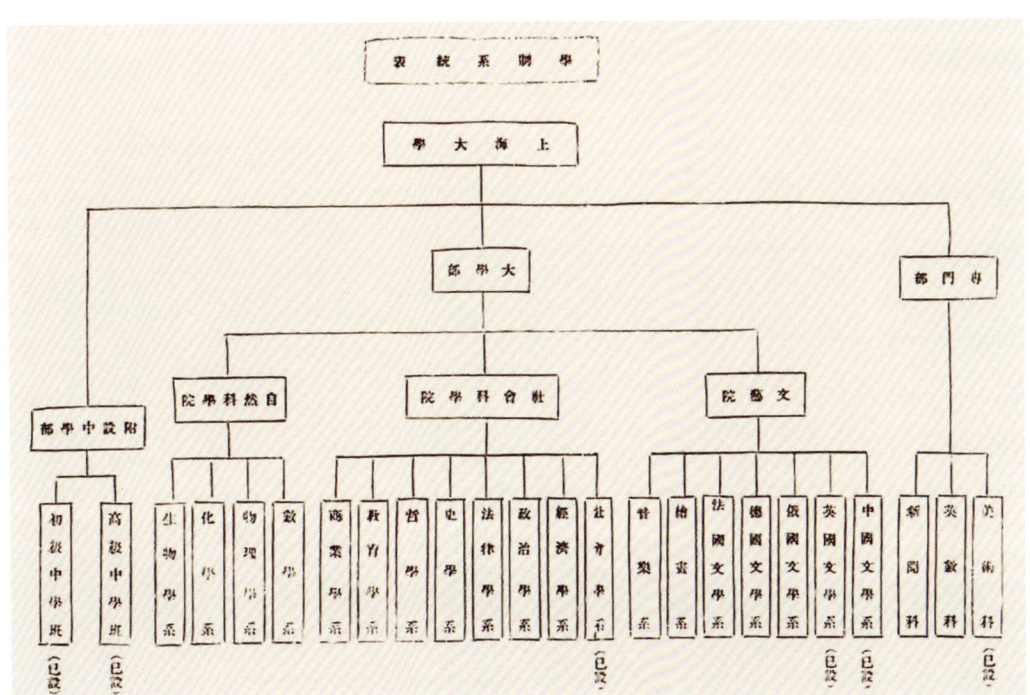

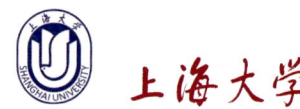

各系课程表（部分）

Course Schedule of Each Department (Partial)

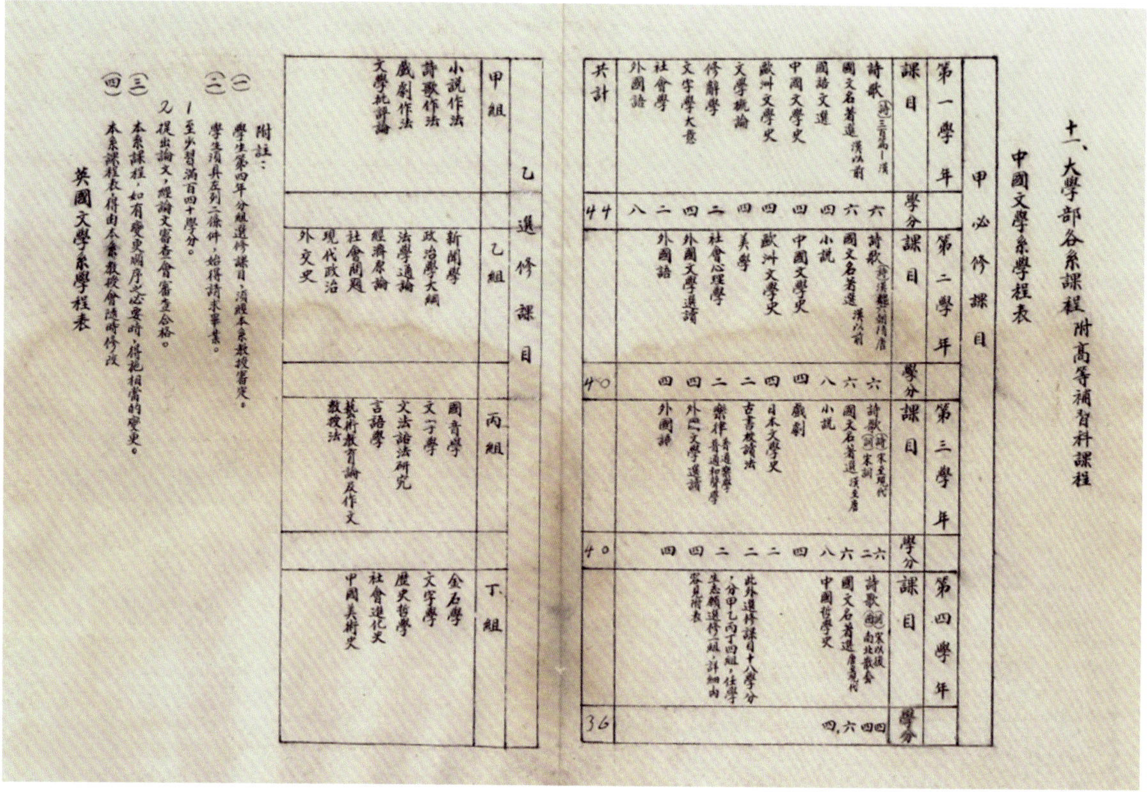

十、大學部各系課程 附高等補習科課程

中國文學系學程表

甲 必修課目

第一學年

課目	學分
詩歌（詩）三百篇—漢	六
國文名著選 漢以前	六
國語文選	四
中國文學史	四
歐洲文學史	四
文學概論	四
修辭學	二
文字學大意	四
社會學	二
外國語	八
共計	44

第二學年

課目	學分
詩歌（詩）漢魏六朝隋唐	六
國文名著選 漢以前	六
小說	八
中國文學史	四
歐洲文學史	四
美學	二
社會心理學	二
外國文學選讀	四
外國語	四
共計	40

第三學年

課目	學分
詩歌（詩）宋至現代（詞）宋詞	二六
國文名著選 漢至唐	六
小說	八
戲劇	四
日本文學史	二
古書校讀法	二
樂律 音韻學 音韻拓學	二
外國文學選讀	四
外國語	四
共計	40

第四學年

課目	學分
詩歌（詞）宋以後（曲）南北散套	四,六四四
國文名著選 唐至現代	
中國哲學史	
此外選修課目十八學分，分甲乙丙丁四組，任學生志願選修一組，詳細由參見附表	
共計	36

乙 選修課目

甲組	乙組	丙組	丁組
小說作法	新聞學	國音學	金石學
詩歌作法	政治學大綱	文字學	文字學
戲劇作法	法學通論	文法論法研究	歷史哲學
文學批評論	經濟原論	言語學	社會進化史
	社會問題	藝術教育論及作文教授法	中國美術史
	現代政治		
	外交史		

附註：

㈠學生第四年分組選修課目，須經本系教授審定。

㈡學生須具左列二條件，始得請求畢業。

1 至少習滿百四十學分。

乙 提出論文，經論文審查會審查合格。

㈢本系課程，如有變更彌序之必要時，得施相當的變更。

㈣本系課程表，得由本系教授會隨時修改

英國文學系學程表

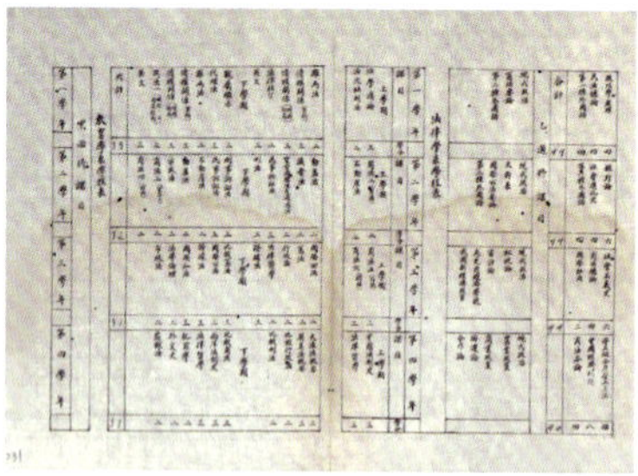

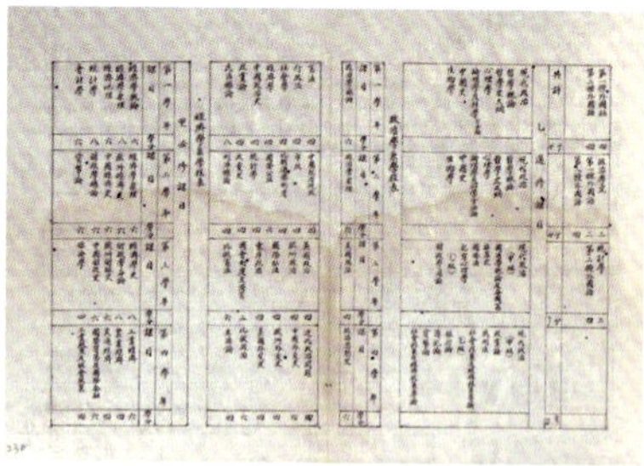

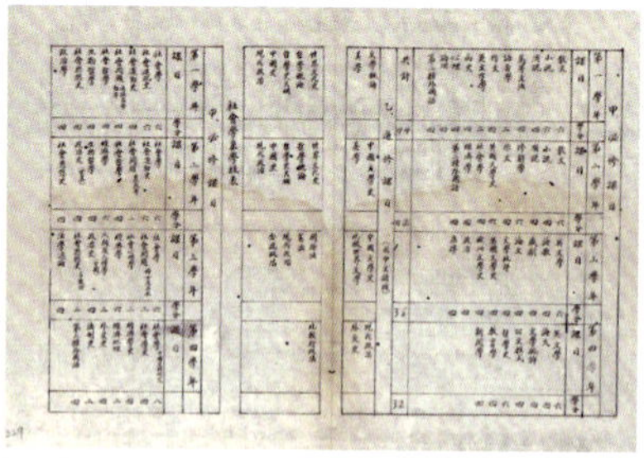

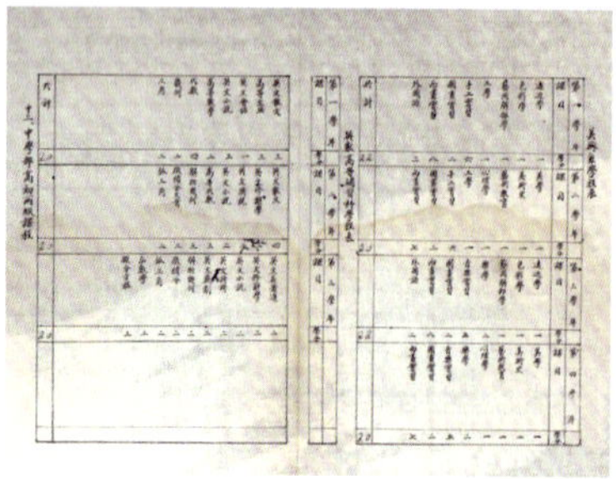

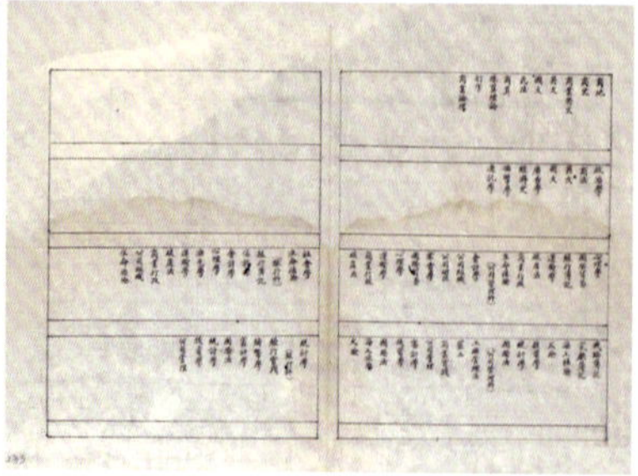

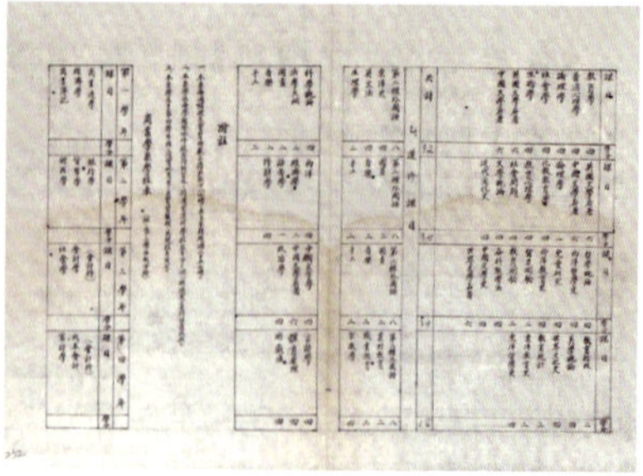

（七）改设中学部　Middle School Division

1923 年 4 月，上海大学附设"普通科"改制为"中学部"。中学部除事务总属于大学部之校务处，其教务、训育皆由中学部独立主持。

In April 1923, the General Department affiliated to SHU was restructured into the Middle School Division.

历任中学部主任一览
Chairs of the Middle School Division

职　务	姓　名	任职时间
中学部主任	陈德徵	1923 年 4 月—1924 年 1 月
	杨明轩（杨荃骏）	1924 年 1 月—1925 年 3 月
	刘薰宇	1925 年 3—8 月
	侯绍裘	1925 年 8 月—1927 年 4 月
中学部代理主任	张作人	1927 年 4—5 月

陈德徵（1899—1951），浙江浦江人。国民党元老。1923 年 4 月，任上海大学中学部主任兼图书室主任；同年 8 月，当选上海大学最高决策机构评议会评议员。

Chen Dezheng (1899-1951) served as Chair of the Middle School Division and Library Director of SHU in April 1923 and a member of the Senate, the highest decision-making body of SHU, in August 1923.

在上海街头的上海大学附属中学（中学部）指示牌
The signpost of the Middle School Affiliated to SHU (Middle School Division) on a street in Shanghai

杨明轩（1891—1967），原名荃骏，陕西户县人。1924年1月，任上海大学中学部主任。1926年12月，加入中国共产党。新中国成立后，任全国人大常务委员会副委员长。

Yang Mingxuan (1891-1967) served as Chair of the Middle School Division of SHU in January 1924. After the founding of the PRC, he served as Vice Chairman of the Standing Committee of the National People's Congress.

刘薰宇（1896—1967），贵州贵阳人。1925年3月，任上海大学中学部主任。

Liu Xunyu (1896-1967) served as Chair of the Middle School Division of SHU in March 1925.

侯绍裘（1896—1927），上海松江人。1923年秋，加入中国共产党。1925年，历任上海大学中学部副主任、主任。1926年3月，任上海大学行政委员会委员。1927年3月，参加上海工人第三次武装起义的组织工作；同月，当选上海特别市临时政府委员。

Hou Shaoqiu (1896-1927) served as Chair of the Middle School Division of SHU in 1925 and a member of the Administrative Committee of SHU in March 1926.

张作人（1900—1991），江苏泰兴人。1925年2月，任上海大学中学部教员。1927年4月，任上海大学中学部代理主任。

Zhang Zuoren (1900-1991) became a professor of SHU in February 1925 and served as Acting Chair of the Middle School Division of SHU in April 1927.

第一部分　风云际会　青云发轫

（八）校风开放包容　An Open and Inclusive School Culture

1. 举办特别讲座、暑期讲习会、夏令讲学会等演讲活动
Various Lectures and Workshops

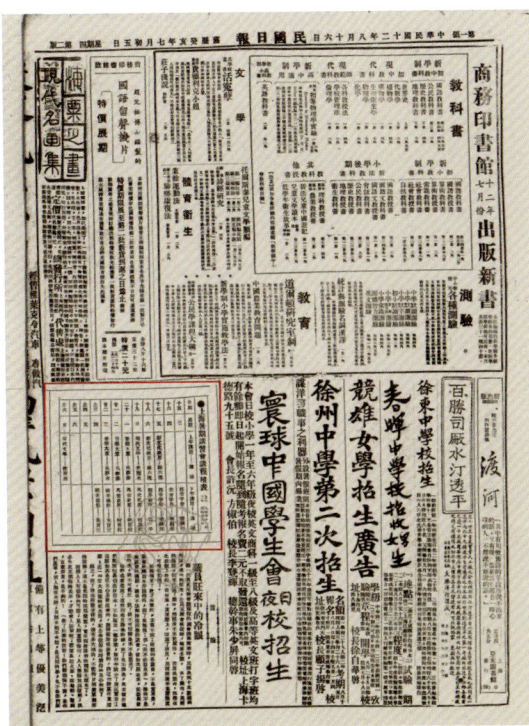

1923 年 8 月 16 日，《民国日报》刊登上海大学《上海暑期讲习会讲程续表》

"Continued Table of Lecture Programs of Shanghai Summer Workshop", reported by *The Republic Daily*, August 16, 1923

2. 组织中国孤星社、中山主义研究会等学生社团
Student Associations

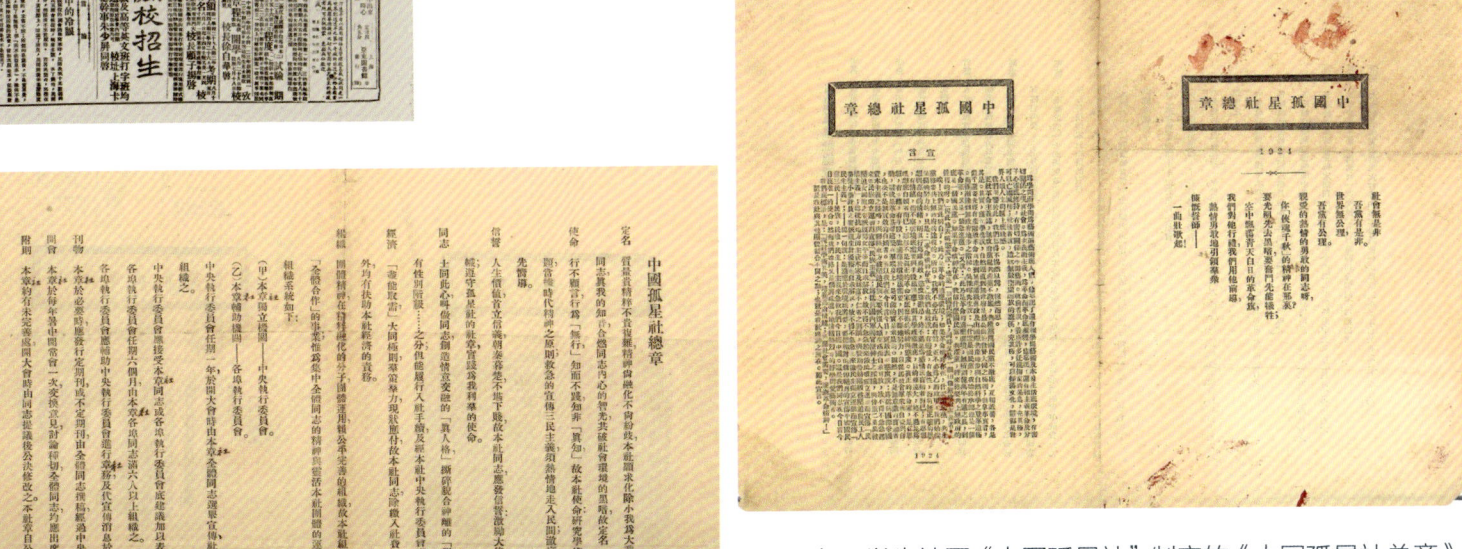

1924 年，学生社团"中国孤星社"制定的《中国孤星社总章》

"The Constitution of the Neptune Association" formulated by the Neptune Association of SHU, 1924

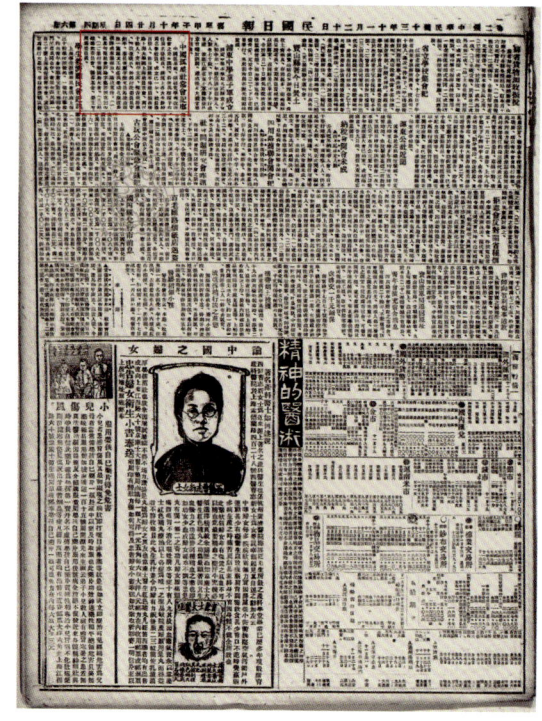

1924年11月20日,《民国日报》刊登有关"中国孤星社"的消息:公推吴稚晖、于右任为名誉社长,请沪上各大学教授为名誉社员,成立一年,社员达百余人

The news of the Neptune Association of SHU reported by *The Republic Daily*, November 20, 1924

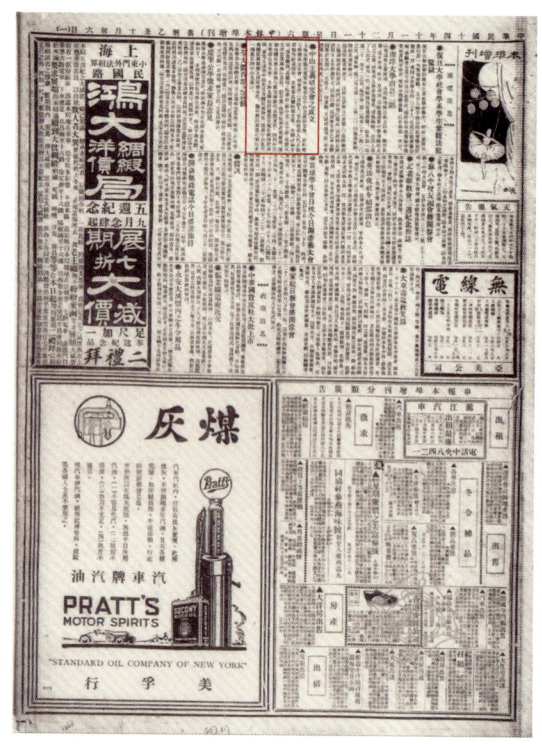

1925年11月21日,《申报》刊登"中山主义研究会"成立的消息

The news that Sun Yat-sen's Doctrine Research Institute was founded, reported by *Shun Pao*, November 21, 1925

学生社团组织一览
Student Associations

社团名称	成立时间
美术科毕业同学会	1923年5月25日
探美画会	1923年10月8日
英文演说会	1923年10月
三民主义研究会	1923年11月
社会问题研究会	1923年11月
青凤文学会	1923年11月
湖波文艺研究会	1923年11月30日
中国孤星社	1924年1月
春风文学会	1924年2月
上海大学附设英文义务学校	1924年3月1日
英文学系二年级英文文学会	1924年3月
上海大学平民学校	1924年3月31日
上大初中阅书报社	1924年4月6日
平民教育委员会	1924年4月
甲子艺术会	1924年6月4日
春雷文学社	1924年11月
社会科学研究会	1924年
上大演说练习会	1925年3月25日
中山主义研究会	1925年11月
心群文艺社	1926年春

3. 开展文艺活动
Artistic Activities

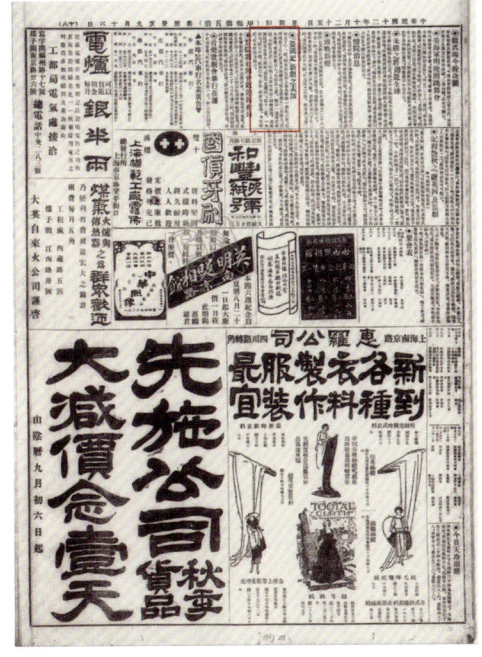

1923年10月25日，《申报》刊登上海大学学生演出《盗国记》的消息

SHU students performed a new drama *Memoirs of a Usurper*, reported by *Shun Pao*, October 25, 1923.

4. 创办校园刊物
Founding Campus Publications

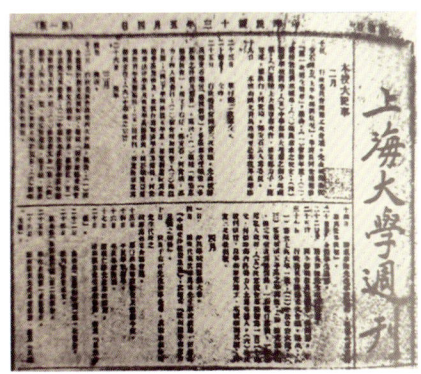

《上海大学周刊》为校刊，于1924年5月4日创刊，陈望道为编辑主任。第一期刊登于右任的《〈上海大学一览〉弁言》和邓中夏的《上大的使命》

Shanghai University Weekly, the school newspaper, started on May 4, 1924, Chen Wangdao serving as Head Editor

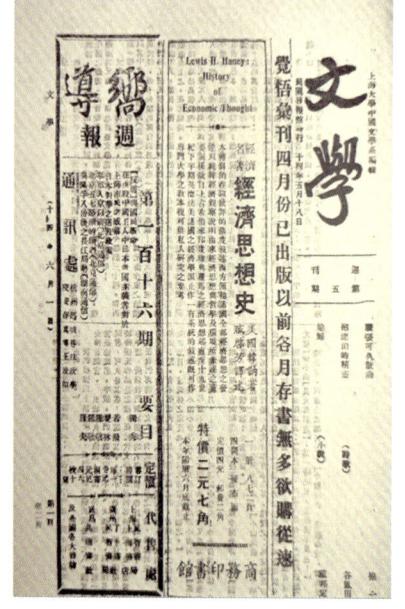

《文学》于 1925 年 4 月 27 日创刊，为上海大学中国文学系编辑，作为《民国日报》的文艺副刊之一随报发行

Literature, edited by the Chinese Literature Department of SHU, was started on April 27, 1925.

《上海大学三周纪念特刊》于 1925 年 10 月 23 日发行，由上海大学学生会宣传部编辑

The Special Issue Commemorating the Third Anniversary of Shanghai University, edited by the SHU Student Union, was published on October 23, 1925.

《上大附中》为上海大学附中学生会主办的半月刊

SHU Affiliated High School Biweekly, edited by the Student Union of the High School Affiliated to SHU

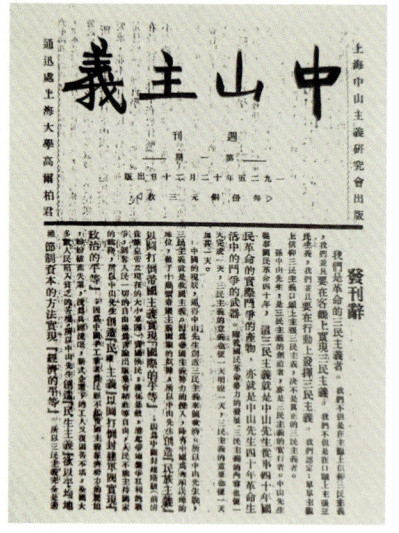

《中山主义》于 1925 年 12 月 20 日创刊，为上海大学中山主义研究会主办的周刊，是上海大学宣传革命和新三民主义的一个阵地。第一期发表由瞿秋白演讲，秦邦宪（博古）、崔小立记录的《国民革命与阶级争斗》

Sun Yat-sen's Doctrine, sponsored by Sun Yat-sen's Doctrine Research Institute of SHU, was started on December 20, 1925.

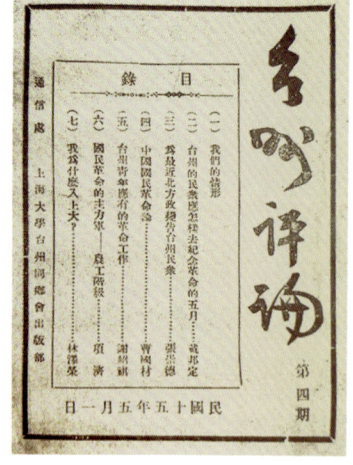

《台州评论》为上海大学台州同乡会主办的刊物

Taizhou Review, a journal sponsored by Taizhou Association of SHU

（九）校址变迁　Relocations of Campuses

校舍变迁情况一览
Relocations of Campus Buildings

校　舍	地　　址	使用时间
青云里校舍	闸北青岛路（后改名青云路）青云里（今东宝兴路青云路一带）	1922年10月23日—1924年2月
西摩路校舍（第一院）	西摩路132号（今陕西北路南阳路口）	1924年2月—1925年6月
时应里校舍（第二院和学生宿舍）	西摩路522—527号（今陕西北路299弄一带）	1924年3月—1925年6月
甄庆里学生宿舍	新闸路戈登路（今江宁路）口东南侧	1924年3月—1925年6月
敦裕里学生宿舍	紧邻时应里南侧（今陕西北路277—287弄附近）	1924年3月—1925年6月
勤业女子师范学校临时办事处	西门方浜桥（今中华路方浜西路口）	1925年6月
方斜路东安里临时校舍	西门方斜路东安里18号、29号（今方斜路362弄）	1925年6—9月
中兴路德润坊临时办公处	闸北中兴路德润坊8号（今公兴路中兴路口）	1925年7—9月
师寿坊临时校舍	闸北青云路师寿坊（今青云路167弄附近）	1925年9月—1927年3月
江湾校舍	圣堂路、奎照路一带（今奎照路、广粤路、凉城路一带）	1927年3月—5月3日

1. 青云里校舍时期（1922年10月—1924年2月）
School Buildings in Qingyun Lane (October 1922-February 1924)

青云路青云里校舍旧影
School Buildings in Qingyun Lane, Qingyun Road

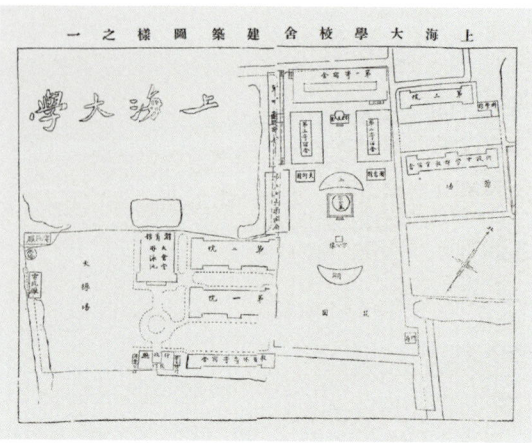

上海大学遗址（青云路青云里校舍）于1987年被列为上海市纪念地点（今上海市第六十中学位置）
The former site of Shanghai University (School Buildings in Qingyun Lane) was designated as "Memorial Site under the Protection of Shanghai Municipality" (today's Shanghai No. 60 Middle School) in 1987.

1923年8月12日，学校召开首次评议会，议决在闸北宋园（今闸北公园）建社会科学院、图书馆及学生宿舍。但该方案未能付诸实施
SHU convened the council and decided to build a social science academy, a library and student dormitories in Song Yuan (today's Zhabei Park) on August 12, 1923. But the plan failed to be implemented.

2. 西摩路校舍时期（1924年2月—1925年6月）
School Buildings on Seymour Road (February 1924-June 1925)

西摩路校舍旧影（今陕西北路南阳路口位置）
School Buildings on Seymour Road (at today's intersection of North Shaanxi Road and Nanyang Road)

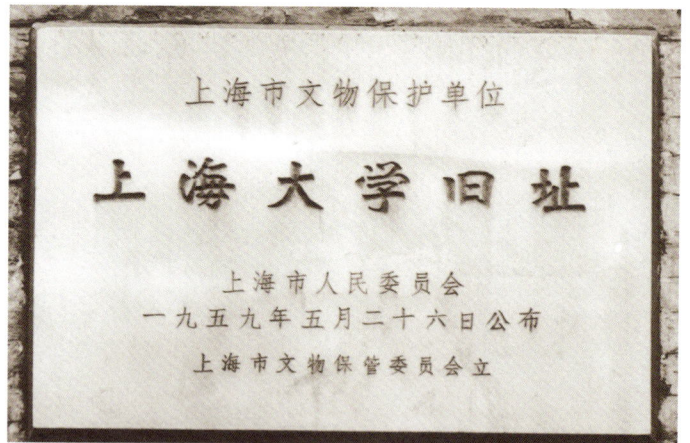

上海大学旧址（西摩路校舍）于1959年被列为上海市文物保护单位
The former site of Shanghai University (School Buildings on Seymour Road) was designated as "Shanghai Culture Relic Protection Site" in 1959.

第一部分　风云际会　青云发轫

于右任校长刚上任，就拿出自筹经费1万元用以办学。1923年2月，孙中山批准广州国民政府每月拨款1000元补助学校。1924年7月，于右任致函中国国民党中央执行委员会，提请自8月起将学校补助款增至每月5000元。该申请未获批准。

President Yu Youren actively raised funds to improve school facilities.

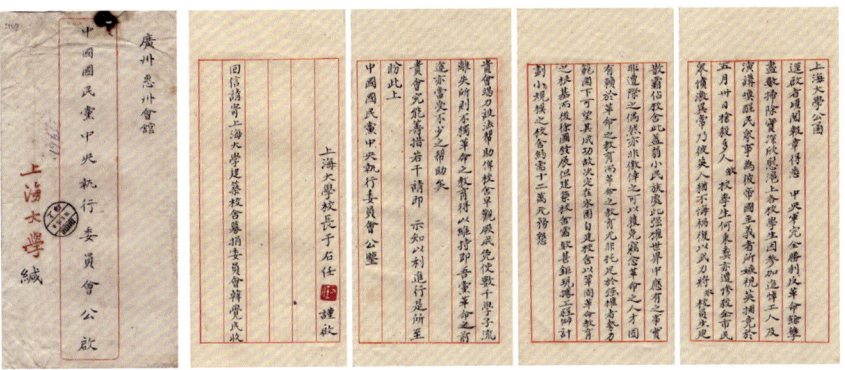

1925年6月18日，于右任致函中国国民党中央执行委员会，请求筹措建筑校舍经费

On June 18, 1925, Yu Youren sent a letter to the Central Executive Committee of the KMT, requesting funds for building school premises.

时应里师生宿舍旧影
Dormitories in Shiying Lane

3. 方斜路东安里临时校舍时期（1925年6—9月）

Temporary School Buildings in Dong'an Lane, Fangxie Road (June-September 1925)

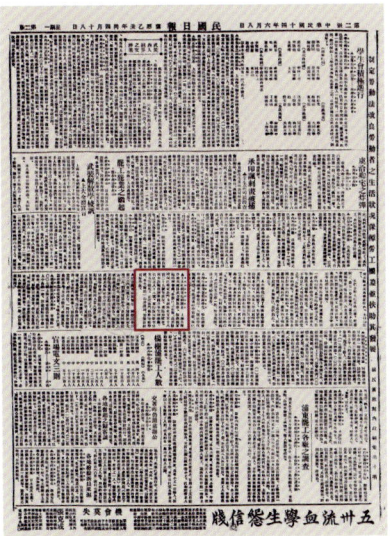

1925年6月8日，《民国日报》刊登上海大学"已租定西门方斜路东安里十八号、二十九号等房屋为临时校舍"的消息

The news that "SHU rented temporary school buildings in Dong'an Lane", reported by *The Republican Daily*, June 8, 1925

4. 师寿坊临时校舍时期（1925年9月—1927年3月）
Temporary School Buildings in Shishou Lane (September 1925-March 1927)

青云路师寿坊临时校舍旧影
Temporary School Buildings in Shishou Lane

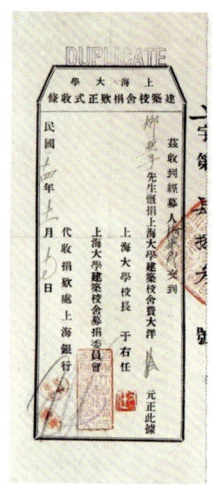

1925年11月17日，社会贤达柳亚子捐助上海大学建筑校舍费收条
A receipt for the donation by Liu Yazi, a respected figure in society, for the construction of school buildings of SHU, November 17, 1925

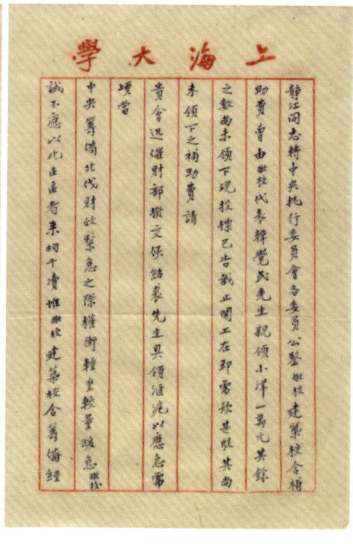

1926年6月26日，于右任致函张静江转国民党中央执行委员会各委员，催拨建筑上海大学江湾校舍补助费
A letter from Yu Youren to Zhang Jingjiang, asking Zhang to forward the letter to all the members of the Central Executive Committee of the KMT, urging the allocation of subsidies for the construction of the Jiangwan campus of SHU, June 26, 1926

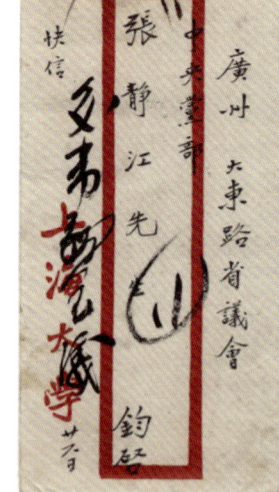

5. 江湾校舍时期（1927年3—5月）
School Buildings in Jiangwan Lane (March-May 1927)

1927年5月，上海大学江湾校舍被国民党当局武力封闭并成为国立劳动大学农学院校舍。图为国立劳动大学校门旧影
The Jiangwan campus was forcefully closed by the KMT and became the campus of Agricultural College of National Labor University in May, 1927.

第一部分　风云际会　青云发轫

二、教学演讲　名师云集
Outstanding Professors and Renowned Orators

上海大学锐意革新，广延名师，一大批名师、名流和著名学者来校任职任教和演讲，包括共产党人李大钊、李达、李汉俊、李季、陈望道、邵力子、施存统、沈雁冰（茅盾）、沈泽民、邓中夏、瞿秋白、蔡和森、张太雷、恽代英、任弼时、萧楚女、侯绍裘、田汉、蒋光慈、安体诚、杨贤江、张秋人、董亦湘、彭述之、刘含初、韩觉民、高语罕、卜世畸（卜士奇）、萧朴生、郑超麟、何味辛、张伯简、许德良、沈志远（沈观澜）、梅电龙（梅龚彬）、潘念之等。

SHU was committed to innovation and actively recruited renowned scholars and celebrities to serve and give lectures.

（一）教学名师　Outstanding Professors

1923年7月30日，在给胡适的信中，瞿秋白写道："既就了上大的事，便要用些精神，负些责任。我有一点意见，已经做了一篇文章，寄给平伯，平伯见先生时，想必要说起的。我们和平伯都希望上大能成南方的新文化运动中心。"

Qu Qiubai wrote a letter to Hu Shi, hoping that SHU would become the center of the new cultural movement in the south, on July 30, 1923.

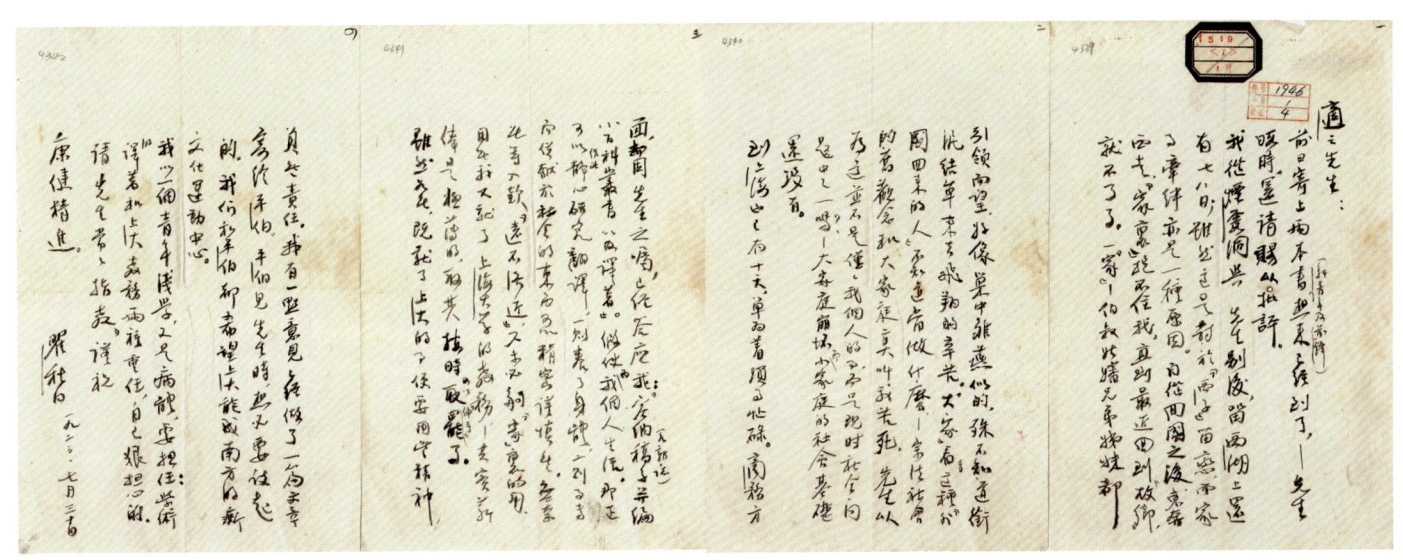

1924年6月,上海大学教职员合影。前排左起:洪野(1)、陈抱一(2)、陈望道(3)、杨明轩(6)、刘大白(7)、于右任(8)、邵力子(10)、何世桢(13)、邓中夏(16);中排左起:陈铁庵(3)、李瑞峰(5)、瞿秋白(8);后排左起:许德良(1)、周建人(2)、沈雁冰(3)、田汉(7)、施存统(8)、韩觉民(9)、向浒(10)、翁吉云(11)、邱青钱(邱清泉,半工半读)(12)

Group photo of SHU faculty, June 1924

1. 社会学系
The Sociology Department

任弼时(1904—1950),湖南汨罗人。伟大的马克思主义者,杰出的中国无产阶级革命家、政治家、组织家,中国共产党和中国人民解放军的卓越领导人,以毛泽东同志为核心的中国共产党第一代中央领导集体的重要成员。1922年初,加入中国共产党。1924年8月,任上海大学社会学系教授。1927年7月,任第四届共青团中央书记。新中国成立后,任中共中央书记处书记、共青团中央名誉主席。

Ren Bishi (1904-1950) became a professor of SHU in August 1924 and served as Secretary of the 4th Central Committee of the Communist Youth League in July 1927.

第一部分　风云际会　青云发轫

李达（1890—1966），湖南永州人。中国共产党发起组织成员。哲学家，马克思主义传播的先驱者。1921年，出席中共一大，当选中央局宣传主任。1924年8月，任上海大学社会学系教授。后任黄埔军校武汉分校代理政治总教官。新中国成立后，任湖南大学校长、武汉大学校长。

Li Da (1890-1966) became a professor of SHU in August 1924. He was one of the delegates of the First National Congress of the CPC, 1921.

李汉俊（1890—1927），湖北潜江人。中国共产党发起组织成员。1920年12月，任发起组织的代理书记。1921年，出席中共一大。1926年春，任上海大学社会学系教授。

Li Hanjun (1890-1927) became a professor of SHU in 1926. He was one of the delegates of the First National Congress of the CPC, 1921.

杨贤江（1895—1931），浙江慈溪人。教育理论家，青年教育家。1922年，加入中国共产党。1923年，任上海大学社会学系教授、中学部初高中人文科主任。1924年1月，任上海地方兼区执委会委员。1925年1月，参与创建中共商务印书馆支部，任支部书记。1926年3月，任上海大学行政委员会委员。

Yang Xianjiang (1895-1931) became a professor of SHU in 1923 and served as a member of the Administrative Committee of SHU in 1926.

沈泽民（1900—1933），浙江桐乡人。中国无产阶级革命家。中国共产党发起组织成员。沈雁冰胞弟。1923年底，任上海大学社会学系教授。五卅惨案后，任《热血日报》编辑。1931年1月，任中共中央宣传部部长。

Shen Zemin (1900-1933), the younger brother of Shen Yanbing, became a professor of SHU in 1923. He served as the Minister of the Publicity Department of the Central Committee of the CPC in January 1931.

  Shanghai University

张太雷（1898—1927），江苏常州人。中国无产阶级革命家和早期领导人。1920年10月，加入北京中国共产党早期组织。1924年8月，任上海大学社会学系教授。1925年1月，当选第三届共青团中央总书记。1927年，领导广州起义。

Zhang Tailei (1898-1927) became a professor of SHU in August 1924. He served as Secretary-General of the 3rd Central Committee of the Communist Youth League of China Central Committee in January 1925.

周建人（1888—1984），浙江绍兴人。鲁迅胞弟。1924年春，任上海大学社会学系教授。1948年4月，加入中国共产党。新中国成立后，任全国人大常务委员会副委员长、全国政协副主席。

Zhou Jianren (1888-1984), the younger brother of Lu Xun, became a professor of SHU in 1924. After the founding of the PRC, he served as Vice Chairman of the Standing Committee of the National People's Congress and Vice Chairman of the Chinese People's Political Consultative Conference (CPPCC).

郑超麟（1901—1998），福建漳平人。翻译家。1924年春，加入中国共产党；同年，翻译布哈林所著《共产主义ABC》。同期任上海大学社会学系教授。五卅惨案后，任《热血日报》编辑。1927年，任中共湖北省委宣传部部长。

Zheng Chaolin (1901-1998) became a professor of SHU in 1924 and Minister of the Publicity Department of the Hubei Provincial Party Committee in 1927.

恽代英（1895—1931），江苏武进人。中国无产阶级革命家，中国共产党早期青年运动领导人。1921年，加入中国共产党。1923年夏，任上海大学社会学系教授。1925年4月，任上海大学行政委员会委员。1926—1927年，任黄埔军校政治主任教官、武汉分校政治总教官。参加南昌起义、广州起义。后任中共中央宣传部秘书长、组织部秘书长。

Yun Daiying (1895-1931) became a professor of SHU in 1923 and served as a chief instructor of HMA from 1926 to 1927.

第一部分　风云际会　青云发轫

高语罕（1888—1948），安徽寿县人。中国共产党的早期领导人。1921年10月，加入中国共产党。1922年8月，加入中共旅德支部。1925年9月，任上海大学社会学系教授；同年12月，任黄埔军校政治教官。

Gao Yuhan (1888-1948) became a professor of SHU and a political instructor of HMA in 1925.

郭沫若（1892—1978），四川乐山人。1925年，任上海大学社会学系教授。1927年，参加南昌起义；同年，加入中国共产党。新中国成立后，任全国人大常务委员会副委员长、全国政协副主席。

Guo Moruo (1892-1978) became a professor of SHU in 1925. After the founding of the PRC, he served as Vice Chairman of the Standing Committee of the National People's Congress and Vice Chairman of the National Committee of the CPPCC.

萧朴生（1897—1926），四川德阳人。1922年，加入中国共产党。1925年初，当选中共旅欧支部执行委员会书记；同年8月回国，任上海大学社会学系教授。

Xiao Pusheng (1897-1926) became a professor of SHU in 1925.

彭述之（1895—1983），湖南邵阳人。1921年冬，加入中国共产党，是中共莫斯科支部负责人之一。1924年，任上海大学社会学系教授。1925年，在中共四大当选中央执行委员、中央局委员。

Peng Shuzhi (1895-1983) became a professor of SHU in 1924. He was elected as a member of the Central Executive Committee and the Central Bureau at the 4th National Congress of the CPC in 1925.

董亦湘（1896—1939），江苏常州人。1922年，加入中国共产党。1923年7月，参与创建中共商务印书馆小组，任组长。1924年，任上海大学社会学系教授。

Dong Yixiang (1896-1939) became a professor of SHU in 1924. He was the group leader of the CPC work group at the Commercial Press in July 1923.

蒋光慈（1901—1931），安徽六安人。作家。1921年，加入中国共产党。1924年，任上海大学社会学系教授。

Jiang Guangci (1901-1931), a renowned writer, became a professor of SHU in 1924.

蔡和森（1895—1931），湖南双峰人。中国无产阶级革命家，中国共产党早期领导人。1915年，与毛泽东一起组织新民学会，创办《湘江评论》，参加五四运动。1921年，与周恩来、赵世炎等筹组中共旅欧早期组织；同年12月，加入中国共产党。1922年起，任中共中央机关报《向导》周报主编。1923年秋，任上海大学社会学系教授。为五卅运动的领导人之一。1927年，任中共中央秘书长。

Cai Hesen (1895-1931) became a professor of SHU in 1923 and served as Secretary-General of the Central Committee of the CPC in 1927.

2. 中国文学系
The Chinese Literature Department

田汉（1898—1968），湖南长沙人。戏剧活动家，剧作家。1923年8月，任上海大学中国文学系教授。1932年，加入中国共产党。

Tian Han (1898-1968), a renowned dramatist, became a professor of SHU in 1923.

朱自清（1898—1948），浙江绍兴人。散文家，诗人，古典文学学者。曾任上海大学中国文学系教授。

Zhu Ziqing (1898-1948), a well-known essayist and poet, once served as a professor of SHU.

任中敏（1897—1991），江苏扬州人。戏曲史家，戏曲理论家。曾任上海大学中国文学系教授。

Ren Zhongmin (1897-1991), a theorist of traditional Chinese opera, once served as a professor of SHU.

刘大白（1880—1932），浙江绍兴人。诗人。1924年春，任上海大学中国文学系教授。1925年4月，任上海大学行政委员会委员。

Liu Dabai (1880-1932), a famous poet, became a professor of SHU in 1924.

Shanghai University

沈雁冰（1896—1981），笔名茅盾，浙江桐乡人。中国共产党发起组织成员。1922年7月，任上海地方兼区执委会委员。1923年5月，任上海大学中国文学系教授。1925年4月，任上海大学行政委员会委员。新中国成立后，任全国政协副主席、文化部部长。

Shen Yanbing (1896-1981), known by the pen name of Mao Dun, a member of Shanghai Communist Group, became a professor of SHU in 1923. He later served as Vice President of National Committee of the CPPCC and Minister of Culture.

周予同（1898—1981），浙江瑞安人。经学史家。曾任上海大学中国文学系教授。

Zhou Yutong (1898-1981), a historian of classical studies, once served as a professor of SHU.

赵景深（1902—1985），浙江丽水人。戏曲史家，戏曲理论家。1925年9月，任上海大学中国文学系教授。

Zhao Jingshen (1902-1985), a theorist of traditional Chinese opera, became a professor of SHU in 1925.

1925年9月，于右任聘赵景深为上海大学文艺院中国文学系教授的聘书

The Letter of Appointment from Yu Youren appointing Zhao Jingshen as a professor in the Chinese Literature Department of the College of Arts at SHU, September 1925

第一部分　风云际会　青云发轫

胡朴安（1878—1947），安徽泾县人。语言文字学家。1924年春，任上海大学中国文学系教授。

Hu Pu'an (1878-1947), a linguist, became a professor of SHU in 1924.

俞平伯（1900—1990），浙江德清人。作家，古典文学学者，红学家。1923年8月，任上海大学中国文学系教授。

Yu Pingbo (1900-1990), a writer and scholar of classical literature, became a professor of SHU in August 1923.

傅东华（1893—1971），浙江金华人。翻译家。1924年春，任上海大学中国文学系教授。

Fu Donghua (1893-1971), a translator, became a professor of SHU in 1924.

谢六逸（1898—1945），贵州贵阳人。中国新闻教育事业的开拓者之一。1926年，任上海大学中国文学系教授。

Xie Liuyi (1898-1945), one of the founders of modern journalism education of China, became a professor of SHU in 1926.

3. 英国文学系
The English Literature Department

朱光潜（1897—1986），安徽桐城人。美学家。1923 年后，任上海大学英国文学系教授。

Zhu Guangqian (1897-1986), an aesthetician, became a professor of SHU in 1923.

朱复（1898—1982），上海人。1925 年 2 月，任上海大学英国文学系教授；同年 4 月，任上海大学行政委员会委员。

Zhu Fu (1898-1982) became a professor of SHU and a member of the Administrative Committee of SHU in 1925.

何世枚（1896—1975），安徽望江人。何世桢胞弟。1924 年春，任上海大学英国文学系教授。

He Shimei (1896-1975), the younger brother of He Shizhen, became a professor of SHU in 1924.

4. 政治学系
The Politics Department

杨杏佛（1893—1933），江西清江（今樟树）人。爱国民主人士。1924 年 8 月，任上海大学政治学系教授；同年 11 月，任孙中山秘书。

Yang Xingfo (1893-1933) became a professor of SHU in August 1924 and served as the secretary of Sun Yat-sen in November of the same year.

5. 美术科
The Fine Arts Section

万古蟾（1900—1995），江苏南京人。美术片导演，中国动画片的创始人之一。1923年，任上海大学美术科教授。

Wan Guchan (1900-1995), an art film director and one of the founders of Chinese animated films, became a professor of SHU in 1923.

万籁天（1899—1977），湖北武昌人。话剧、电影导演。1924年，任上海大学美术科教授。

Wan Laitian (1899-1977), a film director, became a professor of SHU in 1924.

吴梦非（1893—1979），浙江东阳人。音乐教育家。1924年，任上海大学美术科教授。

Wu Mengfei (1893-1979), a music educator, became a professor of SHU in 1924.

陈抱一（1893—1945），广东新会人。画家，美术教育家。曾任上海大学美术科教授。

Chen Baoyi (1893-1945), a painter and art educator, once served as a professor of SHU.

6. 中学部
Middle School Division

丰子恺（1898—1975），浙江桐乡人。画家，文学家，美术和音乐教育家。1925年3月，任上海大学中学部教员。

Feng Zikai (1898-1975), a painter, writer and educator in fine arts and music, became a professor of SHU in 1925.

许德良（1900—1991），江苏苏州人。1922年，加入中国共产党。1924年春，任上海大学庶务员兼中学部英文教员。新中国成立后，任上海中医学院副院长。

Xu Deliang (1900-1991) became a professor of SHU in 1924. After the founding of the PRC, he served as Vice President of Shanghai University of Traditional Chinese Medicine.

沈观澜（1902—1965），又名志远，浙江萧山人。1925年3月，任上海大学中学部教员；同年，加入中国共产党。1926年，任上海大学中学部教务副主任。新中国成立后，任上海市政协副主席。

Shen Guanlan (1902-1965) became a professor of SHU in 1925. After the founding of the PRC, he served as Vice Chairman of the Shanghai Municipal Committee of the CPPCC.

周水平（1894—1926），江苏江阴人。1924年，任上海大学中学部体育教员。1925年春，加入中国共产党。

Zhou Shuiping (1894-1926) became a professor of SHU in 1924.

梅电龙（1900—1975），又名龚彬，湖北黄梅人。1925年，加入中国共产党；同年，参与创建中共徐家汇支部和中共徐家汇独立支部，分别任支部书记。五卅运动期间，为上海学生运动负责人。1926年3月，任上海大学中学部教员；同年，参加北伐，任国民革命军第40军第12师政治部主任。后参加南昌起义。新中国成立后，任全国政协副秘书长。

Mei Dianlong (1900-1975) became a professor of SHU in 1926. After the founding of the PRC, he served as Deputy Secretary-General of the National Committee of the CPPCC.

曹聚仁（1900—1972），浙江兰溪人。记者，作家。1925年3月，任上海大学中学部教员。

Cao Juren (1900-1972), a journalist and writer, became a professor of SHU in 1925.

潘念之（1902—1988），浙江新昌人。法学家。1925年，加入中国共产党；同年，任上海大学中学部教员。新中国成立后，任华东政法学院副院长。

Pan Nianzhi (1902-1988), a jurist, became a professor of SHU in 1925.

历任教职员一览表（部分）
Faculty and Administrative Staff (Partial)

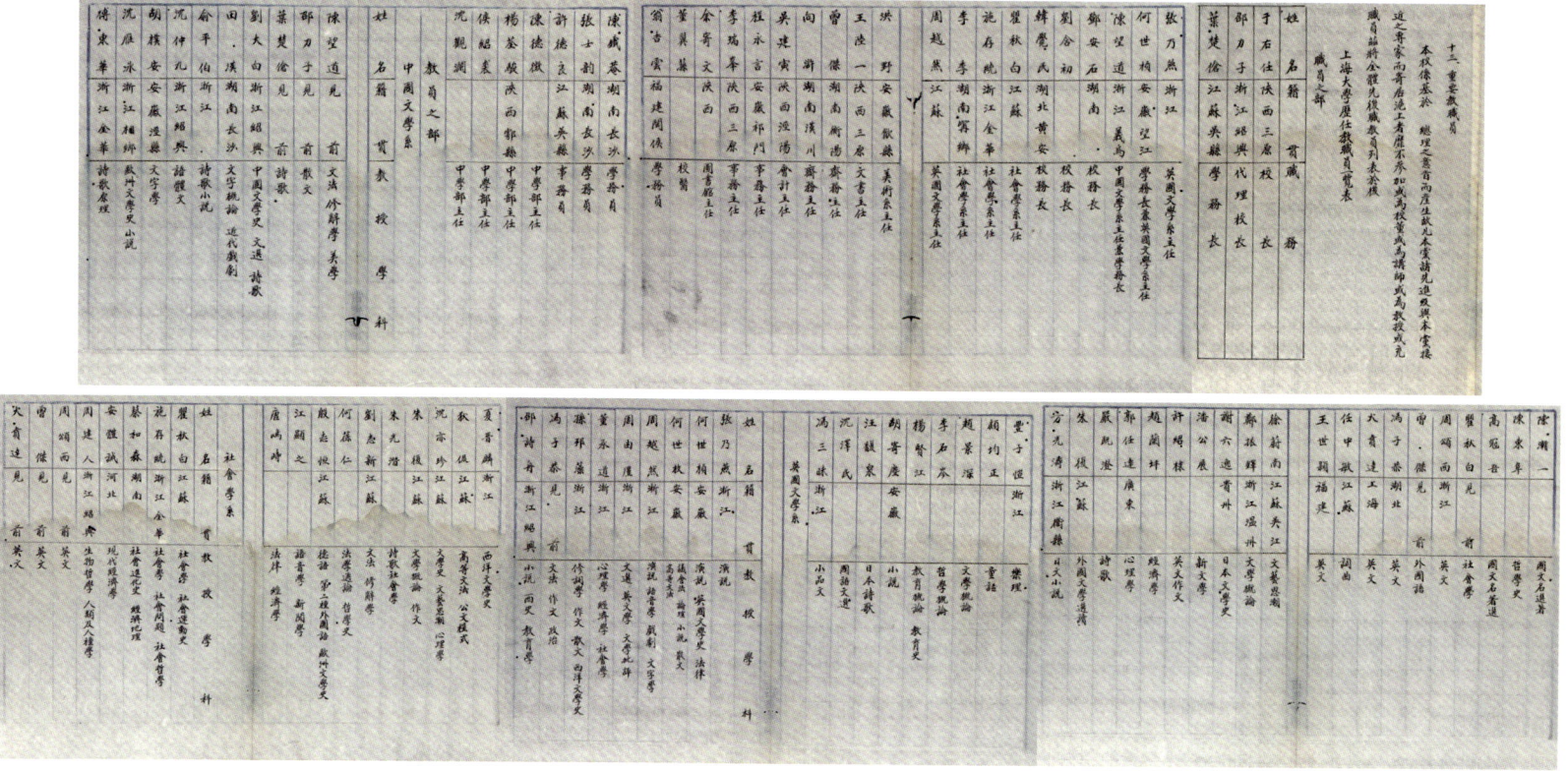

（二）演讲名人　Renowned Orators

"特别讲座教授"名单一览
Distinguished Visiting Professors

身　份	姓　名
上海大学教授	李大钊　郭沫若　杨杏佛　朱光潜　朱自清　赵景深　戴季陶 胡汉民　左舜生　黄葆钺　王登云　朱　湘　万籁天　周予同
上海大学校董	张　继　章太炎　马君武　汪精卫
其他文化精英和政界名流	胡　适　刘仁静　廖仲恺　邓演达　吴玉章 李权时　吴稚晖　沈玄庐　胡愈之　褚理堂

第一部分 风云际会 青云发轫

三、人才培养　济济一堂
Excellent Talent Cultivation

上海大学吸引四方热血青年影从云集，为中国革命和建设汇聚、培养了一大批杰出人才。

SHU attracted passionate young people from all over, gathering and cultivating a large number of outstanding talents for China's revolution and development.

1923年7月，上海大学美术科图音、图工组毕业生在宋园（今闸北公园）宋教仁墓前合影

Graduates from the Fine Arts Section of SHU in front of the tomb of Song Jiaoren in Song Garden (now Zhabei Park), July 1923

1923年7月，上海大学美术科第一届毕业生合影

The first graduates from the Fine Arts Section of SHU, July 1923

1924年春,上海大学全体学生合影
All the students of SHU, 1924

1926年7月1日,上海大学中国文学系、英国文学系丙寅级毕业生合影(中坐长髯者为校长于右任)
Graduation photo of the 1926 Class of the Chinese Literature Department and the English Literature Department, July 1, 1926
(President Yu Youren, the one with long beard in the middle)

学生名录（部分）
Student Roaster (Partial)

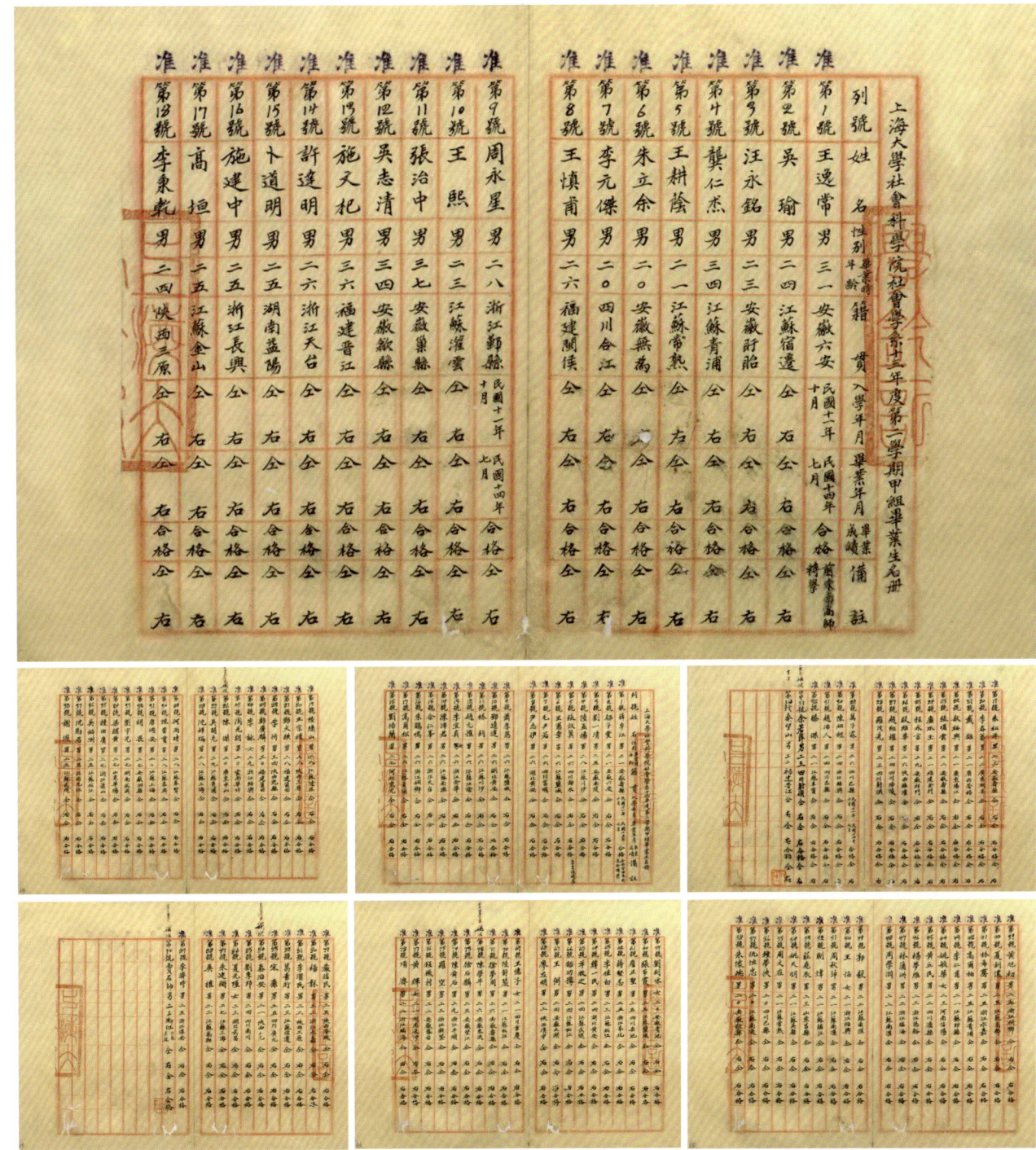

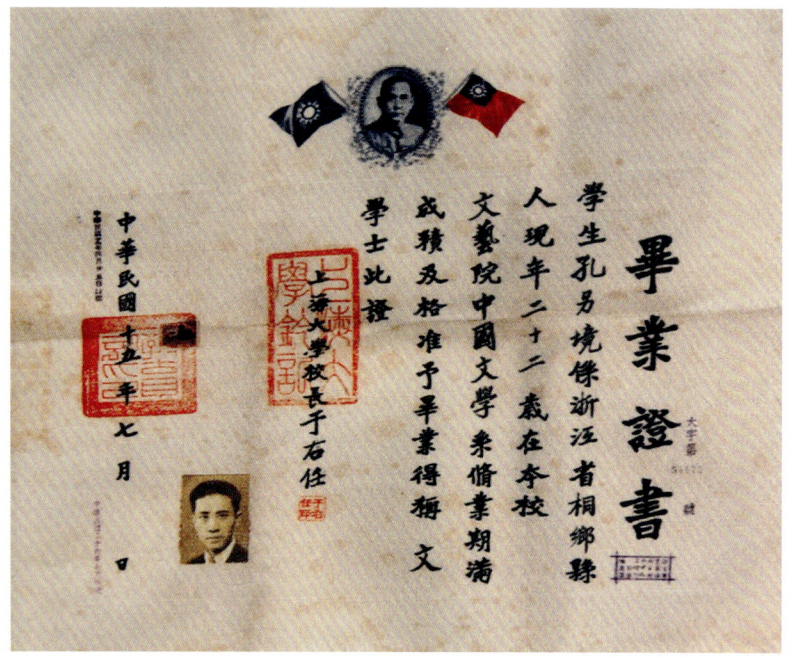

中国文学系孔另境毕业证书

The Graduation Certificate of Kong Lingjing from the Chinese Literature Department

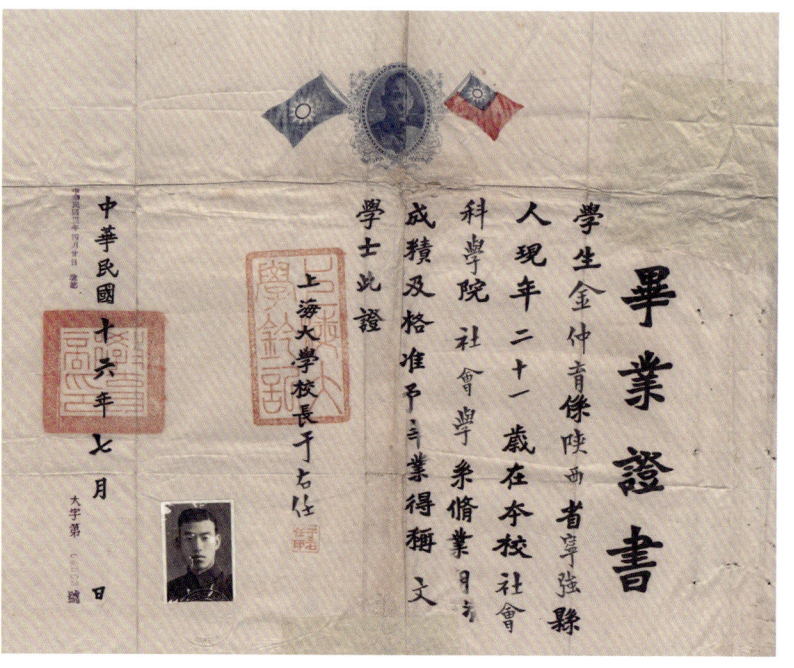

社会学系金仲育毕业证书

The Graduation Certificate of Jin Zhongyu from the Sociology Department

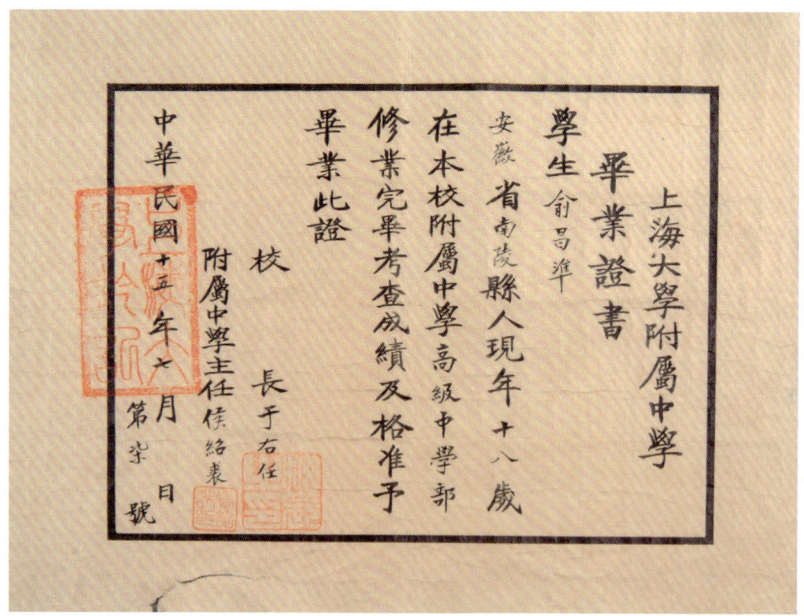

中学部俞昌准毕业证书

The Graduation Certificate of Yu Changzhun from the Middle School Division

第一部分　风云际会　青云发轫

四、革命堡垒　红色学府
Revolutionary Stronghold and Red Academy

上海大学集聚了一批中国共产党的早期党员和领导人，积极宣传和传播马克思列宁主义。上海大学师生在中共中央、共青团中央和全国学联担任领导工作，并奔赴全国各地帮助建立中共地方基层党组织。上海大学师生领导平民教育和工人运动，投身上海工人三次武装起义，广泛开展反帝反封建斗争。

SHU gathered a group of early members and leaders of the CPC, who actively publicized and disseminated Marxism-Leninism. Teachers and students of SHU held leading positions in the Central Committee of the CPC, the Central Committee of the Communist Youth League and the National Students' Federation, and were actively dedicated to anti-imperialist and anti-feudal fights.

（一）宣传和传播马克思列宁主义　Spreading and Popularizing Marxism-Leninism

1. 创办中国共产党最早的宣传刊物
Establishing the Earliest Propaganda Publications of the CPC

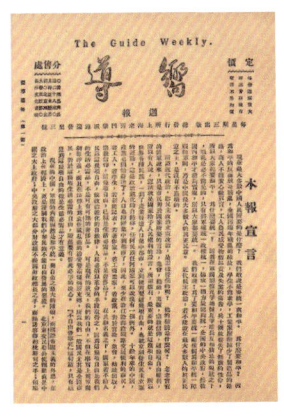

《向导》周报是中国共产党于1922年9月13日创办的第一份中央机关报，由蔡和森担任首任主编

The Guide Weekly, the first official newspaper of the CPC, was founded on September 13, 1922. Cai Hesen served as the first Chief Editor.

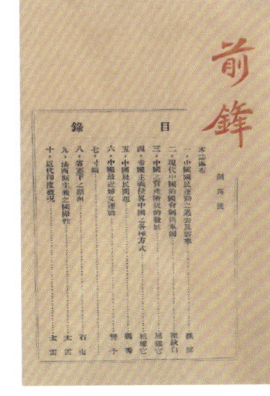

《前锋》月刊是中国共产党于1923年7月1日创办的机关刊物，由瞿秋白担任主编

Vanguard, the monthly official journal of the CPC, was founded on July 1, 1923. Qu Qiubai served as Chief Editor.

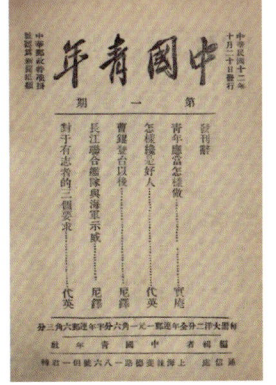

《中国青年》周刊是中国社会主义青年团于1923年10月20日创办的机关刊物，由恽代英担任主编

China Youth, a weekly publication, was founded by the Socialist Youth League on October 20, 1923. Yun Daiying served as Chief Editor.

2. 编撰出版中国共产党早期宣传马克思主义和社会主义理论的专著
Compiling and Publishing Monographs on the Early Publicity of Marxist and Socialist Theories by the CPC

上海大学是中国最早系统讲授马克思主义和社会主义理论的高等学府。1924年，上海书店陆续出版《社会科学讲义》1—4集，其中收有上海大学教授瞿秋白的《现代社会学》《社会哲学概论》、安体诚的《现代经济学》、施存统的《社会运动史》《社会思想史》《社会问题》等讲义。这些讲义，既是学习社会学、社会哲学的教材，也是马克思主义理论的启蒙读物，在社会上产生了很大影响。

SHU was the first institution of higher education in China to systematically introduce Marxist and socialist theories. In 1924, Shanghai Bookstore published *Lectures on Social Sciences* (Volumes 1-4), among which were influential works by professors of SHU.

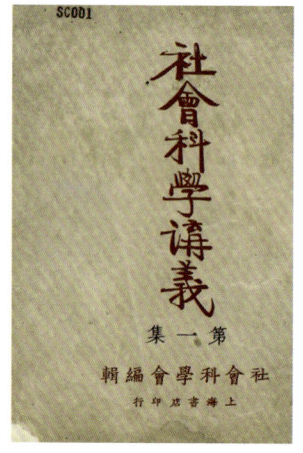

《社会科学讲义》
Lectures on Social Philosophy

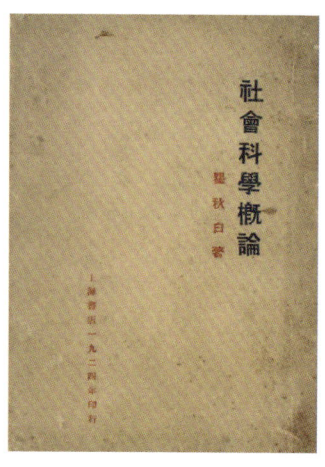

瞿秋白著《社会科学概论》
Introduction to Social Philosophy by Qu Qiubai

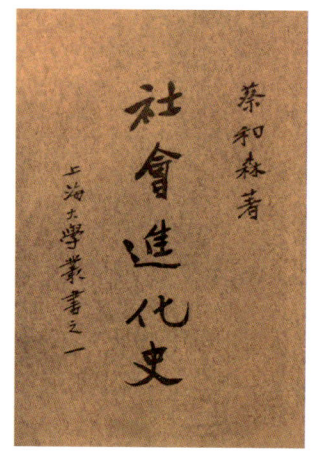

蔡和森著《社会进化史》是中国运用马列主义阐述社会发展的奠基之作，书名由校长于右任题签

The History of Social Evolution by Cai Hesen is a founding book in China that applies Marxism-Leninism to expound on social development. The book title was inscribed by President Yu Youren.

3. 在报刊上发表马克思列宁主义相关译著
Publishing Translation Works Related to Marxism-Leninism

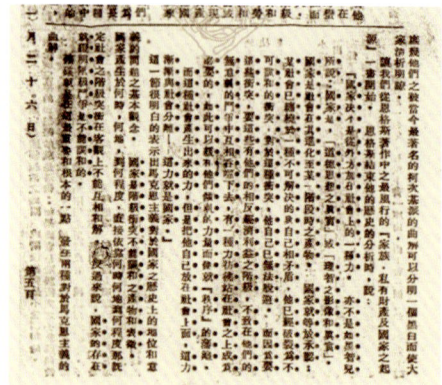

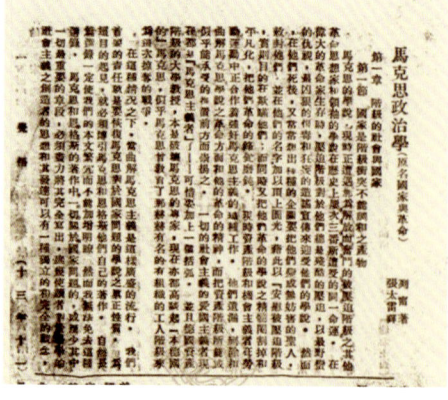

张太雷翻译列宁所著的《国家与革命》第一章，以《马克思政治学》为题，1924年11月26—29日在《民国日报》副刊《觉悟》上连载

The first chapter of *The State and Revolution* by Vladimir Lenin, translated by Zhang Tailei, was published with the title "Marx's Politics" on *Enlightenment*, a supplement of *The Republican Daily*, from November 26 to 29, 1924

（二）担任中共中央、共青团中央和全国学联的领导工作
Leading Work in the Central Committee of the CPC, the Central Committee of the Communist Youth League and the All-China Students' Federation

1. 担任中共中央的领导工作
Leading Work in the Central Committee of the CPC

在中共中央第二至第四届委员会任职的上海大学师生一览

SHU Teachers and Students Serving in the 2nd to 4th Central Committees of the CPC

中共中央委员会	姓　名	担任职务
第二届 （1922年7月—1923年6月）	邓中夏	执行委员
	蔡和森	执行委员
第三届 （1923年6月—1925年1月）	蔡和森	执行委员
	李大钊	执行委员
	邓中夏	职工运动委员会书记
第四届 （1925年1月—1927年4月）	李大钊	执行委员
	蔡和森	执行委员
	瞿秋白	执行委员、 中央局常务委员
	彭述之	执行委员、宣传部主任
	杨之华（女）	妇女部主任

2. 担任中国社会主义青年团（共青团）中央的领导工作
Leading Work in the Central Committee of the Communist Youth League

在共青团中央第一至第三届委员会任职的上海大学师生一览
SHU Teachers and Students Serving on the 1st to 3rd Central Committees of the Communist Youth League

青年团（共青团）中央委员会	姓　名	担任职务
第一届 （1922年5月—1923年8月）	施存统	书记
	张太雷	执行委员、经济部主任、宣传部主任
	蔡和森	执行委员、宣传部主任
	贺　昌	执行委员、经济部主任
第二届 （1923年8月—1925年1月）	邓中夏	委员长
	恽代英	执行委员、宣传部主任、学生部主任
	张秋人	执行委员、农工部主任
	卜世畸	执行委员、学生部主任、农工部主任
	施存统	执行委员
第三届 （1925年1月—1927年5月）	张太雷	总书记
	任弼时	代理总书记、执行委员
	恽代英	执行委员、宣传部主任、学生部主任
	贺　昌	执行委员、工农部主任
	张秋人	执行委员、非基督教部主任
	张伯简	代理工农部主任
	杨之华（女）	妇女运动委员会书记

第一部分　风云际会　青云发轫

贺昌（1906—1935），山西柳林人。1923年7月，加入中国共产党；同年9月，进入上海大学学习。曾任共青团中央执行委员、经济部主任、工农部主任和共青团上海地委书记。后参加南昌起义、广州起义。1929年，任中共广东省委书记，协助邓小平策划百色起义。1933年，任中国工农红军总政治部代主任。

He Chang (1906-1935) entered SHU in 1923. In 1929, he served as Secretary of the Guangdong Provincial Committee of the CPC and assisted Deng Xiaoping in planning the Baise Uprising. In 1933, he served as Acting Director of the General Political Department of the Chinese Workers' and Peasants' Red Army.

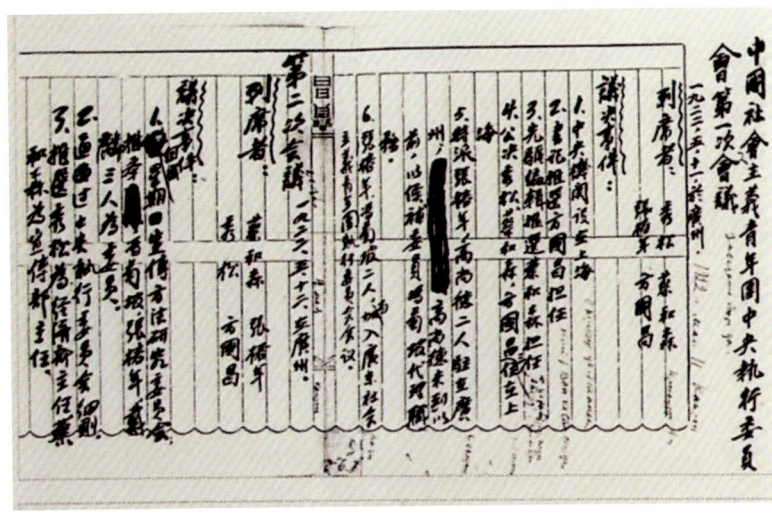

邓中夏、施存统、张太雷、蔡和森等人是中国社会主义青年团的主要创始人。图为1922年5月11日中国社会主义青年团中央执行委员会的会议记录（部分）

Meeting Minutes of the Central Executive Committee of the Socialist Youth League of China, founded by Deng Zhongxia, Shi Cuntong, Zhang Tailei, Cai Hesen, etc., May 11, 1922

1924年3月，中国社会主义青年团中央二届二次扩大会议在上海召开。图为邓中夏（前排右1）、恽代英（后排右2）、卜世畸（前排左1）和部分与会者在上海合影

Group photo of Deng Zhongxia (first from right in the front row), Yun Daiying (second from right in the back row), Bu ShiJi (first from left in the front row) and some other participants of the Second Enlarged Meeting of the Second Central Committee of the Socialist Youth League of China in Shanghai, March 1924

3. 担任中华全国学生联合会总会（全国学联）的领导工作
Leading Work in the All-China Students' Federation

1919年6月16日至8月5日，全国学联第一次代表大会在上海召开，邓中夏出席会议。图为成立大会合影

Group photo taken at the founding conference of the First National Congress of the All-China Students' Federation in Shanghai from June 16 to August 5, 1919, which Deng Zhongxia attended

在全国学联第六至第八届委员会任职的上海大学学生一览
SHU Students Serving on the 6th to 8th Committees of the All-China Students' Federation

全国学联委员会	姓　名	担任职务
第六届（1924年8月—1925年6月）	刘一清	委员长
第七届（1925年6月—1926年7月）	李硕勋	委员长、党团书记
	刘峻山	宣传部部长
第八届（1926年7月—1927年7月）	刘披云（刘荣简）	委员长
	李硕勋	党团书记
	何成湘	秘书长

　　李硕勋（1903—1931），四川高县人。1923年，进入上海大学社会学系学习。1924年，加入中国共产党。五卅运动期间，当选第七届全国学联委员长、党团书记。1926年1月，参与创建中华全国学生联合总会独立支部，任支部书记。后参加南昌起义，任起义军第11军第25师党代表兼政治部主任。1930年起，任中共中央军委委员、中共江南省委军委书记、中共两广省委军委书记。

　　Li Shuoxun (1903-1931) entered the Sociology Department of SHU in 1923.

第一部分　风云际会　青云发轫

刘披云（1905—1983），又名荣简，四川岳池人。1925年，进入上海大学学习；同年，加入中国共产党。1926年，任第八届全国学联委员长。1927年，任中共四川省委常委兼宣传部部长。新中国成立后，任云南省副省长。

Liu Piyun (1905-1983) entered SHU in 1925. After the founding of the PRC, he served as Vice Governor of Yunnan Province.

刘峻山（1899—1985），江西吉安人。1924年，进入上海大学学习；同年，加入中国共产党。1925年，任上海学联党团书记。1926年，任全国学联常务委员兼宣传部部长。新中国成立后，任江西省人民政府体育运动委员会副主任、民盟江西省委副主任委员。

Liu Junshan (1899-1985) entered SHU in 1924. After the founding of the PRC, he served as Deputy Director of the Sports Commission of People's Government of Jiangxi Province and Deputy Chairman of the Jiangxi Provincial Committee of China Democratic League.

（三）建立中国共产党最活跃的基层组织
Building the Most Active Grassroots Organizations of the CPC

1. 担任中共上海地方执行委员会兼上海区执行委员会的领导工作
Leading Work in the Shanghai Local Executive Committee of the CPC and Concurrently in the Shanghai Regional Executive Committee of the CPC

1921年12月，中共上海地方委员会（上海地委）成立，直属中共中央领导，陈望道、张太雷先后出任书记。

1922年7月，上海地委改组为中共上海地方执行委员会兼上海区执行委员会（简称上海地方兼区执委），领导上海市及江苏、浙江两省的工作。邓中夏曾任委员长，沈雁冰、沈泽民、杨贤江曾任委员。

In December 1921, the Shanghai Local Committee of the CPC (Shanghai Local Committee) was established, directly under the leadership of the Central Committee of the CPC. Chen Wangdao and Zhang Tailei successively served as secretaries.

In July 1922, the Shanghai Local Committee was reorganized into the Shanghai Local Executive Committee of the CPC and concurrently the Shanghai Regional Executive Committee of the CPC (referred to as the Shanghai Local and Regional Executive Committee), leading the revolutionary work in Shanghai as well as that in Jiangsu and Zhejiang provinces. Deng Zhongxia once served as Chairman; Shen Yanbing, Shen Zemin and Yang Xianjiang once served as members.

2. 建立中共上海地区第一党小组
Establishing the First Party Group in Shanghai

1923年7月，上海地方兼区执委将全市53名党员按居住地建立四个党小组，第一组为上海大学组，组员11人，其中上海大学师生有9人：邓中夏、瞿秋白、张太雷、施存统、许德良、王一知（女）、贺昌、严信民、黄让之。

上海大学师生先后担任组长的有：许德良、施存统、王一知（女）、黄让之、陈比难（陈碧兰，女）、刘华（刘剑华）、张景曾。

1925年初，根据中共四大党章规定，在中共小组基础上组建中共支部。中共上海大学支部成立，初期由施存统任负责人。

In July 1923, the Shanghai Local and Regional Executive Committee established four Party groups for the 53 Party members in the city based on their places of residence. The first group was the SHU group, consisting of 11 members, nine of whom were teachers and students from SHU. Seven teachers and students from SHU successively served as group leaders.

3. 建立中共上海地区上海大学独立支部
Establishing an Independent CPC Branch at SHU

1926年3月，中共上海大学独立支部成立，直属上海区执委领导。高尔柏担任独立支部首任书记。

In March 1926, the independent CPC branch at SHU was established. Gao Erbai served as the first Secretary.

中共上海大学独立支部历任书记一览
Secretaries of the Independent CPC Branch at SHU

姓　名	任职时间
高尔柏	1926年3—8月
张晓柳	1926年9月—冬
张　耘	1926年冬
党伯弧	1927年2—5月

高尔柏（1901—1986），上海青浦人。1924年9月，进入上海大学社会学系学习；同年，加入中国共产党。1925年，任上海大学中学部教员、训育主任、社会科主任。1926年3月，任中共上海大学独立支部首任书记。

Gao Erbai (1901-1986) entered SHU in September 1924. He served as the first Secretary of the independent CPC branch at SHU in March 1926.

4. 建立共青团上海大学特别支部
Establishing a Special Branch of the Communist Youth League at SHU

1925年11月，共青团上海大学特别支部成立。阳翰笙（欧阳继修）担任特别支部首任书记。

In November 1925, the special branch of the Communist Youth League at SHU was established. Yang Hansheng (Ouyang Jixiu) served as the first Secretary.

共青团上海大学特别支部历任书记一览
List of Secretaries of the Special Branch of the Communist Youth League at SHU

姓　名	任职时间
阳翰笙	1925年11—12月
马　英	1925年12月—1926年6月
陈怀璞	1926年6—8月
刘披云	1926年9月—1927年5月

阳翰笙（1902—1993），原名欧阳本义，字继修，四川高县人。电影剧作家，作家，戏剧家。1924年，进入上海大学社会学系学习。1925年，加入中国共产党；同年，任中共闸北部委书记、共青团上海大学特别支部首任书记。后参加南昌起义。新中国成立后，任总理办公室副主任、全国文联党组书记。

Yang Hansheng (1902-1993) entered SHU in 1924. After the founding of the PRC, he served as Deputy Director of the Premier's Office and Secretary of the Party Leadership Group of the China Federation of Literary and Art Circles.

（四）播撒革命火种，帮助各地建立中共地方基层党组织
Spreading Flames of Revolution

在地方党团基层组织中作为创建者或领导者的上海大学师生一览（部分）

SHU Teachers and Students as Founders or Leaders of Local Grassroots Organizations of the CPC and the Communist Youth League (Partial)

地　区	基层组织	创建者或领导者
上海 （6个）	中共商务印书馆组	董亦湘
	中共商务印书馆支部	杨贤江
	中共徐家汇支部	梅电龙
	中共公共支部	张伯简
	中共徐家汇独立支部	梅电龙
	中华全国学生联合总会独立支部	李硕勋
安徽 （12个）	中共寿县小甸集特别支部	曹蕴真　薛卓汉　徐梦周　方运炽（方英）等
	中共安庆支部	王步文　濮德治
	中共寿县淮上中学补习社支部	胡允恭　吴云　吴震等
	中共寿县瓦埠小学支部	方运炽
	中共寿县窑口集特别支部	薛卓汉
	中共阜阳小组	周传鼎　周传业
	中共高皇特别支部	程锡简
	中共六安特别支部	王绍虞
	中共南陵县特别支部	俞昌准
	中国社会主义青年团寿县支部	薛卓汉　徐梦秋
	中国社会主义青年团淮上青年社	吴云
	共青团安庆特别支部	徐梦秋　薛卓汉

续表

浙江 （8个）	中共宁波小组	张秋人
	中共象山支部	贺威圣
	中共沙村支部	沙文求
	中共宁海中学支部	蒋如琮
	中共临海县特别支部	张崇文
	中共天台特别支部	蒋如琮
	中共兰溪临时特别支部	童玉堂
	中国社会主义青年团宁波支部	张秋人
江苏 （3个）	中共常熟特别支部	周文在
	中共横山桥支部	包焕赓
	青年团无锡特别支部	张秋人
广东 （2个）	中共琼崖地方执行委员会	王文明
	中共邓仲支部	陈垂斌　郭儒灏
福建 （2个）	中共漳州支部	翁泽生
	共青团漳州支部	翁泽生
江西 （5个）	中共吉安小组	罗石冰　曾延生
	中共延福支部	罗石冰
	中共吉安特别支部	罗石冰
	中共革坂小组	汪佑春
	中国社会主义青年团永修支部	王环心
山东 （1个）	中共曹州支部	徐鹏翥
河南 （1个）	中共南阳支部	杨士颖
辽宁 （2个）	中共奉天支部	吴　霆
	青年团奉天特别支部	吴　霆

续表

陕西 （10个）	中共西安特别支部	安体诚
	中共三原特别支部	张仲实
	中共郃县支部	杜嗣尧
	中共郃县委员会	杜嗣尧
	中共洋县小组	尚辛友　阎灵初
	中国社会主义青年团赤水特别支部	武止戈
	中国社会主义青年团西安支部	武止戈　邹　均
	共青团三原特别支部	李秉乾
	共青团澄城特别支部	王超北
	共青团肤施（延安）四中支部	王超北
重庆 （1个）	中共双江支部	雷晓晖（女）

曹蕴真（1901—1927），安徽寿县人。1922年春，加入中国共产党。1923年秋，进入上海大学社会学系学习；同年12月，回乡参与创建中共寿县小甸集特别支部，任支部书记。

Cao Yunzhen (1901-1927) entered SHU in 1923.

徐梦周（1904—1944），安徽寿县人。曾在上海大学英国文学系学习。1922年，加入中国共产党。1923年，回乡参与创建中共寿县小甸集特别支部，任宣传委员。1928年1月，任中共陕西省委常委、秘书长。

Xu Mengzhou (1904-1944) once studied at SHU.

第一部分　风云际会　青云发轫

方运炽（1906—1932），又名方英，安徽寿县人。1923年，进入上海大学社会学系学习，其间加入中国共产党。后回乡参与创建中共寿县小甸集特别支部、中共寿县瓦埠小学支部。1929年，领导安徽独山暴动。1931年，任鄂豫皖中央分局特委书记、中共皖西北道委书记。

Fang Yunchi (1906-1932) entered SHU in 1923.

王步文（1898—1931），安徽岳西人。1923年，加入中国共产党；同年12月，参与创建中共安庆支部，任组织委员。1924年，进入上海大学社会学系学习。1927年，参加上海工人第三次武装起义。1930年9月，任中共安徽省委首任书记。

Wang Buwen (1898-1931) entered SHU in 1924.

濮德治（1905—1997），安徽安庆人。陈独秀表弟。1923年，加入中国共产党；同年12月，回乡参与创建中共安庆支部，任宣传委员。1924年，进入上海大学英国文学系学习。

Pu Dezhi (1905-1997), cousin of Chen Duxiu, entered SHU in 1924.

胡允恭（1902—1991），安徽寿县人。1923年，进入上海大学社会学系学习；同年，加入中国共产党。1924年夏，回乡与吴云、吴震等创建中共寿县淮上中学补习社支部。1931年10月，任中共山东省委书记。新中国成立后，任福建师范学院院长。

Hu Yungong (1902-1991) entered SHU in 1923.

吴云（1903—1978），安徽凤台人。吴震胞兄。1923年夏，进入上海大学社会学系学习；同年，加入中国共产党。1924年夏，回乡参与创建中共寿县淮上中学补习社支部、中国社会主义青年团淮上青年社。1930年12月，任中共凤台县委书记。

Wu Yun (1903-1978) entered SHU in 1923.

周传鼎（1905—1929），安徽阜阳人。周传业胞兄。1924年，加入中国共产党。1925年2月，进入上海大学中学部学习；同年夏，与周传业一起回乡创建中共阜阳小组。1928年2月，参加中共领导的以阜阳为中心的四九起义，点燃皖北的革命烈火。

Zhou Chuanding (1905-1929) entered SHU in 1925.

周传业（1907—1929），安徽阜阳人。周传鼎胞弟。1924年，加入中国共产党。1925年7月，进入上海大学社会学系学习；同年夏，与周传鼎一起回乡创建中共阜阳小组。1928年2月，参加中共领导的以阜阳为中心的四九起义，点燃皖北的革命烈火。

Zhou Chuanye (1905-1929) entered SHU in 1925.

程锡简（1903—1931），安徽凤台人。1922年，进入上海大学学习。1923年，加入中国共产党。1924年，回乡参与创建中共高皇特别支部，任支部书记。后参加南昌起义。

Cheng Xijian (1903-1931) entered SHU in 1922.

王绍虞（1897—1928），安徽六安人。1923年，进入上海大学学习。1924年，加入中国共产党。1925年冬，回乡参与创建中共六安特别支部，任支部书记。

Wang Shaoyu (1897-1928) entered SHU in 1923.

俞昌准（1907—1928），安徽南陵人。1925年7月，进入上海大学中学部学习。1926年，加入中国共产党；同年，回乡参与创建中共南陵县特别支部，任宣传委员兼秘书。1928年1月，领导成立安徽第一个红色农民运动政权南芜边区苏维埃政府并任副主席。

Yu Changzhun (1907-1928) entered SHU in 1925.

贺威圣（1902—1926），浙江象山人。1924年春，进入上海大学社会学系学习；同年，加入中国共产党。在学期间，回乡参与创建中共象山支部。1925年，任共青团闸北部委书记。1926年，任中共杭州地委书记。

He Weisheng (1902-1926) entered SHU in 1924.

沙文求（1904—1928），浙江宁波人。1925年春，进入上海大学社会学系学习；同年，加入中国共产党。1926年初，回乡参与创建中共沙村支部，任支部书记。

Sha Wenqiu (1904-1928) entered SHU in 1925.

第一部分　风云际会　青云发轫

蒋如琮（1898—1961），浙江三门人。1925年，进入上海大学社会学系学习；同年9月，加入中国共产党。1926年9月，回乡参与创建中共宁海中学支部，任支部书记。1927年，参加南昌起义；同年11月，创建参与中共天台特别支部，任支部书记。

Jiang Rucong (1898-1961) entered SHU in 1925.

张崇文（1906—1995），浙江临海人。张崇德胞弟。1926年，进入上海大学社会学系学习；同年，加入中国共产党，回乡参与创建中共临海县特别支部并任支部书记。新中国成立后，任铁道兵政治部副主任。1955年，获少将军衔。

Zhang Chongwen (1906-1995) entered SHU in 1926.

童玉堂（1905—1951），浙江兰溪人。1925年，进入上海大学社会学系学习。1926年，加入中国共产党。1927年2月，回乡参与创建中共兰溪临时特别支部，任支部书记。

Tong Yutang (1905-1951) entered SHU in 1925.

周文在（1906—1994），江苏常熟人。1925年，进入上海大学中学部学习；同年，加入中国共产党。1926年，参与创建中共常熟特别支部。后参加南昌起义。新中国成立后，任江苏省政协副主席。1955年，获少将军衔。

Zhou Wenzai (1906-1994) entered SHU in 1925.

包焕赓（1907—1947），江苏武进人。1925年，进入上海大学社会学系学习；同年，加入中国共产党。1926年春，回乡参与创建中共横山桥支部，任支部书记。

Bao Huangeng (1907-1947) entered SHU in 1925.

王文明（1894—1930），广东琼海（今属海南）人。1922年秋，加入中国共产党。1924年秋，进入上海大学社会学系学习。1926年6月，参与创建中共琼崖地方执行委员会，任地委书记。后开辟母瑞山农村革命根据地，是海南岛地区党组织和革命根据地的创始人。

Wang Wenming (1894-1930) entered SHU in 1924.

陈垂斌（1902—1933），广东三亚（今属海南）人。1924年，进入上海大学社会学系学习；同年，加入中国共产党。1926年，任中共琼崖地委委员兼组织部部长；同年，参与创建中共邓仲支部，任支部书记。

Chen Chuibin (1902-1933) entered SHU in 1924.

郭儒灏（1903—1990），广东琼海（今属海南）人。1925年9月，进入上海大学社会学系学习；同年，加入中国共产党。1926年，参与创建中共邓仲支部。

Guo Ruhao (1903-1990) entered SHU in 1925.

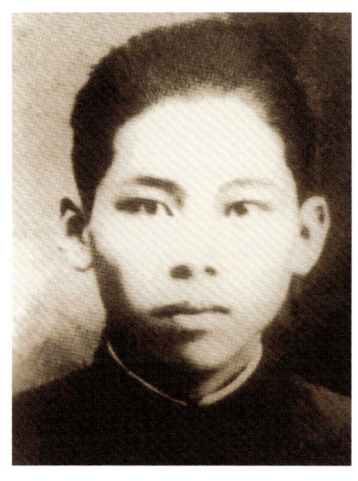

翁泽生（1903—1939），福建厦门人。1925年初，进入上海大学学习；同年7月，加入中国共产党。1926—1927年，参与创建共青团漳州支部、中共漳州支部。1928年，参与创立台湾共产党。1932年，奉调上海负责台共与中共中央的联络工作；同年，任中华全国总工会党团秘书长。

Weng Zesheng (1903-1939) entered SHU in 1925.

罗石冰（1896—1931），江西吉安人。1924年2月，进入上海大学社会学系学习；同年，加入中国共产党。1926年，回乡参与创建中共吉安小组、中共延福支部和中共吉安特别支部；同年4月，任中共江西地委书记。后参加南昌起义。

Luo Shibing (1896-1931) entered SHU in 1924.

曾延生（1897—1928），江西吉安人。1924年，进入上海大学社会学系学习；同年，加入中国共产党。1925年12月，任共青团引翔港部委书记。1926年，回乡参与创建中共吉安小组；同年11月，任中共九江地委书记。后参加南昌起义。

Zeng Yansheng (1897-1928) entered SHU in 1924.

汪佑春（1898—1933），江西上饶人。1922年10月，进入上海大学学习。1926年，加入中国共产党。1927年，参加南昌起义；同年，回乡参与创建中共革坂小组，任组长。

Wang Youchun (1898-1933) entered SHU in 1922.

王环心（1901—1927），江西永修人。1922年10月，进入上海大学中国文学系学习。1923年12月，回乡参与创建中国社会主义青年团永修支部。1924年4月，加入中国共产党。1926—1927年，任中共永修支部书记、地委书记、县委书记。

Wang Huanxin (1901-1927) entered SHU in 1922.

徐鹏翥（1902—1976），山东成武人。1923年9月，进入上海大学社会学系学习。1927年3月，加入中国共产党；同年10月，回乡参与创建中共曹州支部，任支部书记。

Xu Pengzhu (1902-1976) entered SHU in 1923.

杨士颖（1903—1931），河南南阳人。1924年，进入上海大学英国文学系学习，其间加入中国共产党。1926年5月，回乡参与创建中共南阳支部。

Yang Shiying (1903-1931) entered SHU in 1924.

吴霆（1905—1937），安徽凤台人。1923年夏，进入上海大学社会学系学习；同年，加入中国共产党。在学期间，兼任平民学校委员会委员、教员。1925年，参与创建共青团奉天特别支部、中共奉天支部，分别任支部书记。1926年10月，任共青团北满地委书记。

Wu Ting (1905-1937) entered SHU in 1923.

张仲实（1903—1987），陕西陇县人。马列主义著作翻译家。1925年，加入中国共产党；同年12月，参与创建中共三原特别支部，任支部书记。1926年，进入上海大学社会学系学习。

Zhang Zhongshi (1903-1987) entered SHU in 1926.

杜嗣尧（1900—1969），陕西榆林人。1924年秋，加入中国共产党。1925年秋，进入上海大学学习。1926年夏，参与创建中共葭县支部，任支部书记。1927年7月，参与创建中共葭县委员会，任县委书记。新中国成立后，任陕西省政协副秘书长。

Du Siyao (1900-1969) entered SHU in 1925.

尚辛友（1903—1937），陕西洋县人。1924年，加入中国共产党。1926年初，进入上海大学学习。1929年8月，回乡参与创建中共洋县小组，任组长。

Shang Xinyou (1903-1937) entered SHU in 1926.

阎灵初（1904—1930），陕西洋县人。1924年，进入上海大学学习。1926年，加入中国共产党。1929年8月，回乡参与创建中共洋县小组。

Yan Lingchu (1904-1930) entered SHU in 1924.

武止戈（1902—1933），陕西渭南人。1923年初，加入中国共产党。1924年初，进入上海大学英国文学系学习；同年，参与创建中国社会主义青年团赤水特别支部和中国社会主义青年团西安支部（第一团支部）。

Wu Zhige (1902-1933) entered SHU in 1924.

李秉乾（1901—1966），又名子健，陕西三原人。1923年，进入上海大学社会学系学习。1924年，加入中国共产党；同年夏，回乡参与创建中国社会主义青年团三原特别支部。1927年，任中共陕西省委常委、宣传部部长。

Li Bingqian (1901-1966) entered SHU in 1923.

王超北（1903—1985），陕西澄城人。1923年，进入上海大学学习。1925年，加入中国共产党；同年，参与创建共青团澄城特别支部和共青团肤施（延安）四中支部，后任肤施支部书记。四一二反革命政变后，在上海中央局特科从事情报工作。1939年，任中共中央西安情报处处长。

Wang Chaobei (1903-1985) entered SHU in 1923.

雷晓晖（1905—2005），女，四川安岳人。1925年7月，进入上海大学社会学系学习；同年12月，加入中国共产党。1928年初，参与创建中共双江支部。1931年9月，在李硕勋就义后，把李硕勋夫人赵君陶和一双儿女接到家中一起生活半年多。

Lei Xiaohui (1905-2005) entered SHU in 1925.

（五）领导平民教育、妇女解放和非基督教运动
Leading Mass Education, Women's Liberation and Anti-Imperialism Movements

1. 开展平民教育
Carrying out Mass Education

1924年4月，在邓中夏的倡导下，开办上海大学平民学校。卜世畸、林钧先后任平民学校主任，刘华、程永言、王秋心等人担任平民学校执行委员，担任教职员的有40余人。

邓中夏还动员和组织学生刘华、何秉彝、杨之华（女）、张琴秋（女）等，在沪东杨树浦和沪西小沙渡创办工人补习学校（平民学校）。张琴秋（女）担任沪东杨树浦平民学校校长，刘华担任沪西工友俱乐部副主任。

In April 1924, under the initiative of Deng Zhongxia, the Mass School of SHU was established.

杨树浦平民学校旧址——平凉路韬朋路（今通北路）惟兴里900号

The former site of the Mass School of SHU

沪西工友俱乐部旧址——槟榔路德昌里旧影（今安远路278—280号位置）

The former site of Club for Workers in West Shanghai

Shanghai University

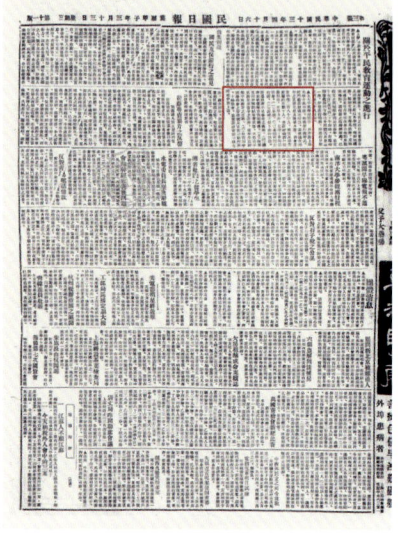

1924年4月16日,《民国日报》刊登《上大平民学校开学》

The news "The Mass School of Shanghai University starts", reported by *The Republic Daily*, April 16, 1924

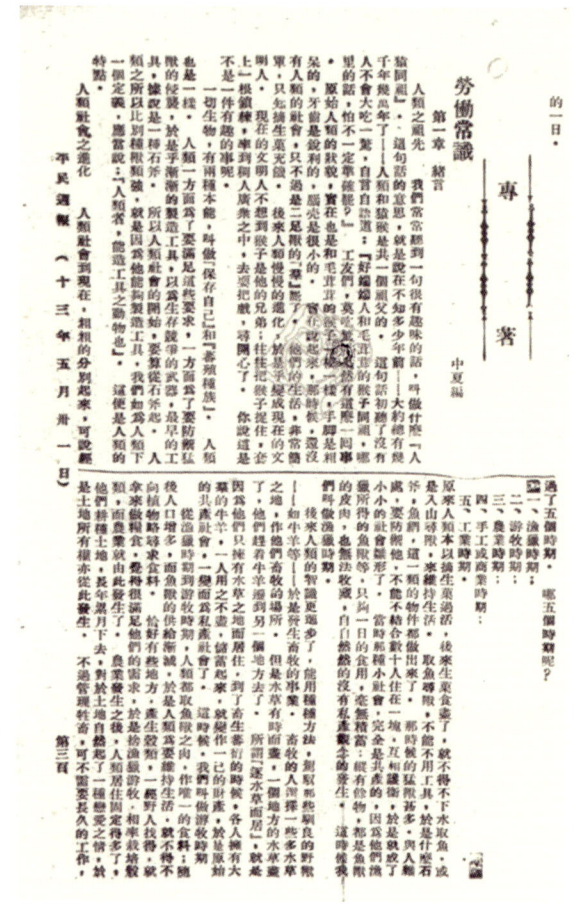

1924年5月31日,《民国日报》副刊《平民周报》刊登邓中夏编写的平民学校教材《劳动常识》

"General Knowledge of Labor", teaching material edited by Deng Zhongxia, reported by *The Mass Weekly*, a supplement of *The Republican Daily*, May 31, 1924

卜世畸（1902—1964），又名士奇、士琦、士畸，湖南益阳人。1921年，加入中国共产党。1922年冬，任上海大学俄文教员。1924年4月，任上海大学平民学校主任。

Bu Shiji (1902-1964) served as Director of the Mass School of SHU in April 1924.

张琴秋（1904—1968），女，浙江桐乡人。1923年底，进入上海大学社会学系学习。1924年11月，加入中国共产党；同年，在杨树浦创办平民学校，任校长。后任中共川陕省委妇女部部长、红四方面军总政治部主任。新中国成立后，任纺织工业部副部长。

Zhang Qinqiu (1904-1968) entered SHU in 1923. She served as President of the Mass School in Yangshupu in 1924.

2. 领导妇女解放运动
Leading Women's Liberation Movements

上海大学女学生王一知、张琴秋、杨之华、钟复光、陈比难、丁郁等，在中共中央妇女部部长向警予的领导下，从事妇女解放运动。

Female SHU students such as Wang Yizhi, Zhang Qinqiu, Yang Zhihua, Zhong Fuguang, Chen Binan and Ding Yu engaged in women's liberation movements under the leadership of Xiang Jingyu, head of the Women's Department of the Central Committee of the CPC.

在中共上海区委担任妇女工作领导职务的上海大学女学生一览
（1925年8月—1927年6月）

Female SHU Students Leading Women's Work in the Shanghai District Committee of the CPC
(August 1925-June 1927)

担任职务		姓　名
妇女运动委员会	书记	陈比难　钟复光　刘尊一
	主任	丁　郁　陈比难　刘尊一　王亚璋
妇女部	主任	杨之华　陈比难　丁　郁　刘尊一

王一知（1901—1991），女，湖南芷江人，1922年2月，进入上海平民女校学习；同年8月，加入中国共产党。1923年夏，进入上海大学学习。1925年底，任广州妇女协会宣传部主任，主编《光明》周刊。新中国成立后，任上海吴淞中学校长、北京一〇一中学校长。

Wang Yizhi (1901-1991), a pioneer in women's liberation movements, entered SHU in 1923.

杨之华（1901—1973），女，浙江杭州人。1919年，参加五四运动。1924年，进入上海大学社会学系学习；同年，加入中国共产党。1925年，任中共中央妇女部主任、上海各界妇女联合会主任。1926年，任中共上海区委妇女部主任、共青团中央妇女运动委员会书记。新中国成立后，任全国妇联副主席。

Yang Zhihua (1900-1973), a pioneer in women's liberation movements, entered SHU in 1924.

钟复光（1903—1992），女，重庆江津人。1923年，进入上海大学社会学系学习。1924年冬，加入中国共产党。1925年，任中共上海区委妇女运动委员会书记。新中国成立后，任北京经济学院图书馆主任。

Zhong Fuguang (1903-1992) entered SHU in 1923. After the founding of the PRC, she served as Director of the library at Beijing Institute of Economics.

王亚璋（1902—1990），女，浙江定海人。1924年，进入上海大学学习。1925年1月，加入中国共产党。1927年，任中共上海区委妇女运动委员会书记；同年，在中共五大当选中央候补委员。

Wang Yazhang (1902-1990) entered SHU in 1924. In 1927, she was elected an alternate member of the Central Committee at the 5th National Congress of the CPC.

3. 投身非基督教运动

Joining Anti-Imperialism Movements

非基督教运动是由中国社会主义青年团发起的反对帝国主义利用宗教进行文化侵略的群众运动。1924年8月，上海非基督教同盟成立，上海大学张秋人、柯柏年（李春蕃）、高尔柏任执行委员。1925年1月，张秋人任第三届共青团中央非基督教部主任；同年11月，上大非基督教同盟会成立。其间，梅电龙任共青团上海地委非基督教运动委员会书记，柯柏年、饶漱石、翁泽生等人在党组织的领导下，投身非基督教运动的宣传和组织工作。

Led by the CPC, SHU teachers and students actively participated in Anti-Imperialism movements.

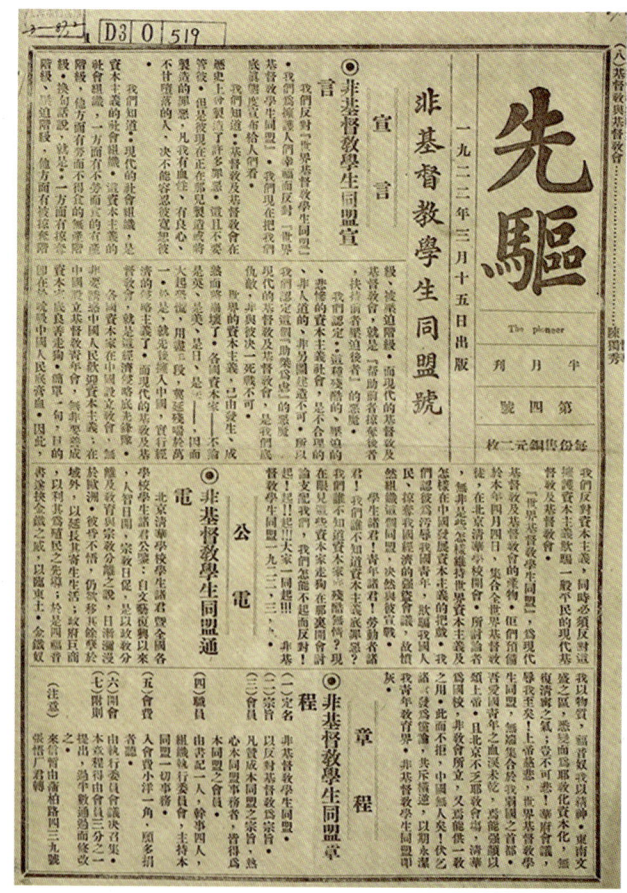

1922年3月15日，由施存统任主编的中国社会主义青年团机关刊物《先驱》第四期刊登"非基督教学生同盟号"

On March 15, 1922, the fourth issue of *The Pioneer*, the official publication of the Socialist Youth League of China, with Shi Cuntong as Chief Editor, carried "The Special Issue of the Anti-Imperialism Students' Alliance".

第一部分　风云际会　青云发轫

张秋人（1898—1928），浙江诸暨人。1922年，加入中国共产党。1923年5月，任上海大学英文教授兼中学部英文教员。1924年，参与创建中共宁波小组、中国社会主义青年团宁波支部等。后任共青团中央执行委员、农工部主任、非基督教部主任和共青团上海地委书记。1927年，任中共浙江省委书记。

Zhang Qiuren (1898-1928) became a professor of SHU in 1923 and served as Secretary of Zhejiang Provincial Committee of the CPC.

柯柏年（1904—1985），原名李春蕃，广东潮州人。1923年，进入上海大学社会学系学习，其间加入中国共产党，并从事上海大学非基督教同盟会工作。新中国成立后，任外交部首任美澳司司长，驻罗马尼亚、丹麦大使。

Ke Bainian (1904-1985) entered SHU in 1923 and worked for the SHU Anti-Imperialism Alliance during his study at SHU.

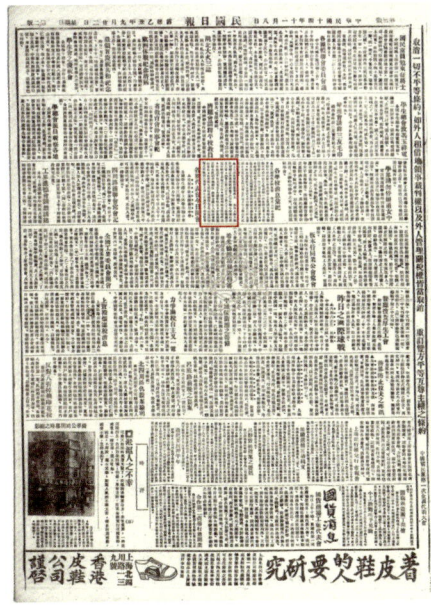

1925年11月8日，《民国日报》刊登《上大非基督教同盟会成立》：饶漱石等五人当选执行委员

The Republican Daily reported the founding of the SHU Anti-Imperialism Alliance on November 8, 1925.

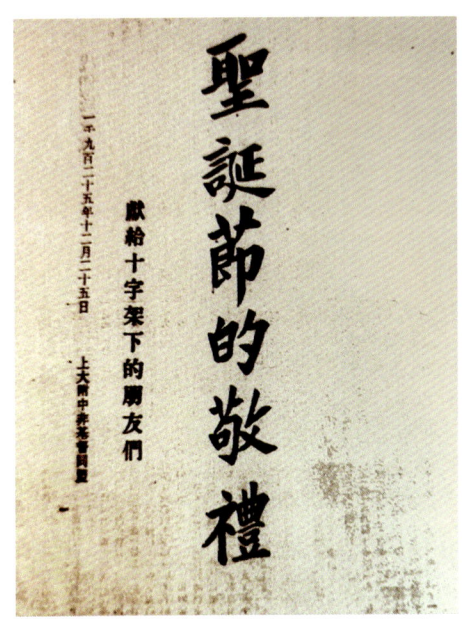

《圣诞节的敬礼》于1925年12月25日创办，是上大附中非基督教同盟编辑的宣传反对基督教言论的刊物

The Christmas Salute, compiled by the Affiliated High School of SHU, was started on December 25, 1925.

（六）践行统一战线 Practicing the United Front

1. 拥护孙中山联俄、联共、扶助农工三大政策
Supporting Sun Yat-sen

　　1924年1月20—30日，在孙中山主持下，中国国民党在广州召开第一次全国代表大会，通过共产党人参加起草的以反帝反封建为主要内容的宣言，事实上确立了联俄、联共、扶助农工的三大革命政策。大会的召开标志着第一次国共合作正式形成。大会选举产生中国国民党中央执行委员会，李大钊、于右任等人当选中央执行委员，毛泽东、瞿秋白等人当选候补执行委员。

The Communists at SHU supported Sun Yat-sen and worked with the KMT.

中国国民党第一次全国代表大会场景
The First National Congress of the KMT

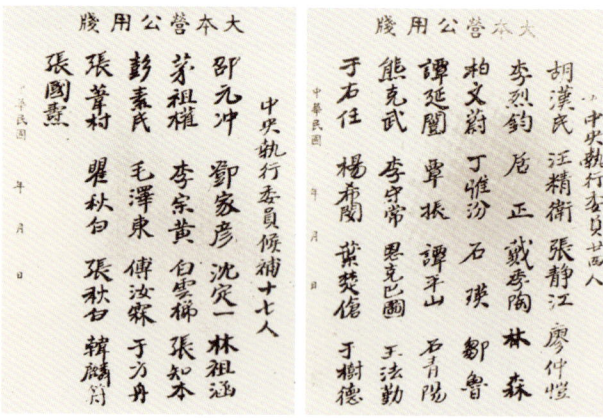

孙中山手书的国民党第一届中央执行委员会委员和候补委员名单
List of members and alternate members of the first Central Executive Committee of the KMT, written by Sun Yat-sen

1926年3月，上海大学师生出席纪念孙中山逝世一周年盛大集会
SHU teachers and students attending the parade commemorating Sun Yat-sen's death, March 1926

2. 参与国民党上海执行部工作
Participating in the Work of the KMT Executive Department in Shanghai

国民党上海执行部于1924年2月设立,统辖江浙皖赣沪的国民党党务工作。胡汉民、于右任、叶楚伧等人分任各部部长;共产党人毛泽东、罗章龙、王荷波、恽代英、邵力子等人分任各部秘书,邓中夏任工农部干事,施存统、沈泽民、韩觉民任宣传部干事。

The CPC members and the KMT veterans of SHU worked in different sections of the KMT Executive Department in Shanghai.

国民党上海执行部旧址——环龙路44号(今南昌路180号)

The former site of the Shanghai Executive Department of the KMT—No. 44 Huanlong Road (now No. 180 Nanchang Road)

1924年5月5日,毛泽东(后排左2)与邓中夏(前排左1)、沈泽民(后排左4)、恽代英(后排右3)、邵力子(后排右2)等国民党上海执行部人员出席庆祝孙中山就任非常大总统三周年活动,在莫里爱路29号(今香山路7号)孙中山寓所合影

SHU teachers celebrating the anniversary of Sun Yat-sen's inauguration as President of the Cantonese Government, May 5, 1924

1924年12月30日,中国国民党上海市第一区第二分部执行委员会秘书施存统致上海执行部呈报第一区分部成立以及执行委员、候补委员名单

A report by Shi Cuntong to the KMT Executive Department in Shanghai, December 30, 1924

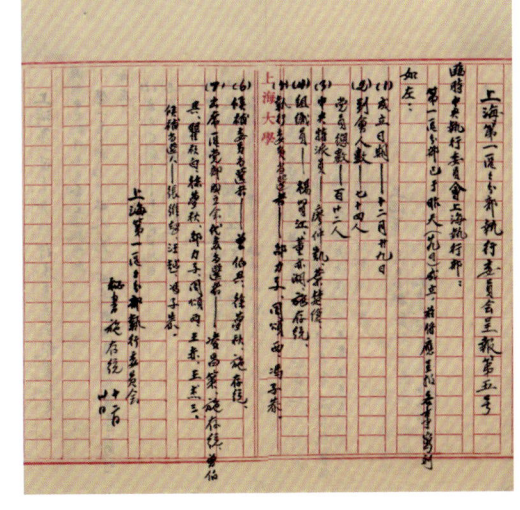

3. 与国民党右派展开斗争
Fighting Against the Rightists of the KMT

1924年10月10日，上海各界举行纪念辛亥革命13周年国民大会。上海大学学生黄仁遭国民党右派指使的流氓殴打，被推下高台，当即昏迷，后不治身亡。

黄仁惨案在社会上引起巨大反响。上海大学召开了黄仁烈士追悼大会，由陈望道主持会议。上海大学学生会发表通电，揭露惨案真相。瞿秋白组织了反对国民党右派暴行的"行动委员会"。陈独秀、恽代英、邓中夏、施存统等分别撰文，发表于《向导》《中国青年》等报刊，严厉谴责国民党右派的暴行。

Huang Ren, an SHU student, was killed by the rightists of the KMT in the national assembly commemorating the 13th anniversary of the 1911 Revolution at Tianhou Palace, October 10, 1924. The Huang Ren Massacre elicited a significant public outcry across the society.

黄仁（1904—1924），四川富顺人。1924年9月，进入上海大学社会学系学习；同年，加入中国共产党。是在国共合作时期上海大学最早牺牲的革命青年。

Huang Ren (1904-1924) entered SHU in 1924. He was the first SHU student who sacrificed during the cooperation period of the KMT and the CPC.

惨案发生地——北河南路天后宫旧址旧影（今河南北路天潼路西南角位置）
Tianhou Palace on North Henan Road (Located now at the southwest corner of Tiantong Road and North Henan Road), where the massacre took place

第一部分　风云际会　青云发轫

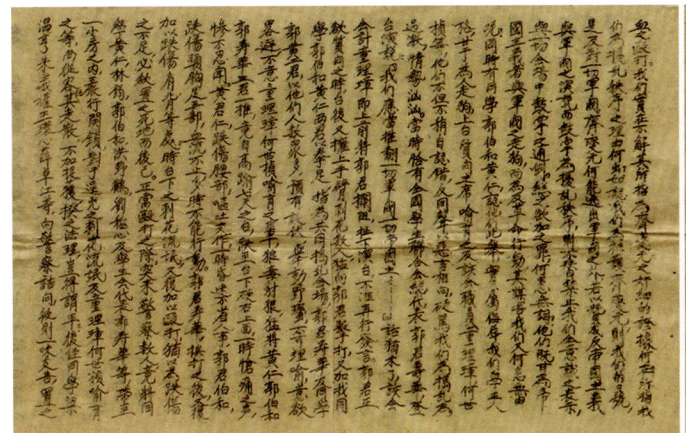
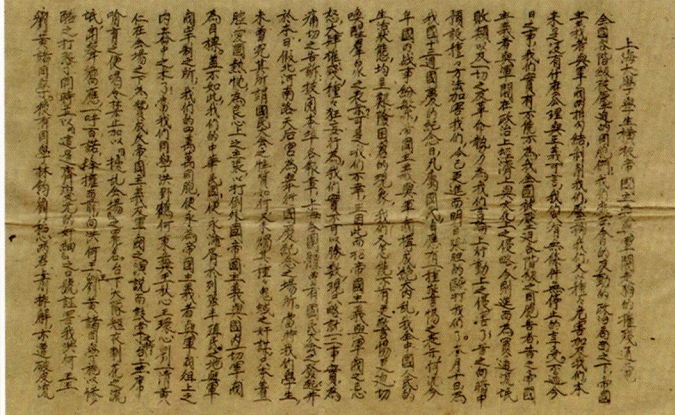
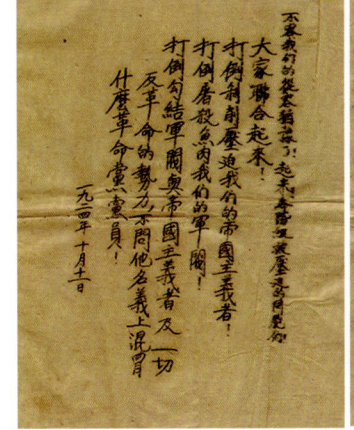

1924年10月11日，上海大学学生会发表《上海大学学生横被帝国主义与军阀走狗摧残的通电》，揭露惨案真相
"The Telegram on the Brutal Suppression of Students at Shanghai University by Imperialists and Lackeys of Warlords" by the Student Union of SHU, exposing the truth of the massacre, October 11, 1924

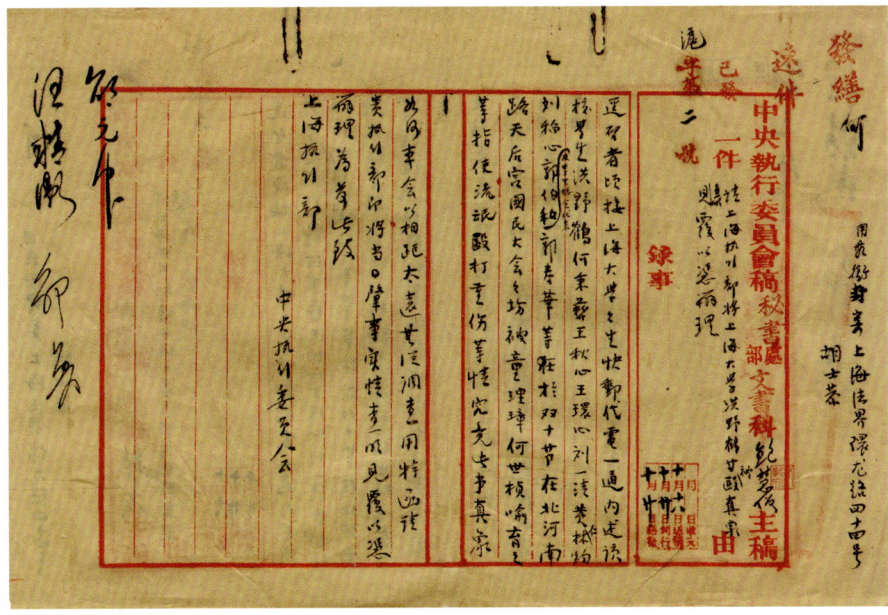

1924年10月，中国国民党中央执行委员会致上海执行部，请将上海大学洪野鹤等被殴真相查明的函件
The letter from the Central Executive Committee of the KMT to the Executive Department in Shanghai, requesting to find out the truth about the assault on Hong Yehe and others from SHU, October 1924

4. 到农民运动讲习所任教、学习
Teaching and Studying in Workshops of Peasant Movement

广州农民运动讲习所创办于 1924 年 7 月，是共产党人彭湃等倡议、经中国国民党中央执行委员会通过而开办的培训农民运动干部的学校。至 1926 年 9 月，共举办了六届，毛泽东任第六届农讲所所长。1927 年 3 月，毛泽东等人创办武昌中央农民运动讲习所。上海大学部分师生赴农民运动讲习所或担任教员，或学习深造。

The workshops of peasant movement was established by the CPC in Guangzhou and Wuchang to train peasant cadres in 1924 and 1927. Some SHU teachers and students lectured or studied in the workshops.

第六届广州农民运动讲习所旧址——惠爱东路番禺学宫（今广州中山四路 42 号）
The former site of the 6th Guangzhou Workshop of Peasant Movement - Panyu Xuegong on East Huiai Road (now No. 42 Zhongshan 4 Road, Guangzhou)

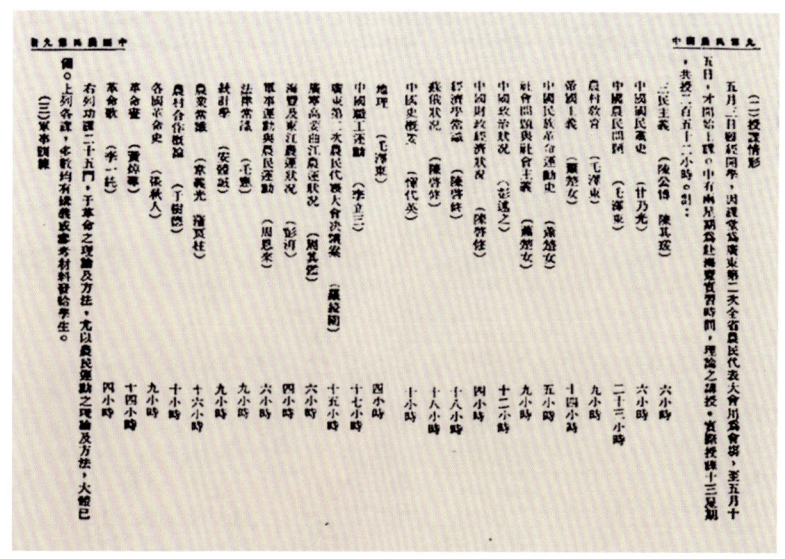

第六届广州农民运动讲习所授课表
Teaching schedule of the 6th Guangzhou Workshop of Peasant Movement

在农民运动讲习所任教、学习的上海大学师生一览
SHU Teachers and Students Who Lectured or Studied in Workshops of Peasant Movement

身　份	姓　名
第六届广州农民运动讲习所教员	萧楚女　高语罕　彭述之　恽代英　张秋人 安体诚　施存统　邓中夏　张太雷　张伯简
武昌中央农民运动讲习所教员	瞿秋白　恽代英　李达　李汉俊　张太雷　郭沫若
农民运动讲习所学员	薛卓汉　邓果白　尚辛友　汪佑春　王述绩　胡宏让

萧楚女（1893—1927），湖北武汉人。中国共产党早期青年运动领导人。早年参加武昌起义、五四运动。1922年，加入中国共产党。1925年5月，任上海大学教授。1926年，赴广州协助毛泽东编辑《政治周报》；同年，任第六届广州农民运动讲习所教务长。

Xiao Chunü (1893-1927), leader of the youth movement in the early period of the CPC, served as a professor of SHU in 1925.

薛卓汉（1898—1931），安徽寿县人。1923年秋，进入上海大学社会学系学习；同年，加入中国共产党。后回乡参与创建中共寿县小甸集特别支部、中共寿县窑口集特别支部、中国社会主义青年团寿县支部、共青团安庆特别支部。1925年，进入第五届广州农民运动讲习所学习。1926年，参加北伐；同年，任第六届广州农民运动讲习所所长毛泽东的秘书。1930年，赴鄂豫皖苏区任红1军政治部副主任。

Xue Zhuohan (1898-1931) entered SHU in 1923. He served as Deputy Director of the Political Department of the First Army of the Chinese Red Army in 1930.

（七）派赴苏联学习　Going to Study in the Soviet Union

派赴苏联学习的上海大学师生一览
SHU Teachers and Students Dispatched to Study in the Soviet Union

学校名称	姓　名
莫斯科中山大学	王嘉祥（王稼祥）　杨尚昆　秦邦宪　蔡和森　董亦湘　沈观澜　沈泽民　杨之华（女） 张琴秋（女）　方运炽　崔小立　何尚志　吉国桢　武止戈　邹　均　陈伯达 张崇文　张崇德　瞿景白　谢飞英（谢雪红）（女）　张仲实　任卓宣　罗石冰 林登岳　王陆一　于芝秀（女）　王友直　罗世文　李秉乾　陶　淮　郭肇唐 李锦蓉（女）
莫斯科东方大学	龙大道　关向应　谢飞英（女）　林木森（林木顺）　卜世畸　李德昭（李得钊） 李　季　张伯简　郑超麟　蒋光慈　张仲实　濮德治　严信民　徐梦秋　陈　明 糜文浩　张景曾　许乃昌

1925年11月，谢雪红（前排右2）、林木顺（后排右1）赴莫斯科东方大学前合影
Xie Xuehong (second from right in the front row) and Lin Mushun (first from right in the back row) before going to Moscow, November 1925

第一部分　风云际会　青云发轫

王稼祥（1906—1974），原名嘉祥，安徽泾县人。中国无产阶级革命家，中国共产党和中国人民解放军领导人。1925年，进入上海大学中学部学习并任学生会主席；同年11月，赴莫斯科中山大学学习。1928年，加入中国共产党。1938年8月，任中共中央军委副主席、总政治部主任。新中国成立后，任外交部副部长、中共中央对外联络部部长、中共中央书记处书记。

Wang Jiaxiang (1906-1974) entered SHU in 1925. After the founding of the PRC, he served as Deputy Minister of Foreign Affairs.

杨尚昆（1907—1998），四川潼南（今属重庆）人。中国无产阶级革命家、政治家、军事家，中华人民共和国、中国人民解放军领导人。1926年，加入中国共产党；同年夏，进入上海大学社会学系学习；同年11月，赴莫斯科中山大学学习。长期担任中央军委秘书长和中共中央办公厅主任。1988年，当选中华人民共和国主席。

Yang Shangkun (1907-1998) entered SHU in 1926. He was elected President of the PRC in 1988.

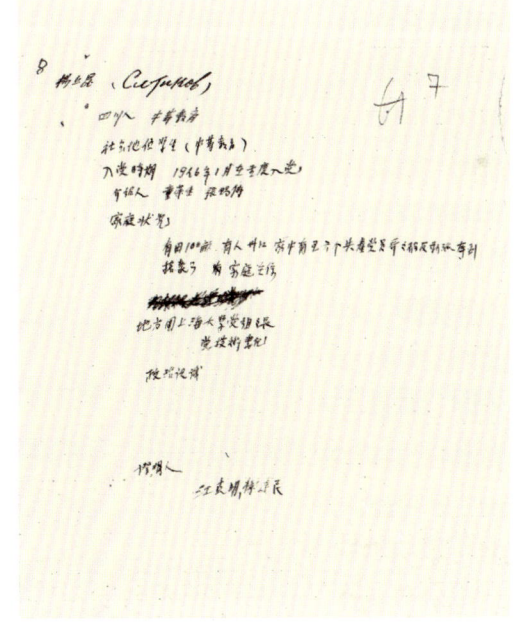

王嘉祥（王稼祥）赴苏联留学时的登记材料
Registration materials of Wang Jiaxiang for overseas study in the Soviet Union

杨尚昆赴苏联留学时的登记材料
Registration materials of Yang Shangkun for overseas study in the Soviet Union

谢雪红（1901—1970），女，又名飞英，福建泉州人。1925年8月，加入中国共产党；同年9月，进入上海大学社会学系学习；同年底，赴莫斯科东方大学学习，后转入莫斯科中山大学。1928年，与台湾籍的林木顺、翁泽生等一起创立台湾共产党，任台共中央委员。新中国成立后，任台湾民主自治同盟总部理事会主席。

Xie Xuehong (1901-1970) entered SHU in 1925.

李得钊（1905—1936），又名德昭，浙江永嘉人。1925年7月，进入上海大学社会学系学习；同年，加入中国共产党，并赴莫斯科东方大学学习。1928年，在共青团中央任职。后在中共中央特科秘书处、总务部和上海中央局任职。

Li Dezhao (1905-1936) entered SHU in 1925.

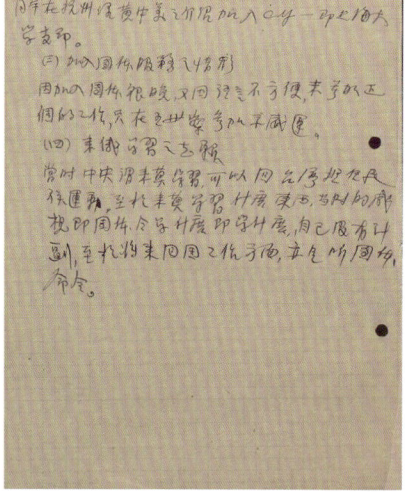

谢飞英（谢雪红）赴苏联留学时的登记材料
Registration materials of Xie Feiying (Xie Xuehong) for overseas study in the Soviet Union

 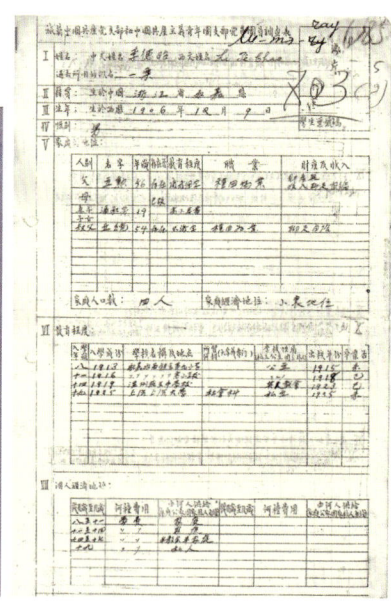

李德昭（李得钊）赴苏联留学时的登记材料
Registration materials of Li Dezhao for overseas study in the Soviet Union

秦邦宪（1907—1946），又名博古，江苏无锡人。中国无产阶级革命家。1925年9月，进入上海大学社会学系学习；同年10月，加入中国共产党。1926年11月，赴莫斯科中山大学学习。1931年9月，任中共临时中央负责人。1935年1月遵义会议后，任红军总政治部代理主任。

Qin Bangxian (1907-1946) entered SHU in 1925.

关向应（1902—1946），辽宁金州人。1924年5月，进入上海大学学习；同年冬，赴莫斯科东方大学学习。1925年1月，加入中国共产党。1928年7月，当选第五届共青团中央书记。1931年11月，当选中共中央军委委员。

Guan Xiangying (1902-1946) entered SHU in 1924.

林木顺（1905—？），又名木森，台湾南投人。1925年8月，加入中国共产党；同年9月，进入上海大学社会学系学习；同年底，赴莫斯科东方大学学习。1928年，与台湾籍的谢雪红、翁泽生等一起创立台湾共产党，任台共中央书记长。

Lin Mushun (1905-?) entered SHU in 1925.

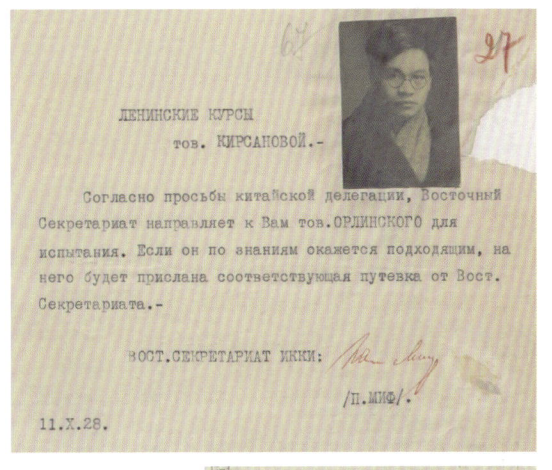

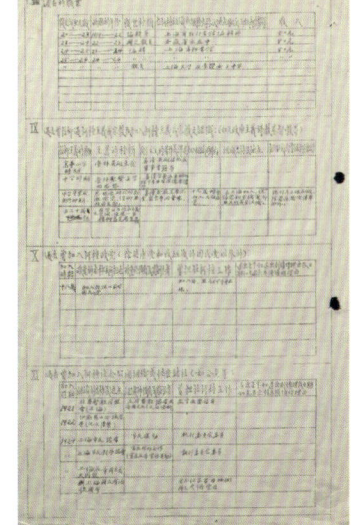

董亦湘赴苏联留学时的登记材料

Registration materials of Dong Yixiang for overseas study in the Soviet Union

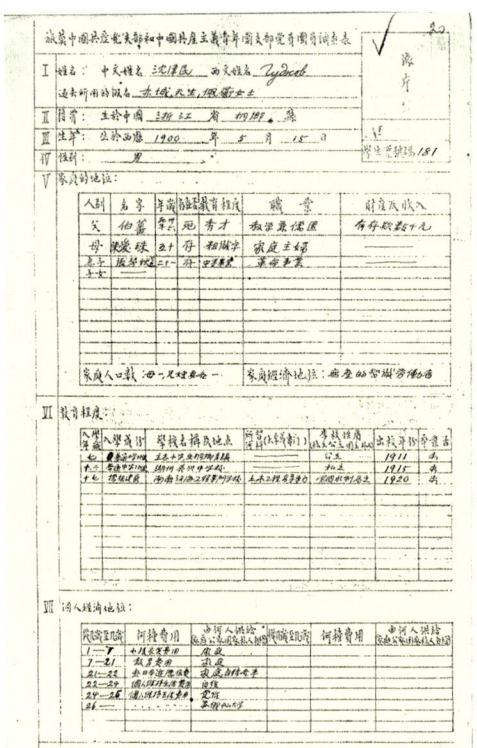

沈泽民赴苏联留学时的登记材料
Registration materials of Shen Zemin for overseas study in the Soviet Union

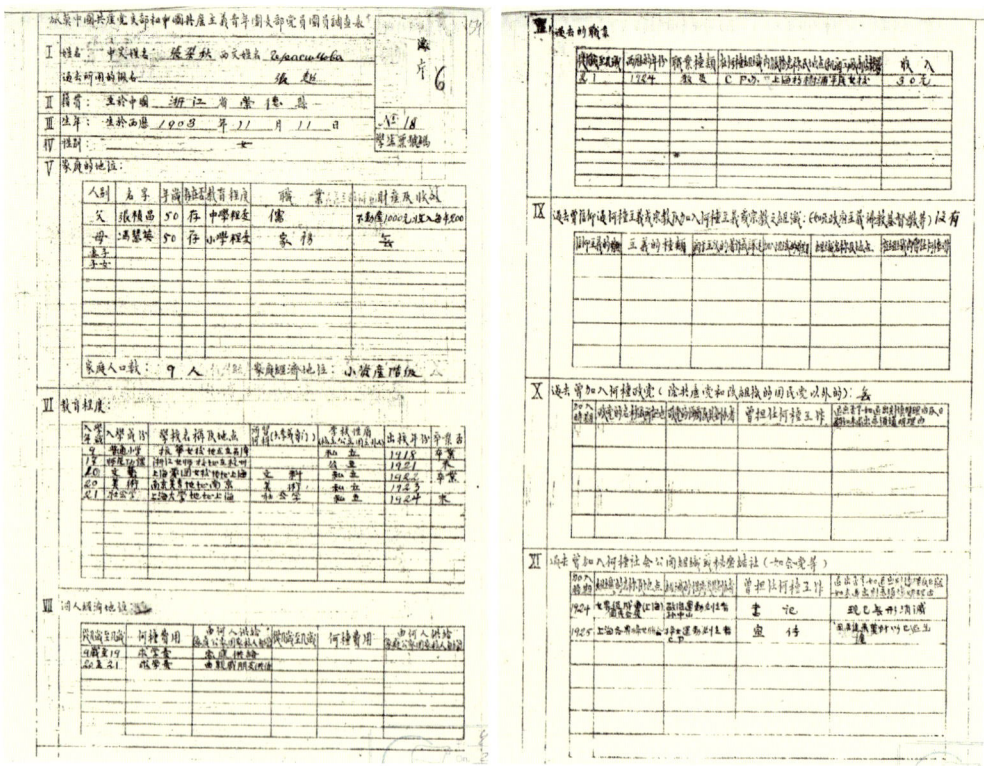

张琴秋赴苏联留学时的登记材料
Registration materials of Zhang Qinqiu for overseas study in the Soviet Union

（八）参加上海工人三次武装起义　Joining Three Armed Uprisings of Workers in Shanghai

为了配合北伐军进军上海，1926年秋至1927年春，中共中央和上海区委发动并组织上海工人，连续举行了三次武装起义。上海大学师生积极参与其中：余泽鸿、何洛等人配合工人起义组织学生军，直接参加战斗；龙大道、郭伯和、顾作霖、林钧、刘披云等人参与指挥第三次武装起义；侯绍裘、杨贤江、张秋人、杨之华（女）等人协助周恩来、罗亦农等领导的起义工作。

SHU teachers and students took part in three armed uprisings of workers in Shanghai in the wake of the Northern Expedition.

1. 参加上海工人三次武装起义的师生
SHU Teachers and Students in Three Armed Uprisings of Workers in Shanghai

中共上海区委派上海大学学生党团员到各区担任训练工人纠察队的工作。图为上海工人第三次武装起义时工人纠察队在操练
The workers drilling during the third armed uprising of workers in Shanghai

参加上海工人三次武装起义的上海大学师生一览
SHU Teachers and Students in Three Armed Uprisings of Workers in Shanghai

次　别	姓　名
上海工人第一次武装起义	龙大道　杨尚昆　秦邦宪　余泽鸿　何　洛　杨之华（女）　冯三昧 张崇文　张崇德　康　生（赵　容）　刘锡吾　党维蓉　刘披云　杨振铎
上海工人第二次武装起义	龙大道　何　洛　杨之华（女）　许德良　张崇德　康　生　党维蓉
上海工人第三次武装起义	郭伯和　顾作霖　林　钧　杨贤江　龙大道　余泽鸿　糜文浩　何　洛　王稼祥　杨之华（女） 陈比难（女）　侯绍裘　张秋人　许德良　张崇德　葛　琴（女）　康　生　王步文　刘披云 杨振铎　沈方中（女）　党维蓉　薛尚实　尚辛友　贾南坡　阎灵初　熊寿祺　张树德

张崇德（1903—？），浙江临海人。张崇文胞兄。1924年，进入上海大学英国文学系学习兼中学部英文教员。五卅运动期间，加入中国共产党。参加上海工人三次武装起义。

Zhang Chongde (1903-?) entered SHU in 1924. He joined the three uprisings.

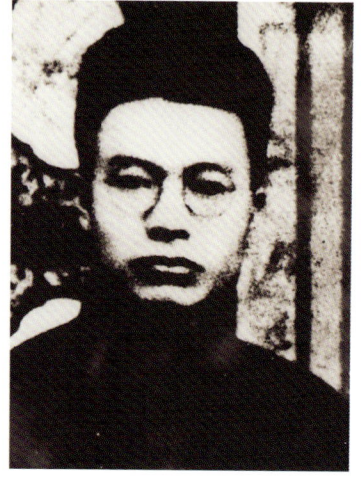

龙大道（1901—1931），贵州锦屏人。1922年冬，进入上海大学学习。1923年11月，加入中国共产党。参加上海工人三次武装起义。后任中共浙江省委常委、代理省委书记，上海总工会秘书长。

Long Dadao (1901-1931) entered SHU in 1922. He joined the three uprisings.

郭伯和（1900—1927），四川南溪人。1923年，进入上海大学学习。1924年，加入中国共产党。1925年11月，任中共小沙渡部委书记。1927年，参加上海工人第三次武装起义；同年，任中共江苏省委组织部部长。

Guo Bohe (1900-1927) entered SHU in 1923. He worked for the third uprising in 1927.

顾作霖（1908—1934），上海嘉定人。中国无产阶级革命家。1922年，进入上海大学社会学系学习。1926年，加入中国共产党；同年，任中共杨树浦部委委员、共青团杨树浦部委书记。1927年，参加上海工人第三次武装起义。1934年1月，在中共六大当选中央政治局委员，后任中国工农红军总政治部代理主任。

Gu Zuolin (1908-1934) entered SHU in 1922. He worked for the third uprising in 1927.

余泽鸿（1903—1935），四川长宁人。1924年9月，进入上海大学社会学系学习。1925年春，加入中国共产党；同年，任中共上海学联党团书记，参加领导五卅运动。1927年，参加上海工人第三次武装起义。1929年夏，接替邓小平任中共中央秘书长。

Yu Zehong (1903-1935) entered SHU in 1924. He worked for the third uprising in 1927.

第一部分　风云际会　青云发轫

刘锡吾（1904—1970），河南孟县人。1925年，进入上海大学社会学系学习，其间加入中国共产党。1926年，参加上海工人第一次武装起义。新中国成立后，任中共吉林省委书记。

Liu Xiwu (1904-1970) entered SHU in 1925. He worked for the first uprising in 1926.

薛尚实（1902—1977），广东梅州人。1926年秋，进入上海大学社会学系学习。1927年，参加上海工人第三次武装起义。1928年2月，加入中国共产党。新中国成立后，任中共青岛市委书记、同济大学党委书记兼校长。

Xue Shangshi (1902-1977) entered SHU in 1926. He worked for the third uprising in 1927.

党维蓉（1908—1931），陕西富平人。1925年，进入上海大学社会学系学习；同年秋，加入中国共产党。参加上海工人三次武装起义。后任中共上海沪西区委组织部部长、青岛市委书记。

Dang Weirong (1908-1931) entered SHU in 1925. He joined the three uprisings.

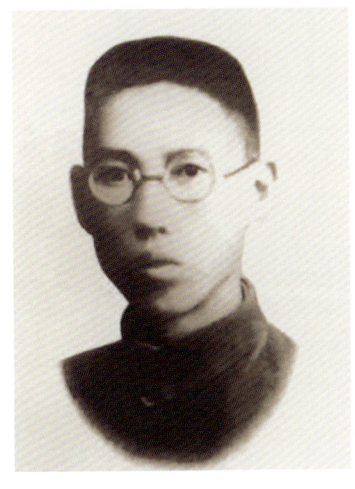

杨振铎（1905—1933），山西芮城人。1925年，加入中国共产党。1926年，进入上海大学社会学系学习。1927年，参加上海工人第三次武装起义。后任共青团江苏省委书记、上海沪中区行委书记。

Yang Zhenduo (1905-1933) entered SHU in 1926. He worked for the third uprising in 1927.

糜文浩（1901—1927），江苏无锡人。1923年，进入上海大学社会学系学习；同年，加入中国共产党。1927年，参加上海工人第三次武装起义，任上海总工会机关报《平民日报》编辑部主任。

Mi Wenhao (1901-1927) entered SHU in 1923. He worked for the third uprising in 1927.

2. 在上海特别市临时市政府中任职
Serving in Temporary Shanghai Special City Government

上海工人第三次武装起义成功后，1927年3月22日，成立上海特别市临时市政府。上海市民代表会议选出上海特别市临时市政府委员19人，其中包括上海大学中学部主任侯绍裘和学生林钧、何洛3人，林钧兼任秘书长。

On March 22, 1927, the Shanghai Municipal People's Congress elected 19 members of the Temporary Shanghai Special City Government, including three teachers and students from SHU. Lin Jun served as Secretary-General.

上海特别市临时市政府旧址——蓬莱路171号
The former site of the Temporary Shanghai Special City Government—No. 171 Penglai Road

1927年3月，侯绍裘（后排左2）、林钧（后排左1）、何洛（前排左1）在上海特别市临时市政府召开第一次执行委员会常委会议时合影
The first standing committee meeting of the Temporary Shanghai Special City Government, March 1927

　　林钧（1896—1944），上海川沙人。1924年7月，进入上海大学社会学系学习；同年，加入中国共产党。1925年，任上海学界、工商界五卅烈士丧葬筹备处主任。1927年3月，当选上海特别市临时市政府委员兼秘书长。后参加南昌起义。

Lin Jun (1896-1944) entered SHU in 1924. In March 1927, he was elected Secretary-General of the Temporary Shanghai Special City Government.

五、文有上大　武有黄埔
SHU, as Prestigious as HMA

1924年6月，孙中山在共产国际和中国共产党的帮助下，在广州黄埔创办陆军军官学校（简称黄埔军校）。在大革命时期，上海大学和黄埔军校为反帝反封建做出了巨大的贡献，当时就有"文有上大，武有黄埔"之说。

SHU and HMA were the most important talent-training bases during the Great Revolution. The two were closely linked during the revolutionary years.

（一）上海大学是黄埔军校第一期考生复试场所
SHU as the Venue for the Second-Round Examination of the First-Batch Candidates of HMA

1924年3月12日，国民党上海执行部在上海大学举行黄埔军校第一期新生录取考试。施存统、陈望道、恽代英等人担任监考工作，于右任、叶楚伧、戴季陶等人担任阅卷工作。

On March 12, 1924, the Shanghai Executive Department of the KMT held the admission examination for the first-batch candidates of HMA at SHU.

陆军军官学校（黄埔军校）
Huangpu Military Academy

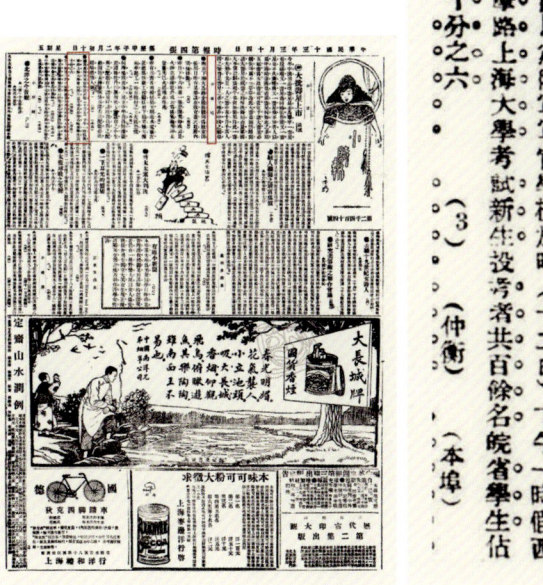

1924年3月14日，《时报》刊登消息："国民党陆军军官学校于昨（十二日）下午一时假西摩路上海大学考试，新生投考者共百余名，皖省学生占十分之六。"

The report on the examination by *Times*, March 14, 1924

（二）赴黄埔军校任职任教　SHU Teachers and Students at HMA

黄埔军校政治部办公室
An office of the Political Department of HMA

赴黄埔军校任职任教的上海大学师生
SHU Teachers and Students at HMA

姓　名	曾在上海大学身份	在黄埔军校身份
邵力子	代理校长、教授	秘书长、政治部主任
戴季陶	经济学系教授	政治部主任
邵元冲	教授	政治教官、政治部代理主任
卜世畸	教授	政治部代理主任
恽代英	社会学系教授	政治主任教官
高语罕	社会学系教授	政治教官、入伍生部少将党代表
施存统	社会学系主任	政治教官、武汉分校政治部主任
李　达	社会学系教授	武汉分校代理政治总教官
安体诚	教授	政治教官、政治部宣传科科长
郭沫若	社会学系教授	政治教官
萧楚女	教授	政治教官
张秋人	教授	政治教官
任卓宣	社会学系教授	政治教官
胡汉民	教授	政治教官
瞿秋白	教务长兼社会学系主任	武汉分校政治教官
李汉俊	社会学系教授	武汉分校政治教官
陶希圣	社会学系教授	武汉分校政治教官
沈雁冰	中国文学系教授	武汉分校政治教官
向　浒	斋务员	武汉分校排长

续表

张治中	社会学系学生	第三期入伍生代理总队长、军官团团长
许继慎	社会学系学生	教导团连长、第三期学生队队长
曹 渊	学生	教导团学生连党代表
邱清泉	英国文学系学生	第五期入伍生工兵营第三连连长
钟复光（女）	社会学系学生	武汉分校女生队政治指导员
周士冕	社会学系学生	第四期入伍生团区队附
王逸常	社会学系学生	第一军政治部上校组织科科长
阳翰笙	社会学系学生	政治教官
罗髫渔	社会学系学生	政治教官
吴 云	社会学系学生	政治教官
张庆孚	英国文学系学生	政治教官
曹蕴真	社会学系学生	政治部宣传科员
胡允恭	社会学系学生	政治部科员
白明善	学生	政治部宣传科科员
梁伯隆	社会学系学生	军需官

张治中（1890—1969），安徽巢湖人。爱国民主人士。1923年，进入上海大学社会学系学习。1924年初，任黄埔军校第三期入伍生代理总队长、军官团团长。1926年，任黄埔军校武汉分校教育长。新中国成立后，任全国人大常务委员会副委员长、国防委员会副主席。

Zhang Zhizhong (1890-1969) entered SHU in 1923. He served as Provost of HMA Wuhan Branch in 1926.

安体诚（1896—1927），河北唐山人。1922年，加入中国共产党。1924年春，任上海大学教授。1925年，参与创建中共西安特别支部，任支部书记。1926年，任黄埔军校政治教官。

An Ticheng (1896-1927) became a professor of SHU in 1924 and served as a political instructor of HMA in 1926.

向浒（1898—1983），湖北汉川人。1923年秋，任上海大学斋务员。1924年，加入中国共产党。曾赴黄埔军校第四期学习。后参加北伐、南昌起义。

Xiang Hu (1898-1983) entered SHU in 1923 and once studied at HMA.

（三）转入黄埔军校学习　Transferring to HMA

黄埔军校的学生在上课
A class at HMA

从上海大学转入黄埔军校学习的师生（部分）
SHU Teachers and Students Transferring to HMA (Partial)

期　数	姓　名
第一期	曹　渊　许继慎　杨溥泉　张其雄　徐石麟　曹蕴真 王逸常　尚辛友　谭肇明　刘仲言　周士冕　曹利生
第二期	邱清泉　蔡鸿猷　吴　震　梁伯隆
第三期	程锡简　皮言智　斯　励
第四期	李逸民　季步高　吴维中　胡睦修　蒋坚忍　向　浒　王子伟　田动云
第五期	杨　达
第六期	周文在　余　拯　周秋萍（周大根）

第一部分　风云际会　青云发轫

张其雄（1902—1926），湖北广济人。1922年，加入中国共产党。曾在上海大学社会学系学习。1924年，赴黄埔军校第一期学习。后参加东征、北伐，任国民革命军第8军政治部副主任，授陆军少将军衔。

Zhang Qixiong (1902-1926) once studied at SHU. He transferred to HMA in 1924.

徐石麟（1901—1976），安徽望江人。1923年8月，进入上海大学中国文学系学习。1924年，赴黄埔军校第一期学习。后参加北伐，任国民革命军第4军第10师28团营长。1927年，参加南昌起义，后任中央军校教导总队团长、副旅长。

Xu Shilin (1901-1976) entered SHU in 1923. He transferred to HMA in 1924.

邱清泉（1902—1949），原名青钱，浙江永嘉人。1923年8月，进入上海大学英国文学系学习。1924年，赴黄埔军校第二期学习。后参加北伐，任国民革命军第4军连党代表。抗日战争期间，参加淞沪会战、南京保卫战、昆仑关战役。

Qiu Qingquan (1902-1949) entered SHU in 1923. He transferred to HMA in 1924.

李逸民（1904—1982），浙江龙泉人。1922年10月，进入上海大学中国文学系学习。1925年9月，加入中国共产党。曾赴黄埔军校第四期学习。1927年，参加北伐，任国民革命军第11军第24师教导大队政治指导员；同年，参加南昌起义。新中国成立后，任中国人民解放军总政治部文化部部长。1955年，获少将军衔。

Li Yimin (1904-1982) entered SHU in 1922. Later he studied at HMA.

季步高（1906—1928），浙江龙泉人。1922年10月，进入上海大学中国文学系学习。1925年9月，加入中国共产党。曾赴黄埔军校第四期学习。1927年11月，参加广州起义。1928年1月，任中共广州市委书记。

Ji Bugao (1906-1928) entered SHU in 1922. He once studied at HMA.

周大根（1906—1938），又名秋萍，江苏南汇（今属上海）人。1924年，进入上海大学社会学系学习。后赴黄埔军校武汉分校第六期学习。1927年，参加南昌起义；同年9月，加入中国共产党。1928年8月，任中共南汇县委首任书记。

Zhou Dagen (1906-1938) entered SHU in 1924. Later he studied at HMA.

（四）参加北伐 Participating in the Northern Expedition

1926 年，黄埔军校第四期学生分赴北伐前线
HMA students in the Northern Expedition, 1926

在北伐军任职的上海大学师生（部分）
SHU Teachers and Students Serving in the Northern Expeditionary Army (Partial)

姓　名	曾在上海大学身份	在北伐军职务
于右任	校长	联军副总司令
邵力子	代理校长、教授	总司令部秘书长
郭沫若	社会学系教授	总政治部副主任
高冠吾	中国文学系教授	第 10 军副军长
梅电龙	附中教员	第 40 军第 12 师政治部主任
李达	社会学系教授	总政治部编审委员会主席
杨贤江	社会学系教授	总政治部"革命军日报"社社长
韩觉民	总务主任	总政治部秘书
张厉生	教授	第 10 军政治部秘书
许绍棣	教员	后方总政治部秘书
蒋坚忍	社会学系学生	第 26 军政治部主任
罗髫渔	社会学系学生	第 11 军政治部代理主任
张其雄	社会学系学生	第 8 军政治部副主任兼秘书长
李硕勋	社会学系学生	第 4 军第 25 师政治部主任
于忠迪	社会学系学生	第 6 军第 19 师政治部主任
张庆孚	英国文学系学生	第 35 军第 2 师政治部主任、第 19 军师政治部主任兼秘书长
陈兴霖	学生	第 11 军第 24 师政治部主任
周士冕	社会学系学生	第 3 师政治部主任
张治中	社会学系学生	总司令部副官长

续表

许继慎	社会学系学生	第4军叶挺独立团第2营营长、第24师第72团团长
杨 达	社会学系学生	第3军军官教导团参谋长
曹 渊	学生	第4军叶挺独立团第1营营长
杨溥泉	社会学系学生	第4军营长
徐石麟	中国文学系学生	第4军第10师第28团营长
邱清泉	英国文学系学生	第4军连党代表
田动云	社会学系学生	连党代表、团政治指导员
王子伟	社会学系学生	第17军总部参谋、第2师炮兵团连长
何挺颖	社会学系学生	第8军第3师团指导员
胡允恭	社会学系学生	第4军第12师第35团政治指导员
李逸民	中国文学系学生	第11军第24师教导大队政治指导员
胡睦修	美术科学生	第1军第1师第59团第11连排长
邹 均	社会学系学生	联军驻陕总部驻武汉全权代表
柯柏年	社会学系学生	第3军政治教官
梁伯隆	社会学系学生	总政治部政训员、宣传队长
孔另境	中国文学系学生	前敌总指挥部宣传科科长
蒋如琮	社会学系学生	东路总指挥部宣传科科长
陈 明	社会学系学生	东路总指挥部情报股股长
黄让之	中国文学系学生	总政治部宣传科股长
罗化千	社会学系学生	总政治部宣传干事
陶光潮（陶光朝）	社会学系学生	第3军政治部宣传干事
郭 毅	社会学系学生	第36军某师政治部宣传干事
杨士颖	英国文学系学生	第4军政治部宣传干事
李炳祥	经济学系学生	第4军顾问团翻译

于忠迪（1903—1928），湖南临澧人。曾在上海大学学习，其间加入中国共产党。1926年，参加北伐，任国民革命军第6军第19师政治部主任。

Yu Zhongdi (1903-1928) once studied at SHU. He participated in the Northern Expedition in 1926.

许继慎（1901—1931），安徽六安人。中国工农红军早期杰出将领，军事家。1923年秋，进入上海大学社会学系学习。1924年，加入中国共产党。参加两次东征、北伐。1926年起，任国民革命军第4军叶挺独立团第2营营长、第24师第72团团长。1930年，任鄂豫皖红军第1军军长。

Xu Jishen (1901-1931) entered SHU in 1923. He participated in the two Eastern Expeditions and the Northern Expedition.

杨达（1902—1928），四川彭州人。1925年初，进入上海大学社会学系学习；同年，加入中国共产党。1926年，参加北伐，在朱德领导的国民革命军第3军军官教导团任参谋长。后参加南昌起义。

Yang Da (1902-1928) entered SHU in 1925. He participated in the Northern Expedition in 1926.

曹渊（1902—1926），安徽寿县人。1923年，进入上海大学学习。1924年，赴黄埔军校第一期学习，毕业后留任教导团学生连党代表；同年，加入中国共产党。后参加北伐，任国民革命军第4军叶挺独立团第1营营长。

Cao Yuan (1902-1926) entered SHU in 1923. He participated in the Northern Expedition.

杨溥泉（1900—1927），安徽六安人。1924年春，进入上海大学社会学系学习；同年，加入中国共产党。后参加北伐，任国民革命军第4军营长。1927年，参加南昌起义，任第11军副团长。

Yang Puquan (1900-1927) entered SHU in 1924. Later he participated in the Northern Expedition.

何挺颖（1905—1929），陕西南郑人。1925年，进入上海大学社会学系学习；同年冬，加入中国共产党。后参加北伐，任国民革命军第8师团指导员。1927年9月，参加秋收起义，随毛泽东率部创建井冈山革命根据地，是黄洋界保卫战指挥员之一。

He Tingying (1905-1929) entered SHU in 1925. Later he participated in the Northern Expedition.

邹均（1900—1930），陕西富平人。1923年夏，加入中国共产党。1924年初，进入上海大学社会学系学习；同年，参与创建中国社会主义青年团西安支部（第二团支部）。1927年，参加北伐，任国民革命军联军驻陕总部驻武汉全权代表。1930年夏，任中共河南省委军委书记。

Zou Jun (1900-1930) entered SHU in 1924. He participated in the Northern Expedition in 1927.

六、五四北大　五卅上大
SHU, as Revolutionary as PKU

1925年5月15日，上海内外棉七厂工人顾正红被日本资本家枪杀，成为五卅运动导火线。30日，中国共产党领导的反对帝国主义暴行的五卅运动在上海爆发，并迅速席卷全国。当时就有"上海大学是五卅运动的策源地""北有五四时期的北大，南有五卅时期的上大"之说。

The worker Gu Zhenghong was shot dead by a Japanese at a cotton mill on May 15, 1925, triggering the May Thirtieth Movement. SHU teachers and students acted as the vanguard and main force in the movement. Back then a saying went like this: "In the North Was Peking University in the May Fourth Movement; in the South Was Shanghai University in the May Thirtieth Movement."

（一）五卅运动的策源地　Leading May Thirtieth Movement

恽代英、侯绍裘担任五卅运动示威游行的正、副指挥，蔡和森、沈雁冰、杨之华（女）等领导上大师生400余人组成38个演讲团，分布在南京路的福建路至河南路段，进行演讲和散发传单。上海大学瞿景白、崔小立、周文在、钟复光（女）、丁郁（女）等多名学生被捕，何秉彝当场中弹身亡。

SHU teachers and students participated in demonstrations and parades during the May Thirtieth Movement.

五卅惨案现场
The scene of the May Thirtieth Massacre

游行学生在南京路永安公司前散发传单
Demonstrating students distributing leaflets on Nanjing Road

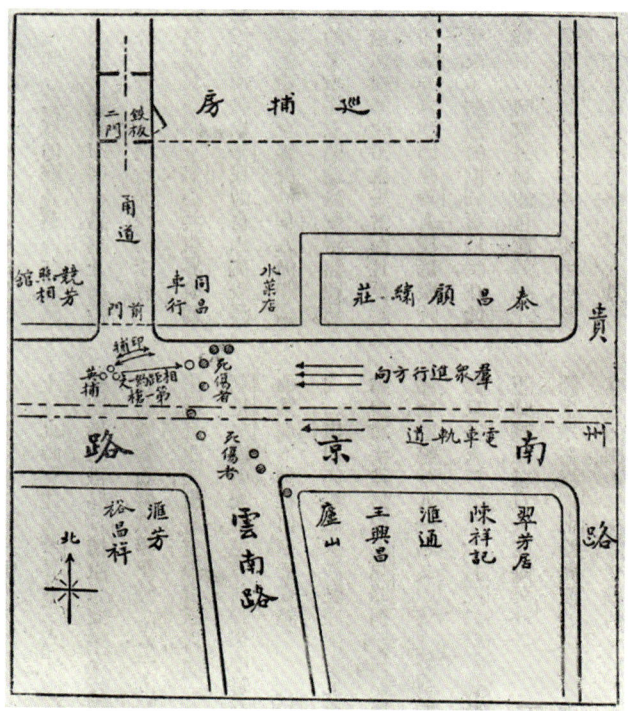

五卅惨案地形图
A scene map of the May Thirtieth Massacre

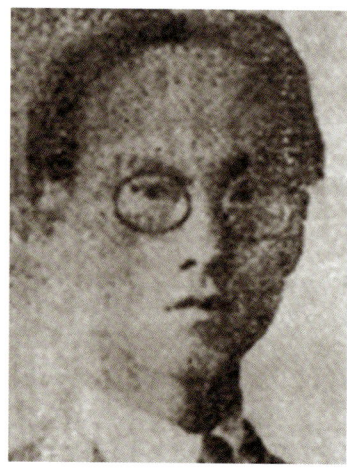

何秉彝（1902—1925），字念兹，四川彭州人。1924年7月，进入上海大学社会学系学习。1925年，加入中国共产党；同年，任共青团上海地委组织主任。五卅运动时担任示威演讲指挥总部的联络员。

He Bingyi (1902-1925) entered SHU in July 1924. He served as a liaison officer at the headquarter for the demonstration and speech command during the May Thirtieth Movement.

在五卅运动中伤亡及被捕的上海大学学生一览
SHU Students Killed, Injured or Arrested during the May Thirtieth Movement

（1）死亡名单

何秉彝，5月30日，弹由背入，31日下午死于仁济医院。

（2）伤者名单

瞿景白（1906—1929），江苏常州人。瞿秋白胞弟。1924年，加入中国共产党。1925年春，进入上海大学社会学系学习；同年12月，任共青团杨树浦部委书记。

Qu Jingbai (1906-1929), the younger brother of Qu Qiubai, entered SHU in 1925. In December of the same year, he served as Secretary of the Yangshupu Committee of the Communist Youth League.

姓 名	时 间	伤 情	备 注
于 达	5月30日	弹掠膝盖	现未愈
赵治人	5月30日	重伤未愈	在南京路被击
郭肇唐	5月30日	轻伤已愈	在南京路被棍打伤
吴稽天	5月30日	同上	同上
吴 瑜	5月30日	同上	在先施公司门前被打
罗总纲	5月31日	同上	在南京路被打了两次
刘从文	5月31日	同上	在南京路上
杨一达	5月31日	重伤未愈	棍伤脑部
姜礼达	5月31日	轻伤已愈	在南京路被棍打
方 山	5月31日	轻伤	在南京路调查被捕打
马会云	5月31日	轻伤	在南京路上被踢伤
谢秉琼	6月4日	轻伤	被西捕棍打
汪惟勗	6月4日	轻伤	被美海军强占学校时挨打

（3）被捕名单

姓　名	时　间	被拘情形	备　注
朱义权	5月24日	追悼顾正红，被拘普陀捕房	5月30日交保金百元释放
韩步先	同上	同上	同上
赵震宾（秉）	同上	同上	同上
江锦维	同上	同上	5月30日交保释放
瞿景白	5月30日	在南京路被捕	押老闸捕房
杨恩圣	同上	同上	同上
王宇春	同上	同上	同上
蔡鸿烈	同上	在南京路演讲	于6月2日铺保交百元释放
董儒京	同上	同上	同上
符育英	同上	同上	于5月31日交保金5元
黎　白	同上	同上	同上
黎伯光	同上	同上	同上
尹敦招	同上	同上	同上
郑则龙	同上	同上	同上
王国钧	同上	同上	同上
黎元撰	同上	同上	同上
沈起英	同上	在南京路演讲，被拘老闸捕房	6月2日交保金5元，宣判无罪
安剑平	同上	同上	同上
梁郁华	同上	同上	同上
张以民	同上	同上	同上
朱鹄鸣	同上	同上	同上
周文在	同上	同上	同上
张书德	同上	同上	同上

续表

姓名	时间	被拘情形	备注
林树江	同上	同上	同上
陈庆翰	5月30日	在南京路演讲，被拘老闸捕房	因被捕太多，被打一顿后释放
张先梅	同上	同上	当日释放
毛钟胤	同上	同上	讯问后关了5小时释放
黄　骅	同上	同上	同上
丁　郁	同上	同上	同上
崔小立	同上	同上	同上
李葆真	同上	同上	捕后一小时释出
钟复光	同上	同上	同上
丁复娟	同上	同上	同上
沈淑班	同上	同上	同上
蔡鸿生	同上	同上	同上
李霭白	同上	同上	与瞿景白同时释放
陈铁梅（陈企荫）	同上	同上	
洪世华	同上	同上	5月31日释出

（原载《上大五卅特刊》1925年6月15日第4版）

注：5月30日被拘捕于南京路老闸捕房的，因人满当时即驱逐出来者有130余人。5月31日被捕于当时即释放者有60余人

(Originally recorded in The Special Issue of Shanghai University on the May Thirtieth Movement, June 15, 1925, Page 4)

1925年6月，西摩路校舍被公共租界当局武装占领，上海大学师生被迫离校；同年8月9日，*The Shanghai Sunday Times* 报道："位于西摩路132号的上海大学被称为'布尔什维克主义的温床'。"

School buildings on Seymour Road, occupied by the authorities of the International Settlement with armed forces, June 1925. "Shanghai University, located at No. 132 Seymour Road, is known as the 'Breeding Ground of Bolshevism'", reported by *The Shanghai Sunday Times* on August 9, 1925.

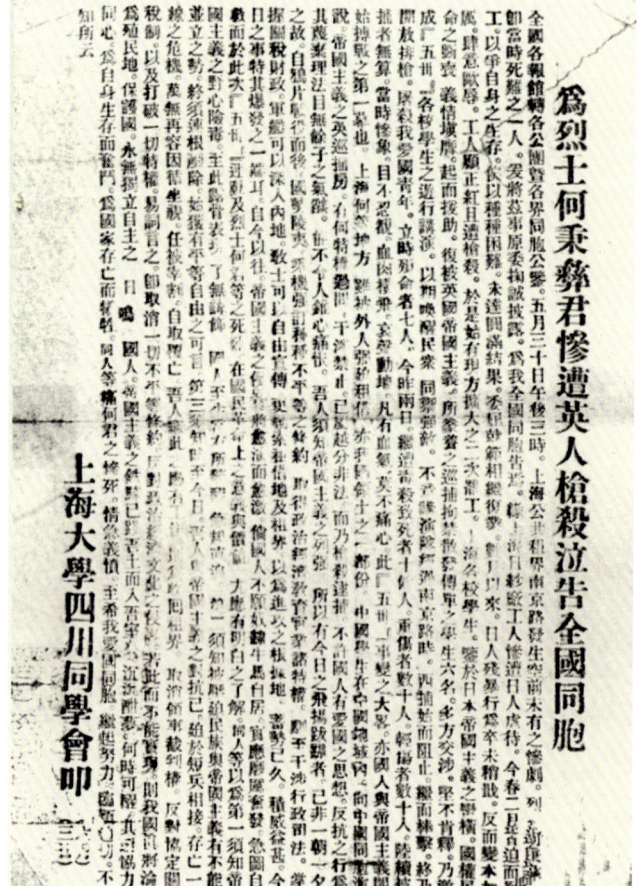

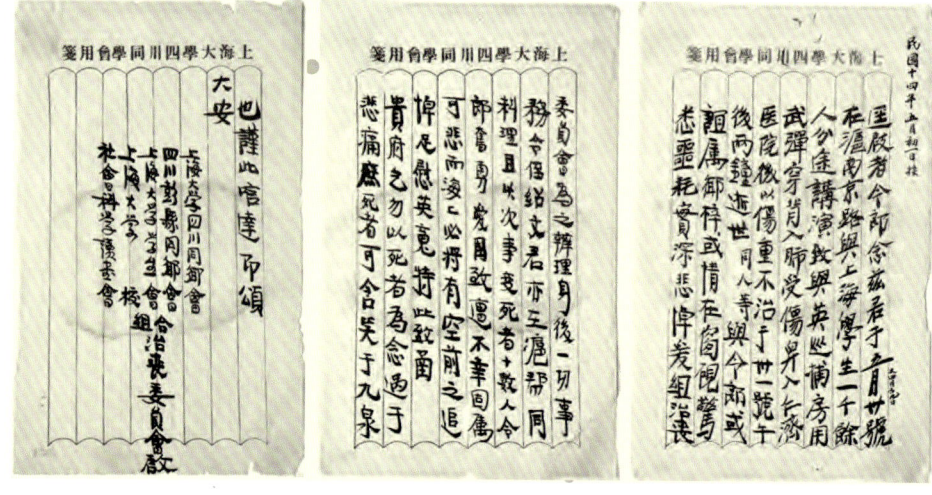

上海大学四川同乡会等致何秉彝（何念兹）家属的慰问信

A letter of condolence from the Sichuan Students Association of SHU to the family of He Bingyi (He Nianzi)

1925年6月3日，上海大学四川同学会印发《为烈士何秉彝君惨遭英人枪杀泣告全国同胞》的悼文

The elegy "Weeping to Compatriots Nationwide over the Tragic Shooting of Martyr He Bingyi by the British" printed and distributed by the Sichuan Students Association of SHU, June 3, 1925

第一部分　风云际会　青云发轫

1925年6月30日，"五卅"死难烈士追悼大会举行，到会者逾20万人
A memorial meeting for the martyrs in the May Thirtieth Massacre, June 30, 1925

1925年9月7日，北洋政府外交部特派江苏交涉员许沅呈文，详述"上海大学被租界海军搜索发生损失要求赔偿据情陈请汇案"。图为1925年9月10日，加盖北洋政府外交部总长沈瑞麟"沈阅"章后的公文（局部）
The document elaborating on "the losses of SHU due to a search by the concession navy and the request for compensation", September 7, 1925

《上大五卅特刊》于1925年6月15日创刊，为上海大学学生会在五卅运动爆发后创办，共出8期。刊头由校长于右任题写
The Special Issue of Shanghai University on the May Thirtieth Movement, launched on June 15, 1925

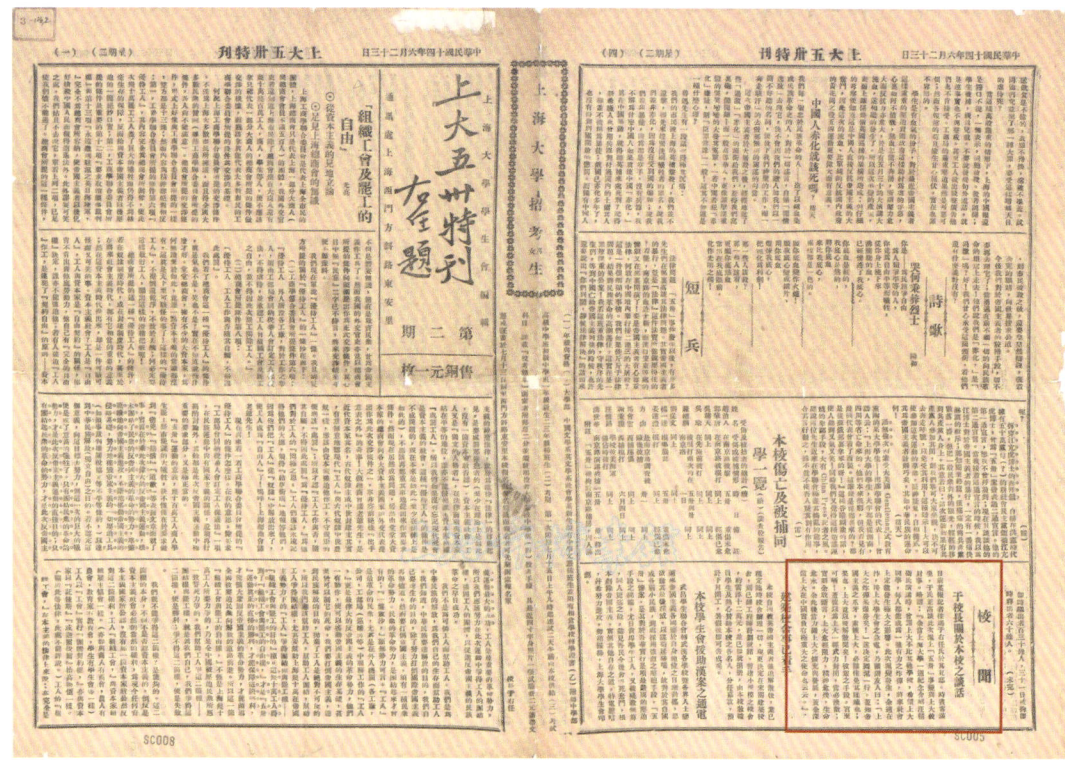

1925年6月23日,《上大五卅特刊》第2期刊登《于校长关于本校之谈话》:"曾谓上大不比其他学校,希望上大同学,每人都能成为一强有力之炸弹,将来社会上定能发生极大之影响。……余此后当力图上大之扩充与发展,盖余深信上大在中国实负有极重大之使命也。"

The report "President Yu's Remarks on Shanghai University" in *The Special Issue of Shanghai University on the May Thirtieth Movement*, June 23, 1925

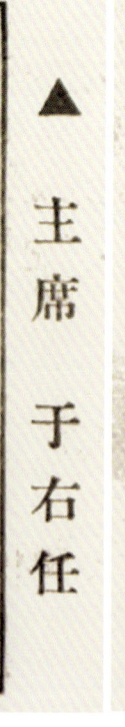
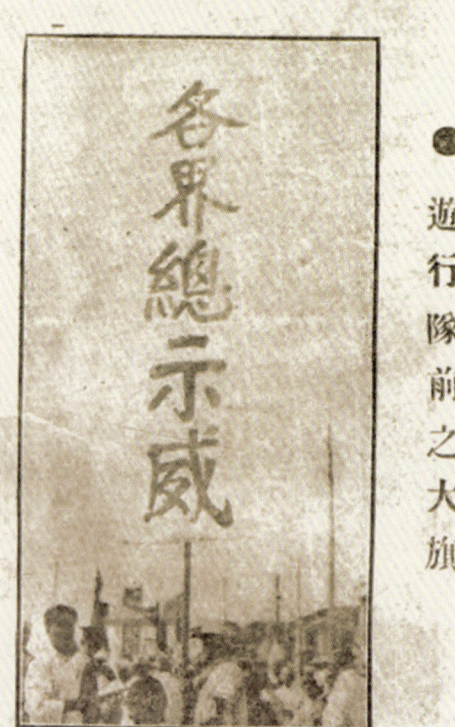

北京各界民众在天安门举行全国总示威,声援上海五卅运动。于右任担任大会主席,披露五卅惨案景状

People from all walks of life in Beijing held a national general demonstration at Tian'anmen to show their support for the May Thirtieth Movement in Shanghai. Yu Youren served as Chairman of the meeting to disclose the details of the May Thirtieth Massacre.

第一部分　风云际会　青云发轫

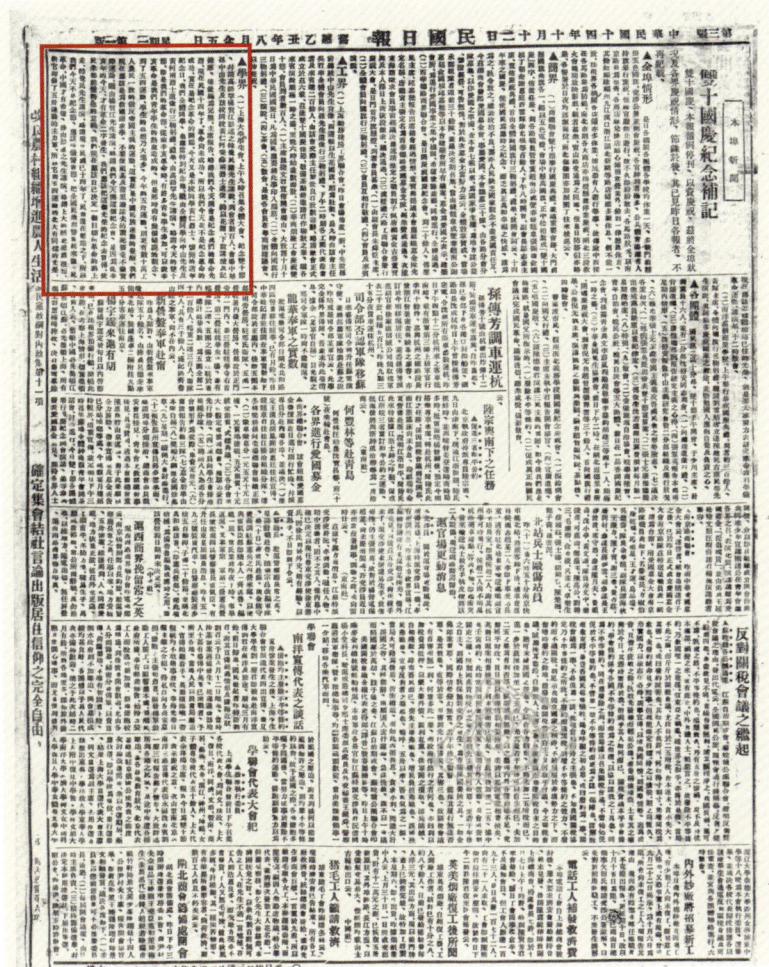

1925年10月12日,《民国日报》记载彭述之演讲内容中称:"它（上海大学）却做了五卅运动的主力军,所以它与五四运动的北大有同样的光荣。"

On October 12, 1925, *The Republic Daily* recorded Peng Shuzhi's speech that "It (SHU) became the main force in the May Thirtieth Movement. Therefore, it enjoys the same glory as PKU in the May Fourth Movement."

五卅运动中上海大学学生朱有才刻印传单用的钢板（中共一大纪念馆藏）

The steel stencil used by Zhu Youcai, an SHU student, to print leaflets during the May Thirtieth Movement

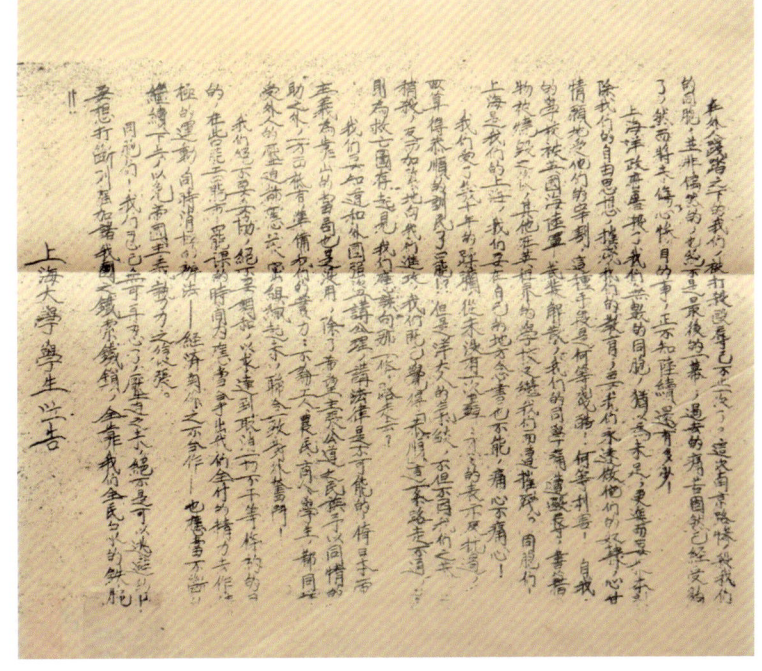

五卅运动中上海大学学生印发的油印传单

Mimeographed leaflets printed and distributed by SHU students during the May Thirtieth Movement

（二）在上海总工会任职　Serving in Shanghai Federation of Trade Unions

1925年5月31日，上海总工会正式成立，李立三任委员长、刘华任副委员长、刘少奇任总务科主任。

The Shanghai Federation of Trade Unions was established on May 31, 1925, with Li Lisan as Chairman, Liu Hua Vice Chairman, and Liu Shaoqi Director of General Affairs.

上海总工会领导工人罢工
The strike led by Shanghai Federation of Trade Unions

上海总工会旧址——宝山里2号（今宝山路403弄2号）
The former site of Shanghai Federation of Trade Unions - No.2 Baoshan Lane (now No. 2 Lane 403, Baoshan Road)

刘华（1899—1925），字剑华，四川宜宾人。1923年8月，进入上海大学中学部学习，其间任上海大学学生会执行委员、四川同学会主席。1924年，加入中国共产党。1925年1月，任第四届中共中央职工委员会委员；同年2月，任"二月罢工"前沿总指挥；同年6月，任上海总工会副委员长。

Liu Hua (1899-1925) entered SHU in 1923. In June 1925, he served as Vice Chairman of Shanghai Federation of Trade Unions.

第一部分　风云际会　青云发轫

（三）编辑出版中国共产党第一张日报——《热血日报》
Founding the First Daily Newspaper of the CPC—*Rexue Daily*

为加强五卅运动中的反帝宣传，中共中央创办了《热血日报》。该报是中共创办的第一张日报，于 1925 年 6 月 4 日创刊，由瞿秋白任主编，沈泽民、郑超麟、何味辛 3 人任编辑，张伯简负责筹办和发行。

Rexue Daily, the first daily newspaper of the CPC, was founded after the May Thirtieth Massacre to fight against reactionary authorities. Qu Qiubai served as Chief Editor.

何味辛（1905—1986），上海松江人。编辑。1925 年，加入中国共产党；同年，任上海大学教授。五卅惨案后，任《热血日报》编辑。

He Weixin (1905-1986) became a professor of SHU in 1925. He served as an editor of *Rexue Daily* after the May Thirtieth Massacre.

张伯简（1898—1926），云南剑川人。1921 年冬，加入中国共产党。1924 年，任上海大学教授；同年，任中共中央出版部首任书记。1925 年 1 月，参与创建中共公共支部，任支部书记。五卅惨案后，负责《热血日报》的筹办和发行。1925 年，任中共广东区执行委员会委员、军委书记。

Zhang Bojian (1898-1926) was in charge of the preparation and distribution of *Rexue Daily*.

《热血日报》创刊号
The inaugural issue of *Rexue Daily*

七、追认学籍　筹划复校
Recognition of Student Status and Re-operation of SHU

自1927年5月上海大学被封后，国民政府教育部不承认上海大学学生学籍，致使曾在上海大学求学的近两千名学生在就业、晋级等方面受到不公平待遇。1936年，于右任校长为争取学生学籍资格，与国民党当局一再交涉，终获认定。上海大学毕业生追认学籍后，多地纷纷成立上海大学同学会，进行复校活动。

After SHU was closed by the KMT authorities in May 1927, the Ministry of Education of the KMT Government refused to recognize the student status of SHU. In view of such unfair treatments, Yu Youren, President of SHU, repeatedly negotiated with the authorities, and finally in 1936, SHU won back the official recognition of student status and equal treatments with national universities.

（一）追认上海大学学生学籍，与国立大学同等待遇
Winning Back Recognition of Student Status and Equal Treatments

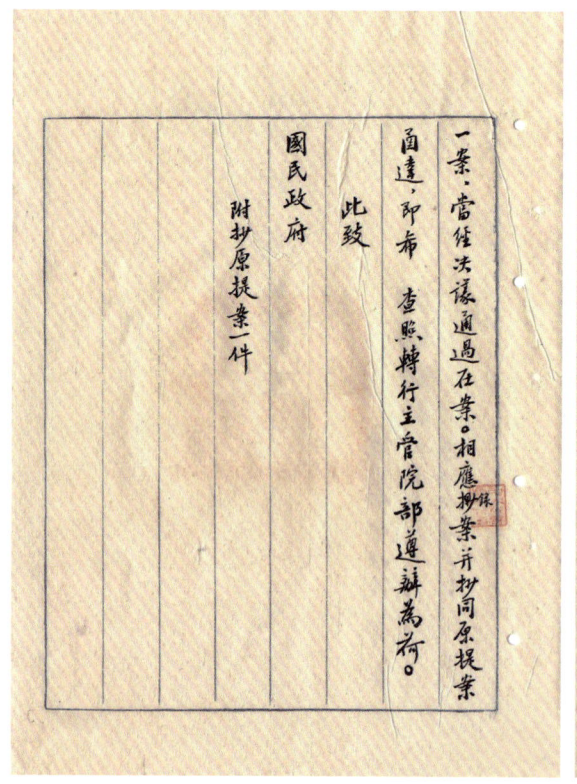
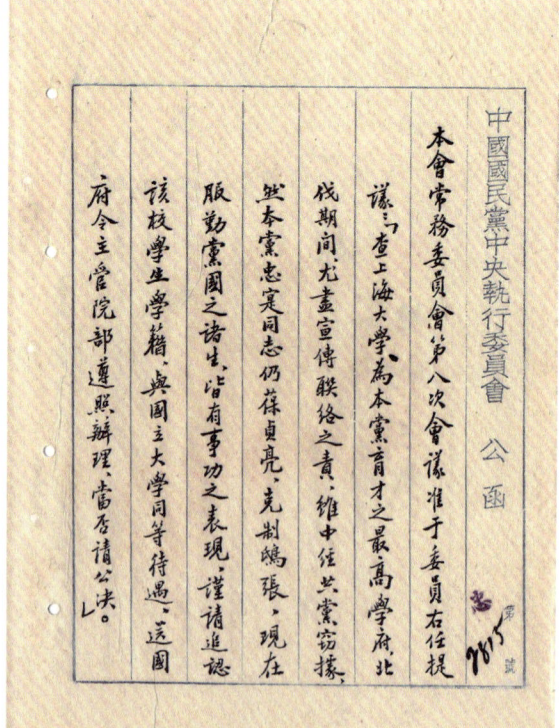

1936年3月，国民党中央执行委员会常务委员会第八次会议通过"追认上海大学学生学籍，与国立大学同等待遇"的决定

The approval letter on "Recognition of Student Status of Shanghai University Students and Equal Treatments with National Universities", March 1936

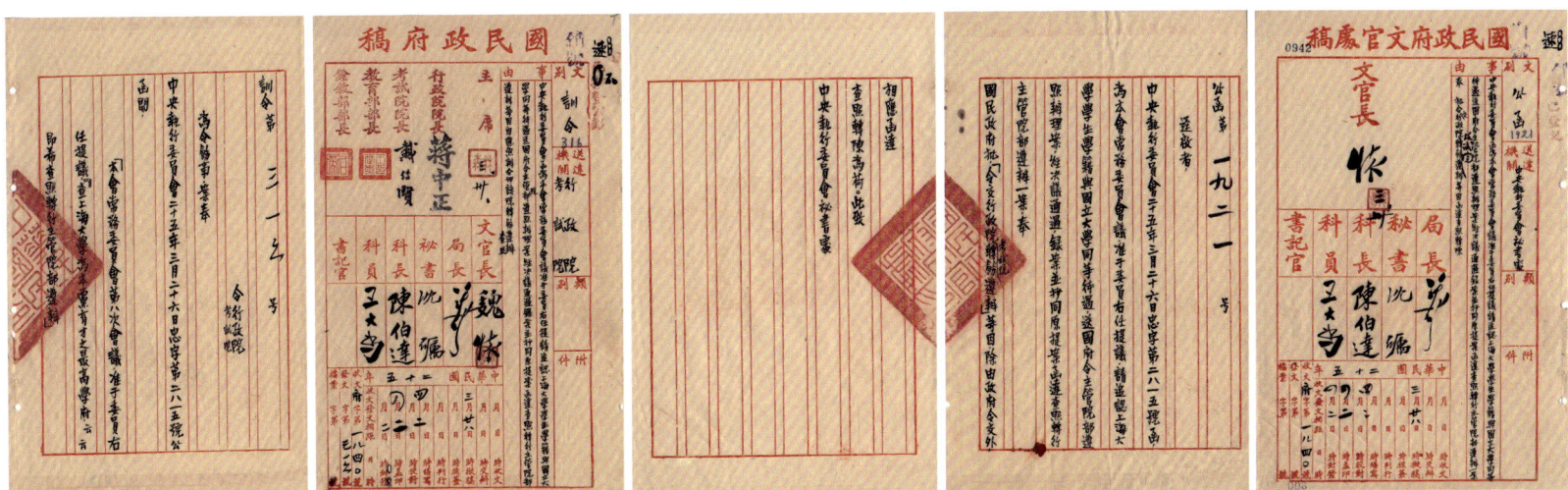

1936年4月,国民政府就"追认上海大学学生学籍,与国立大学同等待遇"决议,送达行政院、考试院的训令和国民党中央执行委员会秘书处的公函

KMT Government's Resolution on the "Recognition of Student Status of Shanghai University Students and Equal Treatments with National Universities", April 1936

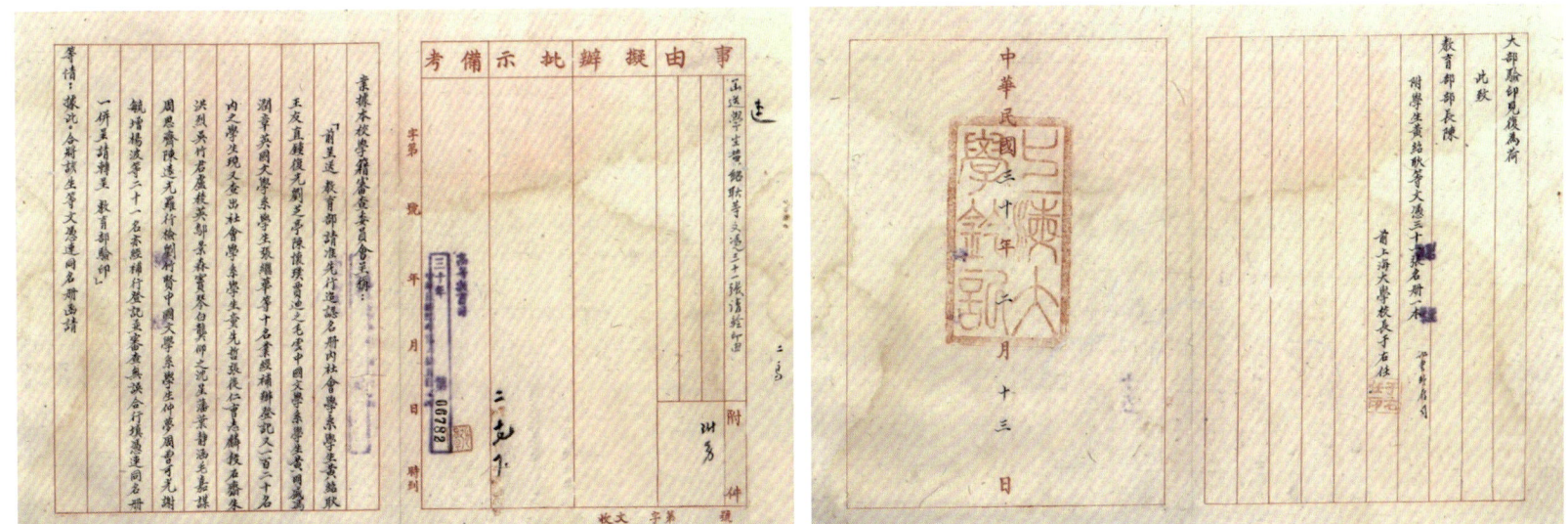

1941年2月13日,于右任校长致函国民政府教育部提请为上海大学黄绍耿等31名学生文凭验印

A letter by President Yu Youren to the Ministry of Education of the KMT Government, requesting to verify the diplomas of 31 SHU students, February 13, 1941

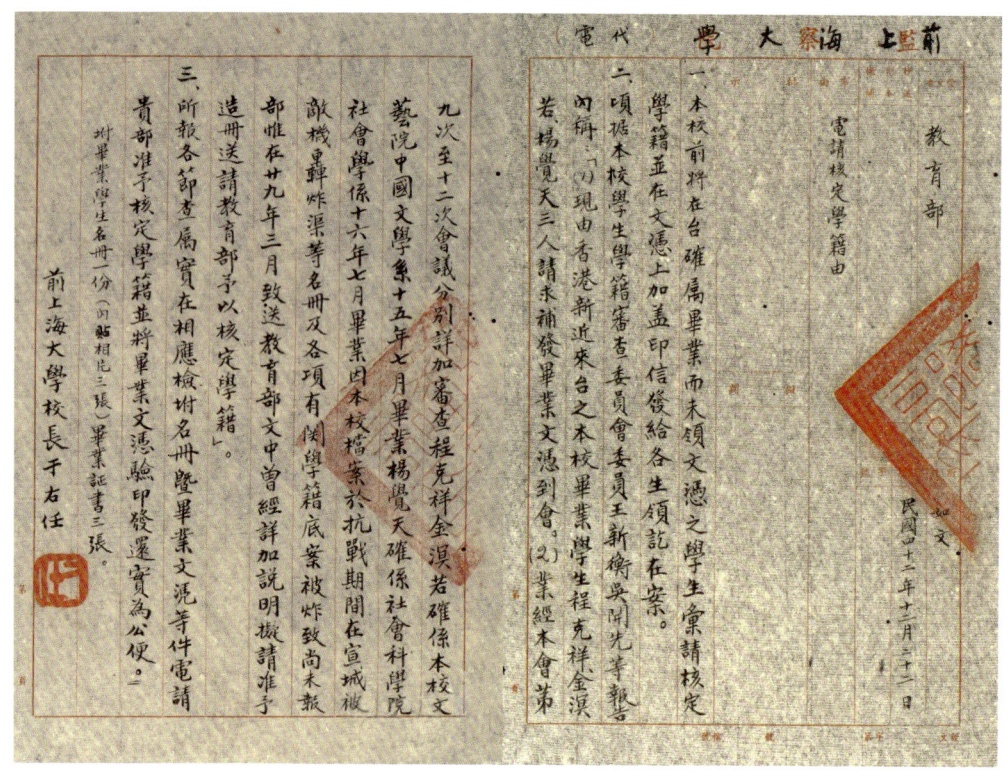

1953年12月22日，于右任提请为上海大学学生程克祥、金溟若和杨觉天核定学籍并将毕业文凭验印发还

A letter by President Yu Youren to the Ministry of Education of the KMT Government, requesting to verify the diplomas of SHU students, December 22, 1953

1955年9月6日，于右任提请为上海大学1925年毕业学生蒋振河核查学历并准予更名为蒋瑞清

A letter by Yu Youren to the Ministry of Education of the KMT Government, requesting to verify the academic credential of Jiang Zhenhe, an SHU graduate, and approve his name change to Jiang Ruiqing, September 6, 1955

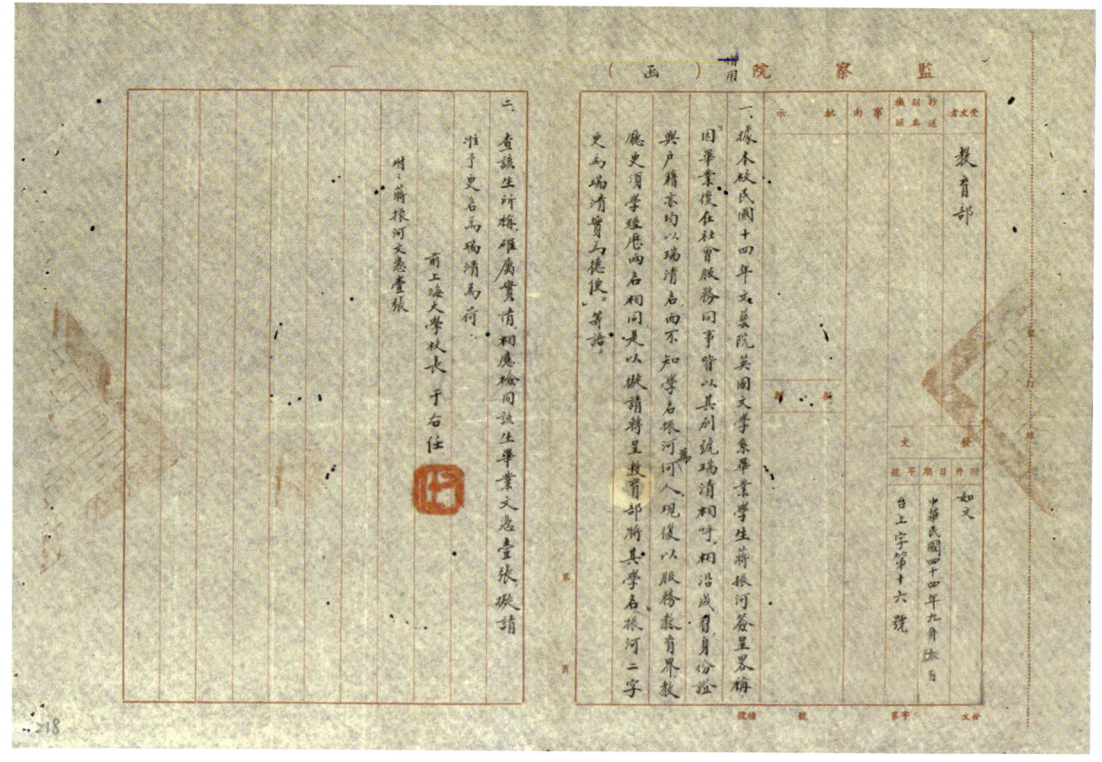

第一部分　风云际会　青云发轫

（二）成立上海大学同学会　Establishing SHU Alumni Associations

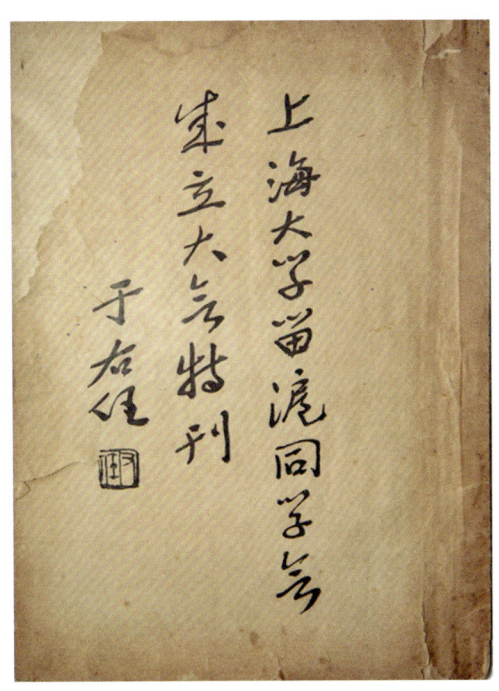

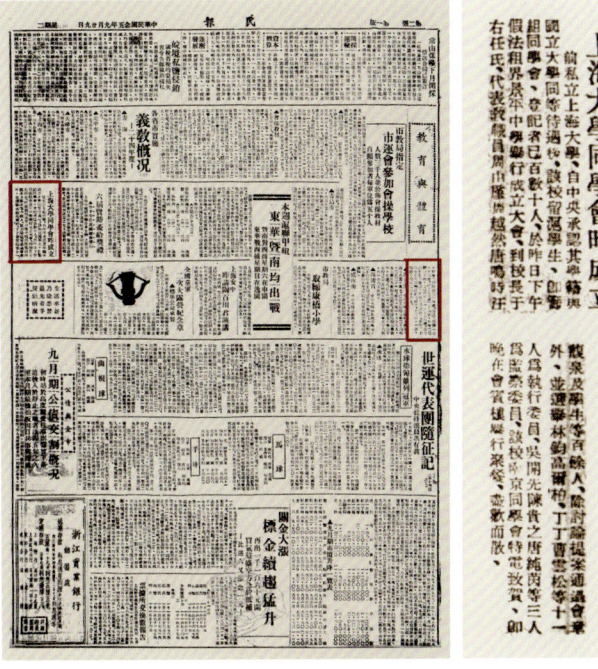

1936年9月29日，《民报》刊登《上海大学同学会昨成立》
The news that "The Shanghai University Alumni Association Was Established Yesterday", reported by *Min Pao*, September 29, 1936

1936年9月28日，上海大学留沪同学会成立。于右任为《上海大学留沪同学会成立大会特刊》题写刊名
Cover of *The Special Issue on Establishing Shanghai University Alumni Association in Shanghai*, inscribed by Yu Youren, 1936

20世纪50年代，台北市上海大学同学会成立，于右任出席
The inauguration of the SHU Alumni Association in Taipei in the 1950s, attended by Yu Youren

（三）力促复校　Striving for the Re-operation of SHU

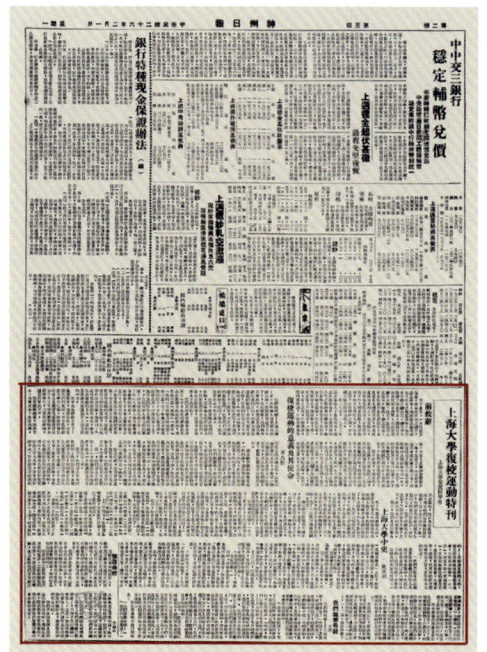
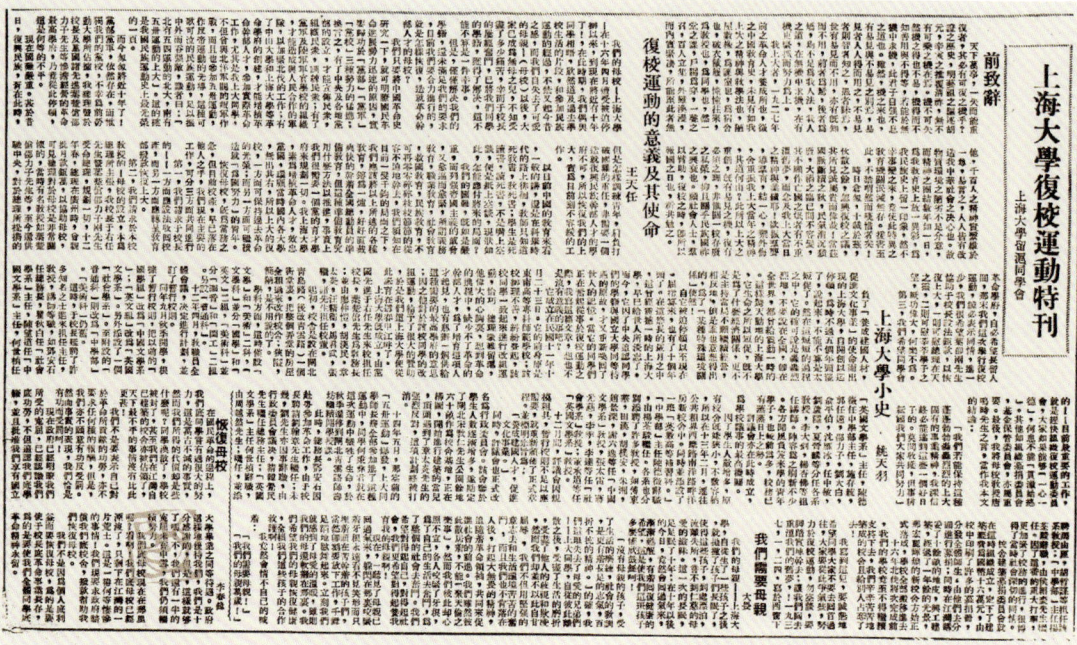

1937年2月1日，《神州日报》刊登上海大学留沪同学会编《上海大学复校运动特刊》
"The Special Issue on the Movement to Re-open Shanghai University", reported by *Shenzhou Daily*, February 1, 1937

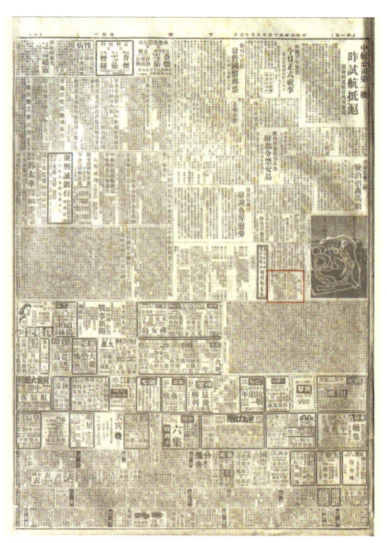

1945年9月17日，《申报》刊登上海大学复校招生简讯
"Notice on Re-enrollment of Shanghai University", reported by *Shun Pao*, September 17, 1945

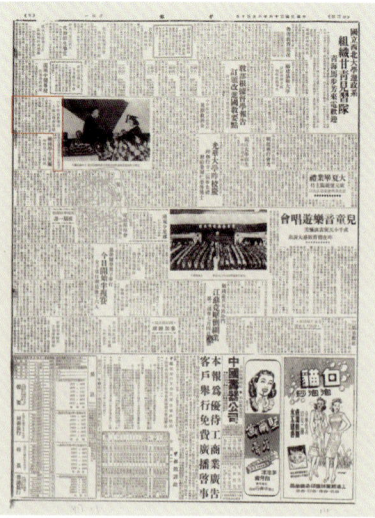

1947年6月30日，《申报》刊登《二十年前旧学府上海大学将重建》
"Shanghai University to Be Re-operated", reported by *Shun Pao*, June 30, 1947

八、知名校友　映照前路
Notable Alumni

曾经在上海大学工作或学习过的校友，怀揣理想，奋斗在各自的人生轨迹中。他们中有中国共产党的创建者和领导人，有为国捐躯的烈士，有著名的学者，有杰出的作家、剧作家、画家、诗人等。

The alumni who once worked or studied at SHU, with ideals in their hearts, were all striving in their lives. Among them were founders and leaders of the CPC, martyrs who sacrificed their lives for the country, renowned scholars, outstanding writers, playwrights, painters and poets.

（一）新中国成立前为革命献身的部分校友
Notable Alumni Sacrificing for Revolution (Partial)

皮言智（1901—1926），安徽英山（今属湖北）人。1924年，进入上海大学社会学系学习，后加入中国共产党。参加东征。

Pi Yanzhi (1901-1926) entered SHU in 1924.

张应春（1901—1927），女，江苏吴江人。1925年，进入上海大学学习；同年11月，加入中国共产党。1926年3月，创办并主编《吴江妇女》。

Zhang Yingchun (1901-1927) entered SHU in 1925.

Shanghai University

何洛（？—1927），重庆涪陵人。曾在上海大学社会学系学习。1927年3月，当选上海特别市临时市政府委员。

He Luo (? -1927) once studied at SHU.

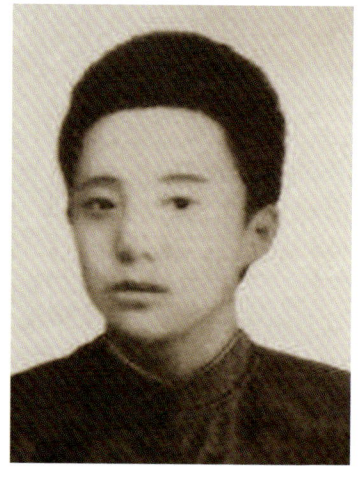

李清漪（1902—1927），山东沂水人。1923年，进入上海大学社会学系学习。1924年，加入中国共产党。五卅惨案后，根据党组织安排，随于右任北上策应北伐，从事军运工作。

Li Qingyi (1902-1927) entered SHU in 1923.

贾南坡（1904—1927），浙江金华人。曾在上海大学学习。1924年，加入中国共产党。1926年，任共青团上海闸北区委宣传部部长。

Jia Nanpo (1904-1927) once studied at SHU.

龚际飞（1903—1927），湖南双峰人。1923年秋，进入上海大学英国文学系学习；同年，加入中国共产党。1924年1月，任中共上海地方兼区执行委员会第三组代组长。1926年4月，赴长沙领导全省学生运动。

Gong Jifei (1903-1927) entered SHU in 1923.

许侠夫（1901—1927），广东文昌（今属海南）人。1924年，进入上海大学社会学系学习。1925年秋，加入中国共产党。1926年，任中共琼崖地委委员兼宣传部部长。1927年7月，任琼崖讨逆革命军第五路军党代表。

Xu Xiafu (1901-1927) entered SHU in 1924.

黄昌炜（1899—1928），广东琼海（今属海南）人。1922年，进入上海大学学习，后加入中国共产党。1926年6月，任共青团琼崖地委书记。

Huang Changwei (1899-1928) entered SHU in 1922.

第一部分　风云际会　青云发轫

蔡鸿猷（1897—1928），浙江缙云人。1922年，加入中国共产党。曾在上海大学学习。后任国民革命军连党代表。参加两次东征。

Cai Hongyou (1897-1928) once studied at SHU.

赵祚传（1903—1929），云南大姚人。1925年，进入上海大学学习。1926年，加入中国共产党。1927年，任云南省特委书记。

Zhao Zuochuan (1903-1929) entered SHU in 1925.

师集贤（1899—1930），陕西合阳人。1922年10月，进入上海大学美术科学习；同年，加入中国共产党。

Shi Jixian (1899-1930) entered SHU in 1922.

梁伯隆（1904—1930），四川江安人。1924年，加入中国共产党。1925年，进入上海大学社会学系学习。后参加北伐、南昌起义。

Liang Bolong (1904-1930) entered SHU in 1924.

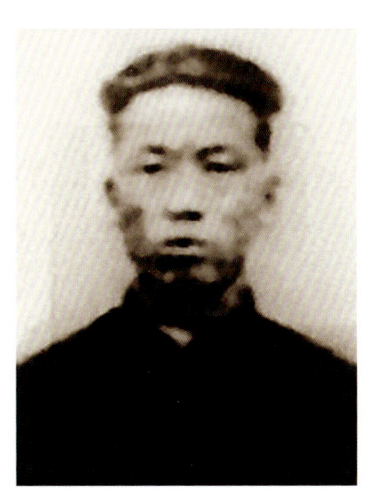

马凌山（1902—1931），陕西合阳人。1924年初，进入上海大学社会学系学习。1926年，加入中国共产党。1927年4月，任中共兰州特别支部宣传委员。

Ma Lingshan (1902-1931) entered SHU in 1924.

刘晓浦（1903—1931），山东沂水人。1923年，进入上海大学社会学系学习；同年，加入中国共产党。1927年后，任中共江苏省委组织部部长、中共山东省委执行委员兼秘书长。

Liu Xiaopu (1903-1931) entered SHU in 1923.

刘一梦（1905—1931），山东沂水人。1923年，进入上海大学社会学系学习；同年，加入中国共产党。1928年，任共青团山东省委书记。

Liu Yimeng (1905-1931) entered SHU in 1923.

何尚志（1897—1931），陕西铜川人。1923年秋，进入上海大学中国文学系学习。1924年，加入中国共产党。1931年，参与创建鄂北苏区，任红9军第26师参谋长。

He Shangzhi (1897-1931) entered SHU in 1923.

吉国桢（1899—1932），陕西华县人。1924年夏，进入上海大学社会学系学习。1926年，加入中国共产党。1931年，任中共河南省委书记。

Ji Guozhen (1899-1932) entered SHU in 1924.

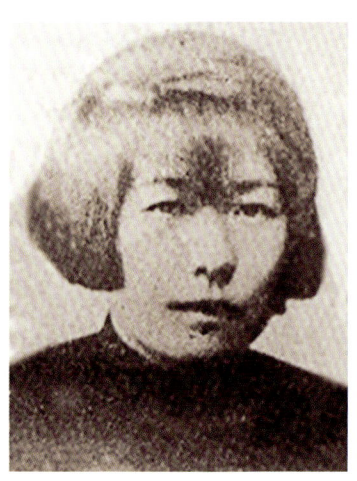

沈方中（1900—1932），女，浙江长兴人。1925年9月，进入上海大学社会学系学习。1926年，深入杨树浦、吴淞、闸北等地从事妇女工作。1927年，加入中国共产党。

Shen Fangzhong (1900-1932) entered SHU in 1925.

佘埃生（1896—1932），又名佘惠，湖南慈利人。1923年，进入上海大学英国文学系学习，后加入中国共产党。参加北伐、南昌起义、百色起义。

She Aisheng (1896-1932) entered SHU in 1923.

吴祥宝（1904—1933），女，又名静焘，江苏武进人。曾在上海大学中学部学习。四一二反革命政变后，与丈夫余泽鸿一起工作。后赴中央苏区任建宁中心县委宣传部部长、妇委书记。

Wu Xiangbao (1904-1933) once studied at SHU.

第一部分　风云际会　青云发轫

孟芳洲（1905—1933），陕西洛川人。1925年冬，进入上海大学社会学系学习。1926年，加入中国共产党。1932年11月，任中共陕南特委书记。

Meng Fangzhou (1905-1933) entered SHU in 1925.

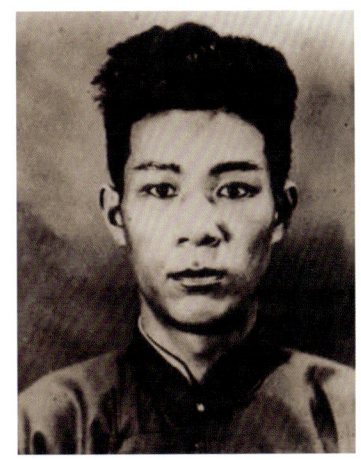

吴振鹏（1906—1933），安徽怀宁人。1925年，进入上海大学社会学系学习；同年，加入中国共产党。后任共青团江苏省（兼上海市）委书记、共青团中央宣传部部长。

Wu Zhenpeng (1906-1933) entered SHU in 1925.

黄让之（1902—1934），安徽天长人。1923年，进入上海大学中国文学系学习；同年，加入中国共产党。1924年夏，回家乡开设图书室，传播马克思主义。

Huang Rangzhi (1902-1934) entered SHU in 1923.

蔡威（1907—1936），福建宁德人。1925年，进入上海大学学习。1926年，加入中国共产党。1932年，任红四方面军总指挥部通信电台台长、通信站站长。

Cai Wei (1907-1936) entered SHU in 1925.

张景曾（1898—1937），河北蠡县人。1923年秋，进入上海大学学习；同年11月，加入中国共产党。1928年，任中共河南省委书记。

Zhang Jingzeng (1898-1937) entered SHU in 1923.

吴维中（1902—1937），江苏武进人。1925年，进入上海大学学习并加入中国共产党。后参加北伐、南昌起义。1927年10月，任中共武进县委常委兼军委书记。

Wu Weizhong (1902-1937) entered SHU in 1925.

蒲克敏（1903—1939），陕西蒲城人。1925年，进入上海大学社会学系学习并加入中国共产党。1927年，任中共西安市委书记。1928年，任中共陕西省委常委。

Pu Kemin (1903-1939) entered SHU in 1925.

崔小立（1901—1941），浙江宁波人。1924年春，进入上海大学社会学系学习，其间发表大量宣传马克思主义和反帝反军阀的文章。1925年5月，加入中国共产党。

Cui Xiaoli (1901-1941) entered SHU in 1924.

陈明（1902—1941），福建龙岩人。1925年，进入上海大学社会学系学习并加入中国共产党。后参加北伐。1927年，任中共闽南特委书记、中共福建临时省委书记。

Chen Ming (1902-1941) entered SHU in 1925.

罗世文（1904—1946），四川威远人。1925年，进入上海大学社会学系学习；同年，加入中国共产党。后任中共四川省委军委书记、省委书记。

Luo Shiwen (1904-1946) entered SHU in 1925.

恽代英革命烈士证明书

Martyrdom Certificate of Yun Daiying

沙文求革命烈士证明书

Martyrdom Certificate of Sha Wenqiu

（二）新中国成立后任重要领导职务的部分校友
Notable Alumni in Important PRC Leadership

张奚若（1889—1973），陕西大荔人。1924年8月，任上海大学政治学系主任。新中国成立后，任教育部部长。

Zhang Xiruo (1889-1973) served as Head of the Political Science Department at SHU in August 1924.

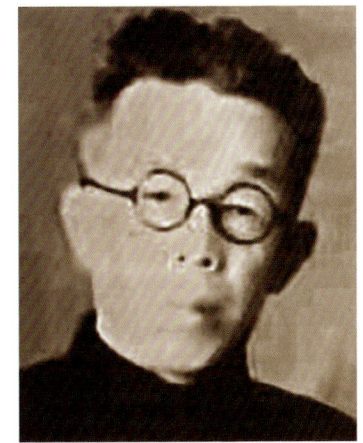

黄欧东（1905—1993），江西永丰人。1925年6月，加入中国共产党。1926年，进入上海大学社会学系学习。后参加南昌起义。新中国成立后，任中共辽宁省委第一书记、辽宁省省长。

Huang Oudong (1905-1993) entered SHU in 1926.

郑振铎（1898—1958），福建长乐人。1923年，任上海大学中国文学系教授。新中国成立后，任文化部副部长。

Zheng Zhenduo (1898-1958) became a professor of SHU in 1923.

何成湘（1900—1967），四川珙县人。1922年，进入上海大学学习。1924年，加入中国共产党。1926年，任全国学联秘书长、共青团江浙区委秘书长。后任共青团江苏省委书记。新中国成立后，任甘肃省副省长。

He Chengxiang (1900-1967) entered SHU in 1922.

张庆孚（1901—1968），江苏江阴人。曾在上海大学英国文学系学习。1925年，加入中国共产党。为宋时轮入党介绍人。新中国成立后，任林垦部党组副书记、林业部副部长。

Zhang Qingfu (1901-1968) once studied at SHU.

徐雪寒（1911—2005），浙江慈溪人。1925年，进入上海大学中学部学习。1926年，加入中国共产党；同年，任中共杭州地委组织部部长。新中国成立后，任对外贸易部副部长。

Xu Xuehan (1911-2005) entered SHU in 1925.

黄玠然（1901—2004），浙江浦江人。1926年，进入上海大学社会学系学习；同年，加入中国共产党。1927年初，任陈独秀秘书。新中国成立后，任全国工商联党组副书记、中央工商行政管理局副局长。

Huang Jieran (1901-2004) entered SHU in 1926.

李宇超（1906—1968），山东诸城人。1925年，进入上海大学学习。1926年，加入中国共产党。新中国成立后，任山东省副省长。

Li Yuchao (1906-1968) entered SHU in 1925.

方光焘（1898—1964），又名光涛，浙江衢州人。1924年8月，任上海大学中国文学系教授。新中国成立后，任江苏省文化局局长。

Fang Guangtao (1898-1964) became a professor of SHU in 1924.

第一部分　风云际会　青云发轫

马文彦（1902—1983），陕西三原人。1923年，进入上海大学中国文学系学习；同年，加入中国共产党。1926年5月，经李大钊推荐，陪同于右任赴苏联并任俄文翻译。1927年，任于右任秘书。新中国成立后，任西安市政协副主席。

Ma Wenyan (1902-1983) entered SHU in 1923.

党伯弧（1906—1985），陕西合阳人。1925年，进入上海大学学习；同年，加入中国共产党。新中国成立后，任西安市政协秘书长。

Dang Bohu (1906-1985) entered SHU in 1925.

匡亚明（1906—1996），江苏丹阳人。1926年，进入上海大学中国文学系学习；同年，加入中国共产党。新中国成立后，任东北人民大学党委书记兼校长、南京大学党委书记兼校长。

Kuang Yaming (1906-1996) entered SHU in 1926.

陈林（1902—1990），四川宜宾人。1925年，进入上海大学社会学系学习；同年，加入中国共产党。新中国成立后，任中央民族学院党委书记。

Chen Lin (1902-1990) entered SHU in 1925.

严信民（1902—1988），陕西澄城人。1922年，加入中国共产党。曾在上海大学社会学系学习。1927年，任于右任秘书。新中国成立后，任中央民族学院副院长。

Yan Xinmin (1902-1988) once studied at SHU.

熊寿祺（1906—1971），四川邻水人。1926年秋，进入上海大学中学部学习。1927年，加入中国共产党。1928年，参与创建井冈山革命根据地，参加三次反"围剿"作战。1930年，任中共红四军军委代理书记。新中国成立后，任中央民族学院副院长。

Xiong Shouqi (1906-1971) entered SHU in 1926.

嵇直（1901—1983），江苏镇江人。1922年10月，进入上海大学学习。1925年，加入中国共产党。新中国成立后，任农业部办公厅副主任。

Ji Zhi (1901-1983) entered SHU in 1922.

林淡秋（1906—1981），浙江三门人。1926年，进入上海大学英国文学系学习。1936年，加入中国共产党。新中国成立后，杭州大学副校长、中共浙江省委宣传部副部长。

Lin Danqiu (1906-1981) entered SHU in 1926.

赵君陶（1903—1985），女，重庆酉阳人。1925年，进入上海大学社会学系学习。1926年，加入中国共产党；同年，任湖北妇女学会宣传部部长。新中国成立后，参与创办北京化工学院并任副院长。

Zhao Juntao (1903-1985) entered SHU in 1925.

第一部分　风云际会　青云发轫

（三）文化界名人（部分校友）　　Notable Alumni in the Cultural Field (Partial)

戈公振（1890—1935），江苏东台人。新闻记者，新闻学者。曾任上海大学教授。

Ge Gongzhen (1890-1935) once served as a professor at SHU.

丁玲（1904—1986），女，湖南临澧人。作家。1923年，进入上海大学中国文学系学习。1932年，加入中国共产党并任左联党团书记。

Ding Ling (1904-1986) entered SHU in 1923.

孔另境（1904—1972），浙江桐乡人。作家。沈雁冰内弟。1923年，进入上海大学中国文学系学习。1925年，加入中国共产党。

Kong Lingjing (1904-1972) entered SHU in 1923.

沉樱（1907—1988），女，原名陈瑛，山东潍县人。作家。1925年，进入上海大学中国文学系学习。

Chen Ying (1907-1988) entered SHU in 1925.

孟超（1902—1976），山东诸城人。作家。1924年秋，进入上海大学中国文学系学习。1926年，加入中国共产党。

Meng Chao (1902-1976) entered SHU in 1924.

施蛰存（1905—2003），浙江杭州人。作家，翻译家，古典文学学者。1923年9月，进入上海大学中国文学系学习。

Shi Zhecun (1905-2003) entered SHU in 1923.

葛琴（1907—1995），女，江苏宜兴人。作家，编剧。曾在上海大学学习，并在工人夜校任教。1926年11月，加入中国共产党。

Ge Qin (1907-1995) once studied at SHU.

董每戡（1907—1980），浙江温州人。戏剧家。1923年，进入上海大学中国文学系学习，其间加入中国共产党。

Dong Meikan (1907-1980) entered SHU in 1923.

戴望舒（1905—1950），浙江杭州人。诗人。1923年9月，进入上海大学中国文学系学习。

Dai Wangshu (1905-1950) entered SHU in 1923.

第一部分　风云际会　青云发轫

罗尔纲（1901—1997），广西贵港人。历史学家。1926年，进入上海大学社会学系学习。

Luo Ergang (1901-1997) entered SHU in 1926.

罗髫渔（1902—1988），四川兴文人。历史学家。1923年，进入上海大学社会学系学习。1926年，加入中国共产党。

Luo Tiaoyu (1902-1988) entered SHU in 1923.

谭其骧（1911—1992），浙江嘉兴人。历史学家，历史地理学家。1926年夏，进入上海大学社会学系学习。

Tan Qixiang (1911-1992) entered SHU in 1926.

张弦（1898—1936），浙江青田人。现代中国美术界先驱者之一。1923年，毕业于上海大学美术科。

Zhang Xian (1898-1936) graduated from SHU in 1923.

我们学校的历史上，1922—1927年期间里有过一个上海大学。这是我们党最早建立的一个大学，像李鹏同志的父亲就是那个时候的上海大学学生会主席，毕业以后在上海参加了共产党，从事党的地下工作，后来他被国民党杀害在海南岛。还有井冈山黄洋界保卫战的指挥员也是我们上海大学1923年毕业出去的，他牺牲在井冈山，现在的井冈山烈士纪念馆里第一个就是他。没有他们的牺牲，没有那么多革命志士的奉献，我们上海大学提不出那么响亮的名字，这是我们上海大学的光荣。

——1997年5月，钱伟长校长在"迎接香港回归，走向灿烂明天"上海大学学生演讲会上的讲话（摘自《钱伟长文选》第五卷，上海大学出版社2012年版，第331页）

In the history of our university, there was a Shanghai University from 1922 to 1927. That was one of the earliest universities established by our Party. Comrade Li Peng's father was Chairman of the Student Union of Shanghai University at that time. After graduation, he joined the Party in Shanghai and engaged in underground Party activities. Sadly, he was killed by the Kuomintang on Hainan Island. Also, the commander of the Huangyangjie Defense Battle in Jinggangshan, a 1923 graduate of Shanghai University, gave his life for the cause and was the first martyr commemorated at the Jinggangshan Martyrs Memorial Hall. Without their sacrifice and the dedication of countless revolutionary martyrs, we would not have such a distinguished reputation for Shanghai University. This is the glory of Shanghai University.

——Remarks by President Qian Weichang at the "Welcome the Return of Hong Kong and March towards a Brilliant Tomorrow" Speech Contest for SHU Students in May 1997 (Excerpted from Volume 5 of *Selected Works of Qian Weichang*, published by Shanghai University Press in 2012, Page 331)

第二部分

海纳百川　奠基再造

20 世纪 50 年代中期，中央对上海提出，要把上海建成一个具有高度科学技术水平的大城市，成为我国重要的工业基地和科研基地，上海也作出工业生产向高（级）、精（密）、尖（端）方向发展的决策，由此急需大批适应这方面发展的高级专门人才，1958—1960 年，上海科学技术大学、上海计算技术学校（上海科技高等专科学校前身）和上海工学院（上海工业大学前身）相继成立。20 世纪 80 年代改革开放初期，上海进入经济社会转型发展轨道，需要大批具有人文社会科学专业知识的外向型、应用型人才。1983 年，上海的五所大学分校和上海市美术学校合并重建上海大学。

Part II

Integration and Reconstruction

In the mid-1950s, the central government proposed that Shanghai should be developed into a major city with advanced scientific and technological capabilities, serving as an important industrial and research base for the country. In response, Shanghai decided to steer its industrial production toward high-end, precision and cutting-edge directions. This shift created an urgent need for a large number of highly specialized talents to support such development. From 1958 to 1960, Shanghai University of Science and Technology, Shanghai School of Computing Technology (the predecessor of Shanghai College of Science and Technology), and Shanghai Institute of Technology (the predecessor of Shanghai University of Technology) were founded successively. In 1983, by merging Shanghai Fine Arts College and five branches of existing institutions, Shanghai University was re-founded to join in the current of cultivating comprehensive talents.

一、上海工业大学（1960—1994）
Shanghai University of Technology (SUT, 1960-1994)

前身上海工学院，创办于 1960 年，是上海市属高等学校。

The predecessor, Shanghai Institute of Technology, was established in 1960 as a municipal university under the Shanghai Municipal People's Government.

（一）学校成立　Founding of SUT

1958 年，上海根据工业发展需要，对应 8 个工业局成立了 8 所高等专科学校。为了培养这些学校所急需的师资，1960 年 3 月，上海市委决定筹办上海工业师范学院。1960 年 7 月，教育部党组批复上海市委，同意建立上海工学院。上海市委成立了以上海交通大学校长谢邦治为主任委员、上海市委工业部副部长李华为副主任委员的筹备委员会，还将筹备中的上海工业师范学院并入上海工学院，旨在为上海培养高、精、尖工业发展需要的工程技术人才。1960 年 9 月，上海市委任命李华担任上海工学院院长兼党委书记，当月举行了上海工学院成立暨开学典礼。1972 年 4 月，工学院有两个专业并入上海科学技术大学，其余与上海机械学院合并，成为上海机械学院（总部）。1979 年 1 月，经国务院批准，恢复上海工学院建制，并改名为上海工业大学。1982 年 9 月，中共中央组织部同意钱伟长担任上海工业大学校长。1994 年，学校已成为一所以工为主，理、管、文相结合的多学科市属重点高校。

In 1958, in response to the needs of industrial development, Shanghai established eight specialized colleges corresponding to its eight industrial bureaus. To address the urgent demand for faculty at these institutions, the Shanghai Municipal Committee decided in March 1960 to establish the Shanghai Normal College of Technology. In July 1960, the Party Leadership Group of the Ministry of Education approved the establishment of Shanghai Institute of Technology. In September 1960, the founding and opening ceremony of the institute was held. In April 1972, two of the institute's programs were merged into Shanghai University of Science and Technology, while the rest were combined with Shanghai Mechanical College, becoming the headquarters of Shanghai Mechanical College. In January 1979, Shanghai Institute of Technology was renamed SUT. In September 1982, the Organization Department of the CPC Central Committee appointed Qian Weichang to be President of SUT. By 1994, the university had developed into a multidisciplinary key institution, focusing primarily on engineering while integrating science, management and humanities.

1960年9月30日，举行上海工学院成立大会暨开学典礼，教师代表朱家骏发言
Teacher representative Zhu Jiajun delivering a speech at the founding and opening ceremony of Shanghai Institute of Technology, September 30, 1960

1960年10月6日，《解放日报》刊登上海工学院正式成立的消息
Jiefang Daily reporting on the official establishment of Shanghai Institute of Technology, October 6, 1960

中共中央华东局书记魏文伯于1965年为上海工学院题写的校名
The name of Shanghai Institute of Technology inscribed by Wei Wenbo, Secretary of the East China Bureau of the CPC Central Committee, 1965

1979年1月28日，《解放日报》刊登上海工业大学成立的消息
Jiefang Daily reporting on the establishment of SUT, January 28, 1979

1990年10月14日，举行庆祝工大建校30周年大会（右起：原校党委组织部部长李中臣、校党委副书记黄祥豫、原校党委副书记朱晓初、原校党委宣传部部长朱志豪、原工学院副院长林立、校党委书记兼常务副校长郑令德、校党委副书记兼副校长赵耀华、副校长孔先豪、原校党委副书记兼副校长傅赤先）
Celebration of the 30th anniversary of the founding of SUT, October 14, 1990

（二）校园变迁　Relocations of Campuses

20 世纪 20 年代，基督教南浸信会传教士万应远在北宝兴路底置地筑屋，1924 年建成"浸会庄"，门牌号为北宝兴路 150 号。庄内南北向的道路（现广延路）将这方地域（现上海大学延长校区）分隔为东部和西部。在东部，1925 年以后晏摩氏女中和沪江大学附中相继迁入，1952 年两校合并为上海市北郊中学并于 1956 年迁出；接着，此地又相继成为上海第一师范学院（1958 年迁出）、上海交通大学分部和上海交通大学工农预科的校舍；1960 年秋上海工学院在此成立，校门门牌号为延长路 149 号，学校成立初与上海交通大学分部及工农预科共用校舍；1962 年上海交通大学分部迁出，校舍划归上海工学院，上海交通大学工农预科则改为上海工学院附中；1963 年上海工学院不再办附中，附中迁徙他地办学。在西部，1946 年中华浸会神学院迁入，1950 年停办；1951 年共青团上海团校在此成立；1960 年上海工学院成立初与团校共用校舍，1962 年团校迁出，校舍划归上海工学院。

建校初，校园面积为 220 亩，校舍建筑面积为 5 万平方米；1993 年，校园面积为 516 亩，校舍建筑面积近 19 万平方米。

In the 1920s, Southern Baptist missionary Robert Bryan purchased land and built houses at the end of North Baoxing Road. In 1924, the "Baptist Village" was completed on No.150 North Baoxing Road. A north-south road (now Guangyan Road) within the village divided the original estate (now the Yanchang Campus of SHU) into eastern and western sections. In the eastern section, after 1925, McTyeire Girls' School and the Affiliated High School of the University of Shanghai moved in successively. In 1952, the two schools merged to form Shanghai Beijiao Middle School, which moved out in 1956. Subsequently, the site became the campus of Shanghai First Normal College (which moved out in 1958), the branch campus of Shanghai Jiao Tong University, and the Workers' and Peasants' Preparatory Department of Shanghai Jiao Tong University. In the autumn of 1960, the Shanghai Institute of Technology was established here, with the main gate at No.149 Yanchang Road. Initially, the institute shared the campus with the branch campus of Shanghai Jiao Tong University and the Workers' and Peasants' Preparatory Department. In 1962, the branch campus of Shanghai Jiao Tong University moved out, and the campus was allocated to the Shanghai Institute of Technology. The Workers' and Peasants' Preparatory Department was transformed into the Affiliated High School of the Shanghai Institute of Technology. In 1963, the institute ceased operating the affiliated high school. In the western section, in 1946 the China Baptist Theological Seminary moved in and ceased operations in 1950. In 1951, the Shanghai Youth League School was established here. When the Shanghai Institute of Technology was founded in 1960, it initially shared the campus with the Youth League School. In 1962, the Youth League School moved out, and the campus was allocated to the Shanghai Institute of Technology.

At the time of its establishment, the campus covered an area of 220 mu (about 14.7 hectares), with a building area of 50,000 square meters. By 1993, the campus had expanded to 516 mu (about 34.4 hectares), with a building area of nearly 190,000 square meters.

# 上海大学 Shanghai University

建校初，延长路 149 号校门（上海工学院）。图为首届女学生干部在校门前合影
The first batch of female student leaders in front of the gate of Shanghai Institute of Technology at No.149 Yanchang Road

1983 年，延长路 149 号新修的校门（上海工业大学）
The new gate of SUT at No.149 Yanchang Road, 1983

1972—1978 年，延长路 149 号校门（上海机械学院）
The gate of Shanghai Mechanical Engineering Institute (1972-1978) at No.149 Yanchang Road

西北小楼（1925 年建，原中华浸会神学院校舍）
The Northwest Building (built in 1925)

南大楼（1925 年建，原晏摩氏女中校舍）
The South Building (built in 1925)

第二部分　海纳百川　奠基再造

第一教学楼（1956年建，原上海第一师范学院校舍）
No.1 Teaching Building (built in 1956)

老图书馆（1958年建，原上海交通大学分部校舍）
The old library (built in 1958)

电机楼（1961年建，上海工学院成立后建造的第一栋实验教学楼）
The teaching building of the Electrical Engineering Department (built in 1961)

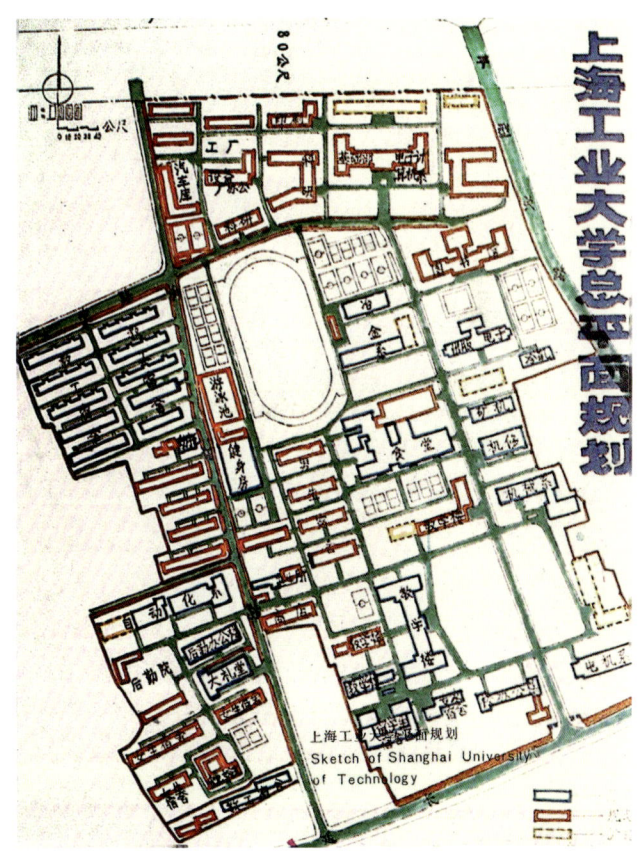

学校平面图（1990年绘制）
Campus map (1990)

（三）学校领导　SUT Leaders

校（院）党政负责人更迭一览
SUT Leaders

职　务	姓　名	任职年月	职　务	姓　名	任职年月
党委书记 核心小组组长 党委书记	李　华 张敬人 陈立富 侯东升 张　华 郑令德 吴程里	1960.7—1963.2 1963.3—1966.12 1971.4—1973.5 1973.6—1978.2 1979.4—1986.5 1986.6—1992.6 1992.6—1994.5	党委副书记 核心小组副组长 党委副书记	傅继生 阮世炯 黄宝生 田君福 徐安桂 鲁巧英 朱晓初 苏　宁 傅赤先 王力平 郑令德 赵耀华 黄祥豫 孙路一	1960.9—1961.6 1961.6—1966.12 1971.4—1972.4 1973.6—1978 1975.11—1978 1975.11—1983.10 1978.10—1983.10 1979.4—1981.8 1981.6—1986.5 1983.10—1985.1 1985.3—1986.5 1986.6—1992.5 1986.6—1993.4 1992.6—1994.5
院　长 校　长	李　华 张敬人 杨慧洁 钱伟长	1960.7—1963.2 1963.3—1966.12 1979.4—1982.9 1982.9—1994.5	副院长 副校长 常务副校长	傅继生 杨仲明 张鲁伯 林　立 宋兰舟 张　华 苏　宁 艾维超 傅赤先 雷凤桐 龚应荣 郑令德 方明伦 刘人怀 赵耀华 孔宪豪 余忠荪 黄　黔 徐匡迪 郑令德 方明伦	1960.9—1961.6 1961.6—1962 1962.1—1966.12 1962.10—1966.12 1979.4—1980.9 1979.4—1983.10 1979.4—1981.8 1979.4—1983.10 1981.6—1986.5 1981.6—1986.2 1981.6—1988.7 1983.10—1985.3 1986.2—1992.7 1986.6—1991.11 1988.7—1992.5 1990.4—1994.5 1991.10—1994.5 1991.10—1994.5 1986.7—1990.2 1990.2—1992.6 1992.7—1994.5

第二部分　海纳百川　奠基再造

张敬人（1905—1970），1963年，任上海工学院党委书记兼院长
Zhang Jingren, Secretary of the Party Committee and President of SUT from 1963

1983年1月，上海市副市长杨恺（右）在上海工业大学欢迎钱伟长校长履任
Shanghai Vice Mayor Yangkai (right) welcoming President Qian Weichang upon his appointment at SUT, January 1983

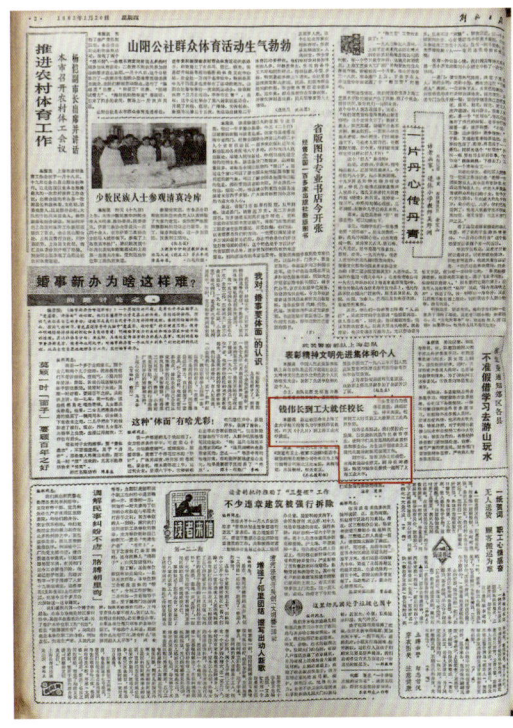

1983年1月20日，《解放日报》刊登钱伟长出任上海工业大学校长的消息
Jiefang Daily reporting on Qian Weichang's assumption of office as SUT President, January 20, 1983

1983年，校党委书记张华（右）和副书记王力平

Secretary of SUT Party Committee Zhang Hua (right) and Deputy Secretary Wang Liping, 1983

1988年10月，校党委书记郑令德（左）、校长钱伟长（中）、常务副校长徐匡迪出席学校第一次系主任沙龙

Secretary of SUT Party Committee Zheng Lingde (left), President Qian Weichang (middle) and Executive Vice President Xu Kuangdi at the first SUT Department Chair Saloon, October 1988

1988年，校领导集体合影（前排左起：校长钱伟长、党委书记郑令德；后排左起：教务长孔宪豪、副校长方明伦、副校长刘人怀、常务副校长徐匡迪、党委副书记黄祥豫、党委副书记兼副校长赵耀华、总务长诸海明、秘书长李金庚）

Group photo of SUT leaders, 1988

1986年5月29日，召开中共上海工业大学第三次代表大会（左起：傅赤先、张华、市教卫工作党委副书记胡绿漪、郑令德）

The Third CPC Congress of SUT, May 29, 1986

第二部分　海纳百川　奠基再造

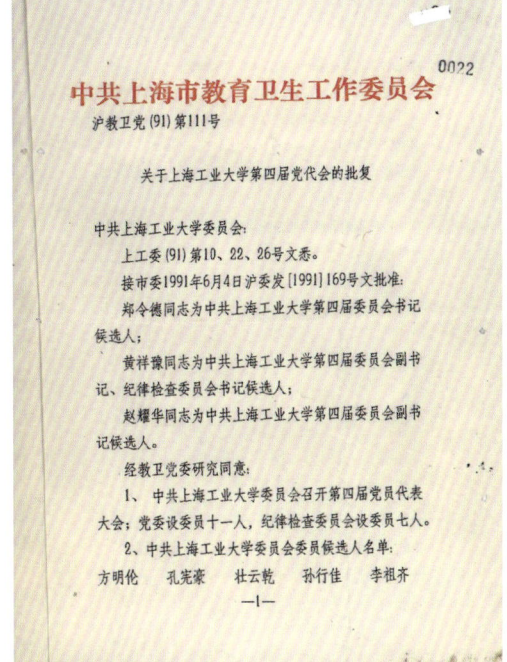

1991年6月5日，中共上海市教育卫生工作委员会关于上海工业大学第四届党代会的批复
The approval on the Fourth CPC Congress of SUT, June 5, 1991

1993年7月25—31日，在全国高校党建工作会议上，学校被中共中央组织部、宣传部和国家教委授予"党的建设和思想政治工作先进普通高等学校"，全国共有33所学校获此殊荣，上海仅上海工业大学1所。图为中共中央总书记、国家主席、中央军委主席江泽民与出席1993年全国高校党建工作会议代表合影（第二排右18：为校党委书记吴程里）
Photo of President Jiang Zemin and representatives at the National Conference on Party Building in Higher Education Institutions, Secretary of SUT Party Committee Wu Chengli in the second row. In July 1993, SUT was entitled "Advanced Higher Education Institution in Party Building and Ideological and Political Work" by the Organization Department and the Publicity Department of the CPC Central Committee as well as the State Education Commission. SUT was the only one that won this title in Shanghai.

（四）领导关怀　Recognition of Leaders

1985年10月18日，中共上海市委书记芮杏文到校视察；同年11月8日，芮杏文出席学校化学化工系学生在上海市青年宫举办的"未来属于保护环境的人们"展览会开幕式

Rui Xingwen, Secretary of the Shanghai Municipal Committee of the CPC, meeting the students of the Department of Chemical Engineering during his visit to SUT, October 18, 1985

1990年8月8日，中共中央总书记、中央军委主席江泽民为上海工业大学建校30周年题词

Inscription by Jiang Zemin, General Secretary of the CPC Central Committee, for the 30th anniversary of SUT, August 8, 1990

1994年1月18日，中共中央政治局委员、国务院副总理李岚清到校视察，称赞学校的综合改革"思路对，步子大，走得稳，效果好"

Li Lanqing, a member of the Political Bureau of the CPC Central Committee and Vice Premier of the State Council, visiting SUT, January 18, 1994

（五）专业、学科设置　Programs and Disciplines

建校初和 1994 年的本科专业设置一览
Undergraduate Programs in 1960 and 1994

年　份	专业名称
1960 年	电机、电器、电磁测量技术及仪表、机械制造工艺及设备、铸造工艺及设备、钢铁冶金、稀有及有色金属冶金、无线电技术及设备、热工仪表
1994 年	电机、电磁测量技术及仪表、应用电子技术、机械设计与制造、电子精密机械、流体传动及控制、机械自动化及机器人、铸造工艺及设备、金属材料与热处理、钢铁冶金、有色金属冶金、金属压力加工、工业电气自动化、工业仪表自动化、广播电视、环境监测、环境工程、精细化工、计算机及应用、计算机软件、工业管理、工业会计、工业外贸、工业与民用建筑（专科）

硕士、博士学位授权点一览
Master's and Doctor's Degree Granting Programs

批　次	获批时间	硕士点	博士点
第一批	1981 年 11 月	固体力学、电机、电磁测量技术及仪表、工业自动化、通信与电子系统、机械制造、机械学、铸造、应用化学	/
第二批	1984 年 1 月	流体力学、钢铁冶金	固体力学
第三批	1986 年 7 月	应用数学、理论电工、计算机应用、电力传动及其自动化、金属材料、热处理和有色金属、冶金	/
第四批	1990 年 12 月	管理工程	电力传动及其自动化、机械学
第五批	1993 年 12 月	流体传动及控制、环境化工	钢铁冶金、流体力学

（六）师资队伍 Faculty

1960—1993 年教师人数及职称情况一览
Faculty Number by Title (1960-1993)

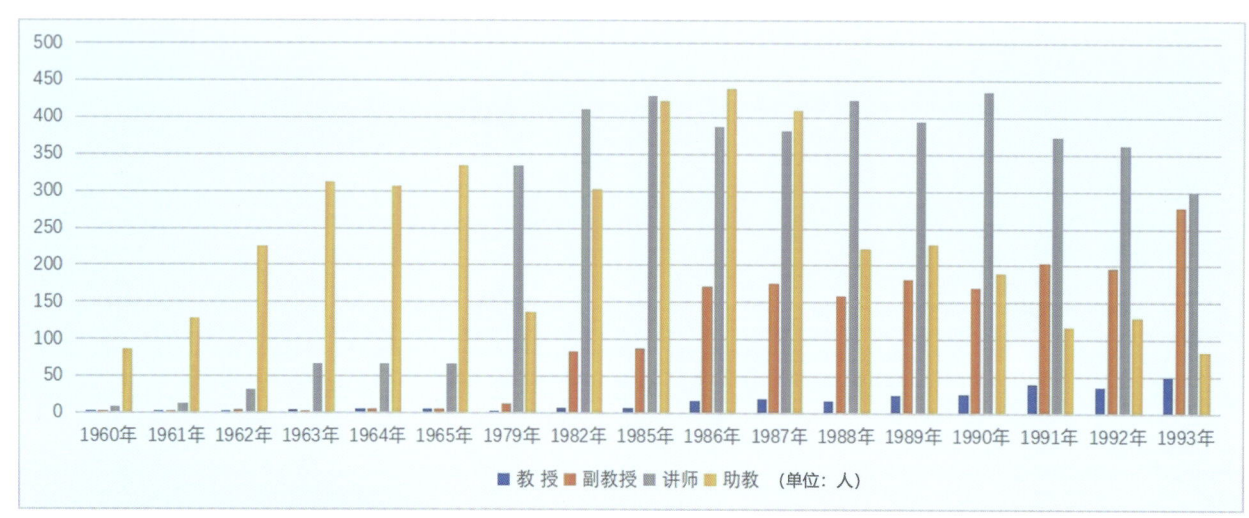

1978 年，学校举办的第一期青年教师进修班合影
Group photo of young teachers attending SUT's first training program, 1978

1985 年，学校基础部全体员工庆祝首届教师节合影（背景是原北大楼）
Group photo of staff from the Basic Education Division celebrating the first Teachers' Day, 1985

第二部分　海纳百川　奠基再造

博士生导师钱伟长教授在上海市应用数学和力学研究所
Professor Qian Weichang at Shanghai Institute of Applied Mathematics and Mechanics

"固体力学"博士生导师刘人怀教授（左2）在指导研究生
Professor Liu Renhuai instructing graduate students

"电力传动及其自动化"博士生导师陈伯时教授在指导青年教师
Professor Chen Boshi instructing young teachers

"机械学"博士生导师张直明教授在为研究生上课
Professor Zhang Zhiming lecturing to graduate students

"钢铁冶金"博士生导师徐匡迪教授在指导研究工作
Professor Xu Kuangdi instructing research work

"流体力学"博士生导师戴世强教授在指导研究生
Professor Dai Shiqiang instructing a graduate student

获全国荣誉称号的教师
Faculty Winning National Honors

荣誉称号	年　度	姓　名
全国教育系统劳动模范	1986	林振汉
全国教育系统劳动模范	1989	徐匡迪
全国教育系统劳动模范	1991	裴仁清
全国优秀教师	1989	张兆扬
全国优秀教师	1991	张侃谕
全国优秀教师	1993	管惠维
全国优秀教师	1993	张文俊

（七）人才培养　Talent Cultivation

　　1960年9月，学校开始招收本科生（五年制）。1966—1969年，停止招生。1970—1976年，招收"工农兵学员"（三年制大学）。1977年，全国恢复高考，开始招收本科生（四年制）。1978年，获批招收研究生资格。1981年，获批"固体力学"等第一批硕士点。1984年，获批第一个博士点。1991年，获批第一个博士后流动站（固体力学）。

　　In September 1960, SUT began enrolling undergraduate students (five-year program). From 1966 to 1969, admissions were suspended. From 1970 to 1976, SUT admitted "worker-peasant-soldier students" (three-year program). In 1977, the national college entrance examination was reinstated, and SUT resumed enrolling undergraduate students (four-year program). In 1978, SUT was granted the qualification to enroll graduate students. In 1981, it was approved to establish its first master's programs, including "Solid Mechanics". In 1984, SUT was granted its first doctoral program. In 1991, it established its first postdoctoral research station (Solid Mechanics).

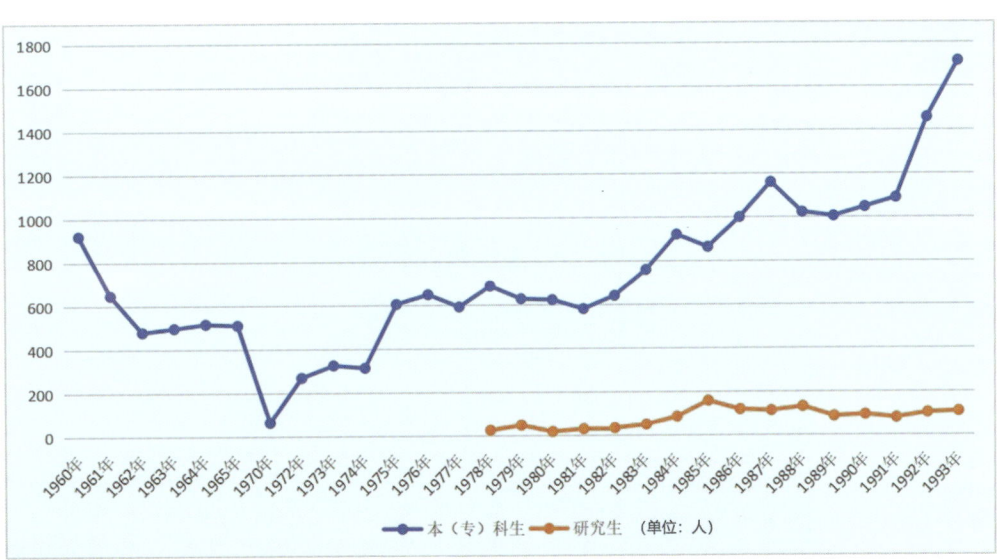

1960—1993年本（专）科、研究生招生人数一览
Number of Enrolled Undergraduate (Vocational) and Graduate Students (1960-1993)

1982年1月，学校八一届本科毕业生合影
Group photo of the class of 1981, January 1982

上海大学 — Shanghai University

上海工业大学1978级研究生毕业合影留念 一九八一年十月

1981年10月，学校首届研究生毕业，和校、系领导合影（前排就座者左2起：副校长龚应荣、校党委副书记兼副校长傅赤先、校党委书记张华、副校长艾维超、副校长雷凤桐）

Graduation photo of the first batch of graduate students with SUT leaders, October 1981

上海工业大学全体博士生留念　1994年4月

1994年4月，学校全体博士生与校领导合影（前排就座者左3起：副校长余忠荪、常务副校长方明伦、校长钱伟长、党委书记吴程里、副校长黄黔）

Group photo of all the doctoral students with SUT leaders, April 1994

第二部分　海纳百川　奠基再造

1988年5月，上海市研究生科技学术协会成立大会在上海工业大学举行（前排就座者左3起：校党委副书记赵耀华、校党委副书记黄祥豫、副校长龚应荣、常务副校长徐匡迪、校党委书记郑令德、校长钱伟长、副校长刘人怀）

The founding conference of Shanghai Science and Technology Academic Association for Postgraduates at SUT, May 1988

1987年6月，在上海工业大学举办中国大学生上海桑塔纳杯篮球邀请赛，上海工业大学男子篮球队获得冠军，校长钱伟长和常务副校长徐匡迪出席开幕式

President Qian Weichang and Executive Vice President Xu Kuangdi at the opening ceremony of Shanghai Santana Cup Basketball Invitation Tournament; SUT men's basketball team winning the championship, June 1987

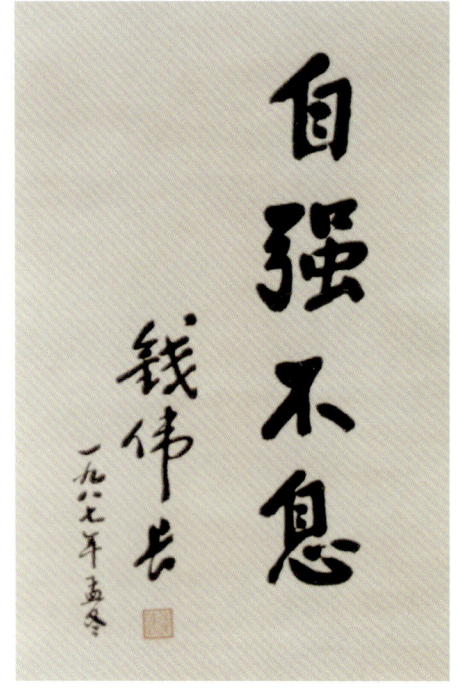

1987年11月，钱伟长校长手书"自强不息"；同年12月25日，学校决定以"自强不息"为校训

President Qian Weichang's calligraphy of the SUT motto "Striving for Self-Perfection", November 1987

上海工业大学教师自编教材《电工教学实习讲义》

Notes on Teaching and Practicing Electrical Engineering, textbook compiled by SUT teachers

1988年5月16日，上海工业大学与上海科学技术大学共同成立计算机学院，成为上海高校创建的首个计算机学院，钱伟长校长邀请清华大学李三立教授担任首任院长

The founding conference for the establishment of the joint School of Computer Science by SUT and Shanghai University of Science and Technology, May 16, 1988

上海工业大学曾使用的铜钟（20世纪七八十年代，电网经常临时停电，为维持学校正常教学秩序，当停电时，上下课时间以敲钟为号）

The bronze bell used by SUT during power failures

（八）科学研究　Scientific Research

1978年全国科学大会召开以后，学校的科研工作蓬勃发展，尤其重视与企业的深度合作。学校的科研人员投入、科研经费、科研项目数逐年增加，1990—1993年，每年的科研经费、三大检索（SCI、EI、ISTP）论文数、获省市级以上奖项、专利获准数在全国地方高校中均名列前茅，在上海高校中名列三甲。

1984年，学校创办上海市应用数学和力学研究所；1992年，学校创办上海工业大学科技园区。学校还先后创办上海机器人研究所、上海色材化学研究所等12个研究所、研究中心，另外还成立了24个研究室。

学校主编并公开发行的学术刊物有《应用数学和力学（英文）》、《上海工业大学学报》；主编的内刊有《高教研究》《人文科学论坛》等。

After the National Science Conference in 1978, the university's research flourished, with a strong emphasis on collaboration with enterprises. Investments in research personnel, funding and projects grew steadily. From 1990 to 1993, the university consistently ranked among the top local universities nationwide and in the top three in Shanghai in annual research funding, the number of papers indexed in major academic databases (SCI, EI, ISTP), provincial and municipal awards, and granted patents.

In 1984, the university established Shanghai Institute of Applied Mathematics and Mechanics, followed by the SUT Science and Technology Park in 1992. Over the years, it founded 12 research institutes and centers, including the Shanghai Robotics Institute and the Shanghai Institute of Color Materials Chemistry, along with 24 research laboratories.

The university also publishes academic journals such as *Applied Mathematics and Mechanics* (English edition) and *Journal of Shanghai University of Technology*, as well as internal publications like *Higher Education Research and Humanities Forum*.

1965—1993年科研经费一览
Research Funds (1965-1993)

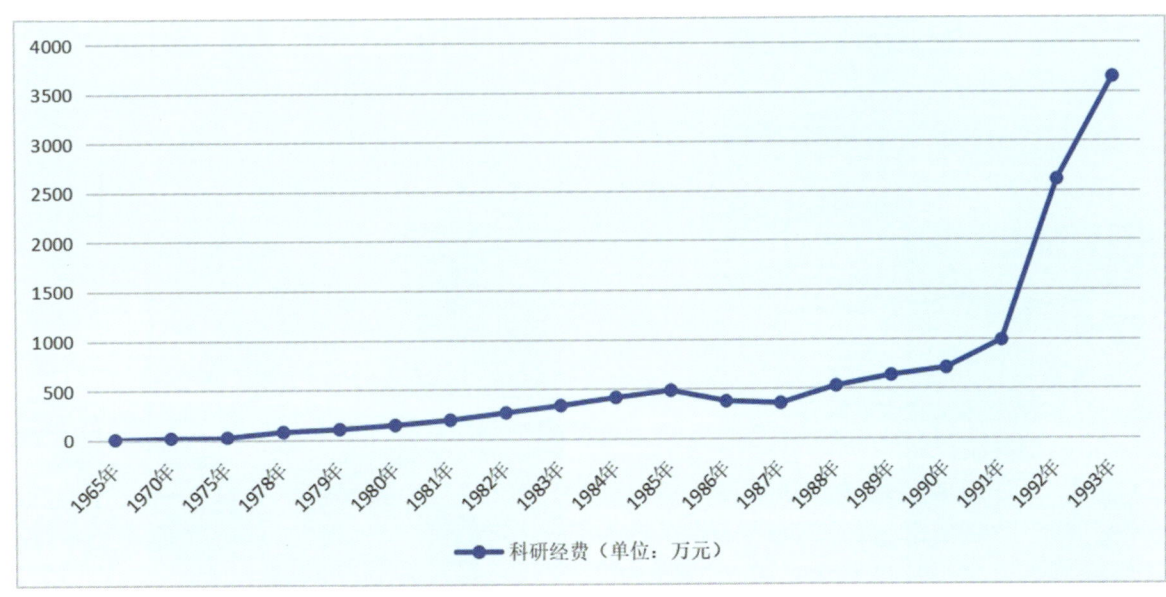

1985—1993年国家自然科学基金项目数量一览
Number of Projects funded by National Natural Science Foundation of China (NSFC), 1985-1993

年度	1985	1986	1987	1988	1989	1990	1991	1992	1993	合计
项目数	1	2	4	12	10	2	13	9	8	61

科研成果获国家级奖项一览
National Achievements in Scientific Research

项目名称	奖项名称	等级	年度	获奖人
绘图曲线规	国家技术发明奖	四等奖	1979	杨秉烈
S76 渣油粘结剂	国家技术发明奖	三等奖	1985	胡彭生
直线异步电机	国家科技进步奖	二等奖	1985	江建中　蔡廷锡　艾维超　胡之光　屠关镇
低温电解渗硫技术	国家科技进步奖	三等奖	1985	余忠荪　张云倩　张万宪　李润宝　肖玉堂
共轭曲面基础研究	国家自然科学奖	三等奖	1987	陈志新
电容式节能吊扇电机优化设计	国家科技进步奖	三等奖	1987	黄永家　杨家琪　林丁生　胡之光
石油机械难加工关键件的切削加工技术	国家科技进步奖	三等奖	1987	周家宝
地质力学地应力测量技术及应用	国家科技进步奖	三等奖	1987	潘立宙　王连捷　廖椿庭　丁原辰
流控式眼玻璃体切割器	国家技术发明奖	三等奖	1987	俞道义　陈银庆　俞丽和　华正清　丁仁根　姜节凯
液压油用磷氮型无灰抗磨剂制备工艺	国家技术发明奖	四等奖	1988	陶德华
GA-121 型整经机	国家科技进步奖	三等奖	1991	蒋洪瑶
氮锆系稳定化变质剂	国家技术发明奖	四等奖	1992	顾焕玉　潘振华　姚德伟

杨秉烈的"绘图曲线规"获 1979 年度国家技术发明奖四等奖
Professor Yang Binglie, winner of the Fourth Prize of the State Technological Invention Award in 1979

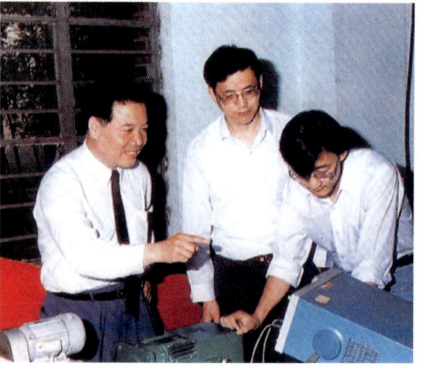

江建中（左）主持的"直线异步电机"获 1985 年度国家科技进步奖二等奖
Jiang Jianzhong's (left) team winning the Second Prize of the State Scientific and Technological Progress Award in 1985

第二部分　海纳百川　奠基再造

余忠荪（右）主持的"低温电解渗硫技术"获 1985 年度国家科技进步奖三等奖

Yu Zhongsun's (right) team winning the Third Prize of the State Scientific and Technological Progress Award in 1985

陈志新的"共轭曲面基础研究"获 1987 年度国家自然科学奖三等奖

Chen Zhixin winning the Third Prize of the National State Science Award in 1987

周家宝的"石油机械难加工关键件的切削加工技术"获 1987 年度国家科技进步奖三等奖

Zhou Jiabao winning the Third Prize of the State Scientific and Technological Progress Award in 1985

潘立宙（中）主持的"地质力学地应力测量技术及应用"获 1987 年度国家科技进步奖三等奖

Pan Lizhou's (center) team winning the Third Prize of the State Scientific and Technological Progress Award in 1987

陈银庆参与的"流控式眼玻璃体切割器"获1987年度国家技术发明奖三等奖

Chen Yinqing, together with other team members, winning the Third Prize of the State Technological Invention Award in 1987

陶德华的"液压油用磷氮型无灰抗磨剂制备工艺"获1988年度国家技术发明奖四等奖

Tao Dehua winning the Fourth Prize of the State Technological Invention Award in 1988

蒋洪瑶的"GA-121型整经机"获1991年度国家科技进步奖三等奖

Jiang Hongyao winning the Third Prize of the State Scientific and Technological Progress Award in 1991

顾焕玉主持的"氮锆系稳定化变质剂"获1992年度国家技术发明奖四等奖

Gu Huanyu's team winning the Fourth Prize of the State Technological Invention Award in 1992

1. 上海市应用数学和力学研究所
Shanghai Institute of Applied Mathematics and Mechanics

1984 年 5 月，钱伟长校长在上海工业大学创办上海市应用数学和力学研究所并任首任所长；同年 11 月，经国家科委批准正式挂牌。

In May 1984, President Qian Weichang established Shanghai Institute of Applied Mathematics and Mechanics at SUT and served as the first director. It was officially unveiled with the approval of National Science and Technology Commission in November the same year.

1984 年 5 月 16 日，钱伟长校长主持上海市应用数学和力学研究所成立大会
President Qian Weichang presiding over the founding conference of Shanghai Institute of Applied Mathematics and Mechanics, May 16, 1984

钱伟长校长于 1980 年创办《应用数学和力学》期刊（中、英文双刊）。图为 1980 年 5 月出版的中文刊创刊号和 1980 年 11 月出版的英文刊创刊号
Applied Mathematics and Mechanics (in both English and Chinese versions), a well-known journal founded by President Qian Weichang in 1980

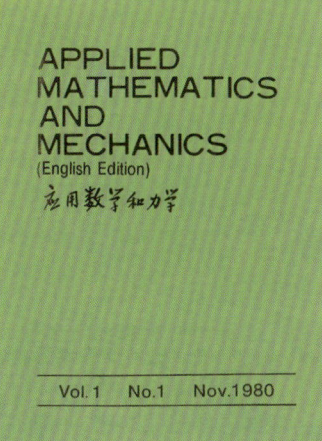

2. 上海工业大学科技园区
SUT Science and Technology Park

1992 年 2 月，经上海市高等教育局同意，上海工业大学创办科技园区，成为继东北大学以后国内第二个大学科技园区。1993 年 9 月，经国家科委批准，上海工业大学科技园区正式列入国家级新技术开发区。

In February 1992, with the consent of the Shanghai Higher Education Bureau, SUT established a science and technology park, the second university science and technology park in China after Northeastern University. In September 1993, with the approval of State Scientific and Technological Commission, the Science and Technology Park was officially listed as a national-level new technology development zone.

1992 年 3 月 27 日，《解放日报》刊登上海工大成立科技园区的消息

Jiefang Daily reporting on the establishment of SUT Science and Technology Park on March 27, 1992

上海工业大学科技园区（1994 年 5 月挂牌为上海大学科技园区）

SUT Science and Technology Park

3. 直线异步电机
Linear Induction Motor

直线异步电机是一种能将电能直接转换成直线运动机械能的电力传动装置。我国直线电机技术的研究始于20世纪70年代，上海工业大学是全国最早研究该技术的单位之一。

Linear induction motor is an electrical transmission device capable of directly converting electrical energy into mechanical energy for linear motion. Research on linear motor technology in China began in the 1970s, and SUT was one of the earliest institutions in the country to study this technology.

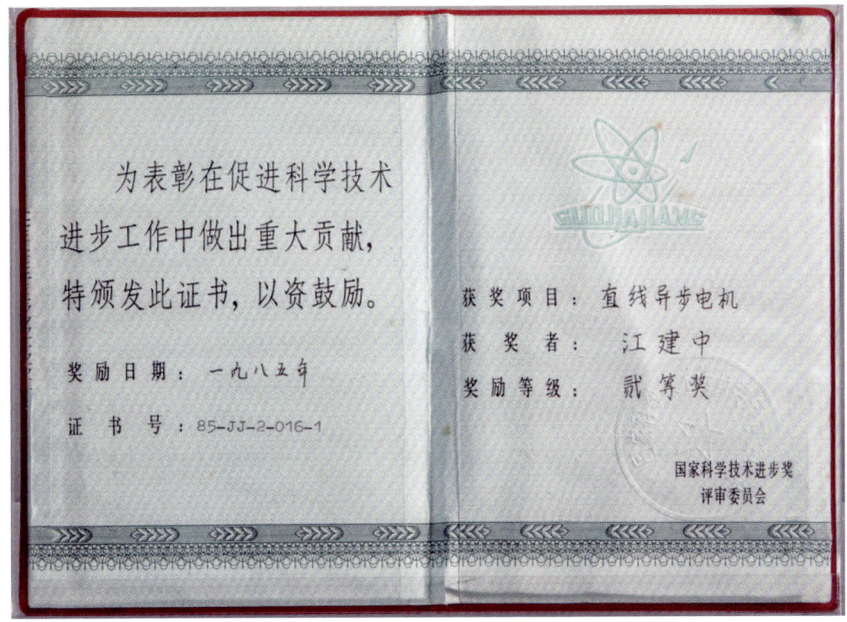

1985年，"直线异步电机"项目获国家科学技术进步奖二等奖
Linear induction motor project winning the Second Prize of the State Scientific and Technological Progress Award in 1985

上海工业大学与上海电机厂合作编写的专著《直线异步电动机》
Linear Induction Motor, co-compiled by SUT and Shanghai Electric Machinery Factory

4. 汉字宏观字形编码（钱码）及中文系统
Macroscopic Chinese Character Shape Encoding (Qian Code) and Chinese Language System

1984年，钱伟长成功开发"汉字宏观字形编码"方案，被称为"钱码"，并推向社会应用。1985年5月，"钱码"获上海市科技进步二等奖。1986年5月，国家标准局组织全国首届汉字输入方法评测，在全国各地选送的34种方案中，"钱码"被评为A类方案；同年，在北京举行的全国编码比赛中，"钱码"因单人输入速度第一获甲等奖。1987年，"钱码"获第三届中国发明展览会银牌。

In 1984, Qian Weichang successfully developed the "Macroscopic Shape Encoding" for Chinese characters, which was known as "Qian Code" and promoted to social applications. In May 1985, "Qian Code" won the Second Prize of Shanghai Scientific and Technological Progress Award. In May 1986, the National Bureau of Standards organized the first national evaluation of Chinese character input methods. Among the 34 selected schemes from all over the country, "Qian Code" was rated as A-class. In the national coding competition held in Beijing in the same year, "Qian Code" won the First Prize for single person input speed. In 1987, "Qian Code" won Silver Medal at the 3rd National Invention Exhibition.

钱伟长研究"钱码"的手稿
Qian Weichang's manuscript of "Qian Code"

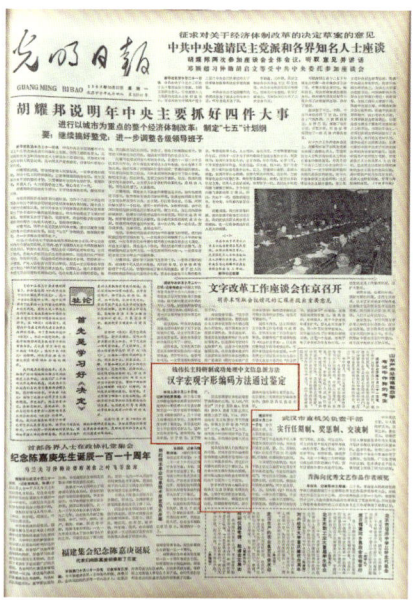

1984年10月22日，《光明日报》刊登钱伟长主持研制的汉字宏观字形编码方法通过鉴定的消息
Guangming Daily reporting on Qian Weichang's Macroscopic Shape Encoding passing the appraisal, October 22, 1984

5. "上海二号"搬运机器人
"Shanghai No.2" Transport Robot

1985年5月9日，上海机器人研究所在上海工业大学成立，这是我国最早开展机器人研发和人才培养的单位之一。1986年，经教育部批准，上海工业大学在全国高校中首先试办本科专业"机械自动化及机器人"，为我国培养了最早一批机器人领域骨干人才。1987年5月17日，"上海二号"搬运机器人研制成功，代表上海参加了第一届全国工业机器人展览会，并获1988年度上海市科技进步一等奖。此后又研制了"上海五号"首台浇筑工业机器人，获上海市科技振兴经济一等奖。

On May 9, 1985, Shanghai Institute of Robotics was established at SUT, one of the earliest units in China to carry out robot research and development and talent cultivation. In 1986, with the approval of the Ministry of Education, SUT firstly piloted the undergraduate major "Mechanical Automation and Robotics", cultivating the earliest group of backbone talents in the field of robotics. On May 17, 1987, "Shanghai No.2" Transport Robot was successfully developed and represented Shanghai at the first National Industrial Robot Exhibition, winning the First Prize of Shanghai Scientific and Technological Progress Award in 1988. Afterwards, the first casting industrial robot "Shanghai No.5" was developed, winning the First Prize of Shanghai Science and Technology for Economic Revitalization Award.

"上海二号"搬运机器人
"Shanghai No.2" Transport Robot

6. 不锈钢冶炼新工艺
New Process for Stainless Steel Metallurgy

上海工业大学徐匡迪教授是我国喷射冶金技术的开拓者，长期从事喷射冶金、钢的二次精炼及"熔融还原"跨世纪新流程研究，对我国钢铁冶金技术的发展作出了重大贡献。

Professor Xu Kuangdi from SUT, pioneer in the field of jet metallurgy in China, has long been engaged in research on jet metallurgy, secondary refining of steel and the cross-century new process of "melt reduction". He has made significant contributions to the development of China's iron and steel metallurgical technology.

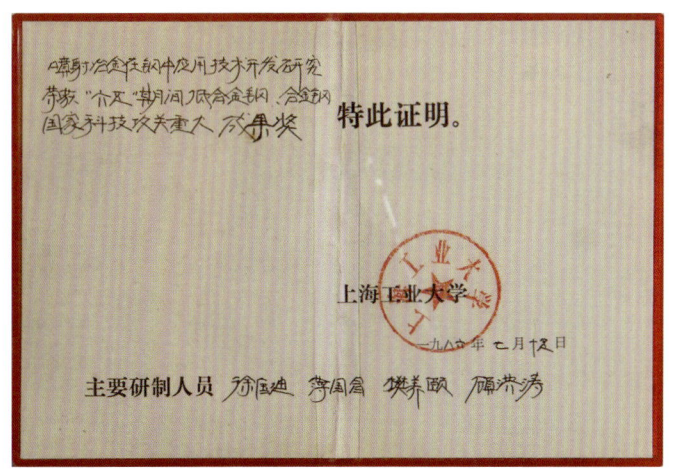

"喷射冶金在钢中应用技术开发研究"项目荣获"六五"期间低合金钢、合金钢国家科技攻关重大成果奖
"Research and Development of Application Technology of Jet Metallurgy in Steel" awarded the Major Scientific and Technological Achievement Award for Low Alloy Steel and Alloy Steel during the "Sixth Five-Year Plan" period

Shanghai University

（九）国际交流　Overseas Exchanges

1966 年，学校曾经接收越南民主共和国的来华进修生。1976 年，开始招收外国来华留学生。1985 年，开始招收外国来华留学研究生。1986 年，开始接收外国来华高级进修生。

改革开放以后，学校积极开展国际交流。据统计，1979—1993 年，学校和 7 个国家或地区的 12 所大学签订了校际合作协议；学校教师出国参加国际学术会议、讲学、访问 343 人次，出国进修、攻读研究生学位 350 人次；应学校邀请来自境外的短期专家 298 人次、长期专家 33 人。1993 年之前，由学校主办或协办的国际会议、国际讲习班 10 种；学校与境外 10 个机构合作科研 18 项。

SUT once admitted trainees from the Democratic Republic of Vietnam in 1966. It began to enroll overseas students in 1976, overseas graduate students in 1985, and senior trainees in 1986.

After the reform and opening-up, SUT actively carried out overseas exchanges. Statistics show that from 1979 to 1993, SUT signed intercollegiate cooperation agreements with 12 universities in 7 countries. Teachers from SUT attended international academic conferences, gave lectures or served as visiting scholars on 343 occasions, and went abroad for further study or to pursue graduate degrees on 350 occasions. At the invitation of SUT, 298 overseas experts paid SUT short-term visits and 33 for long-term visits. Before 1993, SUT had organized or co-organized 10 international conferences or seminars. It also conducted 18 joint research projects with 10 institutions overseas.

1. 来华留学生教育
Education for International Students in China

1976—1993 年留学生招生人数一览

Number of Enrolled International Students (1976-1993)

1990 年，钱伟长校长为优秀外国留学生颁发"好学生"证书

President Qian Weichang awarding the "Good Student" certificate to SUT foreign students, 1990

2. "走出去 请进来"
"Going out, Inviting in"

1984年，徐匡迪教授赴瑞典斯堪的纳维亚·兰塞尔公司任副总工程师、技术经理
Professor Xu Kuangdi working as Deputy Chief Engineer and Technical Manager for an industrial corporation in Sweden, 1984

1991年，上海市高等教育局局长徐匡迪（左5）陪同俄罗斯教育代表团到校参观上海机器人研究所
A Russian education delegation visiting the Shanghai Robotics Institute at SUT, 1991

1985年，香港爱国爱港人士王宽诚创立教育基金会，为国家培养人才；同年，成立了以钱伟长为主任的考选委员会，负责选拔人才，考务办公室设在上海工业大学。图为1986年10月，来自海内外的王宽诚教育基金会考选委员会委员在上海工业大学合影（前排左起：钱临照、陈岱孙、汤佩松、王宽诚、陈省身、钱伟长、吴富恒，后排左起：黄贵康、费孝通、黄丽松、田长霖、张龙翔、薛寿生、王明道）
The committee members of K. C. Wong Education Foundation from home and abroad at SUT, October 1986

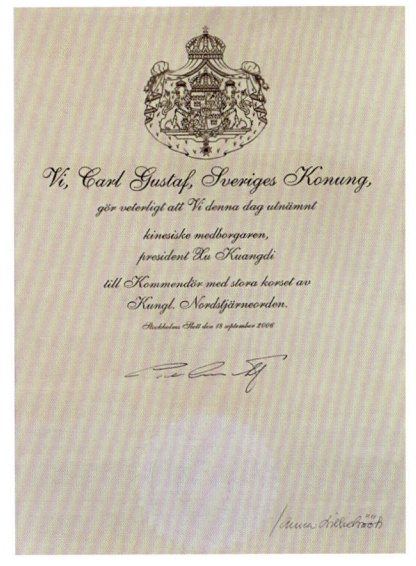

2006年，瑞典驻华大使代表瑞典国王为徐匡迪教授授予北极星大十字司令官勋章，表彰他为促进瑞中友好作出的杰出贡献
Professor Xu Kuangdi awarded the Commander of the Grand Cross of the North Star in recognition of his outstanding contribution to promoting the friendship between Sweden and China, 2006

3. 国际会议
International Conferences

1985年10月28—31日，由中国力学学会、上海市科委和上海工业大学联合主办，钱伟长担任会议指导委员会主席的第一届国际非线性力学会议在上海召开
The First International Conference on Nonlinear Mechanics held in Shanghai, October 28 to 31, 1985

钱伟长与参会的中外力学专家合影
Qian Weichang and experts of mechanics

4. 国际合作办学
International Cooperative Education

1983年，与美国罗切斯特理工学院签订合作办学协议，这是学校第一个校际交流的协议。图为1990年授予美国罗切斯特理工学院院长理查德·罗斯为上海工业大学荣誉博士

Richard Rose, President of Rochester Institute of Technology, receiving an honorary doctorate from SUT, 1990

1987年，校长钱伟长率团访问加拿大蒙特利尔大学工学院，签订两校交流与合作协议书

An agreement signed on exchange and cooperation between the Faculty of Engineering, University of Montreal, Canada and SUT, during a visit led by President Qian Weichang, 1987

（十）勇于改革　争先创新　Deepening Reform and Pursuing Innovation

　　钱伟长校长履任后，完整地提出了办大学要"拆四堵墙"和培养"全面发展的人"的重要思想：要拆除学校与社会之间的墙、教学与科研之间的墙、学院专业之间的墙、教与学之间的墙；我们培养的学生首先是一个全面的人，是一个爱国者，一个辩证唯物主义者，一个有文化艺术修养、道德品质高尚、心灵美好的人，其次才是一个拥有学科、专业知识的人，一个未来的工程师、专门家。钱校长校长的这些重要思想为学校的教育教学改革指明了方向。1991年8月，上海市政府教卫办确定把上海工业大学列为唯一的上海高校综合改革试点单位。1992年6月，上海市高校改革领导小组同意上海工业大学综合改革方案及其实施步骤。

Upon President Qian Weichang's taking office, he proposed the thought of "breaking down four walls" and cultivating "fully developed individuals". Specifically, these ideas called for the removal of the walls between the university and society, between teaching and research, between different faculties and majors, and between teaching and learning. The students should first and foremost be well-rounded individuals, patriots, dialectical materialists, and individuals with cultural and artistic cultivation, noble moral character, and beautiful souls. Secondly, they should be equipped with specialized knowledge and skills, and become future engineers and experts in their respective fields. Such thought provided clear direction for SUT's educational and teaching reforms. In August 1991, SUT was enlisted as the only pilot for comprehensive reform among Shanghai's higher education institutions. In June 1992, SUT's comprehensive reform plan and its implementation steps were approved by the Shanghai Higher Education Reform Leading Group.

1. 在上海事业单位中首先实行"任务—工资总额承包"
"Performance-Salary Contract"

1988年9月12日，常务副校长徐匡迪（右）和人文社会科学部主任分别代表学校和部门签订"任务—工资总额承包"合同
Executive Vice President Xu Kuangdi (right) signing "Performance-Salary Contract" with Chair of Humanities and Social Sciences Division, September 12, 1988

2. 在上海事业单位中首先推行全员聘用合同制
Inclusive Contract System

1992年6月，全体新聘任上岗的中层干部与上海市领导合影（前排左6：中共上海市委常委、市委秘书长王力平）
Group photo of newly appointed cadres with Shanghai municipal and university leaders, June 1992

1992年6月，校党委书记兼常务副校长郑令德（左）向新聘任的校办主任颁发岗位聘任书
Zheng Lingde (left), Secretary of SUT Party Committee and Executive Vice President of SUT, presenting letters of appointment to newly appointed cadres, June 1992

3. 在全国普通高校中率先实行自主招生
Merit-Based Enrollment with Autonomy

1993年5月，推行"面向社会，自主招生，择优录取"招生方法
SUT implementing the policy of "merit-based enrollment with autonomy", May 1993

1993年5月21日，《解放日报》刊登上海工大实行面向社会自主招生的消息
Jiefang Daily reporting on SUT's enrollment with autonomy, May 21, 1993

4. 在上海高校中首先全面推行"三制"（学分制、选课制、短学期制）和"导师""导生"制
Implementation of the "three systems" (Credit System, Elective System and Short Semester System) and Undergraduate Tutorial System

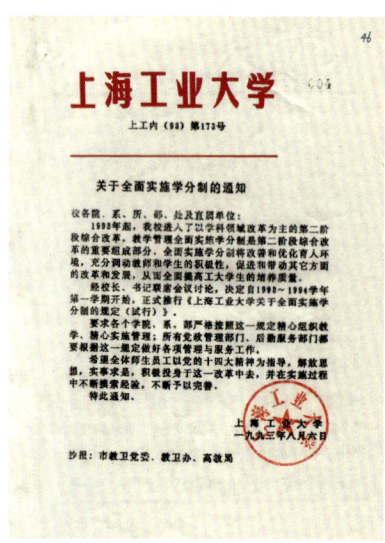

1993年8月6日，学校关于全面实施学分制的通知
A notice on implementing credit system, August 6, 1993

1993年开始每年一编的适用于"三制"的《上海工业大学教学一览（本科）》
SUT Teaching Plan, 1993

第二部分　海纳百川　奠基再造

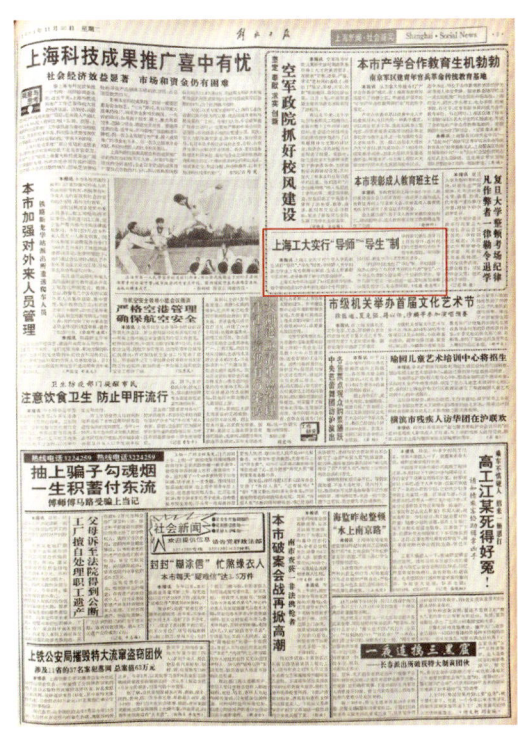

1993年11月30日，《解放日报》刊登上海工大实行"导师""导生"制的消息
Jiefang Daily reporting on SUT's Undergraduate Tutorial System, November 30, 1993

5. 在全国高校中首创学生宿舍管理新模式
——社区管理部
New Model of Dormitory Management
—Community Management Department

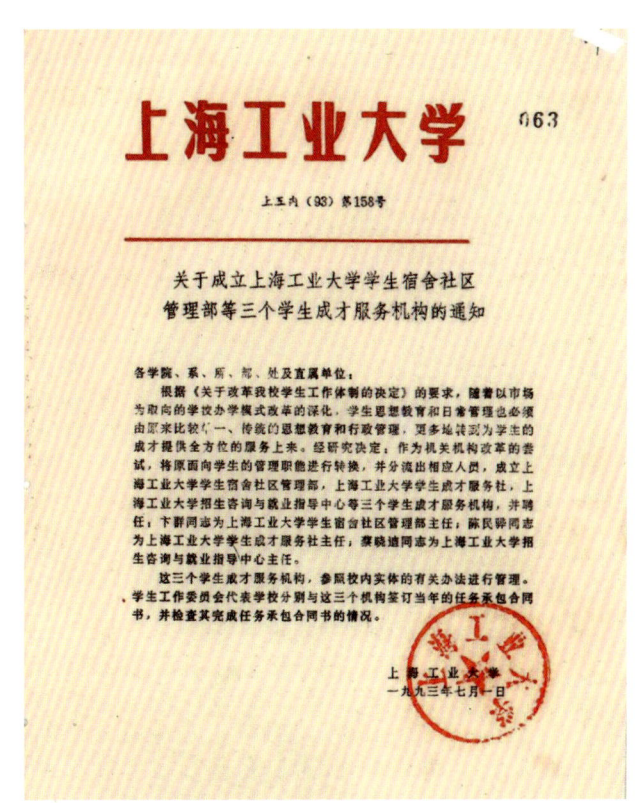

1993年7月1日，关于成立学生宿舍社区管理部等三个学生成才服务机构的通知
A notice on the Establishment of the Student Dormitory Community Management Department and Other Three Student Development Service Institutions, July 1, 1993

（十一）杰出人物　Prominent Figures

钱伟长（1913.10.9—2010.7.30），江苏无锡人。著名科学家、教育家，杰出的社会活动家，中国近代力学奠基人之一。1955年，当选中国科学院学部委员（院士）。1956年，当选波兰科学院外籍院士。历任全国政协第六、第七、第八、第九届副主席，中国民主同盟第五、第六、第七届中央委员会副主席和第七、第八、第九届名誉主席。曾任清华大学副校长、上海工业大学校长、上海市应用数学和力学研究所所长、上海大学校长。

Qian Weichang (October 9, 1913-July 30, 2010) was a scientist, educator, academician of the Chinese Academy of Sciences, Vice Chairman of the 6th-9th National Committee of the CPPCC, Vice Chairman of the 5th-7th Central Committee of the China Democratic League as well as Honorable Chairman of its 7th-9th Central Committee. He served as Provost and Vice President of Tsinghua University, President of SUT, Director of Shanghai Institute of Applied Mathematics and Mechanics and President of SHU.

徐匡迪（1937.12.11—　），浙江崇德（今桐乡）人。钢铁冶金专家，中国工程院院士，美国国家工程院外籍院士，俄罗斯工程科学院外籍院士，瑞典皇家工程院外籍院士。1963年，进入上海工学院冶金工程系工作。1986年，任上海工业大学常务副校长、教授。1992—2001年，历任上海市副市长、中共上海市委副书记、上海市市长。2002—2010年，任中国工程院院长、党组书记。2003年，当选第十届全国政协副主席。

Xu Kuangdi (December 11, 1937-), an expert in iron and steel metallurgy and academician of the Chinese Academy of Engineering, was appointed Executive Vice President of SUT in 1986. Later he served as Deputy Secretary of the Shanghai Municipal Committee on the CPC, Mayor of Shanghai, President of the Chinese Academy of Engineering and Vice Chairman of the 10th CPPCC.

二、上海科学技术大学（1958—1994）

Shanghai University of Science and Technology (SUST, 1958-1994)

创办于 1958 年，是上海市属高等学校。1968 年 8 月前，由中国科学院上海分院主办，1968 年 9 月划归上海市主办。

SUST, established in 1958, was under the leadership of Shanghai Municipal People's Government. Before August 1968, it was operated by Shanghai Office of the Chinese Academy of Sciences, then by Shanghai Municipality from September 1968.

（一）学校成立　Founding of SUST

1958 年 5 月，主管国家科技工作的国务院副总理聂荣臻和中共上海市委第一书记、上海市市长柯庆施在上海研究决定，创建上海科学技术大学，为上海培养"现代最新学科研究人才"和适应高、精、尖工业发展需要的工程技术人才，还决定学校由中国科学院上海办事处（当年 11 月改组为上海分院）主办。学校筹建工作由上海市委书记处候补书记、上海市副市长兼市科委主任、中国科学院上海办事处主任刘述周领导，由办事处副主任兼党委书记王仲良具体负责。学校实现当年筹建、当年招生。1959 年 9 月，上海市委任命周仁为校长、刘芳为副校长兼党委副书记。1994 年，学校已成为一所多科性的、理工结合的市属重点高校。

In May 1958, Nie Rongzhen, the Vice Premier of the State Council in charge of national science and technology work, and Ke Qingshi, the First Secretary of the Shanghai Municipal Committee of the CPC and Mayor of Shanghai, decided to establish SUST, for cultivating "modern research talents in the latest disciplines" and engineering talents to meet the needs of high, precision and cutting-edge industrial development in Shanghai. It was also decided that SUST would be sponsored by the Shanghai Office of the Chinese Academy of Sciences (which was reorganized into the Shanghai Branch in November of that year). The preparatory work went smoothly and SUST was established and began enrollment in the same year. In September 1959, Zhou Ren was appointed President and Liu Fang as Vice President and Deputy Secretary of the Party Committee. By 1994, SUST had become a multidisciplinary key institution of higher education.

上海大学 — Shanghai University

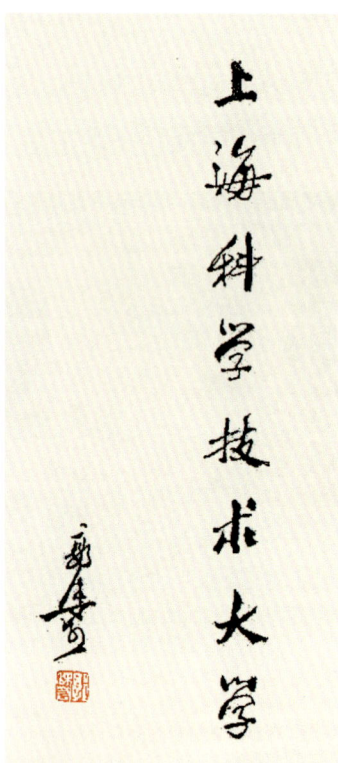

1959年5月，中国科学院院长郭沫若为学校题写校名
The name of SUST, inscribed by Guo Moruo, President of the Chinese Academy of Sciences, May 1959

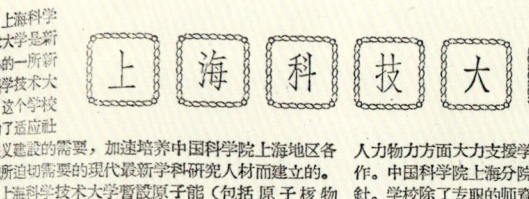

1959年6月17日，《解放日报》刊登上海科技大学招生情况的消息
Jiefang Daily reporting on SUST's enrollment, June 17, 1959

1959年9月12日，校长周仁在新生开学典礼上讲话
President Zhou Ren addressing the opening ceremony of the new school year, September 12, 1959

1989年5月19日，举行庆祝建校30周年大会
Celebration of the 30th anniversary of SUST, May 19, 1989

（三）校园变迁　Relocations of Campuses

　　1958年5月，上海科学技术大学筹备委员会在上海岳阳路320号中国科学院上海办事处院内挂牌；同年9月，在办事处礼堂举行上海科学技术大学1958年新生入学仪式。1959年5月，上海市委批复同意将欧阳路221号（光华大学旧址）作为上海科学技术大学临时校舍，与已在此地的上海机电设计院（现上海航天技术研究院）同处。1960年9月，位于嘉定南门的上海科学技术大学新校园基本建成，学校迁入，校门门牌号为城中路20号。

　　建校初，校园面积为192亩，校舍建筑面积近4.9万平方米；1993年，校园面积为450亩，校舍建筑面积近15.9万平方米。

In May 1958, the "Preparatory Committee for SUST" was established at Shanghai Office of the Chinese Academy of Sciences, located at No.320 Yueyang Road, Shanghai. In September of the same year, the opening ceremony for SUST was held. In May 1959, the Shanghai Municipal Committee approved the use of No.221 Ouyang Road (the former site of Guanghua University) as the temporary campus for SUST, sharing the location with the Shanghai Electromechanical Design Institute (now the Shanghai Academy of Spaceflight Technology), which was already situated there. By September 1960, the new campus of SUST at the south gate of Jiading was largely completed, and SUST moved in, with the campus address being No.20 Chengzhong Road.

At the time of its establishment, the campus area was 192 mu (approximately 12.8 hectares), with a building area of nearly 49,000 square meters. By 1993, the campus had expanded to 450 mu (approximately 30 hectares), with a building area of nearly 159,000 square meters.

1958年5月23日，上海科学技术大学筹备委员会在中国科学院上海办事处院内挂牌
The Preparatory Committee for SUST established at Shanghai Office of the Chinese Academy of Sciences, May 23, 1958

1959年6月，上海科学技术大学在欧阳路221号挂牌
The campus of SUST at No.221 Ouyang Road, June 1959

1960年9月，学校迁至嘉定。图为早期的校门
The gate of SUST in Jiading, September 1960

嘉定城中路20号校门（摄于20世纪80年代）
The gate at No.20 Chengzhong Road, Jiading (photo taken in the 1980s)

建于1960年的第一栋学生宿舍楼
The first dormitory building built in 1960

建于1961年的化学系实验教学楼
The lab building of the Chemistry Department built in 1961

第二部分　海纳百川　奠基再造

建于1966年的无线电电子学系实验教学楼
The lab building of the Radio Electronics Department built in 1966

建于1985年的校标雕塑（寓意办学目标：培养"高、精、尖"人才）
The sculpture of the university logo set up in 1985

建于1993年的联合图书馆
The library built in 1993

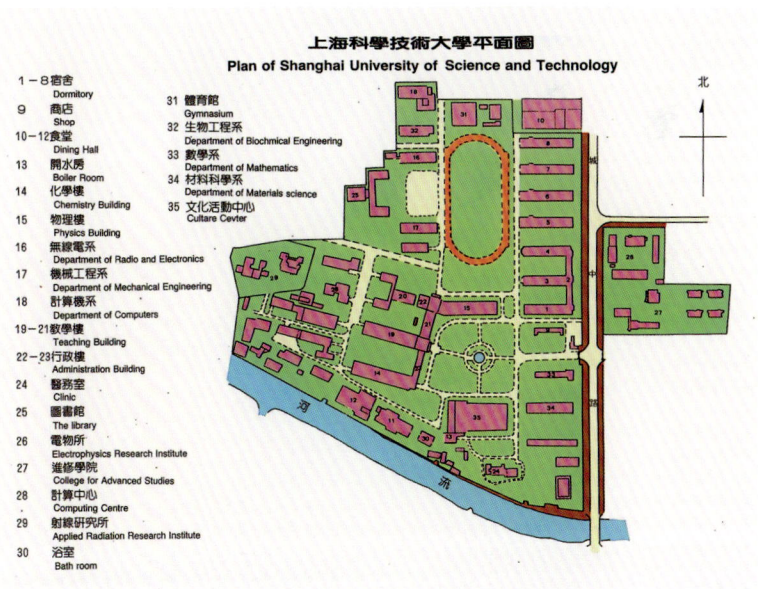

学校平面图（1990年绘制）
Campus map (1990)

（三）学校领导　SUST Leaders

校党政负责人更迭一览
SUST Leaders

职　务	姓　名	任职年月	职　务	姓　名	任职年月
党委书记	刘　芳	1965.7—1966.12	党委副书记	刘　芳	1959.9—1965.7
				董南才	1960.5—1963.1
				荆典谟	1962.7—1966.12
				王力行	1965.5—1966.12
核心小组组长	徐冠彬	1971.5—1973.5	核心小组副组长	萧培南	1971.5—1973.7
				郑子文	1972.8—1973.7
党委书记	马林正	1973.7—1977.10	党委副书记	郑子文	1973.7—1977.10
	张远达	1977.10—1984.2		王家庭	1973.7—1976.10
	沈　诒	1984.2—1986.9		曲　辰	1977.10—1984.2
	吴程里	1988.9—1992.9		林玉凤	1977.10—1989.10
				孙生官	1977.10—1984.2
				殷保津	1980.1—1980.10
				黄为群	1982.7—1984.2
				吴程里	1986.9—1988.9（主持党委工作）
				廖由雄	1986.9—1994.5
				周慕尧	1991.1—1993.7（1992.8起主持党委工作）
				毛杏云	1993.8—1994.5

续表

校　长	周　仁	1959.9—1966.12	副校长	刘　芳	1959.9—1966.12
				徐　鑫	1962.4—1966.12
				荆典谟	1965.7—1966.12
			校革委会副主任	曲　辰	1977.10—1978.7
				林玉凤	1977.10—1978.7
				孙生官	1977.10—1978.7
	杨士法	1978.7—1984.3	副校长	严东生（兼）	1978.7—1984.3
	金柱青	1984.3—1987.3		曲　辰	1978.7—1984.3
	郭本瑜	1987.3—1994.5		孙生官	1978.7—1990.7
名誉校长	严东生	1984.3—1994.5		黄宏嘉	1979.9—1987.3
	黄宏嘉	1987.3—1994.5		卢志杰	1980.1—1985.12
				房明毅	1980.1—1981.11
				钱孝衡	1982.12—1984.3
				郭本瑜	1984.3—1987.3
				王生洪	1984.3—1986.5（后任常务副校长）
				徐得名	1987.8—1994.5
				阚　敏	1987.8—1994.5
				林玉凤	1988.11—1990.2
				高廷春	1990.7—1994.5
				周慕尧	1991.7—1993.12

1959年11月21日，校长周仁主持第一届校务委员会第一次会议，确定办学宗旨和建校方案

President Zhou Ren presiding over the first meeting of the First Council of SUST, November 21, 1959

建校初期，副校长兼党委副书记刘芳（右3）和副教务长兼无线电电子系主任毛启爽（右2）、副教务长兼自动化系主任胡汝鼎（左2）等人讨论专业方向和教学计划

Liu Fang (third from right), Vice President and Deputy Secretary of SUST Party Committee, Mao Qishuang (second from right), Deputy Provost and Chair of the Radio Electronics Department, and Hu Ruding (second from left), Deputy Provost and Chair of the Automation Department, discussing the disciplinary programs and teaching plans

1965年，校党委书记兼副校长刘芳（前排就座者右3）、校党委副书记兼副校长荆典谟（前排就座者右2）与教师在一起

Liu Fang (third from right), Secretary of SUST Party Committee and Vice President, and Jing Dianmo (second from right), Vice Secretary of SUST Party Committee and Vice President, together with teachers, 1965

第二部分 海纳百川 奠基再造

1988年，学校召开学生思想政治工作研讨会（左起：校党委副书记兼副校长林玉凤、校长郭本瑜、校党委书记吴程里）

The seminar on students cultivation, 1988 (from left to right: Deputy Secretary of SUST Party Committee Lin Yufeng, President Guo Benyu, and Secretary of SUST Party Committee Wu Chengli)

1988年9月21日，召开中共上海科学技术大学第三次代表大会（左2：校党委书记吴程里）

The Third CPC Congress of SUST, September 21, 1988

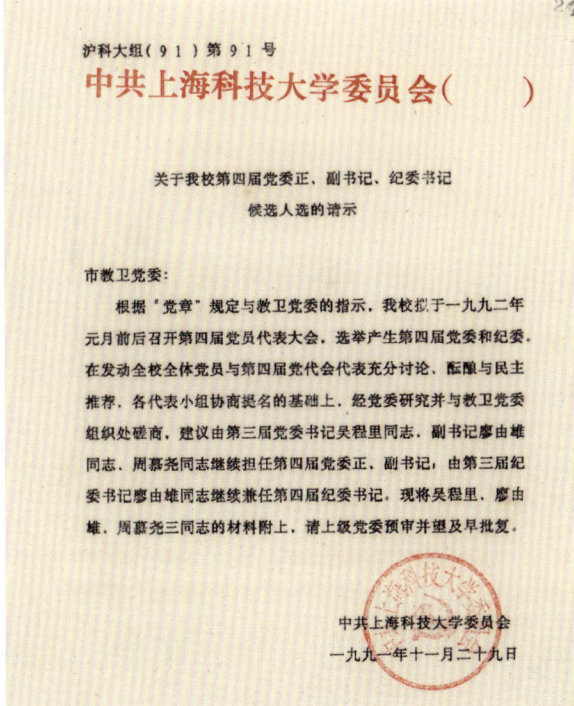

1991年11月29日，关于学校第四届党委正、副书记、纪委书记候选人选的请示

The proposal report for approval of the candidates for SUST Secretary, Deputy Secretary of the Fourth Party Committee, and Secretary of the Commission for Discipline Inspection, November 29, 1991

（四）领导关怀　Recognition of Leaders

1961年10月，中共上海市委候补书记、上海市副市长、中国科学院上海分院院长刘述周（中）到校视察，观看嘉定校园建设规划沙盘，副校长兼党委副书记刘芳（右）陪同

Liu Shuzhou (center), Alternate Secretary of the Shanghai Municipal Committee of the CPC, Vice Mayor of Shanghai, and President of the Chinese Academy of Sciences Shanghai Branch, inspecting SUST, October 1961

1963年，中共上海市委候补书记、教卫部部长杨西光（中）到校视察

Yang Xiguang, Alternate Secretary of the Shanghai Municipal Committee of the CPC and the Minister of Education and Health, inspecting SUST, 1963

（五）专业、学科设置　Programs and Disciplines

建校初和 1994 年的本科专业设置一览
Undergraduate Programs in 1958 and 1994

年　份	专业名称
1958 年	力学、半导体物理、无线电电子学、化学冶金、物理冶金、硅酸盐化学与工学、元素有机化学、放射化学与辐射化学、理化细胞、生物物理化学、植物生理、动物生理
1994 年	电子材料与器件、无机非金属材料、固体物理（金属物理）、半导体物理与器件、磁性物理与器件、光电子技术、应用物理、电磁场与微波技术、无线电技术、电子仪器与测量技术、计算数学、应用数学、电子精密机械、机械设计及制造、精密仪器、自动控制、计算机及应用、计算机软件、生物医学工程及仪器、高分子化学、有机化学、应用化学、生物化工、食品工程、科技英语

硕士、博士学位授权点一览
Master's and Doctor's Degree Granting Programs

批　次	获批时间	硕士点	博士点
第一批	1981 年 11 月	有机化学、无机非金属材料、电磁场与微波技术、物理化学	电磁场与微波技术
第二批	1984 年 1 月	无线电物理与无线电电子学、通信与电子系统、计算数学	无线电物理与无线电电子学
第三批	1986 年 7 月	精密仪器及机械、生物医学仪器及工程、计算机应用、运筹学与控制论、凝聚态物理	计算数学
第四批	1990 年 12 月	金属材料及热处理、自动控制、光学、生物化学工程	运筹学与控制论

（六）师资队伍　Faculty

1959—1993 年教师人数及职称情况一览
Faculty Number by Title (1959-1993)

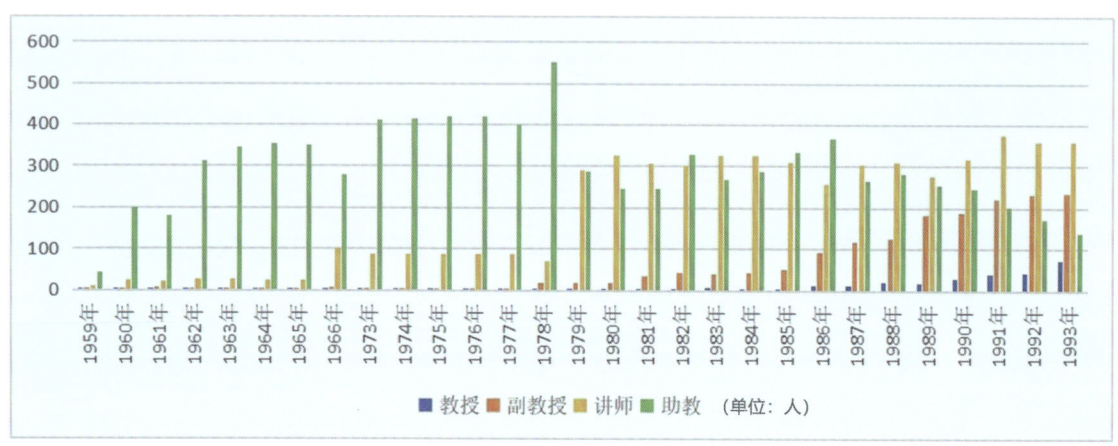

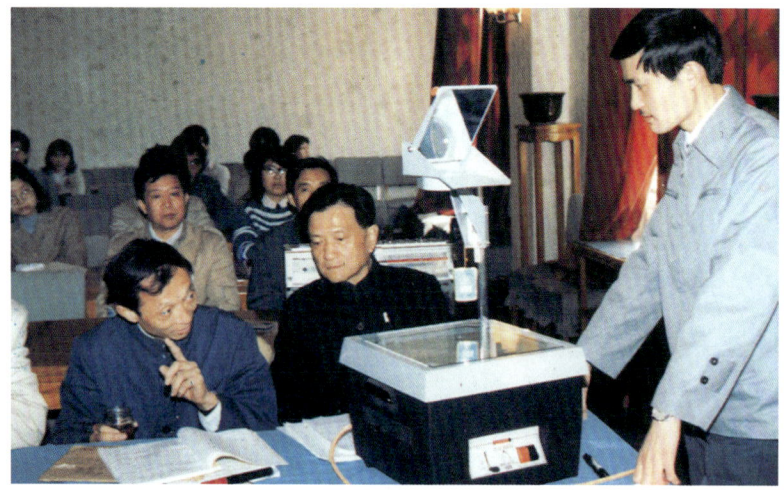

"电磁场与微波技术"博士生导师黄宏嘉教授（中）在主持博士生答辩会

Doctoral supervisor Huang Hongjia (center) presiding over a dissertation defense, 1981

"电磁场与微波技术"博士生导师徐得名教授（右2）与研究生合影

Doctoral supervisor Xu Deming (second from right) and graduate students

"无线电物理与无线电电子学"博士生导师鲍家善教授在指导青年教师
Bao Jiashan, a doctoral supervisor of radio physics and electronics, instructing a young teacher

"计算数学"博士生导师郭本瑜教授（中）在指导研究生
Guo Benyu (center), a doctoral supervisor of computing mathematics, instructing graduate students

"运筹学与控制论"博士生导师郑权教授在指导研究生
Zheng Quan, a doctoral supervisor of operations research and cybernetics, instructing a graduate student

获全国荣誉称号的教师
Faculty Winning National Honors

荣誉称号	年度	姓名
全国"五一"劳动奖章	1986	周幼威
全国"五一"劳动奖章	1993	王保华
全国教育系统劳动模范	1986	邵 俊
全国优秀教师	1989	龚振邦
全国优秀教师	1989	郭本瑜
全国优秀教师	1991	王保华
全国优秀教师	1991	王德人
全国优秀教师	1993	陈体芳
全国优秀教师	1993	陈久康

（七）人才培养　Talent Cultivation

1958年9月，学校开始招收本科生（五年制）。1960—1965年，还招收了工人班学员（五年制本科）。1966—1969年，停止招生。1970—1976年，招收"工农兵学员"（三年制大学）。1977年，全国恢复高考，开始招收本科生（四年制）。1978年，获批招收研究生资格。1981年，获批"电磁场与微波技术"等第一批硕士点，同时获批第一个博士点。1994年，获批第一个博士后流动站（电磁场与微波技术）。

In September 1958, SUST began enrolling undergraduate students (five-year program). From 1960 to 1965, it admitted worker students (five-year undergraduate program). From 1966 to 1969, SUST suspended admissions. From 1970 to 1976, it enrolled "worker-peasant-soldier students" (three-year college program). In 1977, the national college entrance examination was reinstated, and SUST began admitting undergraduate students (four-year program). In 1978, it was granted the qualification to enroll graduate students. In 1981, it was approved for its first master's programs, including Electromagnetic Fields and Microwave Technology, and simultaneously received approval for its first doctoral program. In 1994, SUST established its first postdoctoral research station (Electromagnetic Fields and Microwave Technology).

1. 本科和研究生教育
Undergraduate and Graduate Education

1958—1993年本（专）科、研究生招生人数一览

Number of Enrolled Undergraduate (Vocational) and Graduate Students (1958-1993)

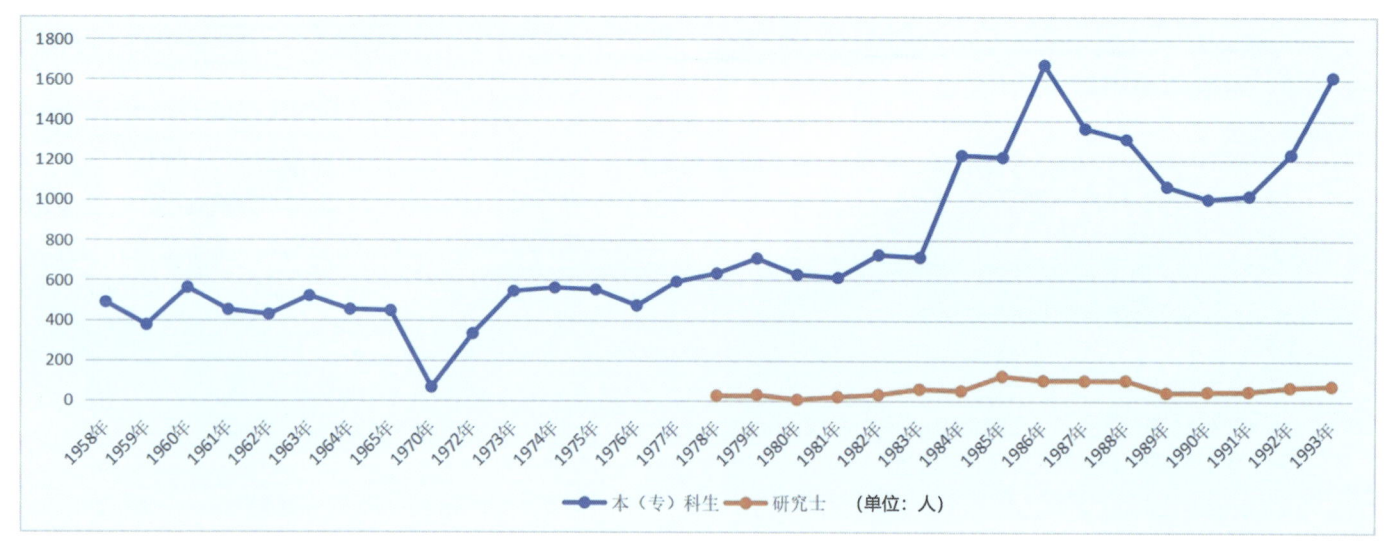

第二部分　海纳百川　奠基再造

1977年8月，学校应届毕业生合影
Graduation photo of undergraduates, August 1977

1981年，学校首届研究生毕业，和导师、校领导合影（前排就座者左7：副校长卢志杰，左8：材料科学系创始人、中国科学院院士邹元爔，左9：党委副书记、副校长曲辰，右3：副校长房明毅，右1：党委副书记林玉凤）
Graduation photo of the first batch of graduate students with supervisors and leaders, 1981

 上海大学　　　　　　　　　　　　　　　　　　　　　　　　　　　Shanghai University

1960年9月，学生们欢快地搬入新校园
Students moving to the new campus happily

1963年，学生在宿舍学习《毛泽东选集》
Students reading *Selected Works of Mao Zedong* at the dorm, 1963

学生在课堂上讨论工程制图
Students discussing engineering drawing

副教务长兼自动化系主任胡汝鼎教授在指导学生
Professor Hu Ruding, Deputy Provost and Chair of the Automation Department, instructing students

第二部分　海纳百川　奠基再造

硅酸盐化学与工学系主任严东生教授在授课
Yan Dongsheng, Chair of the Silicate Chemistry and Engineering Department, giving lectures

1975年，精密机械工程系青年教师王生洪（后排右3）在指导学生毕业设计
Wang Shenghong (third from right in the back row), a young teacher of the Department of Precision Mechanical Engineering, instructing students on their graduation project, 1975

数学系黄育仁教授在指导学生
Huang Yuren, a professor of the Department of Mathematics, instructing students

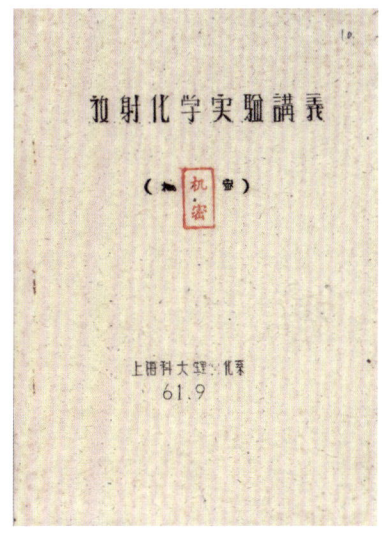

上海科学技术大学教师自编教材《放射化学实验讲义》
Lecture Notes on Radiochemistry Experiments complied by SUST faculty

2. 工人班教育
Worker Student Education

1960年9月21日，中共上海市委候补书记、副市长刘述周到校作报告，强调招收工人班的意义

Liu Shuzhou, Alternate Secretary of the Shanghai Municipal Committee of the CPC and Vice Mayor of Shanghai, reporting on the significance of recruiting workers into SUST, September 21, 1960

党委副书记荆典谟（左2）、教务长毛启爽（右2）和工人班学员在交谈

Deputy Secretary Jing Dianmo (second from left) and Provost Mao Qishuang (second from right) talking with worker students

1965年，工人班首届毕业生、全国著名劳动模范王林鹤毕业设计答辩

Wang Linhe, a graduate of the first Worker Class and a national model worker, defending his graduation thesis, 1965

1965年3月12日，举行工人班首届毕业生毕业典礼

Graduation ceremony of the first Worker Class, March 12, 1965

第二部分　海纳百川　奠基再造

校长周仁向工人班首届毕业生颁发毕业证书
President Zhou Ren presenting graduation certificates to the first graduates from the Worker Class

1965年3月13日，《解放日报》刊登上海科技大学工人班首届学生毕业的消息
Jiefang Daily reporting on the first batch of graduates from the Worker Class of SUST, March 13, 1965

177

（八）科学研究　Scientific Research

　　学校在努力培养人才的同时，坚持不懈地开展科学研究工作，尤其是改革开放以后，科研工作力度大大加强。1984—1994 年，学校累计承担科研课题 3799 项、获得科研经费 10997 万元；在国内外学术刊物上发表论文 7538 篇，其中在国外刊物上发表 938 篇、在国内一级刊物上发表 3160 篇。从 1981 年起，学校有组织地开展各种科技服务活动。1985—1994 年，学校对外签订的技术转让、技术开发、技术咨询、技术服务（包括技术培训）合同金额累计 7013 万元。1980—1993 年，学校获省市级以上科研奖项共 105 项。

　　学校先后建立了上海电子物理研究所、上海光纤技术与现代通信研究所、上海生物医药工程研究所、上海射线应用研究所、上海计算数学与应用数学研究所、科技法研究所，另外还成立了 20 个研究室。

　　学校主编并公开发行的学术刊物有《上海科学技术大学学报》《应用科学学报》《应用数学与计算数学学报》《运筹学》；主编的内刊有《高校科技信息》《高教研究》。

While striving to cultivate talents, SUST has unremittingly conducted scientific research work, especially after the reform and opening up. From 1980 to 1993, SUST won a total of 105 scientific research awards at or above the provincial and municipal levels. It successively established 6 research institutes and 20 research laboratories. Also, it edited and issued 4 academic journals and 2 in-house academic periodicals.

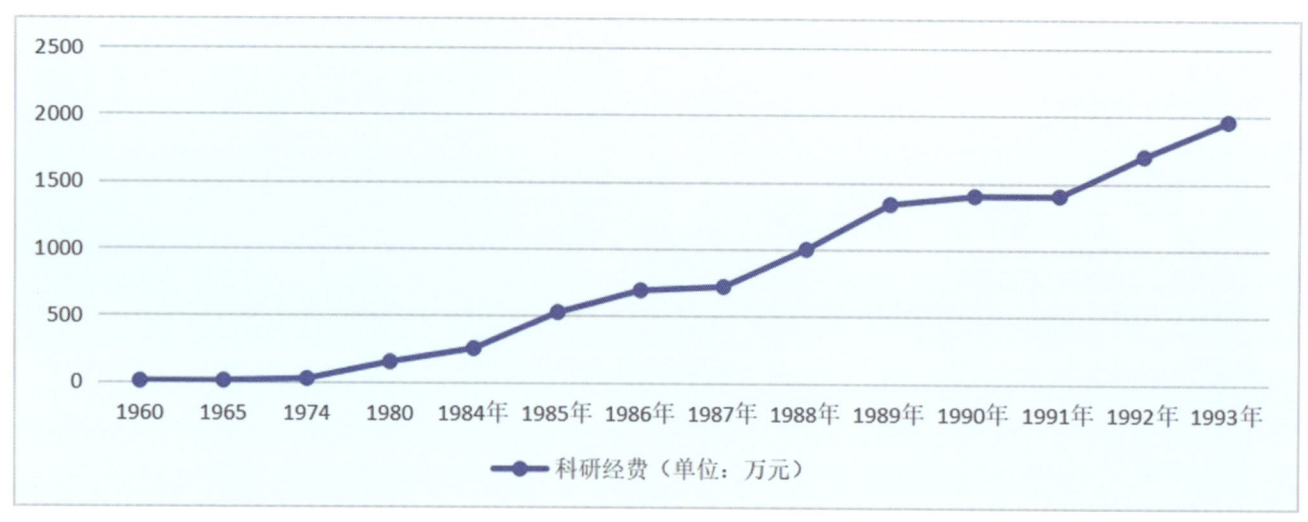

1960—1993 年科研经费一览
Scientific Research Funds (1960-1993)

1985—1993 年国家自然科学基金项目数量一览
Number of Projects Funded by National Natural Science Foundation of China (NSFC), 1985-1993

年　度	1985	1986	1987	1988	1989	1990	1991	1992	1993	合　计
项目数	1	4	5	6	2	2	8	10	4	42

1983—1992 年在全国高校"学术榜"的排名
Place in the "Academic Ranking" of Chinese Universities (1983-1992)

榜次	公布年份	统计年份	SCI、ISTP、ISE 统计		EI 统计		SCI 收录被引证论文		中国科技期刊（1225 种）统计	
			篇数	名次	篇数	名次	篇数	名次	篇数	名次
1	1987	1983—1985	不详	25	13	19	未统计		未统计	
2	1988	1986—1987	15	26	21	19	未统计		未统计	
3	1989	1988	32	27	15	26	15	26	未进入前 50 名	
4	1990	1989	32	32	8	46	未进入前 50 名		134	94
5	1991	1990	39	34	9	39	14	未进入前 50 名	128	98
6	1992	1991	35	38	4	65	未排名		117	126
7	1993	1992	25* 33**	28* 29**	23	32	23	33	138	110

* 据 SCI 统计；** 据 ISTP 统计

科研成果获国家级奖项一览
Projects Winning National Awards

项目名称	奖项名称	等　级	年　度	获奖人
流体力学中的差分方法	全国科学大会"优秀科研成果奖"	/	1978	郭本瑜
红旗渠潜水泵的密封材料	全国科学大会"优秀科研成果奖"	/	1978	周积春　刘文义
膦腈叶立德在合成含氟有机化合物中应用的研究	国家自然科学奖	三等奖	1982	丁维钰
建立国家激光洛氏硬度和表面洛氏硬度基准主测量系统	国家科技进步奖	二等奖	1985	陈明仪　陈久康　孙桂清　王菊荣
K.C 频段二十米卫星地面站天线系统	国家科技进步奖	一等奖	1987	王生洪　龚振邦　吴家麟　郭锡章
模式耦合理论及其在微波和光传输中的应用	国家自然科学奖	二等奖	1987	黄宏嘉
微波介质谐振器材料——A6 陶瓷	国家发明奖	三等奖	1987	方永汉　胡　昂
辐射合成超薄型亲水软接触镜	国家发明奖	二等奖	1988	刘钰铭　杨月琪　阮逸标

续表

氘氚化锂制造技术	国家发明奖	二等奖	1988	毕清华
单模光纤技术	国家科技进步奖	二等奖	1988	黄宏嘉
熔锥型单模光纤无源器件的制造技术与装置	国家发明奖	三等奖	1990	汪道刚
非线性偏微分方程的差分方法和谱方法及其应用	国家教委科技进步奖	一等奖	1990	郭本瑜　马和平　曹伟明

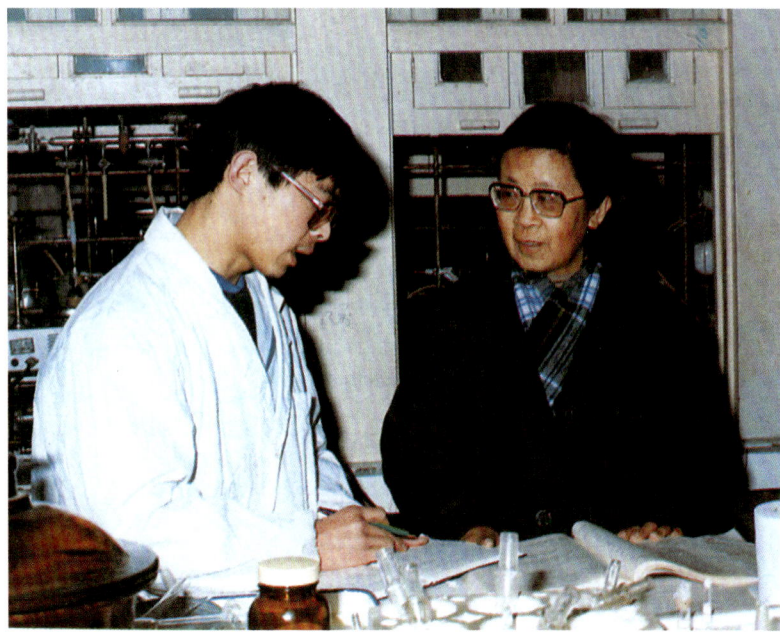

由丁维钰（右）主持、与中国科学院上海有机化学研究所合作完成的"膦胂叶立德在合成含氟有机化合物中应用的研究"获 1982 年度国家自然科学奖三等奖

The project "Study on the Application of Organophosphorus and Organoarsenic Ylides in the Synthesis of Fluoroorganic Compounds" incooperation with Shanghai Organic Institute of the Chinese Academy of Sciences, directed by Ding Weiyu (right), winning the Third Prize of the Natural Science Award in 1982

陈明仪主持的"建立国家激光洛氏硬度和表面洛氏硬度基准主测量系统"获 1985 年度国家科技进步奖二等奖

The project "Establishment of National Laser Rockwell Scale and Surface Rockwell Scale Benchmark Measurement System", directed by Chen Mingyi, winning the Second Prize of the State Scientific and Technological Progress Award in 1985

由王生洪（中）主持、与中国人民解放军总参谋部第五十七研究所合作完成的"K.C 频段二十米卫星地面站天线系统"获 1987 年度国家科技进步奖一等奖

The project "The Ground Station Antenna System of K.C-band 20-meter Satellite" in collaboration with the No.57 Institute of PLA General Staff Department, directed by Wang Shenghong (center), winning the First Prize of the State Scientific and Technological Progress Award in 1987

黄宏嘉院士的"模式耦合理论及其在微波和光传输中的应用"获 1987 年国家自然科学奖二等奖、"单模光纤技术"获 1988 年国家科技进步二等奖

The project "Mode Coupling Theory and Its Application in Microwave and Optical Transmission", directed by Academician Huang Hongjia, winning the Second Prize of the State Natural Science Award in 1987, and "Single-Mode Optical Fiber Technology" the Second Prize of the State Scientific and Technological Progress Award in 1988

方永汉（站立者）、胡昂的"微波介质谐振器材料——A6 陶瓷"获 1987 年度国家发明奖三等奖

The project "The Material of Microwave Dielectric Resonator-A6 Ceramic", co-directed by Fang Yonghan (stand) and Hu Ang, winning the Third Prize of the State Award for Inventions in 1987

刘钰铭（中）主持的"辐射合成超薄型亲水软接触镜"获 1988 年度国家发明奖二等奖

The project "Ultrathin Hydrophilic Soft Contact Lenses Synthesized by Radiation", directed by Liu Yuming (center), winning the Second Prize of the State Award for Inventions in 1988

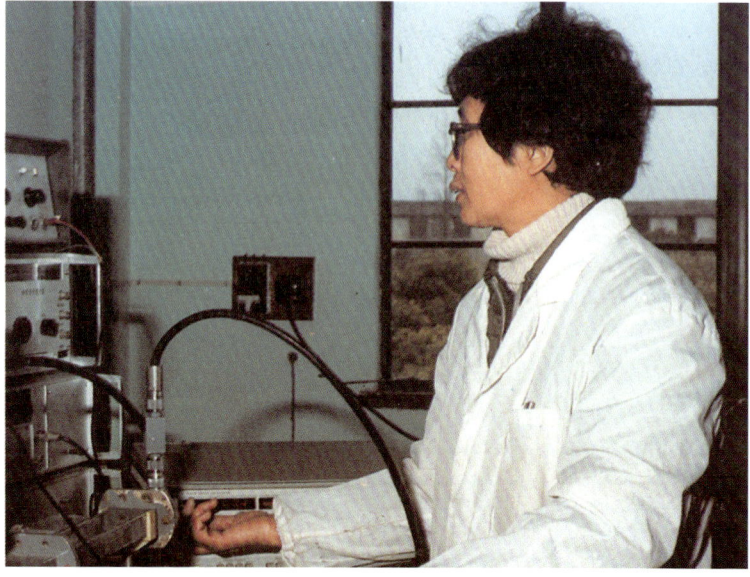

毕清华的"氘氚化锂制造技术"获1988年度国家发明奖二等奖

The project "Manufacturing Technology for Lithium Deuterium Tritide", directed by Bi Qinghua, winning the Second Prize of the State Award for Inventions in 1988

汪道刚的"熔锥型单模光纤无源器件的制造技术与装置"获1990年度国家发明奖三等奖

The project "Manufacturing Technology and Devices of Nonoriginal Devices of Fused-Tapered Single-Mode Optical Fiber", directed by Wang Daogang, winning the Third Prize of the State Award for Inventions in 1990

郭本瑜主持的"非线性偏微分方程的差分方法和谱方法及其应用"获1990年度国家教委科技进步奖一等奖

The project "Differential Method and Spectral Method for Nonlinear Partial Differential Equation and Their Application", directed by Guo Benyu, winning the First Prize of the Scientific and Technological Progress Award of the State Education Commission in 1990

1. 国内第一根"单模光纤"
The First Single-Mode Optical Fiber in China

　　黄宏嘉院士是我国单模光纤技术的开拓者，为我国微波技术及光纤技术的应用与发展作出重要贡献。他于1979年进入上海科学科技大学，1980年在学校创建了国内第一个光纤研究所，并带领科研团队研制成功我国第一根单模光纤。他撰写的《微波原理》是我国第一本微波电子学专著。20世纪90年代，他又创新发明了国际领先的宽带光纤"黄氏波片"。先后荣获1978年全国科学大会重大科研成果奖"突出贡献奖（个人奖）"、1987年国家自然科学奖二等奖、1988年国家科技进步奖二等奖、1998年香港何梁何利科技进步奖。

　　Academician Huang Hongjia, a pioneer of the single-mode optical fiber technology in China, has made important contributions to the application and development of microwave and optical fiber technologies in our country. He successively won "Outstanding Contribution Award (Individual Award)" of the Major Scientific Research Achievements Award at the National Science Conference in 1978, the Second Prize of the State Natural Science Award in 1987, the Second Prize of the State Scientific and Technological Progress Award in 1988, and the Ho Leung Ho Lee Prize for Technological Progress in Hong Kong in 1998.

黄宏嘉（左）1980年主持研制我国新一代单模光纤
Huang Hongjia (left) presiding over the development of China's new-generation single-modeoptical fiber, 1980

1982年6月3日，《解放日报》刊登新一代单模光纤在上海制成的消息
Jiefang Daily reporting on the new-generation single-mode optical fibers development in Shanghai, June 3, 1982

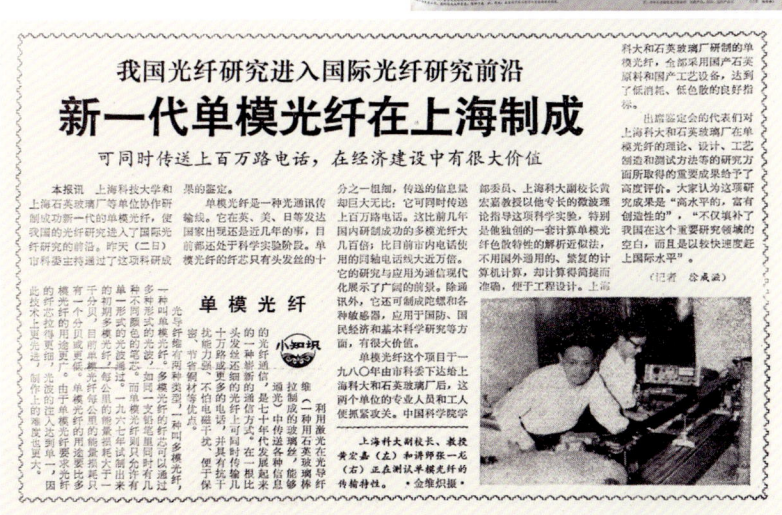

2. 偏微分方程的差分方法
Differential Method for Partial Differential Equation

郭本瑜是中国科学计算事业的重要参与者，主要研究科学计算的方法、理论及其应用。他首创非线性差分格式稳定性理论，并推广到 Banach 空间中具有多个孤立解的非线性算子方程，在国际上称为"G（郭）- 稳定性"。他的研究"不可压缩黏性流的数值计算"获 1978 年全国科学大会重大科技成果奖、"非线性偏微分方程的差分方法和谱方法及应用"获 1995 年国家自然科学奖三等奖。

Guo Benyu is an important participant in China's scientific computing cause, mainly researching the methods, theories and applications of scientific computing. He initiated the stability theory of nonlinear difference schemes and extended it to nonlinear operator equations with multiple isolated solutions in Banach spaces, which is internationally known as "G (Guo)-stability". His research "Numerical Computation of Incompressible Viscous Flow" won the Major Scientific and Technological Achievements Award at the 1978 National Science Conference, and "Differential Method and Spectral Method for Nonlinear Partial Differential Equation and Their Application" won the Third Prize of the State Natural Science Award in 1995.

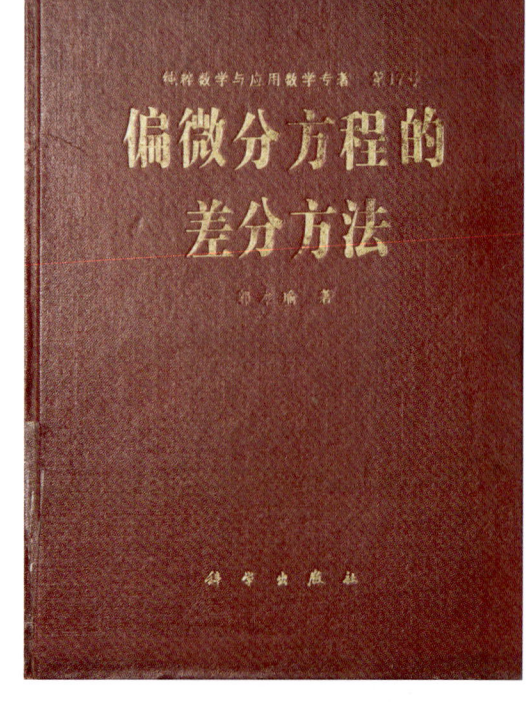

郭本瑜著《偏微分方程的差分方法》
Differential Method for Partial Differential Equation by Guo Benyu

3. K.C 频段 20 米口径卫星地面站天线系统
The Ground Station Antenna System for K.C-Band 20-Meter Satellite

1987 年，王生洪、龚振邦团队与中国人民解放军总参谋部第五十七研究所合作完成的"K.C 频段二十米口径卫星地面站天线系统"获国家科学技术进步奖一等奖，为国家国防事业作出突出贡献。

The project "The Ground Station Antenna System for K.C-Band 20-Meter Satellite" in collaboration withthe No.57 Institute of PLA General Staff Department, directed by Wang Shenghong and Gong Zhenbang, won the First Prize of the State Scientific and Technological Progress Award in 1987.

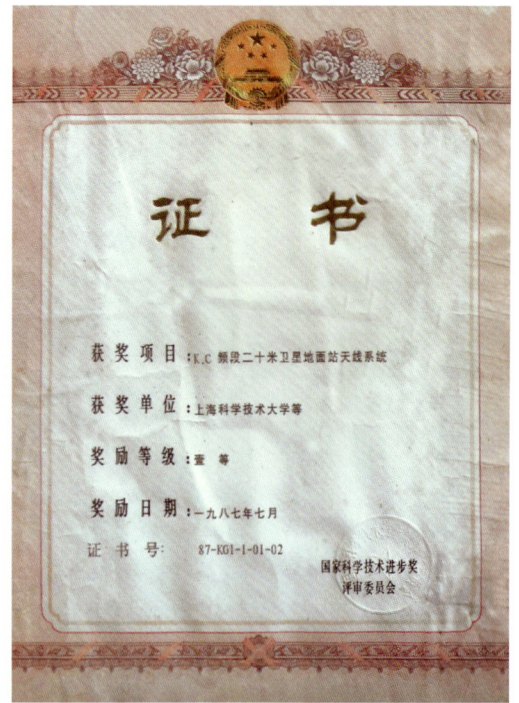

"K.C 频段二十米卫星地面站天线系统"
获 1987 年度国家科技进步奖一等奖
Award Certificate, 1987

4. 中国物理学会、核学会粒子加速器学会
The Particle Accelerator Society of the Chinese Physical Society and the Chinese Nuclear Society

中国物理学会、核学会粒子加速器学会成立于 1980 年 10 月 20 日，是中国物理学会和中国核学会分支机构之一，致力于团结全国广大加速器科技工作者，积极开展粒子加速器方面的学术交流和科学普及工作。其日常办事机构秘书处设在挂靠单位中国科学院高能物理研究所，与上海科学技术大学有着密切合作。

The Particle Accelerator Society of the Chinese Physical Society and the Chinese Nuclear Society was established on October 20, 1980. It was committed to uniting a large number of accelerator scientists and technicians across the country, and actively carrying out academic exchanges and science popularization work in the field of particle accelerators. Its Secretariat was located at the Institute of High Energy Physics, Chinese Academy of Sciences. It had close cooperation with SUST.

1980 年 10 月，中国物理学会、核学会粒子加速器学会成立大会暨学术交流会在上海科学技术大学举行

The Founding Conference of the Particle Accelerator Society of the Chinese Physical Society and the Chinese Nuclear Society at SUST, October 1980

（九）国际交流　Overseas Exchanges

　　1966年，学校曾经接收越南民主共和国的来华进修生。1988年，学校被批准用英语教学招收来华留学生，并于1989年招收了第一批。

　　改革开放以后，学校积极开展国际交流活动。1979—1993年，学校聘请了来自20个国家和地区的长期专家逾30人、短期专家274人次；接待来自31个国家和地区的访问团组312批1064人次；学校教师出国参加国际学术会议、讲学、访问共282批363人次；与德国汉堡哈尔堡工业大学等8所大学签订了校际或系际合作协议；学校还主办了国际学术研讨会、培训班10次。

In 1966, SUST accepted trainees from the Democratic Republic of Vietnam who came to China for further study. In 1988, SUST was approved to recruit international students coming to China and teach them in English, and enrolled the first batch of such students in 1989.

Since the reform and opening up, SUST has actively carried out overseas exchange activities. From 1979 to 1993, it hired more than 30 long-term experts and 274 short-term experts from 20 countries and regions. It received 312 delegations with a total of 1,064 persons from 31 countries and regions. 282 groups of teachers with a total of 363 persons went abroad to participate in international academic conferences, to give lectures, or to conduct visits. It signed inter-school or inter-department cooperation agreements with 8 foreign universities including Hamburg University of Technology in Germany. It also hosted 10 international academic seminars and training courses.

1. 来华留学生教育
Education for International Students in China

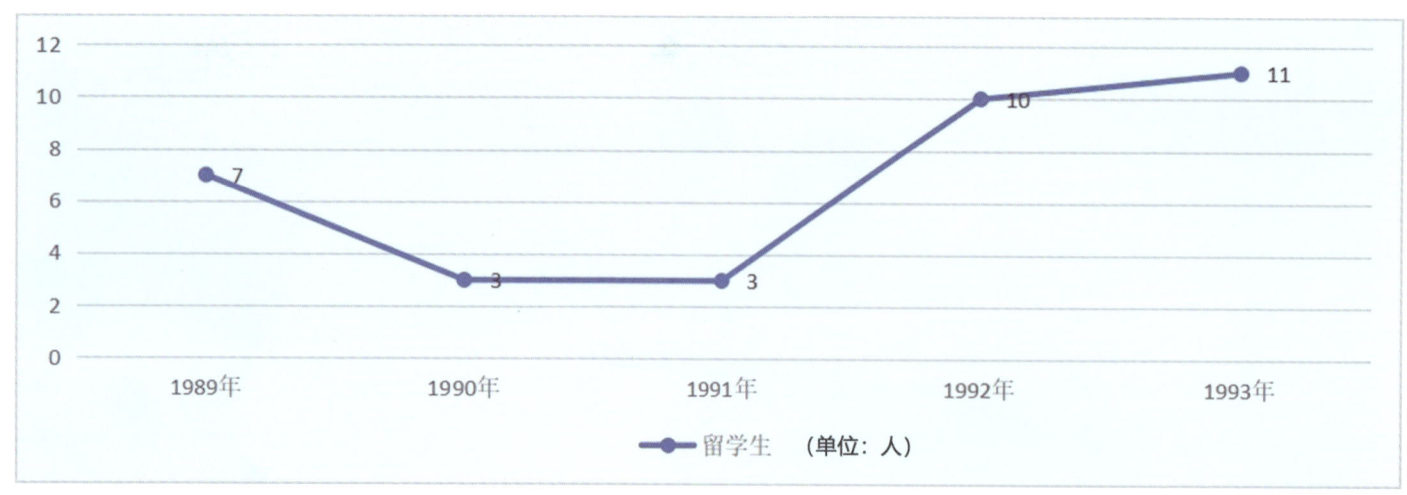

1989—1993年留学生招生人数一览

Number of Enrolled International Students (1989-1993)

1988年，学校被国家教委列为用英语教学招收来华留学博士生的首批试点单位之一。图为首届巴基斯坦来华留学生博士论文答辩（前排就座者左2起：黄宏嘉院士、电子科技大学谢处方教授、鲍家善教授、徐得名教授）

Professors attending the doctoral dissertation defense of the first Pakistani student (from second on the left in the front row: Academician Huang Hongjia from SUST, Professor Xie Chufang from University of Electronic Science and Technology, Professor Bao Jiashan and Professor Xu Deming from SUST). In 1988, SUST was listed by the State Education Commission as one of the first pilot units to recruit English-taught overseas doctoral students.

2. "走出去 请进来"
"Going out, Inviting In"

1988年，校长郭本瑜（左2）和校党委书记吴程里（左1）会见到访的欧共体访华代表团

President Guo Benyu (second from left) and Secretary of SUT Party Committee Wu Chengli (first from left) receiving the visiting delegation of the European Communities, 1988

1990年，副校长徐得名（左3）和到访的外国同行在学校光纤通信实验室探讨科学问题

Vice President Xu Deming (third from left) and visiting scholars discussing scientific issues in the optical fiber communication laboratory, 1990

Shanghai University

1992年，校党委副书记兼副校长周慕尧（右）会见到访的国际原子能机构代表

Zhou Muyao, Deputy Secretary of SUST Party Committee and Vice President of SUST, talking with the visiting representative of the International Atomic Energy Agency, 1992

3. 国际会议、培训班
International Conferences and Training Programs

1985—1991年，联合国原子能机构委托上海科学技术大学射线应用研究所先后举办了三期亚太地区辐射交联技术培训班。图为第一期培训班成员合影

Group photo of trainees of the first training program on radiation technology. From 1985 to 1991, the United Nations Atomic Energy Agency entrusted the Institute of Radiation Application of SUST to hold three training programs for trainees from Asian Pacific areas.

第二部分　海纳百川　莫基再造

1987年，日本鲭江市日中友好协会会长、上海科学技术大学顾问教授山本治（左2）资助上海科学技术大学举办日语进修班、汉语培训班及建造"谊园"宾馆签约仪式举行，副校长孙生官（右2）代表学校签字
Agreement signing ceremony attended by Vice President Sun Shengguan (second from right) and Osamu Yamamoto (second from left), President of the Japan-China Friendship Association of Sabae City and SUST Consultant Professor, 1987

1991年，校长郭本瑜（站立者）主持"上海市—罗纳·阿尔卑斯大区双边光纤科学技术研讨会"
President Guo Benyu presiding over the "Shanghai-France Rhône-Alpes Bilateral Optical Fiber Science and Technology Seminar", 1991

4. 国际合作办学
International Cooperative Education

1991年，举行聘请外籍专家为学校名誉教授暨国外大学授予黄宏嘉院士为名誉博士的授证仪式
Certificate awarding ceremony, 1991. Professor W. A. Gambling was employed as honorary professor of SUST and Academician Huang Hongjia was conferred an honorary DSc degree by the Eurotech, Hawaii.

1991年，与德国汉堡哈尔堡工业大学签订文化教育科技合作协议书，校长郭本瑜（左3）、副校长徐得名（左2）、副校长高廷春（左1）出席签字仪式
Cooperation agreement signing ceremony between SUST and Hamburg University of Technology, 1991

（十）院市共建　所系结合
Joint Efforts of Shanghai Municipal People's Government and the Chinese Academy of Sciences

1958年5月，中共上海市委决定，上海科学技术大学由中国科学院上海办事处主办，市委、市人民委员会各部、委、办、局协同合作。中国科学院上海办事处确定了"全院办校，所系结合，分头包干"的建校方案。

In May 1958, the Shanghai Municipal Committee of the CPC decided that SUST would be mainly operated by Shanghai Office of the Chinese Academy of Sciences, coordinating with all the related parties.

建校初期各系主任一览
Chairs of Early Departments

系　别	主　任	中国科学院任职	备　注
技术物理	谢希德	上海技术物理研究所所长	1980年当选中国科学院学部委员
化学冶金与物理冶金	万　钧	上海冶金研究所党委书记、副所长	
化学冶金与物理冶金	邹元爔（副主任）	上海冶金研究所研究员	1980年当选中国科学院学部委员
硅酸盐化学与工学	严东生	上海硅酸盐研究所副所长	1980年当选中国科学院学部委员，1994年当选中国工程院院士
元素有机化学	汪　猷	上海有机化学研究所副所长	1955年当选中国科学院学部委员
元素有机化学	黄耀曾（副主任）	上海有机化学研究所研究员	
生物物理化学	王应睐	上海生物化学研究所所长	1955年当选中国科学院学部委员
生物物理化学	沈昭文（副主任）	上海生物化学研究所研究员	
工程力学	王希季	上海机电设计院总工程师	1993年当选中国科学院院士，"两弹一星功勋奖章"荣获者
计算数学	李　珩	上海天文台台长	
自动化	胡汝鼎		上海市机电一局原副局长
无线电电子学	毛启爽		上海市市内电话局原副局长

建校初期，副校长兼党委副书记刘芳（中）和生物物理化学系主任王应睐（左2）、系副主任沈昭文（左1）等商量工作

Liu Fang (center), Vice President and Deputy Secretary of SUST Party Committee, Wang Yinglai (second from left), Chair of the Biology, Physics and Chemistry Department, Shen Zhaowen (second from right), Deputy Chair (first from left), discussing the university construction

学生在中国科学院上海生物化学研究所进行毕业作业

Students working on their graduation projects at the Shanghai Institute of Biochemistry, Chinese Academy of Sciences

建校初期，硅酸盐化学与工学系主任严东生（右2）、化学冶金与物理冶金系副主任邹元爔（右3）讨论专业方向和教学计划

Yan Dongsheng (second from right), Chair of the Silicate Chemistry and Engineering Department, and Zou Yuanxi (third from right), Deputy Chair of the Chemical Metallurgy and Physical Metallurgy Department, discussing the disciplinary programs and teaching plans

建校初期，中国科学院上海植物生理研究所所长殷宏章、上海生理研究所所长冯德培、上海生物化学研究所所长王应睐、上海生物化学研究所研究员沈昭文等人研究上海科学技术大学教学计划
Directors from related research institutes of the Chinese Academy of Sciences in Shanghai discussing the teaching plans of SUST

（十一）杰出人物　Prominent Figure

周仁（1892.8.5—1973.12.3），江苏南京人。冶金学家和陶瓷学家，中国钢铁冶金学、陶瓷学的开创者和奠基人之一，中国近代首种学术刊物《科学》和第一个学术团体"中国科学社"的创始人之一。1955年当选中国科学院学部委员（院士）。新中国成立后，历任中国科学院工学实验馆馆长、上海冶金陶瓷研究所所长、上海冶金研究所所长、上海硅酸盐化学与工学研究所所长、中国科学院上海分院副院长等职。1959年9月，任上海科学技术大学首任校长。

Zhou Ren (August 5, 1892- December 3, 1973) was one of the pioneers and founders of iron and steel metallurgy and ceramics in China, and one of the founders of China's first modern academic journal Science and the first academic society, the Science Society of China. In 1955, he was elected as a member of the Chinese Academy of Sciences. After the founding of the PRC, he successively held positions including Director of the Engineering Experiment Hall of the Chinese Academy of Sciences, Director of the Shanghai Institute of Metallurgy and Ceramics, Director of the Shanghai Institute of Metallurgy, Director of the Shanghai Institute of Silicate Chemistry and Engineering, Vice President of the Shanghai Branch of the Chinese Academy of Sciences. In September 1959, he was appointed the first President of SUST.

三、上海大学（1983—1994）
Shanghai University (SHU, 1983-1994)

创办于 1983 年，是上海市属高等学校。

SHU was founded in 1983 as a municipal higher-education institution in Shanghai.

（一）学校成立　Founding of SHU

1978 年召开的全国科学大会为我国科教事业的快速发展开辟了一条前所未有的广阔道路，是年，上海地区有条件的高校根据教育部《关于高等学校扩大招生问题的意见》的精神成立了 13 所大学分校，其中包括复旦大学分校、华东师范大学仪表电子分校、上海外国语学院分院、上海科学技术大学分校和上海机械学院轻工分院。

1983 年 5 月，经教育部批准，上海市政府教卫办着手筹建上海大学，筹备组负责人是上海市高等教育局副局长韩中岳；同年 9 月，上海大学开学。1984 年 4 月，中共上海市委任命孟宪勤为校党委书记；上海市政府任命杜信恩为副校长，主持学校行政工作。学校由上述 5 所分校（院）和上海市美术学校合并组建而成。1993 年 4 月，上海法律高等专科学校加盟上海大学。

The National Science Conference of 1978 paved an unprecedented path for the rapid development of China's science and education endeavors. In May 1983, with the approval of the Ministry of Education, Office of Education and Public Health of Shanghai Municipal People's Government started to prepare for the establishment of SHU. In September of that year, SHU was started. SHU was set up by the merger of six schools (colleges). In April 1993, Shanghai Law College was merged into SHU.

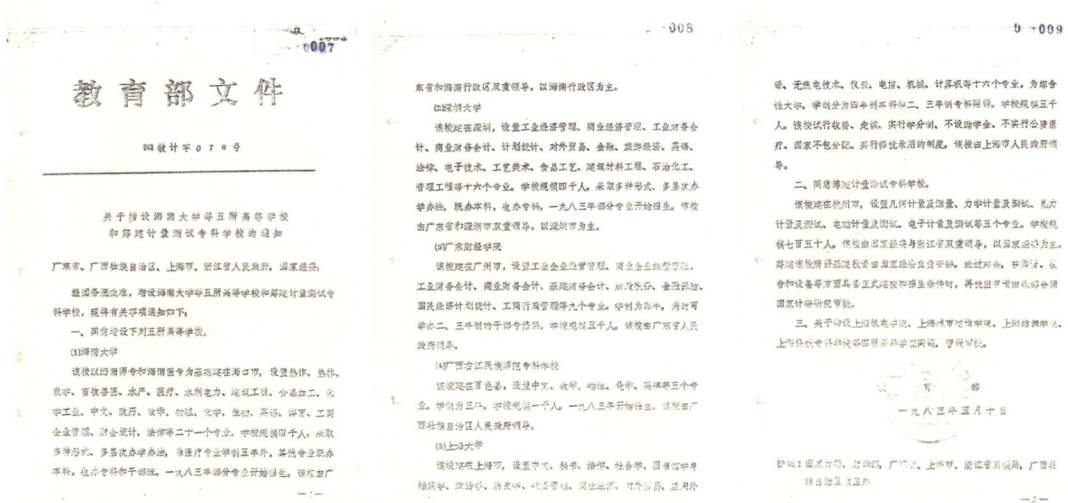

1983 年 5 月 10 日，教育部关于增设上海大学等五所高等学校的通知

A notice from the Ministry of Education on the establishment of five higher education institutions including SHU, May 10, 1983

第二部分 海纳百川 奠基再造

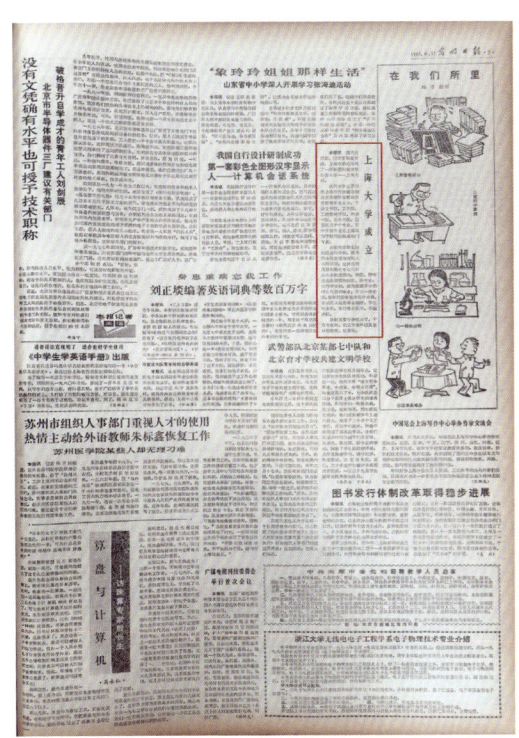

1983年6月11日，《光明日报》刊登上海大学成立的消息
Guangming Daily reporting on the establishment of SHU, June 11, 1983

1983年8月，上海市市长汪道涵为学校题词
An inscription for SHU by Wang Daohan, Mayor of Shanghai, August 1983

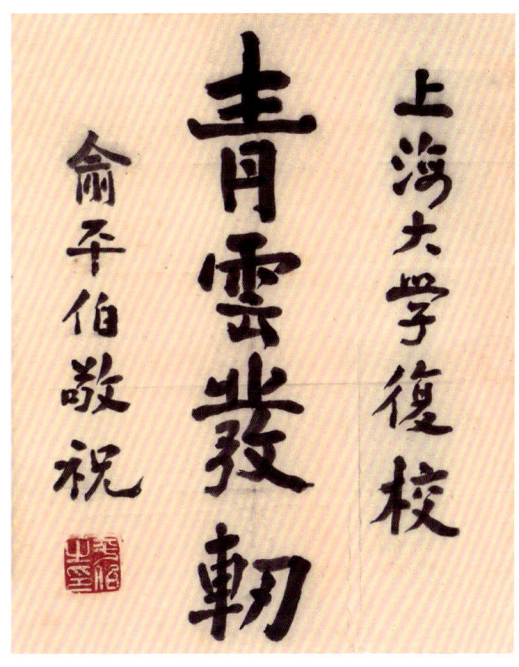

1983年，校友俞平伯为学校题词
An inscription for SHU by alumnus Yu Pingbo, 1983

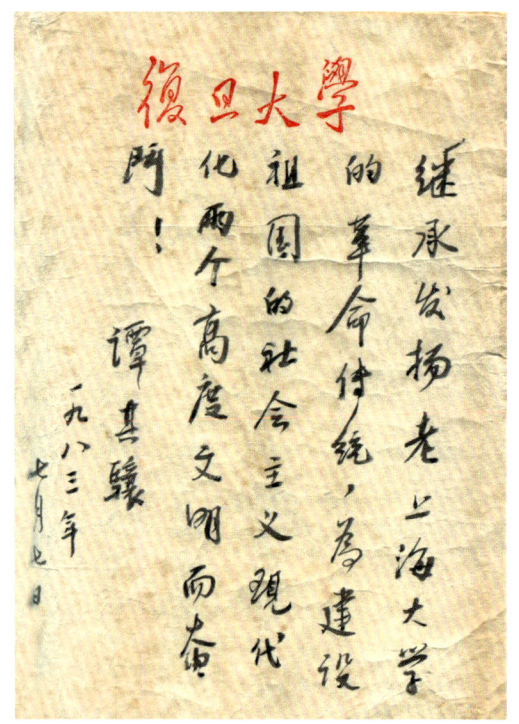

1983年7月,校友谭其骧为学校题词
An inscription for SHU by alumnus Tan Qixiang, July 1983

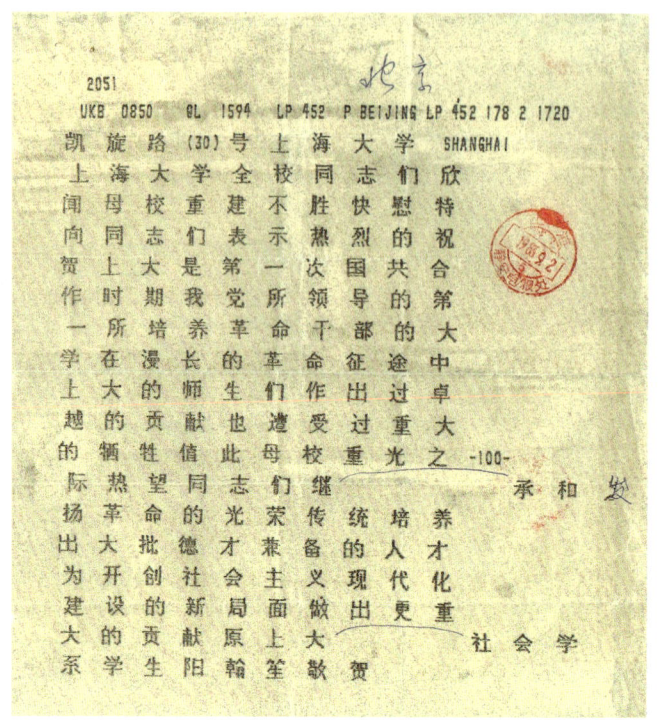

1983年9月,校友阳翰笙给学校发来贺电
Congratulatory message from alumnus Yang Hansheng, September 1983

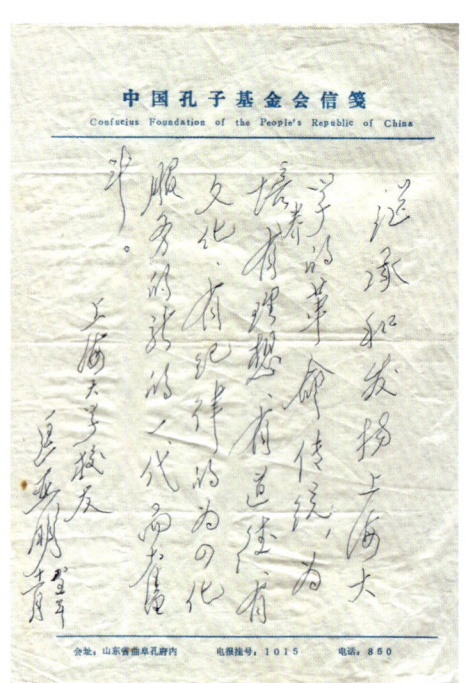

1985年11月,校友匡亚明为学校题词
An inscription for SHU by alumnus Kuang Yaming, November 1985

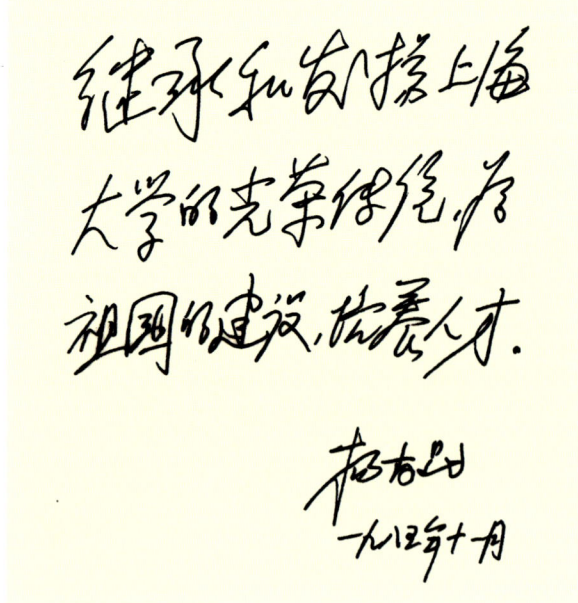

1985年11月,中央军委副主席、校友杨尚昆为学校题词
An inscription for SHU by alumnus Yang Shangkun, Vice Chairman of the CPC Central Military Commission, November 1985

第二部分　海纳百川　奠基再造

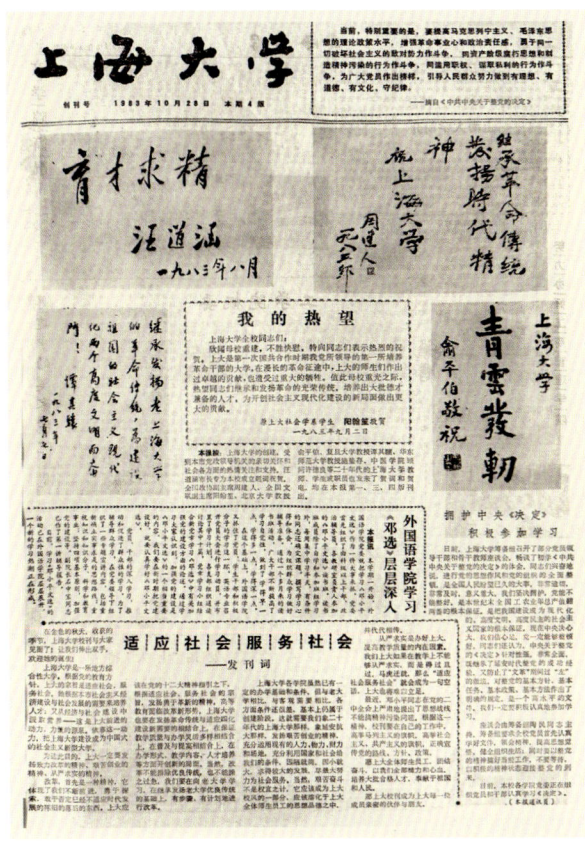

1983 年 10 月 28 日，校报《上海大学》创刊
The first issue of *Shanghai University News*, October 28, 1983

1985 年 5 月，由美术学院副院长任意教授设计的图案确定为上海大学校标。图中一棵新芽萌发的老树干，寓意上海大学重建，六丛枝叶代表当时学校的六所学院
The logo of SHU created in May 1985, picturing a withered tree sprouting with six branches of leaves, signifying a revitalized SHU combined with six branches of colleges and institutes

各学院沿革图（1959—1994）
Evolution of Colleges (1959-1994)

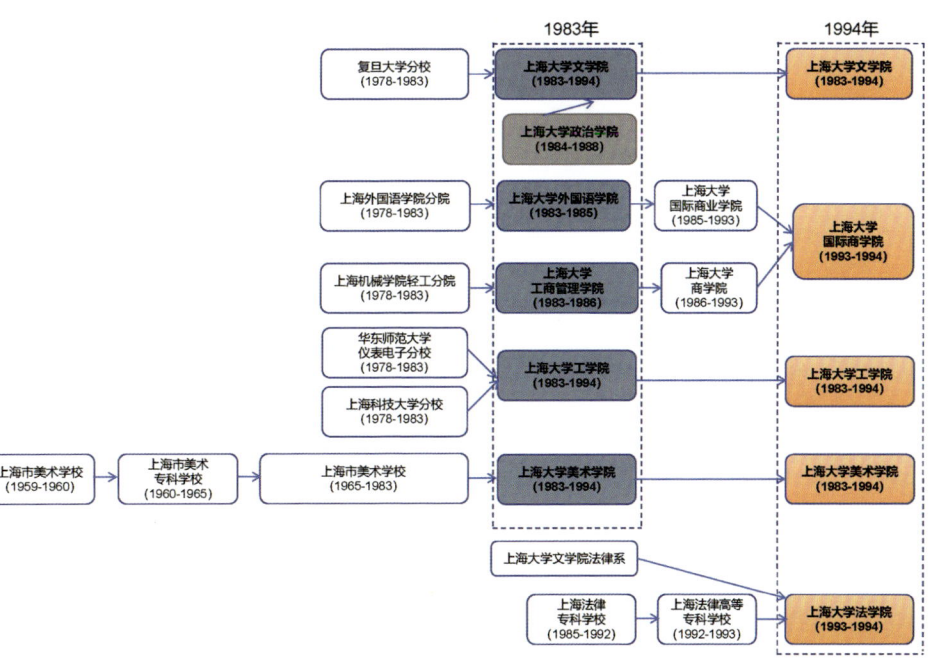

（二）校园变迁　Relocations of Campuses

　　学校刚成立时，下辖文学院、政治学院、工学院、工商管理学院、外国语学院、美术学院，六所学院散布在上海四个区五个地方。1993年，下辖文学院、工学院、国际商学院、法学院、美术学院，五所学院散布在上海五个区六个地方。1983年9月学校正式挂牌时，校部机关在美术学院院内，1987年7月搬至商学院（原工商管理学院）新建综合大楼七楼，校门门牌号为新闸路1220号。

　　建校初，校园面积为65亩，校舍建筑面积约4.1万平方米；1993年，校园面积约294亩，校舍建筑面积约11.5万平方米。

When SHU was newly established, its colleges were scattered across different locations in different districts of Shanghai, the campus covering an area of 65 mu(approximately 43,333 square meters) and the building area premises approximately 41,000 square meters. When SHU was officially established in September 1983, the administrative offices were located within the campus of the Academy of Fine Arts. In July 1987, they relocated to the seventh floor of the newly constructed comprehensive building at the Business School (formerly the School of Business Administration), with the school's entrance address being No.1220 Xinzha Road.

　　In 1993, the campus area was about 294 mu(approximately 196,000 square meters), and the building area premises were approximately 115,000 square meters.

1983年9月1日，上海大学在上海市长宁区凯旋路30号挂牌
SHU at No.30 Kaixuan Road, September 1, 1983

第二部分　海纳百川　奠基再造

1983年，位于上海市虹口区西江湾路547号的文学院
The College of Liberal Arts at No.547 West Jiangwan Road, 1983

1990年2月20日，文学院迁至上海市虹口区三门路661号
The College of Liberal Arts at No.661 Sanmen Road, February 20, 1990

位于上海市徐汇区中山南二路600号的工学院
The College of Engineering at No.600 Second South Zhongshan Road

位于上海市徐汇区蒲西路150号的外国语学院
The School of Foreign Languages at No.150 Puxi Road

Shanghai University

位于上海市静安区新闸路1220号的工商管理学院
The College of Business Administration at No.1220 Xinzha Road

1985年6月10日外国语学院改名为国际商业学院，1986年4月29日工商管理学院改名为商学院，1993年9月10日两个学院合并为国际商学院，并搬至新校区——上海市闵行区莲花路211号。图为当时建设中的莲花路校区
The campus under construction at No.211 Lianhua Road. In 1985, the School of Foreign Languages was renamed the College of International Business. In April 1986, the College of Business Administration was renamed Business School. In September 1993, the two colleges merged into the School of International Business and moved to the new campus at No.211 Lianhua Road

位于上海市松江区外青松公路7989号的法学院
The Law School at No.7989 Waiqingsong Road

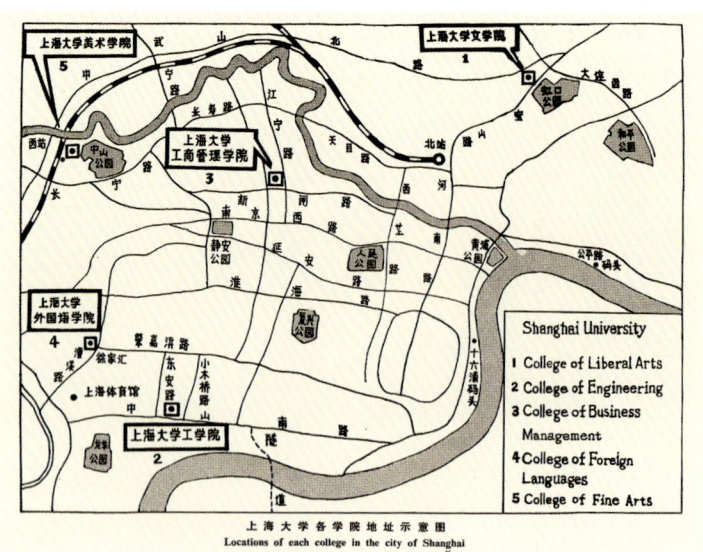

各学院院址示意图（1983）
Location map of colleges, 1983

（三）学校领导　SHU Leaders

校党政负责人更迭一览
SHU Leaders

职　务	姓　名	任职年月	职　务	姓　名	任职年月
党委书记	孟宪勤	1984.4—1993.10	党委副书记	盛善珠 杨慧如	1984.4—1992.11 1992.11—1994.5
校长	王生洪（兼） 杨德广	1987.5—1993.1 1993.1—1994.5	副校长	杜信恩 林炯如 曹仲贤 李明忠	1984.4—1986.12 1986.9—1994.5 1984.4—1994.5 1990.11—1994.5

1988年，校党委书记孟宪勤（左）在美术学院会见参加第三届中日交流作品展的日本友人

Secretary of SHU Party Committee Meng Xianqin (left) meeting with a Japanese visitor at a Sino-Japanese exchange exhibition, 1988

1984年，校领导合影（左起：副校长曹仲贤、副校长杜信恩、校党委书记孟宪勤、校党委副书记盛善珠）

Some SHU leaders in 1984 (from left to right: Vice President Cao Zhongxian, Vice President Du Xin'en, Secretary of SHU Party Committee Meng Xianqin, and Deputy Secretary Sheng Shanzhu)

1993年1月，欢迎杨德广校长到任（左起：副校长李明忠、副校长曹仲贤、校党委副书记杨慧如、杨德广、上海市政府教卫办主任兼高教局局长王生洪、校党委书记孟宪勤、副校长林炯如）

SHU leaders welcoming new President Yang Deguang, January 1993 (from left to right: Vice President Li Mingzhong, Vice President Cao Zhongxian, Deputy Secretary of SHU Party Committee Yang Huiru, Yang Deguang, Director of Office of Education and Public Health of Shanghai Municipal People's Government and Director of Shanghai Higher Education Bureau Wang Shenghong, Secretary of SHU Party Committee Meng Xianqin, and Vice President Lin Jiongru)

1994年5月4日，校长杨德广（中）、校党委副书记杨慧如（右）、副校长曹仲贤（左）出席学校院长书记会议暨92—93年度文明学院评定会议

President Yang Deguang (center), Deputy Secretary of SHU Party Committee Yang Huiru (right), and Vice President Cao Zhongxian (left) at the Appraisal Meeting for Model Colleges, May 4, 1994

（四）领导关怀　Support of Leaders

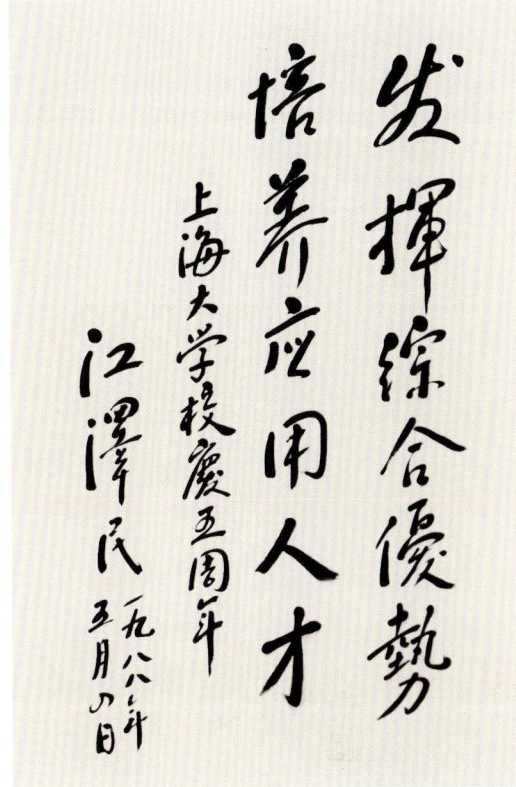

1988年5月4日，中共中央政治局委员、上海市委书记江泽民为学校题词

An inscription to SHU by Jiang Zemin, a member of the Political Bureau of the CPC Central Committee and Secretary of the Shanghai Municipal Party Committee of the CPC, May 4, 1988

1992年3月，国家教委副主任朱开轩（左2）视察建设中的莲花路校区

Zhu Kaixuan (second from left), Deputy Director of the State Education Commission, inspecting SHU, March 1992

（五）专业设置　Programs

建校初各学院本、专科专业设置情况
Undergraduate and Junior Programs in Early Years

学　院	学　历	专业名称
文学院	本科	中文、法律、社会学、图书馆、档案学、历史、考古与博物馆学
文学院	专科	秘书学、政治学
工学院	本科	机械、电子精密机械、生产过程自动化、半导体物理与器件、无线电技术、电信工程、计算机应用、电气技术
工学院	专科	测试技术
外国语学院	专科	英语、日语
工商管理学院	专科	商业经济、财务会计、物资管理
美术学院	本科	绘画、工艺美术

1994 年各学院本、专科专业设置情况
Undergraduate and Junior Programs in 1994

学　院	学　历	专业名称
文学院	本科	汉语言文学、广告学、历史学、社会学、法学、经济法、行政管理、信息学、档案学
文学院	专科	秘书学
工学院	本科	计算机及应用、通信工程、应用电子技术、包装工程、工业外贸、机械电子工程
工学院	专科	安全工程
国际商学院	本科	国际贸易、国际金融、贸易经济、旅游管理、经济信息管理、会计学、管理工程、英语
国际商学院	专科	工商行政管理、日语、食品检验与保鲜
美术学院	本科	中国画、油画、雕塑、环境艺术设计、装潢艺术设计
法学院	本科	劳教法、法学、经济法
法学院	专科	劳动改造法

（六）师资队伍　Faculty

1983—1993 年教师人数及职称情况一览
Faculty Number by Title (1983-1993)

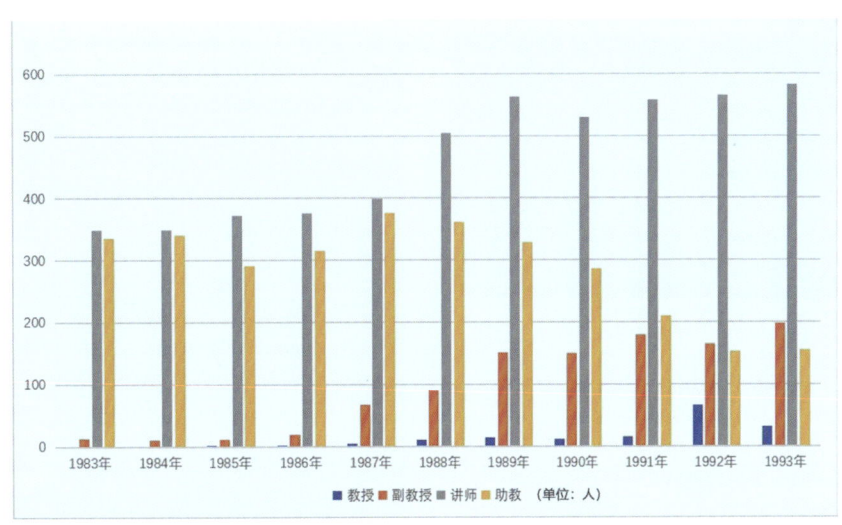

1984 年 10 月 27 日，教育部批复同意授予费孝通教授为上海大学名誉教授。图为 1983 年 12 月 6 日，费孝通教授在上海大学文学院作学术报告

Professor Fei Xiaotong lecturing at the College of Liberal Arts at SHU, December 6, 1983

工学院院长陈大森教授（站立者）在指导学生做实验

Chen Dasen, Dean of the School of Engineering, instructing students on their experiments

国际商学院院长唐豪教授在授课
Professor Tang Hao, Dean of the School of International Business, lecturing to the students

文学院马列主义教研室教师合影
Group photo of teachers from the Marxist-Leninist Teaching and Research Section of the College of Liberal Arts

获全国荣誉称号的教师
Faculty Winning National Honors

荣誉称号	年　度	姓　名
全国教育系统劳动模范	1989	王宇平
全国优秀教师	1989	王乃樑
全国优秀教师	1989	毛忠明
全国优秀教师	1993	何平立

（七）人才培养　Talent Cultivation

1983年9月，学校开始招收本科生（四年制）和专科生（二年制和三年制）。1991年1月，上海市普通高校教育评估工作组进校开展评估工作，认定上海大学"学校办学方向明确，管理正常，学生质量基本适应社会需要，办学条件基本符合有关规定"，评定为"合格"（只分"合格""不合格"两档）。

In September 1983, SHU began to enroll undergraduate students (four-year program) and junior college students (two-year and three-year programs). In January 1991, Education Evaluation Working Group for Higher Education Institutions in Shanghai rated SHU as "qualified" (there were only two grades: "qualified" and "unqualified").

1983—1993年本科、专科招生人数一览
Number of Enrolled Undergraduate and Junior Students (1983-1993)

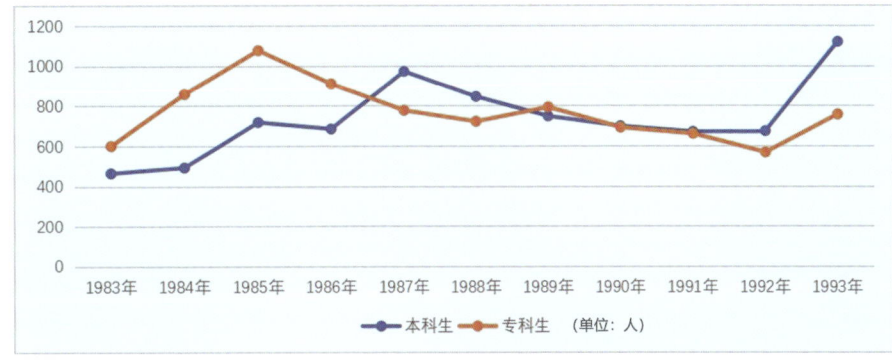

文学院学生在校园文化艺术节上表演
Students from the College of Liberal Arts performing at the Culture and Art Festival

工学院学生进行无线电技术实验

Students from College of Engineering in radio technology experiments

国际商学院学生到美国的商务机构实习

Intern students from the School of International Business at a business organization in the United States

美术学院学生到街上美化环境

Students from the Academy of Fine Arts painting on the street

法学院学生开设模拟法庭

Students from the Law School at a mock court trial

第二部分　海纳百川　奠基再造

1984年4月21日，学校举行第一届运动会
The first sports meeting, April 21, 1984

1987年8月，以商学院学生为主组建的上海大学女子手球队获第四届全国高校手球联赛第一名
The women's handball team of SHU, mainly composed of students from the Business School, winning the first place in the 4th National University Handball League, August 1987

1989年12月，文学院学生团队获上海市宪法知识竞赛二等奖
The student team from the College of Liberal Arts winning the Second Prize in Shanghai Constitution Knowledge Competition, December 1989

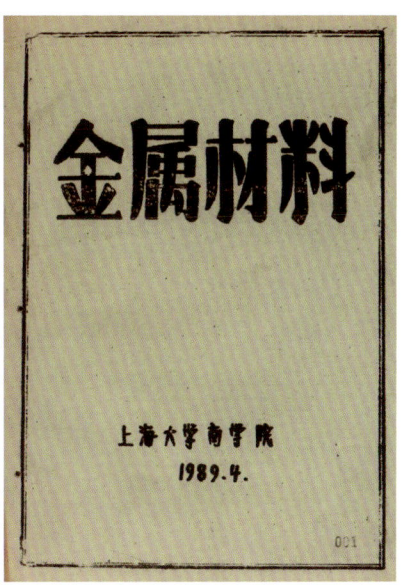

商学院教授自编教材《金属材料》
The textbook *Metal Materials* compiled by teachers from the Business School, 1989

（八）科学研究　Scientific Research

学校科研工作凸显人文社会应用学科的特色，紧密为社会发展服务，着重解决社会现实问题，积极为地方各级政府部门提供决策咨询意见。截至1993年，文学院和国际商学院共承接研究项目353项，其中国家社科基金项目7项、上海市社科基金项目9项；撰写专著657种、译作179种，其中获全国优秀著作奖4种、省市级优秀著作奖27种；撰写论文2000余篇，其中获上海市社科论文奖58篇。法学院共发表论文311篇、论著60种，其中获国家奖论文1篇、论著2种，获省市奖论文11篇、论著6种。

学校努力提升理工科科研能力。1984—1993年，理工科科研经费累计为759万元，1993年的经费是1984年的7.6倍。

学校建立了社会学研究所、中国思想文化研究所、CAD研究所、陶艺研究所、美术研究所，另外还成立了20个研究室。

学校主编并公开发行的学术刊物有《社会》《秘书》《上海大学学报（社会科学版）》《上海大学学报（自然科学版）》；主编的内刊有《教育与研究》。

The scientific research work of SHU highlighted the characteristics of applied disciplines in humanities and social sciences. It closely served the social development, focusing on solving social problems, and actively providing decision-making consultation and suggestions for local government departments at all levels. By 1993, it had undertaken 7 national and 9 municipal research projects, published many awards-winning monographs and academic papers.

SHU also endeavored to enhance its scientific research capabilities in science and engineering. From 1984 to 1993, its cumulative research funds for science and engineering totaled 7.59 million yuan. The funds in 1993 were 7.6 times those in 1984. It established 5 research institutes and 20 research centers. It edited and issued 4 academic journals along with 1 in-house academic periodical.

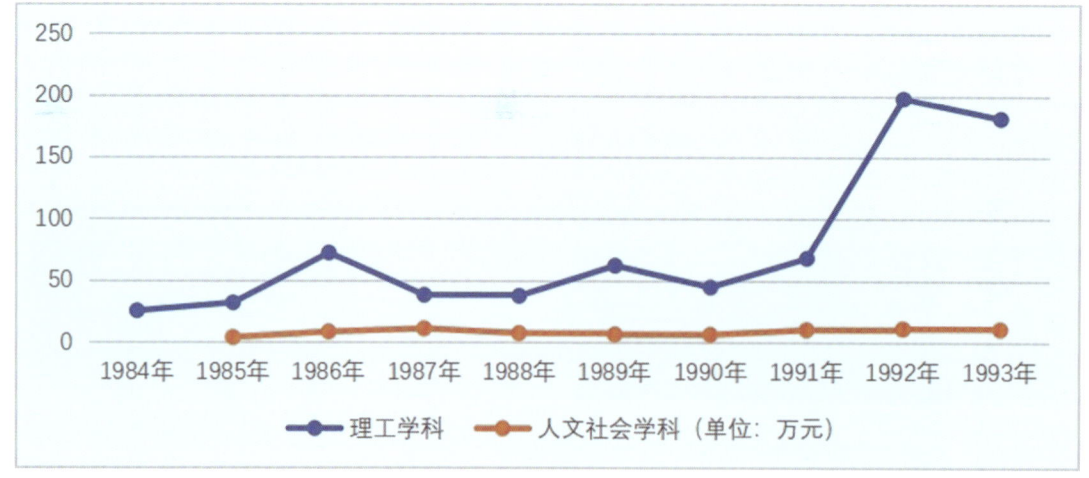

1984—1993年科研经费一览
Research Funds（1984-1993）

国家社科基金项目一览
Projects Funded by the National Office of Philosophy and Social Sciences

项目来源	项目名称	承担部门
"六五"规划重点课题	城市婚姻家庭研究	文学院
"七五"规划重点课题	现阶段中国社会结构研究	文学院
	社区社会保障研究	
	中国十大城市老龄问题研究	
	中国农村婚姻家庭研究	
"八五"规划重点课题	当代中国大陆与港台文学比较研究	美术学院
	中国现阶段文艺经营管理运行机制及模型研究	文学院

人文社会科学著作获奖情况一览
Awards for Monographs in Humanities and Social Sciences

著作名称	获得荣誉	年度	获奖人
《列宁全集》第二版第53卷	中共中央宣传部、中央编译局著作奖	1989	张 坚
公共关系心理学	第二届全国金钥匙奖三等奖	1990	周振明
档案文献保护技术	全国"七五"优秀论著三等奖	1990	宋善玲 等
李心传著作编年	全国古籍图书优秀奖	1991	来可泓
中国历代帝王录	上海市十佳著作	1990	杨剑宇
朋党政治研究	上海市优秀图书二等奖	1993	朱子彦 陈生民
大学德育论	1986—1993年上海市哲学社会科学优秀成果奖三等奖	1993	杨德广

理工科获奖情况一览
Awards for Projects in Science and Engineering

项目名称	获得荣誉	年度	获奖人
SDL型高吸水性聚合物及其应用	上海市科技进步三等奖	1986	杨中一 刘纪明 等
球根花卉小苍兰退化原因与复壮措施的探索	上海市科技进步三等奖	1989	林登正
虹口区商业发展规划研究	上海市科技进步二等奖	1990	周锡樵 章伯虎 等
RX-1型热电池性能智能测试仪	上海市科技进步三等奖	1990	杨桂成 瞿彭志 等
信息科学的积分方程方法和空间偏微分方程的函数论方法	国家教委科技进步三等奖	1992	李明忠

上海大学 / Shanghai University

文学院院长王熙梅教授在进行国家社科"八五"规划重点项目研究
Professor Wang Ximei, Dean of the College of Liberal Arts, working on a national key project

1986年，商学院杨中一（左）、刘纪明等的项目"SDL型高吸水性聚合物及其应用"获上海市科技进步三等奖
The project "SDL-Type Super Absorbent Polymer and Its Applications", directed by Yang Zhongyi (left), Liu Jiming and others from the Business School, winning the Third Prize of Shanghai Scientific and Technological Progress Award, 1986

1990年，商学院周锡樵、章伯虎等的项目"虹口区商业发展规划研究"获上海市科技进步二等奖；商学院杨桂成、瞿彭志等的项目"RX-1型热电池性能智能测试仪"获上海市科技进步三等奖
The project "Research on the Commercial Development Plan of Hongkou District", directed by Zhou Xiqiao, Zhang Bohu and others from the Business School, winning the Second Prize of Shanghai Scientific and Technological Progress Award; the project "RX-1 Intelligent Tester for Thermal Battery Performance", directed by Yang Guicheng, Qu Pengzhi and others from the Business School, winning the Third Prize of Shanghai Scientific and Technological Progress Award, 1990

第二部分　海纳百川　奠基再造

1.《社会》杂志
Sociology

由文学院前身复旦大学分校于 1981 年创刊，是我国最早公开发行的社会学专业期刊。

Sociology is the first academic journal of the discipline in China. It was started by Branch of Fudan University, the predecessor of the College of Liberal Arts of SHU, in 1981.

1980 年 4 月，在复旦大学分校党委书记李庆云（左 1）的推动下，复旦大学分校在全国高校中最早恢复社会学系。图为 1984 年 6 月，上海大学文学院党委书记李庆云主持政治学院成立暨开学典礼，中共上海市委组织部部长曾庆红（左 2）出席
The opening ceremony of the School of Politics, June 1984

1983 年，文学院在上海首开"社会学讲习班"
The first "Sociology Workshop" in Shanghai, held by the College of Liberal Arts of SHU, 1983

《社会》杂志创刊十周年纪念暨社会学理论研讨会
The 10th Anniversary Commemoration of the Founding of *Sociology* and the Symposium on Sociological Theory

《社会》创刊号
The first issue of *Sociology*

2. 《秘书》杂志
Secretary

由文学院于 1983 年创刊，是我国最早公开发行的秘书学专业期刊。

Secretary is the first academic journal of the discipline in China, started by the College of Liberal Arts of SHU in 1983.

文学院主办《秘书》杂志学术研讨会
An academic seminar on *Secretary* held by the College of Liberal Arts

《秘书》创刊号
The first issue of *Secretary*

（九）国际交流　Overseas Exchanges

　　学校积极开展国际学术交流活动，先后与美国、日本、法国、德国、丹麦等国家和地区的十几所高校建立了协作关系。聘请了多位知名学者和专家来校讲学和学术访问，并担任学校的兼职教授，客座教授和顾问教授。学校先后有数十位教师到境外访问、讲学、建立合作研究项目，并取得成果。1989年，学校开始招收外国来华短期培训生。

　　SHU actively conducted international academic exchanges. It successively established collaborative relationship with many universities including those in the United States, Japan, France, Germany, Denmark. In 1989, SHU began to enroll international students for short-term training programs in China.

1985年起，国际商业学院接办上海—旧金山友好城市合作项目——高级经理班。图为1986年11月14日，国际商业学院院长卢关泉（前排右1）出席首期国际高级经理班毕业典礼
Lu Guanquan (first from right), Dean of the College of International Business, at the graduation ceremony of International Senior Management Class, November 14, 1986

1985年，学校与美国纽约市立大学签订第一个校际合作协议；1987年3月，学校又与美国纽约市立大学勃鲁克商业学院合办"商业管理硕士班"。图为1988年6月25日，副校长林炯如（站立者）在美国纽约市立大学发表演讲
Vice President Lin Jiongru giving a talk at the City University of New York, June 25, 1988

1986年11月17日，副校长杜信恩（右）、美术学院院长李天祥（中）和德国柏林艺术高等学校校长乌罗明出席两校校际交流签字仪式
Exchange agreement signing ceremony between Berlin University of Arts and Academy of Fine Arts, November 17, 1986 (from left to right: Ulrich Roloff-Momin, President of Berlin University of Arts; Li Tianxiang, Dean of SHU Academy of Fine Arts; Du Xin'en, Vice President of SHU)

1986年11月24日，学校与日本大阪艺术大学签订校际交流协议书

An exchange agreement signing ceremony with Osaka University of Arts, November 24, 1986

1991年3月1日，学校与日本三城株式会社合作在工学院设立眼镜专业。图为1992年，校长王生洪（中）参加日本三城株式会社向学校赠送光学眼镜仪器交接仪式

President Wang Shenghong (center) attending a donation ceremony, 1992

1993年，国际商学院举办国际学术研讨会

The international symposium held by the School of International Business, 1993

美术学院外国留学生学习中国画

International students learning Chinese painting at SHU Academy of Fine Arts

（十）多项教改　上海首创　Educational Reforms Leading Shanghai Renovation

　　上海市政府在同意市教卫办关于筹建上海大学的批件中指出："上海大学要在教育改革的试验中，不断总结经验，提高教育质量。"与学校成立同时推出的"教育改革试验"具体内容有：收费上学，走读，实行学分制，专科生择优升本科，不设助学金、实行奖学金，不实行公费医疗，毕业不包分配。

In the approval document to establish SHU, Shanghai Municipal People's Government pointed out: "Shanghai University should continuously summarize experiences and improve education quality in experiments of educational reform." In this spirit, SHU has launched a series of "Educational Reform Experiment" since its establishment.

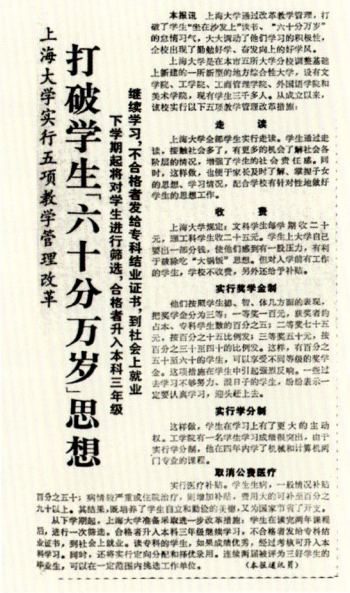

1984年6月24日，《解放日报》刊登上海大学实行教学管理改革的消息
Jiefang Daily reporting on the educational reform of SHU, June 24, 1984

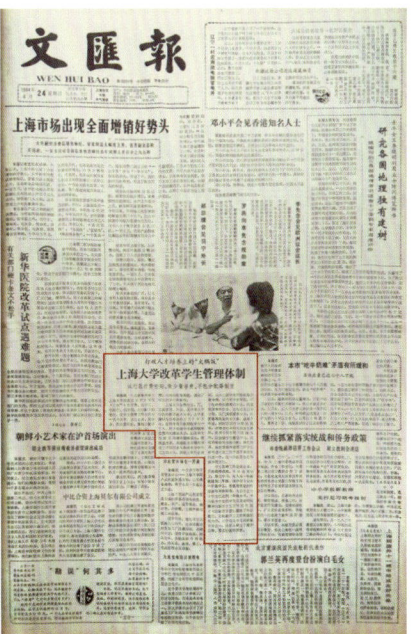

1984年6月24日，《文汇报》刊登上海大学改革学生管理体制的消息
Wenhui Daily reporting on the educational reform of SHU, June 24, 1984

（十一）上海大学美术学院　SHU Academy of Fine Arts

1. 学院沿革
Evolution of the Academy

学院发端于 1959 年 3 月由上海中国画院创立的附设中等美术学校，后更名为上海市美术学校。1960 年 9 月，在上海市委宣传部领导下，经由市文化局和上海中国画院筹划，在上海市美术学校的基础上成立了上海市美术专科学校（本科），由上海市高教局和文化局共管，校址在陕西北路 500 号，当年招收了第一届本科生。1961 年后，按照教育部关于院校调整的要求，学校不再继续招生。1962 年，学校搬至万航渡路 1575 号（圣约翰大学旧址）。1965 年，上海市美术专科学校唯一一届本科生毕业，学校正式停办。为保存上海的美术创作与教育骨干并继续为上海培养美术人才，经上海市高教局和市文化局同意，学校重以上海市美术学校名义办学，同时成立上海市工艺美术训练班（大专）和上海市油画雕塑创作室，并确定上海市美术学校和上海市工艺美术训练班隶属上海市轻工业局，学校搬迁至漕溪北路 502 号（徐家汇土山湾地区）。1970 年，学校又搬迁至天津路 414 号。1983 年，学校成为上海大学美术学院，并搬迁至凯旋路 30 号。

The academy originated from an affiliated secondary art school established by the Shanghai Chinese Painting Academy in March 1959. Later, it was renamed Shanghai Fine Arts School. During the following decade the academy underwent multiple reorganization, relocations and renaming. In 1983, it was set as SHU Academy of Fine Arts and moved to No.30 Kaixuan Road.

2. 校园变迁
Relocations of Campuses

1960 年 9 月，上海市美术专科学校在陕西北路 500 号开学
Shanghai Fine Arts School at No.500 North Shaanxi Road, September 1960

第二部分　海纳百川　奠基再造

1961年，全校共青团员在陕西北路500号校门前合影
Communist Youth League members at No.500 North Shaanxi Road, 1961

1962年，上海市美术专科学校搬至万航渡路1575号
Shanghai Fine Arts School moved to No.1575 Wanhangdu Road, 1962

1965年，上海市美术学校搬至漕溪北路502号（徐家汇土山湾地区）
Shanghai Fine Arts School moved to No.502 Caoxi North Road (Tushanwan area, Xujiahui), 1965

1983年12月至2000年10月，位于上海市凯旋路30号的上海大学美术学院
SHU Academy of Fine Arts at No.30 Kaixuan Road, 1983-2000

3. 师资队伍和人才培养
Faculty and Talent Cultivation

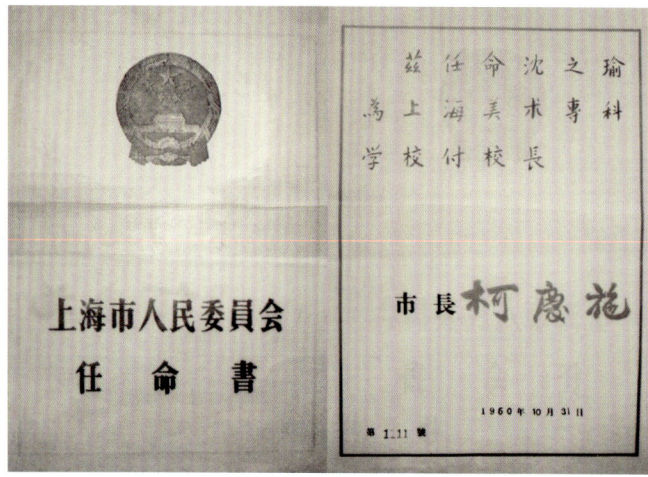

上海市人民委员会任命沈之瑜（1916—1990）为上海市美术专科学校首任副校长（不设正校长）
Shen Zhiyu (1916-1990), the first Vice President of Shanghai Fine Arts School

上海市美术专科学校部分教师合影（前排左1：孟光，右1：李枫；后排左3：周碧初，左5：吴大羽，左6：丁浩，左7：涂克，左10：张充仁，左12：俞云阶）
Group photo of some teachers from Shanghai Fine Arts School

第二部分　海纳百川　奠基再造

学校教师、著名书法家白蕉（中）在学校指导学生书法
Bai Jiao (center), a renowned calligrapher, instructing students

中国画专业师生合影（中排右起：乔木、俞子才、郑慕康、沈凡）
Teachers and students of Chinese painting

1965年8月20日，上海市美术专科学校首届毕业生与全体教师合影（第二排左2起：乔木、张隆基、俞云阶、俞子才、应野平、张充仁、周碧初、郑慕康、陈明、沈凡、唐云、丁浩、李浩、张雪父、沈福根、励俊年、李枫；第三排左7：邱受成，左10：陈家泠，左13：曹有成，左16：孟光）
The Inaugural graduating class of Shanghai Fine Arts School and all the teachers, August 20, 1965

校友陈逸飞（1946—2005），油画家。1965年毕业于上海市美术专科学校
Chen Yifei (1946-2005), a famous oil painter, graduated from Shanghai Fine Arts School in 1965.

4. 美术创作与研究
Art Creation and Research

学院一直是上海美术创作与研究重镇。1983年以后，学院的美术创作与研究经费增长迅速，1984—1993年，共获经费2364万元，1992—1993年的经费是1984年的14.6倍。1984—1993年，学院教师创作的作品在全国或上海市的展评中获得奖项49项，被国家或上海的美术馆、协会收藏的有23项。另外，学院在国内外举办大型展览14场（次）。

The academy has been a major hub for art creation and research in Shanghai. After 1983, the funds for art creation and research of the academy increased rapidly. From 1984 to 1993, a total of 23.64 million yuan was obtained. The funds from 1992 to 1993 were 14.6 times those of 1984. From 1984 to 1993, the works created by the faculty won 49 awards in national or Shanghai exhibitions and evaluations, and 23 of them were collected by national or Shanghai art galleries and associations. In addition, the academy organized 14 large-scale exhibitions at home and abroad.

陈家泠的国画《不染》，获1987年第七届全国美术作品展览银质奖

The traditional Chinese painting "Pure" by Chen Jialing, winning the Silver Award at the 7th National Art Exhibition, 1987

章永浩的雕塑《陈毅纪念铜像》，获1990年上海市陈毅像设计一等奖，耸立于南京东路外滩

The sculpture "Bronze Statue of Chen Yi" by Zhang Yonghao, winning the First Prize in the Design Competition of Chen Yi Statue in Shanghai, 1990

张海平的雕塑《飞虹》，获 1991 年虹桥国际机场雕塑方案一等奖，耸立于虹桥国际机场入口处
The sculpture "Flying Rainbow" by Zhang Haiping, winning the First Prize in the Sculpture Design Competition for Hongqiao International Airport, 1991

在全国美术作品展览获奖的作品一览
Works Winning Awards in National Art Exhibitions

作品名称	获得荣誉	年　度	作　者
《澜沧江畔》（国画）	第六届全国美术作品展览优秀作品奖	1984	应野平
《苏醒》（油画）	第六届全国美术作品展览优秀作品奖	1984	李天祥
《不染》（国画）	第七届全国美术作品展览银奖	1989	陈家泠
《太阳女》（漆画）	第七届全国美术作品展览铜奖	1989	葛春学
《残雪》（油画）	第七届全国美术作品展览铜奖	1989	凌启宁
《少女》（雕塑）	第七届全国美术作品展览作品奖	1989	杨剑平
《中共一大的一员虎将和一位学者——李达》（油画）	建党 70 周年全国美术作品展览银奖	1991	章德明
《白求恩》（雕塑）	建党 70 周年全国美术作品展览铜奖	1991	张海平
《中国共产党的亲密战友——宋庆龄》（雕塑）	建党 70 周年全国美术作品展览铜奖	1991	唐锐鹤

四、上海科技高等专科学校（1959—1994）
Shanghai College of Science and Technology (SCST, 1959-1994)

前身上海计算技术学校（中专），创办于1959年，1981年成为大专，是上海市属高等专科学校。

The predecessor of SCST was Shanghai Computing Technology School (a secondary vocational school) founded in 1959. The school became a junior college in 1981, a municipal higher vocational college in Shanghai.

（一）学校成立　Founding of SCST

1959年2月，中共上海市委教卫部、市科委、中国科学院上海分院以及计算技术研究所共同筹建上海计算技术学校，旨在为上海高校、科研院所和工厂技术部门培养实验技术人才。学校由复旦中学高中部改制而成；同年10月，更名为上海第二科学技术学校。1978年10月，改制为上海科学技术大学分部。1981年12月，成为上海科技专科学校；1992年6月，更名为上海科技高等专科学校。

学校的隶属关系曾多次变更。1959年2月至1969年11月，隶属中国科学院上海分院。1969年12月至1978年9月，隶属上海市仪表电讯工业局。1978年10月至1981年12月，隶属上海科学技术大学。1981年12月23日起，隶属上海市高教局。

In February 1959, the Education and Health Department of the Shanghai Municipal Committee of the CPC decided to transform the senior high school division of Fudan High School into Shanghai Computer Technology School. In October, the school was renamed Shanghai Second Science and Technology School. In December 1981, the school was renamed Shanghai Junior College of Science and Technology (SJCST). In June 1992, it was renamed Shanghai College of Science and Technology.

1989年5月15日，举行庆祝上海科技专科学校建校30周年大会

Celebration ceremony on the 30th anniversary of SJCST, May 15, 1989

（二）校园变迁　Relocations of Campuses

　　1959 年 2 月，中共上海市委决定将位于华山路 1626 号的上海市复旦中学高中部直接改建为上海计算技术学校；同年 10 月，更名为上海第二科学技术学校。1960 年 11 月，学校迁往嘉定东门新建校园，校门门牌号为塔城路 254 号。1993 年底，校门移至金沙路 280 号。

　　建校初，校园面积为 29 亩，校舍建筑面积约 1.9 万平方米；1993 年，校园面积为 117 余亩，校舍建筑面积约 3.9 万平方米。

In February 1959, the Shanghai Municipal Committee of the CPC decided to transform the senior high school department of Shanghai Fudan Middle School located at No.1626 Huashan Road into Shanghai Computing Technology School. In October, it was renamed Shanghai Second Science and Technology School. In November of the following year, the school moved to No.254 Tacheng Road in Jiading District. At the end of 1993, the school was relocated to No.280 Jinsha Road. At the beginning of its establishment, the campus area was 29 mu (approximately 19,333 square meters), and the building area of the school buildings was approximately 19,000 square meters. In 1993, the campus area was over 117 mu (approximately 78,000 square meters), and the building area of the school buildings was approximately 39,000 square meters.

位于嘉定塔城路 254 号的校门
The school gate at No.254 Tacheng Road, Jiading

上海大学
Shanghai University

教学楼
The teaching building

办公楼
The office building

图书馆
The library

（三）学校领导　SCST Leaders

校党政负责人更迭一览
SCST Leaders

职　务	姓　名	任职年月	职　务	姓　名	任职年月
党支部书记	容振华	1959.2—	党支部副书记	马忆冰	1961.11—
	杨文林	1961.11—			
党总支书记	杨文林	1964.1—	党总支副书记	桂荣安	1964.1—
党委书记	庄起良	1971.6—	党委副书记	陈水淼	1971.6—
	巢顺康	1975.8—		杨文林	1971.6—
	陈玉寿 （主持党委工作）	1977.8—			
党总支书记	倪美祥 （主持党总支工作）	1979.4—	党总支副书记	桂荣安	1979.4—
				沙达夫	1979.4—
	倪美祥	1979.7—			
党委书记	倪美祥	1983.5—	党委副书记	唐祥庆	1984.4—
	唐祥庆	1988.7—		陆凤鸣	1987.8—
	汪国铎	1991.6—		蒋乃平	1992.6—
	沈学超	1993.4—			
校长	胡介峰	1959.10—	副校长	容振华	1959.10—
				马忆冰	1960.6—
				杨文林	1964.1—
				杨　锑	1964.3—
领导小组组长	杨文林	1971.2—			
主任	庄启良	1975.8—	副主任	杨文林	1975.8—
				王如群	1975.8—
领导小组组长	桂荣安	1978.12—	领导小组副组长	沙达夫	1978.12—
主任	桂荣安 （主持行政工作）	1979.4—	副主任	沙达夫	1979.4—
				忻福良	1979.4—
	桂荣安	1979.7—			
校长	桂荣安	1983.5—	副校长	忻福良	1984.4—
	钱孝衡	1984.6—		潘道才	1984.4—
	潘道才	1987.8—		刘尚仁	1987.8—
	汪国铎	1993.4—		朱声海	1987.8—
				常增庆	1992.7—

首任校长胡介峰（1903—1963）
Hu Jiefeng (1903-1963), the first President of SCST

1984年，校领导合影（左起：副校长潘道才、校长钱孝衡、党委副书记唐祥庆、副校长忻福良）
Leaders of SJCST (from left to right: Pan Daocai, Qian Xiaoheng, Tang Xiangqing and Xin Fuliang)

1988年，校党委书记唐祥庆（右）和副书记陆凤鸣
Secretary of SJCST Party Committee Tang Xiangqing (right) and Deputy Secretary Lu Fengming, 1988

1988年，校行政领导合影（左起：校长助理常增庆、副校长刘尚仁、校长潘道才、副校长朱声海）
Administrative leaders, 1988 (from left to right: Assistant President Chang Zengqing, Vice President Liu Shangren, President Pan Daocai, and Vice President Zhu Shenghai)

第二部分　海纳百川　奠基再造

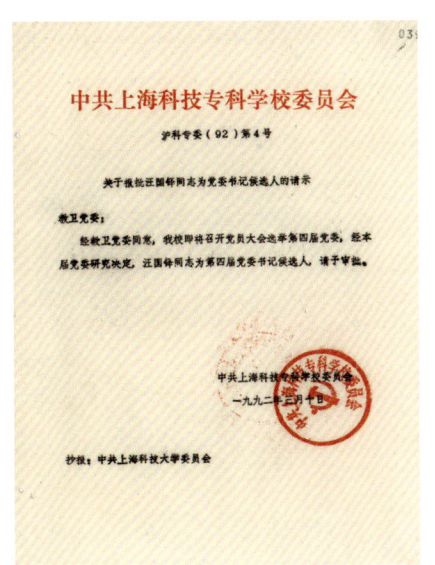

1992年3月10日，关于报批汪国铎同志为党委书记候选人的请示
The proposal report for approval of the candidate for the Secretary of the Fourth Party Committee of SCST, March 10, 1992

1993年，校领导在金沙路280号新校门前合影（左起：党委副书记蒋乃平、党委书记沈学超、校长汪国铎、副校长常增庆）
Leaders of SCST in front of the new gate, 1993 (from left to right: Deputy Secretary of SCST Party Committee Jiang Naiping, Secretary of SCST Party Committee Shen Xuechao, President Wang Guoduo and Vice President Chang Zengqing)

（四）专业设置　Programs

建校初和 1994 年的专业设置情况
Programs in 1961 and 1994

年　份	专业名称
1961	中专：计算机技术、电子学、精密机械、技术物理
1994	大专：电子元器件与应用、无线电技术、检测技术与仪器、微型计算机与应用、机电计量与工艺

（五）师资队伍　Faculty

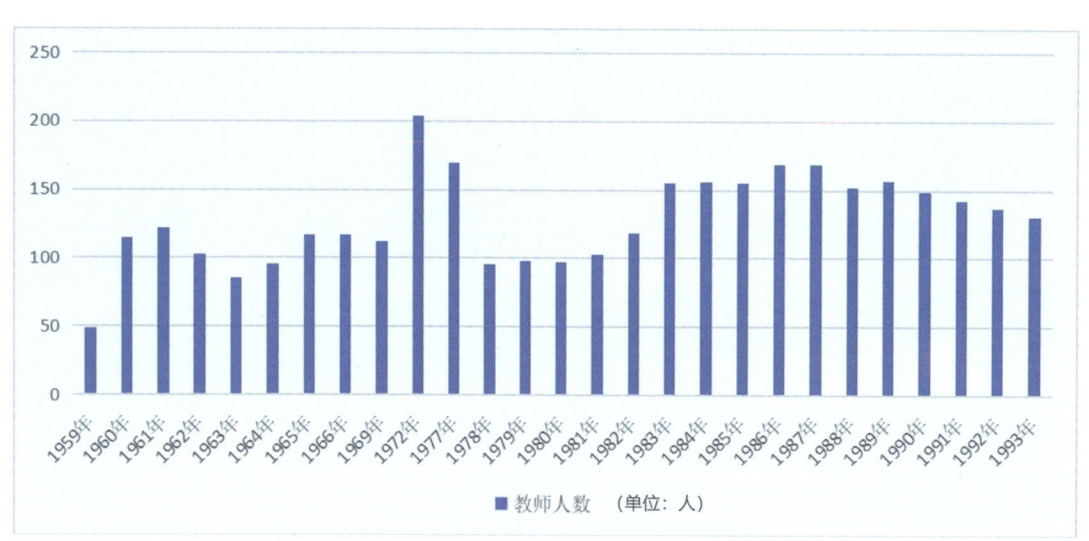

1959—1993 年教师人数一览
Number of Faculty Members (1959-1993)

计算机技术系主任吴震蒙高级工程师在备课
Senior Engineer Wu Zhenmeng, Chair of the Computer Technology Department, preparing for lessons

电子技术系主任张苹迦副教授（中）在主持系务会议
Associate Professor Zhang Pingjia (center), Chair of the Department of Electronic Technology, presiding over the department meeting

技术物理系主任薛鸣鹤副教授（右2）和其他系领导商谈工作
Associate Professor Xue Minghe (second from right), Chair of the Departmentof Technical Physics, discussing with other department leaders

机械技术系主任刘兴东副教授（左1）在指导青年教师
Associate Professor Liu Xingdong (first from left), Chair of the Department of Mechanical Technology, instructing young teachers

获全国荣誉称号的教师
Faculty Winning National Honors

荣誉称号	年　度	姓　名
全国优秀教师	1989	朱锡仁

（六）人才培养　Talent Cultivation

1959—1965 年，学校招收中专生（四年制）。1966—1971 年，停止招生。1972—1977 年，招收大专学历生。1978 年招收了一届本科生（四年制）。1979 年开始招收大专生（三年制）。

From 1959 to 1965, SCST enrolled secondary vocational students (four-year program). From 1966 to 1971, the enrollment was suspended. From 1972 to 1977, SCST enrolled junior college students. In 1978, a class of undergraduate students (four-year program) was enrolled. In 1979, SCST started to enroll junior college students (three-year program).

1959—1993 年中专、大专招生人数一览
Number of Enrolled Secondary Vocational and Junior College Students (1959-1993)

上海大学 — Shanghai University

1960年11月，上海第二科学技术学校首届毕业生合影
The first graduating class of Shanghai Secondary Science and Technology School, November 1960

1988年，学生参加"中国电影之我见"演讲比赛，获上海市三等奖
Students winning the Third Prize in the speech contest "My Views on Chinese Films" in Shanghai, 1988

学生在校办工厂装配电视机
Students assembling TV sets in the school-run factory

学生在进行毕业设计答辩
A student in the graduation defense

第二部分　海纳百川　奠基再造

学生在器件研究室做实验
Students in the device laboratory

学生在机械实验室做实验
Students in the mechanical laboratory

上海科技专科学校教师自编讲义（第一编 声学基础）
Self-compiled Lecture Notes (Part 1: Fundamentals of Acoustics)

（七）科学研究　Scientific Research

学校鼓励教师在搞好教学的基础上参加科研，开展科研、教学、劳动三结合实践。20世纪80年代起，学校设立专门机构和人员从事科研和科技服务工作，大部分科研项目是与企业合作的横向协作项目，属于应用性研究。1990年，学校决定将校办工厂与技术物理系电子器件研究室合并，成立上海科技专科学校科研生产中心，成为教学、科研、生产一体化且经济上独立核算的校办科技产业。

SCST encouraged teachers to integrate scientific research, teaching and practice. Since the 1980s, SCST had established specialized institutions and personnel to engage in scientific research and service work. Most of the scientific research projects were applied research in collaboration with enterprises. In 1990, SJCST merged the university-run factory with the Electronic Device Research Laboratory of the Department of Technical Physics to establish the Scientific Research and Production Center, which integrated teaching, scientific research and production with independent economic accounting.

1986—1993年科研经费一览
Research Funds (1986-1993)

学校科技产业——上海深沪工贸公司成立
The inauguration ceremony of the university-run enterprise—Shanghai Shenhu Industrial Trade Company

（八）国际交流　International Exchanges

1984年5月，副校长忻福良（右）陪同联邦德国驻上海总领事参观学校电教演播室

Consul-General of Federal Germany in Shanghai, accompanied by Vice President Xin Fuliang (right), visiting the audiovisual studio of SJCST, May 1984

1985年，校长钱孝衡（前排右1）与到访的美国艾奥瓦大学谭默教授（前排右2）合影

President Qian Xiaoheng (first from right in the front row) with the visiting professor (second from right in the front row) from the University of Iowa, 1985

1987年1月21日，副校长潘道才（左2）接待到访的英国西格拉摩根高等教育学院院长与夫人

Vice President of West Glamorgan College of Higher Education visiting SJCST, accompanied by President Pan Daocai (second from left), January 21, 1987

（九）学制创新 重在能力　Innovation in Academic System to Value Competence

学校一向重视对学生实际动手能力的培养，改革开放以后，大力推进学制改革，试行多种创新型办学模式，包括选拔优秀生"专升本"、高中与专科五年一贯制（大专班）、专科加本科"三明治"教学模式、校企合作"2 + 1"宝石工艺班。

SCST always attached great importance to cultivating students' practical abilities. After the reform and opening up, it vigorously promoted the reform of the academic system and piloted various innovative models, including selecting outstanding students for the "junior college to undergraduate" program, the five-year consistent system of senior high school and junior college (junior college class), the "sandwich" teaching model of junior college plus undergraduate education, and the "2 + 1" gem-craft class cooperateing with enterprises.

1. 选拔优秀生"专升本"
Transfer Program for Selected Students

1983 年开始，学校与上海科学技术大学合作，选拔优秀专科生转入上海科学技术大学相关的本科专业学习。

In 1983, SJCST began to collaborate with SUST to select outstanding junior college students and transfer them to relevant bachelor's programs at SUST.

1983 年 9 月 2 日，《文汇报》刊登上海科专实行"中间选拔制"的消息
Wenhui Daily reporting on the program of SCST, September 2, 1983

2. 高中与专科五年一贯制（大专班）教学
Five-year Program of Senior High School and Junior College (Junior College Class)

  1985年秋，学校与上海市番禺中学合作，试办五年一贯制（大专班）。前期两年的高中教育课程由番禺中学承担，后期三年的大专班课程到上海科技专科学校完成。

  In the autumn of 1985, SJCST collaborated with Shanghai Panyu High School to pilot the five-year consistent system (junior college class). The first two-year high-school education courses were undertaken by Panyu High School, and the subsequent three-year junior-college courses were completed at SJCST.

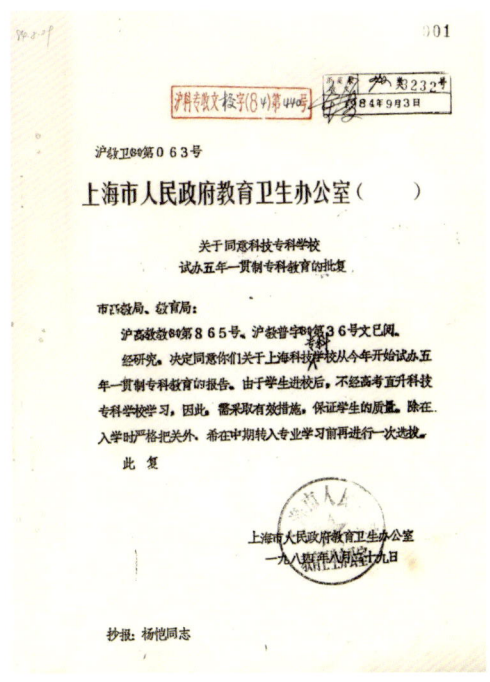

1984年8月29日，上海市人民政府教育卫生办公室关于同意科技专科学校试办五年一贯制专科教育的批复

The approval on the pilot program by Office of Education and Public Health of Shanghai Municipal People's Government, August 29, 1984

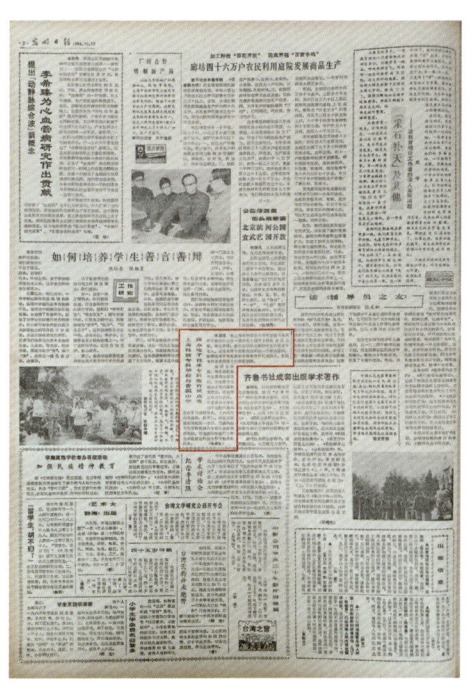

1984年10月12日，《光明日报》刊登上海科技专科学校与番禺中学联办电子技术专科教育试点班的消息

Guangming Daily reporting on the joint pilot class, October 12, 1984

3. 专科加本科"三明治"教学模式
The Pilot "Sandwich" Teaching Model

1988年,学校试办"三明治"教学班,即"3 + 1"本科班,学制四年。实行阶段式教学计划,学生在校学习与下厂实习相间进行,理论教学与实践教学学时之比为1:1,以适应培养工艺型高级技术人才的需要。学生毕业后享受本科毕业生待遇。

In 1988, SJCST initiated a pilot "sandwich" class, also known as the "3 + 1" undergraduate program, with a four-year academic system. This program implemented a phased teaching plan, where students alternated between studying on campus and interning in factories. Graduates of this program were entitled to the same benefits as those of regular undergraduate programs.

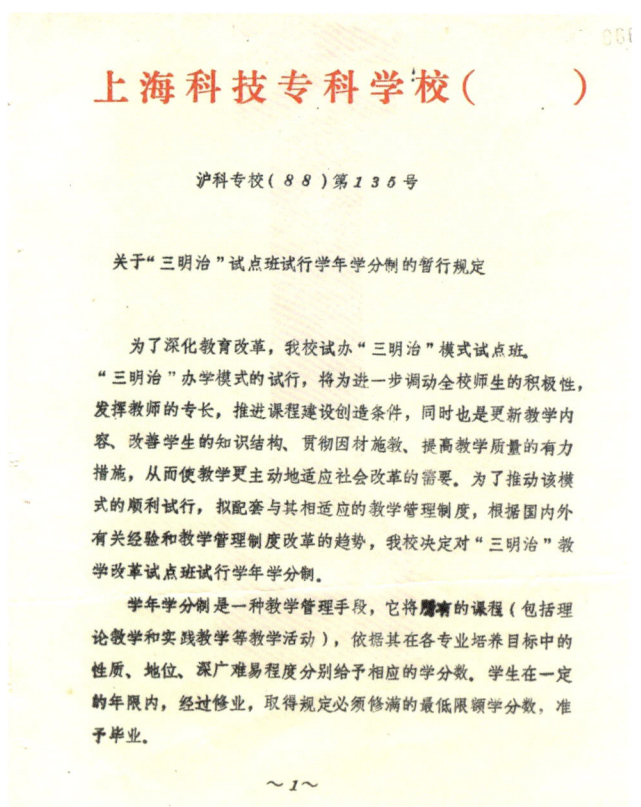

1988年,关于"三明治"试点班试行学年学分制的暂行规定
Interim Provisions for the Trial Implementation of the Credit System in the Pilot "Sandwich" Class, 1988

4. 校企合作"2 + 1"宝石工艺班
"2 + 1" Gem-Craft Class with School-Enterprise Cooperation

1990 年,学校与上海钻石研究资讯中心签订了培养钻石工艺技术人员的协议书。在学校的机电计量与工艺专业中开设钻石加工工艺专业方向,学制三年,其中有一年时间进行生产实习,学生毕业后,发大专毕业证书。

In 1990, SJCST signed an agreement with Shanghai Diamond Research and Information Center to cultivate diamond technicians. A specialized direction in diamond processing technology was set up for majors of Mechanical and Electrical Metrology and Technology. The length of schooling was three years, with one year dedicated to production practice. After graduation, students would be awarded Graduate Certificate of Associate Degree.

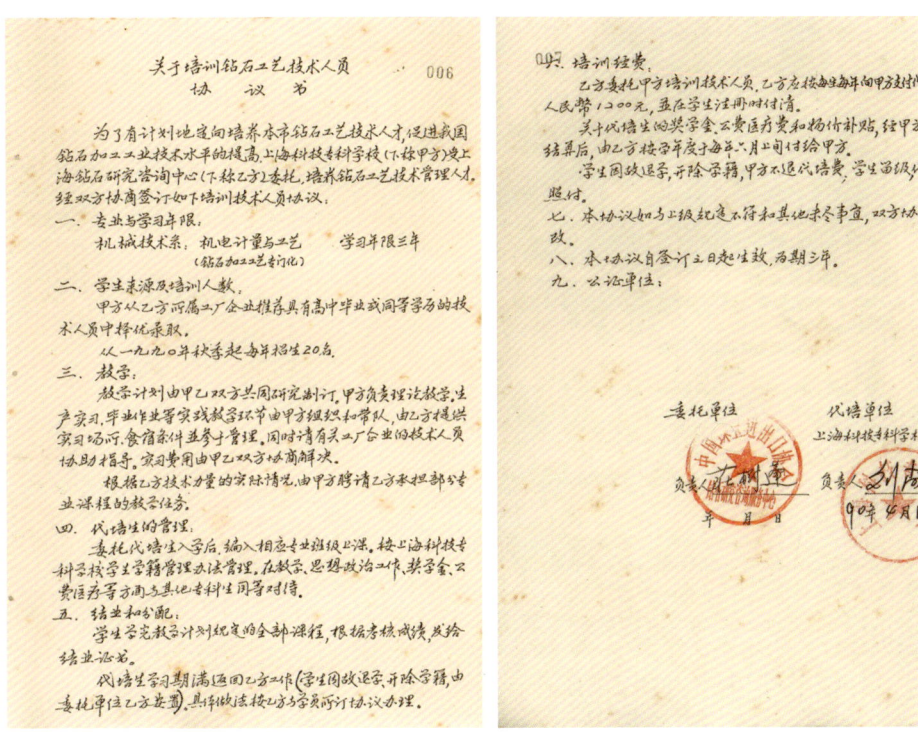

1990 年 4 月 13 日,学校与上海钻石研究资讯中心关于培训钻石工艺技术人员的协议书

Agreement on the Training of Diamond Technicians with Shanghai Diamond Research and Information Center, April 13, 1990

1991 年 9 月 2 日,学校关于举办非学历教育专业"钻石加工工艺"培训班的请示

The proposal report for opening a non-degree training course on "Diamond Processing Technology", September 2, 1991

钱伟长与徐匡迪（油画）
Qian Weichang and Xu Kuangdi (oil painting)

第三部分

自强不息　复兴跨越

为了贯彻中共中央、国务院颁布的《中国教育改革和发展纲要》，优化上海市高等教育布局结构，提高办学效益和教学质量，适应上海市经济建设和社会发展的需要，上海市人民政府决定将上海工业大学、上海科学技术大学、上海大学和上海科技高等专科学校四校合并，建立新的上海大学。1994年4月，国家教委批复同意。这四所学校为上海大学跨入发展新纪元奠定了厚实的基础。

Part III

Pursut of Excellence

In accordance with the "National Plan for Education Reform and Development" issued by the Central Committee of the CPC and the State Council, to optimize the layout of higher education in Shanghai, to improve the efficiency of running schools and teaching quality, and to meet the needs of Shanghai's economic and social development, the Shanghai Municipal People's Government decided to merge SUT, SUST, SHU and SCST to establish a new SHU. In April 1994, the State Education Commission approved the plan. The foundation of these four schools laid a solid foundation for the new SHU to enter a new era of development.

上海大学是教育部与上海市人民政府共建高校、国家"211 工程"重点建设高校、国家"双一流"建设高校。

SHU is jointly built by the Ministry of Education and the Shanghai Municipal People's Government, amongst the list of "Project 211" and "Double First Class" for top national universities.

上海大学校徽　　University Emblem

校徽呈白玉兰的形状，白玉兰是上海市市花。花托为字母"U"形，是大学（University）英文首字母，右花瓣形如海鸥，又是字母"S"，既是上海（Shanghai）英文首字母，又表示腾飞。左花瓣形如数字"1"，表示上海大学争创第一的决心。

The emblem of SHU is in the shape of a white magnolia, the city flower of Shanghai. The flower base is in the shape of the letter "U", representing "University". The right petal resembles a seagull and is also the letter "S", the first letter of "Shanghai" and also symbolizes the university's aspiration to soar. The left petal is shaped like the number "1", indicating SHU's determination to strive for the first place.

2013 年 4 月 18 日，教育部、上海市人民政府共建上海大学协议签字仪式在北京举行，教育部部长、党组书记袁贵仁，上海市市长杨雄出席签约仪式；上海市副市长翁铁慧与教育部副部长鲁昕签署关于共建上海大学的协议

The signing ceremony of the agreement between the Ministry of Education and Shanghai Municipal People's Government on jointly building SHU, April 18, 2013

23 个学科位列软科世界一流学科排名全球前 500（2024 年）
23 Disciplines Ranking in the Top 500 of the 2024 Global Ranking of Academic Subjects

23 个全球前 500 学科的排名区间						
<50	51—75	76—100	101—150	151—200	201—300	401—500
冶金工程	机械工程	控制科学与工程	化学	电力电子工程	数学	经济学
仪器科学	纳米科学与技术	生物医学工程	计算机科学与工程	通信工程	生物工程	心理学
	交通运输工程	化学工程	土木工程	工商管理		
		材料科学与工程	环境科学与工程	管理学		
		能源科学与工程	旅游休闲管理			

ESI 2024 年度上海大学的学科全球引文排名及百分位
ESI 2024 Global Citation Ranking and Percentile of SHU Disciplines

学科名称	2024 年 11 月			2024年9月	2024年7月	2024年5月	2024年3月	2024年1月	备注
	全球引文排名	全球入选 1% 的机构数	全球引文在 1% 机构中的百分位排名	全球引文在 1% 机构中的百分位排名					
工程学	107	2603	4.11	4.28	4.38	4.57	4.94	5.23	2021/5 首次入选 1‰
材料科学	83	1485	5.59	5.85	6.20	6.40	6.85	7.45	2022/11 首次入选 1‰
化学	129	2024	6.37	6.55	6.75	6.88	8.03	8.30	2023/3 首次入选 1‰
计算机科学	118	821	14.37	14.75	15.23	15.28	16.54	17.25	2016/5 首次入选 1%
环境生态学	499	1973	25.29	26.03	26.67	27.40	28.07	29.29	2018/9 首次入选 1%
社会科学	719	2308	31.15	32.35	33.36	35.01	36.75	38.13	2020/3 首次入选 1%
数学	141	383	36.81	37.37	38.50	38.59	38.85	38.83	2013/5 首次入选 1%
临床医学	2989	6518	45.86	47.03	48.37	49.25	51.32	52.91	2013/7 首次入选 1%
物理学	451	956	47.18	48.03	49.95	50.72	49.68	50.93	2018/9 首次入选 1%
生物与生物化学	989	1576	62.75	63.85	65.62	66.87	66.51	68.15	2016/5 首次入选 1%
经济学与商学	364	520	70	72.07	75.90	78.86	85.57	88.52	2023/7 首次入选 1%
植物与动物学	1639	1858	88.21	89.76	91.74	92.89	96.99	99.09	2024/1 首次入选 1%
药理学与毒理学	1212	1337	90.65	94.83	99.69	/	/	/	2024/7 首次入选 1%
地球科学	1104	1120	98.57	/	/	/	/	/	2024/11 首次入选 1%

2017—2024 年上海大学入选 ESI 全球前 1‰ 学科的工程学、材料科学、化学排名百分位变动情况
Variation of the Ranking Percentile of SHU's Engineering, Materials Science and Chemistry in the ESI Global Top 1‰ Disciplines (2017-2024)

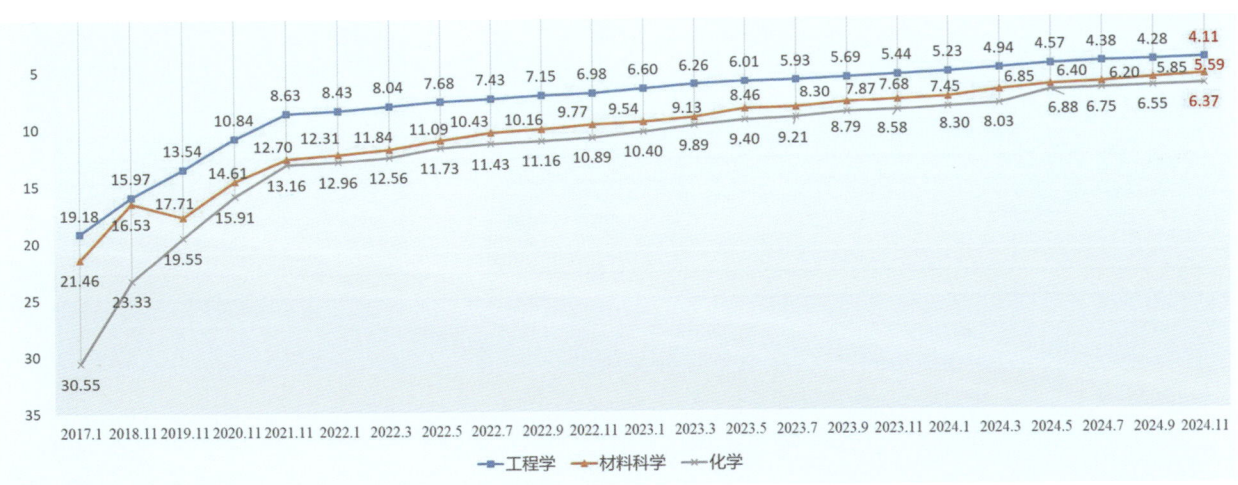

一、上海大学新合并组建
Merger and Establishment

1994年4月22日，中共上海市委通知决定：建立中共上海大学委员会，吴程里任书记；4月25日，国家教委批复上海市政府，同意上海市四所高校合并建立上海大学，原四校建制即予撤销；5月17日，上海市人民政府任命钱伟长为上海大学校长；5月27日，上海市人民政府举行上海大学成立大会。

On April 22, 1994, the Shanghai Municipal Committee of the CPC notified the decision to establish the SHU Committee of the CPC, with Wu Chengli appointed as Secretary. On April 25, the State Education Commission replied to the Shanghai Municipal People's Government, agreeing to the merger of four universities in Shanghai to establish SHU, and the original institutions were abolished. On May 17, the Shanghai Municipal People's Government appointed Qian Weichang as President of SHU. On May 27, the Shanghai Municipal People's Government held the founding ceremony of SHU.

1994年5月27日，上海大学成立大会在上海展览中心友谊会堂举行
The founding conference of SHU at the Friendship Hall of Shanghai Exhibition Center, May 27, 1994

中共上海市委副书记、市长黄菊（右）与钱伟长校长为上海大学揭牌
Huang Ju (right), Mayor of Shanghai, and President Qian Weichang unveiling the new SHU

第三部分　自强不息　复兴跨越

钱伟长校长在上海大学成立大会上讲话，他说："我们上海大学作为一所以'上海'——这样一座世界东方大都市和中国最大的经济中心城市的名字命名的大学，应该在这场跨世纪的伟大变革中作出我们应有的贡献。这是我们全体师生员工的崇高责任，也是我们的无上光荣。当今世界的大城市中，以城市的名字命名的大学有不少，其中也不乏佼佼者。我们上海大学的奋斗目标就是：经过若干年的努力，达到这些优秀大学的水平，与他们并驾齐驱！"

President Qian Weichang delivering a speech at the founding conference of the new SHU, May 27, 1994.

《光明日报》专版刊登祝贺上海大学成立的消息
The special edition on *Guangming Daily* to congratulate the establishment of SHU

1994年5月28日，《解放日报》刊登上海大学正式成立的消息
Jiefang Daily reporting on the official establishment of SHU, May 28, 1994

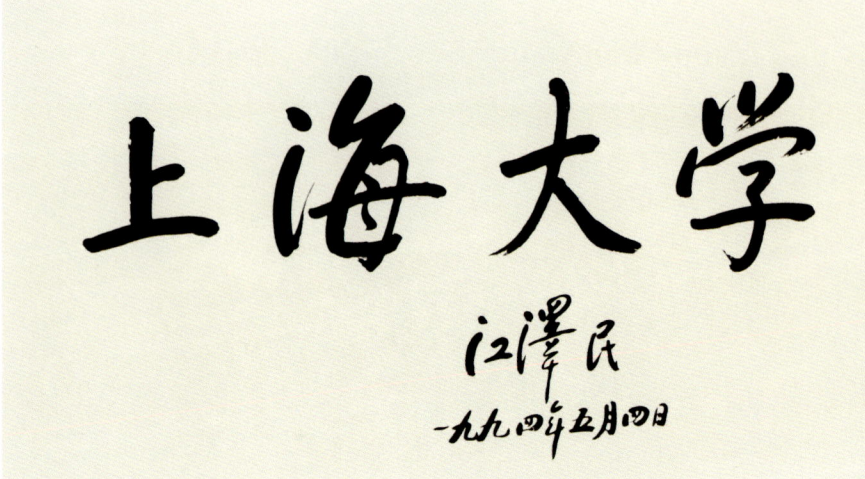

1994年5月4日，中共中央总书记、国家主席、中央军委主席江泽民为上海大学题写校名

The name of SHU calligraphed by Jiang Zemin, General Secretary of the CPC Central Committee, President of the PRC and Chairman of the Central Military Commission, May 1994

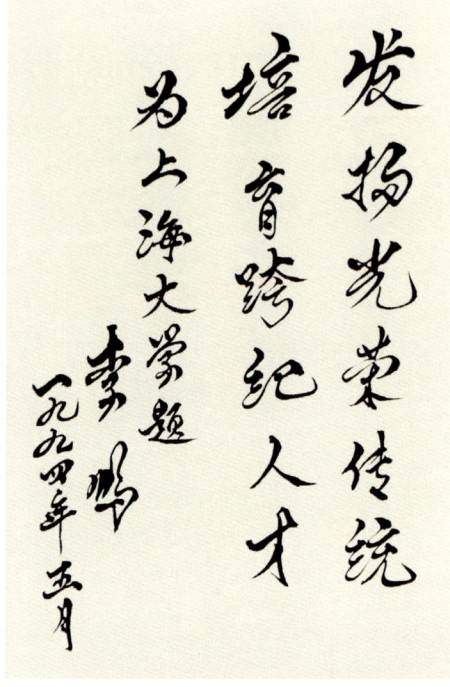

1994年5月，中共中央政治局常委、国务院总理、校友李硕勋与赵君陶之子李鹏为上海大学题词

An inscription for SHU from Li Peng, a member of the Standing Committee of the Political Bureau of the CPC Central Committee and Premier of the State Council, May 1994

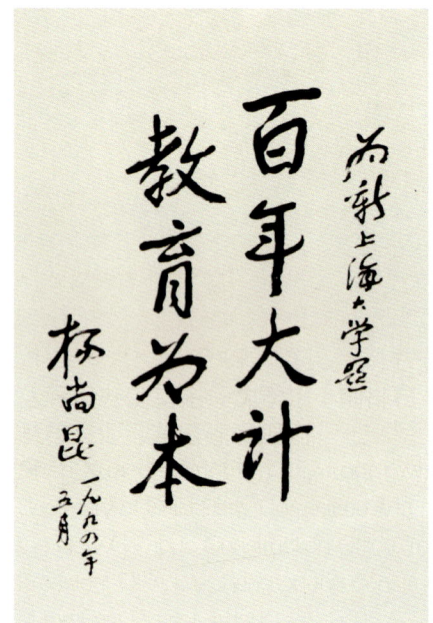

1994年5月，原国家主席、校友杨尚昆为上海大学题词

An inscription for SHU from Yang Shangkun, former President of the PRC and alumnus of SHU, May 1994

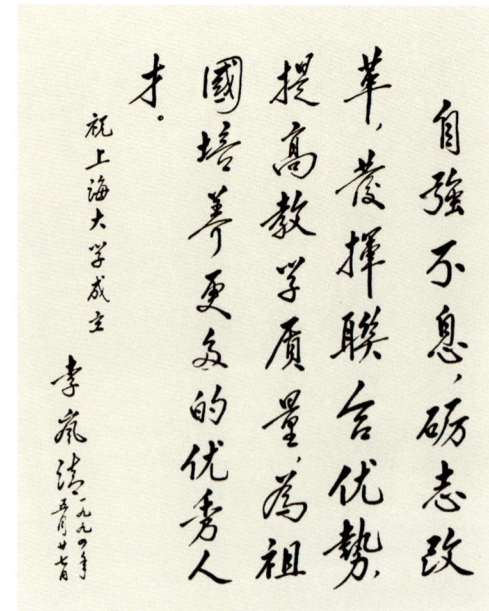

1994年5月27日，中共中央政治局委员、国务院副总理李岚清为上海大学题词

An inscription for SHU from Li Lanqing, a member of the Political Bureau of the CPC Central Committee and Vice Premier of the State Council, May 27, 1994

二、推行"三制" 建立创新性人才培养模式
"Three Systems" and Innovative Talent Cultivation

"三制"(学分制、选课制、短学期制)萌发于钱伟长校长对建立培养创新性人才模式的思考,形成于上海工业大学时期。上海大学新合并组建后,在钱伟长校长的力推下,学校全面实施"三制"。

"Three Systems" (namely, credit system, course selection system and short semester system) originated from President Qian Weichang's thoughts on establishing a model for cultivating innovative talents, and was formed during the period of Shanghai University of Technology. After the new merger and establishment of SHU, with the vigorous promotion of President Qian Weichang, SHU fully implemented the "Three Systems" model.

1994年6月,钱伟长校长在上海大学深化教学改革研讨会上讲话,强调推行"三制"的意义,并要求当年在全校推行(左起:常务副校长杨德广、钱伟长、党委书记吴程里)
President Qian Weichang stressing the importance of "three systems" and requiring to implement them at the Forum on Deepening Educational Reform, June, 1994

1994年5月31日,《文汇报》刊登上海大学教育改革新思路的消息
"New Pathways of SHU's Educational Reform" on *Wenhui Daily*, May 31, 1994

三、调整院系 建设新兴、交叉学科
Faculty Adjustment and Discipline Construction

按照上海市人民政府教卫办关于上海大学必须是"一步到位"实现"紧密型、化合型"合并的要求，学校首先做的是对原四校的院系及专业进行有机整合，充分发挥理工结合、文理渗透、理工文管综合的优势，提高规模效益，努力将学校办成一所高水平的综合型大学。

According to the requirements of Office of Education and Public Health of Shanghai Municipal People's Government that SHU must achieve a "close and integrated" merger in one step, the first thing SHU did was to organically integrate the departments and majors of the original four schools, wisely combining science, engineering, humanities and management, to improve scale efficiency and strive to make SHU a high-level comprehensive university.

整合院系及专业操作步骤示意图
Integration Steps of Departments and Majors

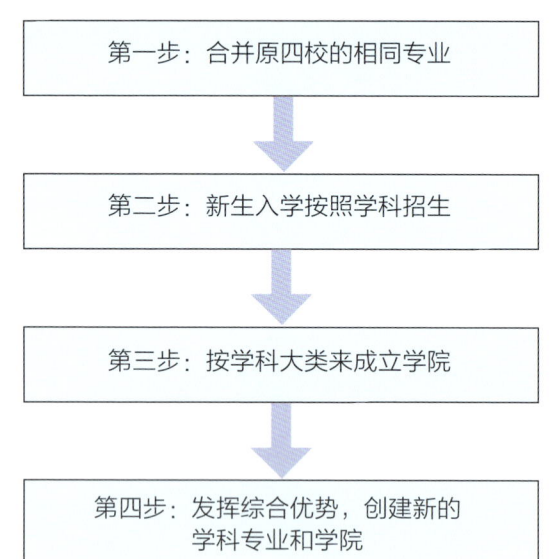

第一步：合并原四校的相同专业

第二步：新生入学按照学科招生

第三步：按学科大类来成立学院

第四步：发挥综合优势，创建新的学科专业和学院

1994—1995 年院系设置一览
Colleges and Departments (1994-1995)

整合形态	学院（系、部）
新建	悉尼工商学院、知识产权学院、理学院、生命科学学院、影视艺术技术学院、社会科学学院、广告学系
重组	计算机工程与科学学院、通信与信息工程学院、自动化学院、机械电子工程学院、化学与化学工程学院、材料科学与工程学院、外国语学院、国际商学院、经济管理学院、国际交流学院、成人教育学院、体育教学部
保留	文学院、法学院、美术学院、建筑工程学院

第三部分　自强不息　复兴跨越

1994年9月，成立上海大学知识产权学院（继北京大学后成立的国内第二个知识产权学院）。图为知识产权学院首届毕业生合影（前排右5起：校党委书记吴程里、常务副校长方明伦、副校长壮云乾）

Group photo of the first graduates from Intellectual Property College, which was established in September 1994

1995年1月4日，成立上海大学理学院，聘请中国科学院院士沈学础担任院长。图为沈学础（中）在理学院主持学科建设研讨会

Academician Shen Xuechu (center) presiding over a discipline construction seminar of the College of Sciences, which was established on January 4, 1995

1995年2月22日，学校与中国科学院生理研究所、细胞生物研究所、植物生理研究所签订合作协议，合作组建上海大学生命科学学院，聘请中国科学院院士杨雄里担任院长

The Signing Ceremony of Cooperation Agreement of the School of Life Sciences of SHU, February 22, 1995

杨雄里在学院"青年成才讲座"上演讲

Academician Yang Xiongli, Dean of the School of Life Sciences of SHU, giving a lecture

1995年4月13日，成立上海大学影视艺术技术学院（国内第一个影视艺术与技术高度融合的学院），聘请电影艺术家谢晋（右3）担任院长，上海市政府同意副市长龚学平担任名誉院长

The foundation of the School of Film and Television Arts and Technology, April 13, 1995

谢晋（坐者右）和学生们在一起

Xie Jin (right in sitting), Dean of the School of Film and Television Arts and Technology, with students

四、"211 工程"建设
"Project 211" Construction

1993 年 2 月，中共中央、国务院印发的《中国教育改革和发展纲要》中指出："为了迎接世界新技术革命的挑战，要集中中央和地方等各方面的力量办好 100 所左右重点大学和一批重点学科、专业，力争在下世纪初，有一批高等学校和学科、专业，在教育质量、科学研究和管理方面，达到世界较高水平。"为贯彻落实纲要精神，国家教委于当年 7 月发文，决定实施"211 工程"计划。1994 年 9 月，上海市市长黄菊在上海市教育工作会议上的讲话中指出："上海除以各种方式支持八所左右在沪中央部委属重点高校进入'211 工程'外，将重点建设好上海大学和上海第二医科大学，支持这两所学校进入'211 工程'，使全市有 10 所左右的高校成为上海和全国培养高层次专门人才、解决经济建设和社会发展重大问题的重要基地，成为一流水准的名牌大学。"1995 年 11 月，国务院批准正式启动国家"211 工程"建设。1996 年 12 月，在上海市人民政府领导下，上海大学跻身"211 工程"。

In February 1993, the Central Committee of the CPC and the State Council issued the "National Plan for Education Reform and Development". The outline stated: "To meet the challenges of the new technological revolution in the world, it is necessary to concentrate the efforts of the central and local governments and all other aspects to run about 100 key universities and a number of key disciplines and majors well so that a number of universities and disciplines can reach a relatively high level in the world in terms of educational quality, scientific research and management by the beginning of the next century." To implement the outline, the State Education Commission issued a document in July of that year, deciding to implement the "Project 211" plan. In September 1994, Huang Ju, Mayor of Shanghai, mentioned in his speech at the Shanghai Education Work Conference that "in addition to supporting about 8 key universities under the central ministries in Shanghai to enter the 'Project 211' in various ways, Shanghai will focus on building SHU and Shanghai Second Medical University, and support these two universities to enter the 'Project 211', so that about 10 universities in the city will become important bases for cultivating high-level specialized talents and solving major problems in economic construction and social development in Shanghai and the whole country, and become first-class universities." In November 1995, the State Council approved the official launch of the national "Project 211" construction. In December 1996, under the leadership of the Shanghai Municipal People's Government, SHU joined the "Project 211" program.

Shanghai University

- 1996年12月25日，专家组通过上海大学"211工程"部门预审。

  On December 25, 1996, the expert group approved the pre-examination of SHU "Project 211".

- 1997年12月29日，专家组通过上海大学"211工程"可行性研究报告和立项审核，上海大学"211工程"建设正式启动。

  On December 29, 1997, the expert group approved the Feasibility Report and Project Approval Review of SHU "Project 211" and SHU officially started the project.

- 2002年3月20日，上海大学"211工程""九五"期间建设项目通过专家组验收。

  On March 20, 2002, the expert group approved the construction projects of SHU "Project 211" and the "Ninth Five-Year Plan".

- 2002年11月，上海大学"211工程"二期建设项目正式立项。

  In November, 2002, the second phase of SHU "Project 211" was approved.

- 2006年6月18日，上海大学"211工程""十五"期间建设项目（二期）通过专家组验收。

  On June 18, 2006, SHU "Project 211" and the "Tenth Five-Year Plan" construction projects (Phase II) were officially approved.

- 2012年3月18日，上海大学"211工程"三期建设通过专家组验收。

  On March 18, 2012, the third phase of SHU "Project 211" was approved by the expert group.

1996年12月23日，举行"211工程"部门预审开幕式，国家教委副主任韦钰（左7）、上海市委副书记陈至立（左5）出席

The opening ceremony of the pre-examination of the "Project 211", December 23, 1996

第三部分　自强不息　复兴跨越

1996年12月25日，中共上海市委副书记、市长徐匡迪在市政府大厦会见上海大学"211工程"部门预审专家组成员（左起：上海市委副书记陈至立，徐匡迪，钱伟长，专家组组长、复旦大学校长杨福家院士）

Shanghai Mayor Xu Kuangdi meeting the pre-examination experts of SHU "Project 211", December 25, 1996

2002年3月19—20日，召开"211工程""九五"期间建设项目（一期）验收会，上海市副市长周慕尧（右3）出席

The acceptance meeting of the "Project 211" and the "Ninth Five-Year Plan" projects (Phase I), March 19-20, 2002

2006年6月17—18日，召开"211工程""十五"期间建设项目（二期）验收会
The acceptance meeting of the "Project 211" and the "Tenth Five-Year Plan" projects (Phase II), June 17-18, 2006

2012年3月18日，召开"211工程"三期建设验收会
The acceptance meeting of the "Project 211" (Phase III), March 18, 2012

五、新校区建设
Construction of the New Campus

1995年12月，中共上海市委书记黄菊在市委六届四次全会的讲话中明确："'九五'期间要集中力量建设上海图书馆新馆、上海大剧院、八万人体育场、新上海大学等，形成一批标志性的教文卫体设施。"1997年6月，在上海市委、市政府主要领导的直接关心下，上海大学新校区（宝山校区）工程正式立项。

学校在确保新校区建设以外，还根据学校学科发展与布局调整需要，有计划地对延长、嘉定、静安等校区进行优化改造。

In December 1995, Huang Ju, Secretary of the Shanghai Municipal Committee of the CPC, explicitly stated in his speech at the Fourth Plenary Session of the Sixth Municipal Committee of the CPC that "during the 'Ninth Five-Year Plan' period, our focus will be on the construction of several landmark projects, including the new Shanghai Library, Shanghai Grand Theater, Shanghai Stadium, new SHU, and other cultural, educational, health and sports facilities." In June 1997, with the direct support of the main leaders of the Shanghai Municipal Committee and the Shanghai Municipal People's Government, the project of the SHU new campus was officially approved. In addition to ensuring the construction of the new Baoshan campus, SHU also planned to optimize and renovate the Yanchang, Jiading, Jing'an and other campuses according to the needs of SHU's discipline development and adjustment.

- 1997年6月28日，上海市计委关于上海大学新校区项目正式立项。

  On June 28, 1997, the Shanghai Municipal Development and Reform Commission officially approved the new SHU campus project.

- 1997年12月26日，举行上海大学新校区建设工程奠基仪式。

  On December 26, 1997, the groundbreaking ceremony of the construction of the new SHU campus was held.

- 1998年5月20日，举行新校区工程开工典礼，第一个建筑群体（院系综合楼）正式开工。

  On May 20, 1998, the groundbreaking ceremony of the new SHU campus project was held, and the first building complex (colleges and departments buildings) officially started construction.

- 1999年8月，新校区（一期）工程基本竣工。

  In August 1999, the first phase of the new campus project was basically completed.

- 1999年9月12日，举行新校区启用暨1999年新生开学典礼。

  On September 12, 1999, the opening ceremony of the new campus and the opening ceremony of the 1999 freshmen were held.

- 2000年8月，新校区（二期）工程基本竣工。

  In August 2000, the second phase of the new campus project was basically completed.

- 2001 年 10 月 24 日，新校区（一期、二期）工程通过专家组验收。

  On October 24, 2001, the new campus (Phase I and Phase II) project passed the expert group's assessment.

- 2006 年 12 月 30 日，新校区扩建（一期）工程开工。

  On December 30, 2006, the expansion project of the new campus (Phase I) began.

- 2008 年 7 月，新校区扩建（一期）工程基本竣工。

  In July 2008, the expansion project of the new campus (Phase I) was basically completed.

- 2010 年 9 月 28 日，新校区扩建（二期）工程开工。

  On September 28, 2010, the expansion project (Phase II) of the new campus began.

- 2012 年 7 月，新校区扩建（二期）工程基本竣工。

  In July 2012, the expansion project of the new campus (Phase II) was basically completed.

- 2015 年 8 月 18 日，新校区扩建（三期）工程开工。

  On August 18, 2015, the expansion project (Phase III) of the new campus began.

- 2017 年 7 月，新校区扩建（三期）工程基本竣工。

  In July 2017, the expansion project of the new campus (Phase III) was basically completed.

- 2022 年 7 月 27 日，新校区扩建（四期）工程开工。

  On July 27, 2022, the expansion project of the new campus (Phase IV) began.

1996 年 2 月 25 日，钱伟长校长与中共上海市委副书记、市长徐匡迪（左），市教委主任郑令德（右）共商新校区选址方案

President Qian Weichang, Mayor Xu Kuangdi (left) and Director of the Municipal Education Commission Zheng Lingde (right) discussing the site selection plan for the new campus, February 25, 1996

1997 年 11 月 11 日，中共上海市委副书记、市长徐匡迪（右 3），市委副书记王力平（左 3），市委秘书长周慕尧（右 2）在钱伟长校长陪同下观看新校区建设规划沙盘

Mayor Xu Kuangdi (third from right), Mr. Wang Liping (third from left) and Mr. Zhou Muyao (second from right), inspecting the sand table of the new campus construction plan accompanied by President Qian Weichang, November 11, 1997

第三部分　自强不息　复兴跨越

1997年12月26日，举行新校区工程奠基仪式，中共上海市委副书记龚学平（中）为奠基石培土

The groundbreaking ceremony for the new campus project, December 26, 1997

1999年9月12日，举行新校区启用暨开学典礼，中共上海市委副书记、市长徐匡迪（前排右7）出席

The opening ceremony of the new campus, September 12, 1999

1999年11月3日，中共中央政治局常委、国务院副总理李岚清（右5）和教育部部长陈至立（右6）在钱伟长校长陪同下视察新校区

Li Lanqing (fifth from right), a member of the Standing Committee of the Political Bureau of the CPC Central Committee and Vice Premier of the State Council, inspecting the new campus accompanied by President Qian Weichang and others, November 3, 1999

2005年8月25日，校党委副书记、新校区建设办公室主任沈学超（前排右）向钱伟长校长汇报东区建设规划

Shen Xuechao (right in the front row), Deputy Secretary of SHU Party Committee and Director of the New Campus Construction Office, reporting to President Qian Weichang on the construction plan of the East District, August 25, 2005

第三部分　自强不息　复兴跨越

2006年12月30日，新校区扩建一期工程项目开工
The groundbreaking ceremony of the first phase of the new campus expansion project, December 30, 2006

2010年9月28日，新校区扩建二期工程项目开工
The groundbreaking ceremony of the second phase of the new campus expansion project, September 28, 2010

2015年8月18日，新校区扩建三期工程项目开工
The groundbreaking ceremony of the third phase of the new campus expansion project, August 18, 2015

2022年7月27日，新校区扩建四期工程项目开工
The groundbreaking ceremony of the fourth phase of the new campus expansion project, July 27, 2022

上海大学　　Shanghai University

校本部（宝山校区）平面图
Baoshan campus map

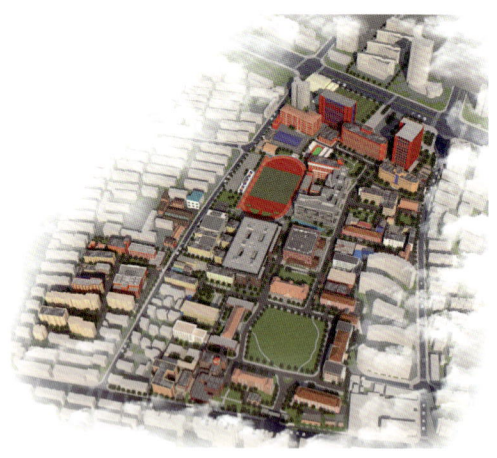

延长校区平面图
Yanchang campus map

嘉定校区平面图
Jiading campus map

新闸路校区平面图
Xinzha Road campus map

六、改革专业技术职务聘任制
Reform on the Promotion System

2001年开始,学校内部管理体制改革以岗位职务聘任制改革为突破口,在上海高校中率先不再执行原来通行的任职资格评审制,全面推行教师系列专业技术职务以聘代评,打破教师职务终身制。

Since 2001, SHU has taken the reform of the promotion system as a breakthrough in its internal administration system reform. It was the first among Shanghai universities to discontinue the previously prevalent qualification review system and fully implement the appointment-based evaluation of professional and technical positions for teachers, breaking the lifelong tenure system for faculty members.

2001年11月,校党委书记、常务副校长方明伦(右5)主持教师系列专业技术职务聘任委员会会议

Fang Minglun (fifth from right), Secretary of SHU Party Committee and Executive Vice President of SHU, presiding over the meeting on the promotion system for the faculty, November 2001

2001年11月26日,《文汇报》刊登上海大学实施教师职务聘任改革的消息

Wenhui Daily reporting on the SHU reform of the promotion system, November 26, 2001

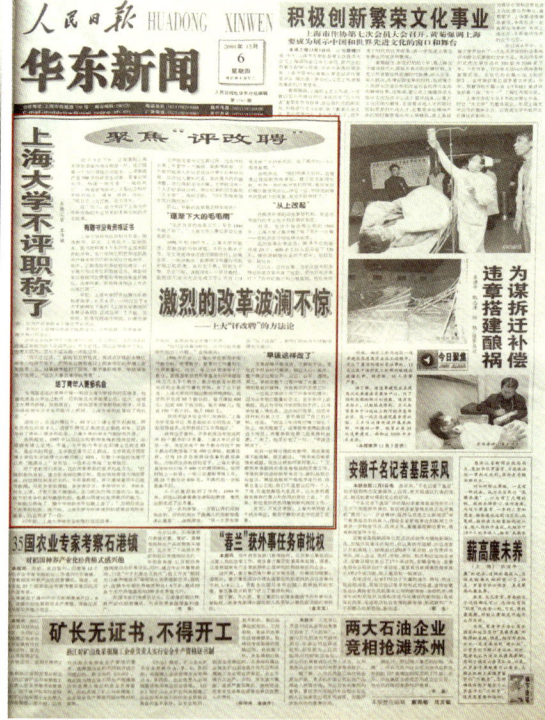

2001年12月6日,《人民日报·华东新闻》头版刊登上海大学教师职务聘任改革的消息

Huadong Views of People's Daily reporting on the SHU promotion reform on the front page, December 6, 2001

七、接受本科教学工作水平评估
Assessment of Undergraduate Teaching Qualification

2003年8月,教育部决定从当年开始用五年左右的时间,对全国普通高校本科教学工作进行一次全面评估,并形成五年一轮的评估制度。上海大学于当年接受首轮评估,于2004年6月获评估结论"优秀"。

In August 2003, the Ministry of Education decided to conduct a comprehensive evaluation of undergraduate teaching work in general higher education institutions across the country over a period of about 5 years and form a 5-year evaluation system. SHU underwent its first round of evaluation that year and was awarded an "excellent" grade in June 2004.

2003年10月20日,举行教育部普通高等学校本科教学工作水平评估上海大学校长汇报会
SHU President reporting on the undergraduate teaching work, October 20, 2003

上海大学
Shanghai University

学校本科教学工作水平评估特色工程示范展示
Exhibitions of characteristic projects in the assessment of undergraduate teaching qualification

2004年6月16日，《教育部办公厅关于公布上海大学等42所高等学校本科教学工作评估结论的通知》中公布上海大学本科教学工作的评估结论为优秀

"Excellent" grade by General Office of the Ministry of Education, June 16, 2004

第三部分 自强不息 复兴跨越

八、确立钱伟长教育思想
Establishment of Qian Weichang's Educational Thought

钱伟长将自己对党的教育方针的深刻理解和对社会、科技、教育发展趋势及其规律的把握相结合，借鉴古今中外优秀教育思想和理论成果，提出一系列独特的教育理念和办学方略，经过上海大学全体师生的长期实践，逐渐形成钱伟长教育思想。

Qian Weichang combined his profound interpretation of the Party's educational policies with his definition of the development trend and laws of society, science and technology, and education, and drew on excellent educational ideas and theoretical achievements from ancient and modern times, both in China and abroad, to propose a series of unique educational concepts and strategies. Through long-term practice by all faculty members and students at SHU, Qian Weichang's educational thought gradually took shape.

2007年1月12日，校党委书记于信汇在学校第一次党代会的工作报告中提出"钱伟长教育思想是上海大学的精神财富"
Yu Xinhui, Secretary of SHU Party Committee, proposed that "Qian Weichang's educational thought is the spiritual wealth of SHU", January 12, 2007

2007年10月9日，校党委副书记忻平（中）主持钱伟长教育思想报告会
Xin Ping (center), Deputy Secretary of SHU Party Committee, presiding over the seminar on Qian Weichang's educational thought, October 9, 2007

钱伟长教育思想概要
Summary of Qian Weichang's Educational Thought

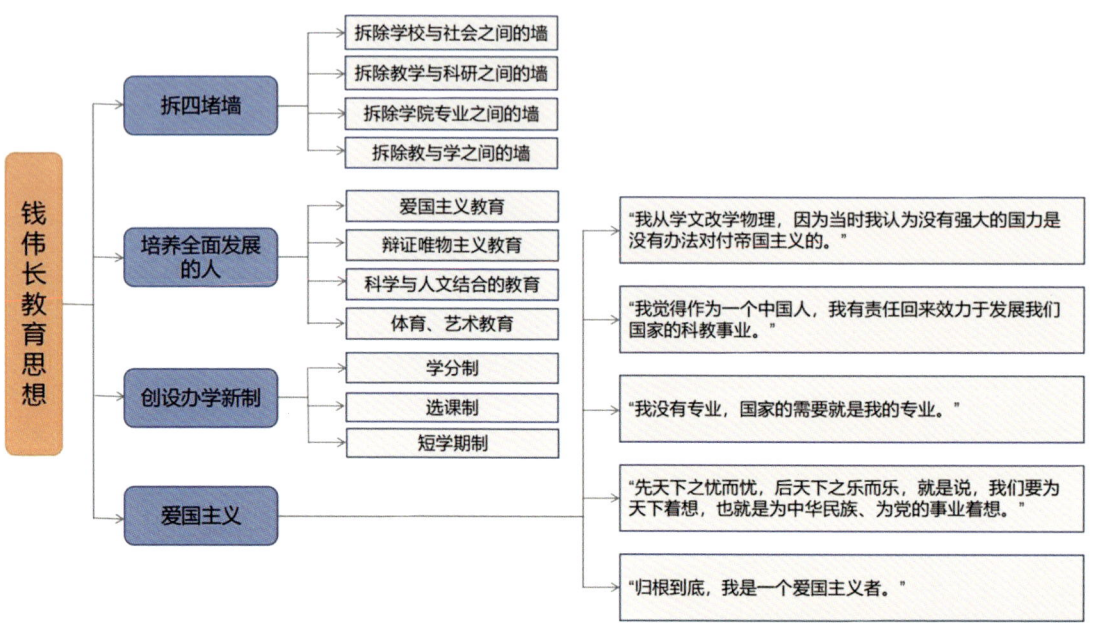

2007年11月23日，第十届全国政协副主席徐匡迪为学校"伟长楼"揭幕
Xu Kuangdi, Vice Chairman of the 10th National Committee of the CPPCC, unveiled the Weichang Building, November 23, 2007

2012年10月，上海大学出版社为纪念钱伟长校长诞辰100周年出版的钱伟长文集
SHU Press published Qian Weichang's collected works to commemorate the 100th anniversary of the birth of President Qian Weichang, October 2012

第三部分　自强不息　复兴跨越

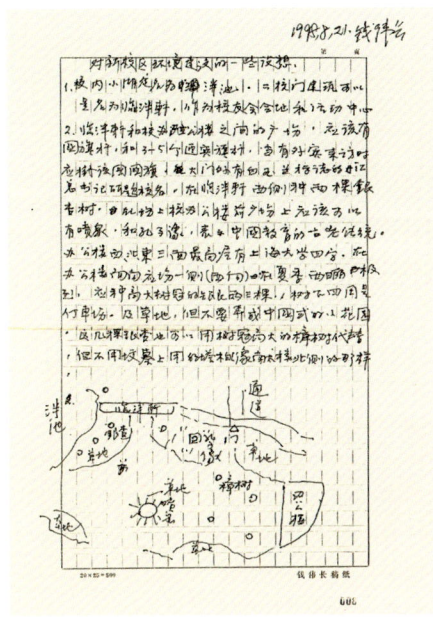
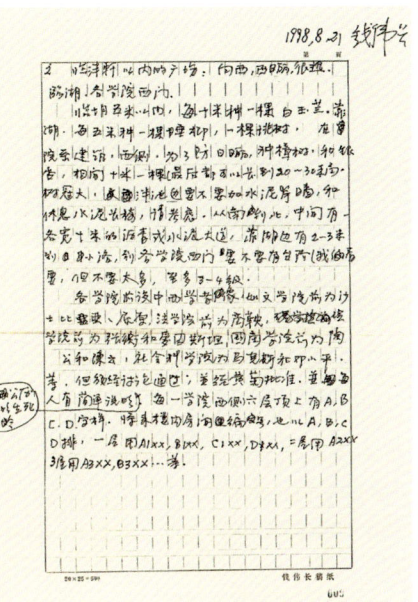

1998年8月21日，钱伟长校长《对新校区环境建设的一些设想》手稿
President Qian Weichang's manuscript of "Some Thoughts on the Construction of the New Campus", August 21, 1998

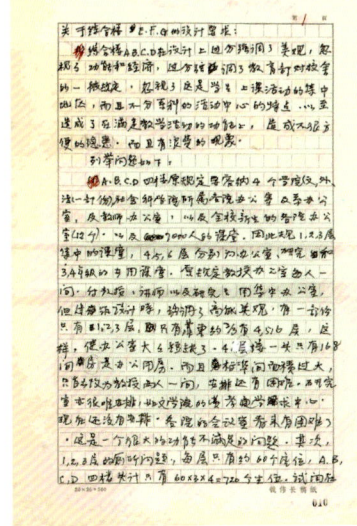
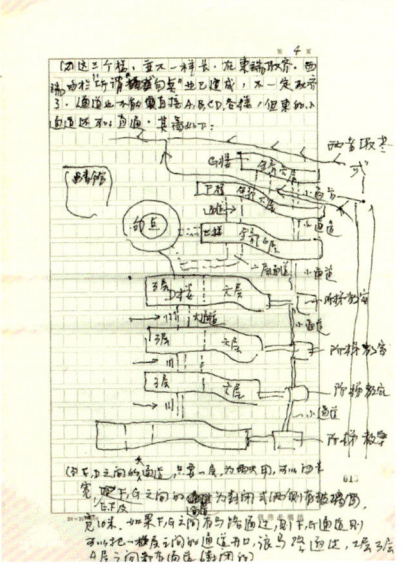

1998年8月21日，钱伟长校长《关于综合楼E、F、G的设计要求》手稿
President Qian Weichang's manuscript of "Design Requirements for Buildings E, F and G", August 21, 1998

上海大学 | Shanghai University

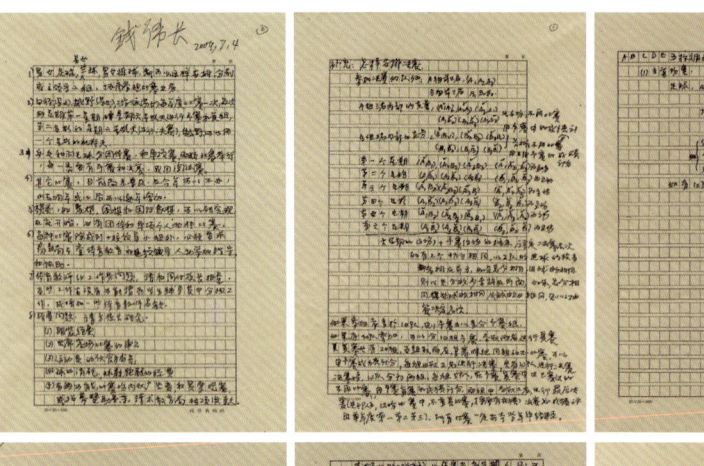

2004年7月4日，钱伟长校长为倡议举办的"钱伟长杯"上海高校大学生足球联赛起草的比赛章程手稿

The manuscript of competition regulations by President Qian Weichang for "Qian Weichang Cup" Collegiate Shanghai Football League, July 4, 2004

钱伟长著《教育和教学问题的思考》
Thinking about the Problems in Education and Teaching by Qian Weichang

钱伟长著《论教育》
On Education by Qian Weichang

九、成立校董事会
Establishment of SHU Board of Trustees

2012年5月，上海大学董事会成立。学校与校董单位、校董会成员建立并发展长期、稳定、全面、紧密的合作关系，助推上海大学向国际知名、国内一流的综合性研究型大学的建设目标迈出更加坚实的步伐。

In May 2012, SHU Board of Trustees was established. SHU has established and developed long-term stable, comprehensive and close cooperative relationships with trustee units and members, helping SHU to march more solidly towards the goal of building an internationally renowned and domestically first-class comprehensive research university.

2012年5月27日，举行校董事会成立大会暨首届校董会第一次会议，第十届全国政协副主席、上海大学终身教授徐匡迪院士当选为首届董事会主席

The inaugural meeting of the SHU Board of Trustees, Academician Xu Kuangdi serving as the first Board Chairman, May 27, 2012

2017年5月27日，举行第二届校董事会第一次会议，中国工程院原副院长、上海大学校友干勇院士担任董事会主席

The first meeting of the second SHU Board of Trustees, Academician Gan Yong serving as the Board Chairman, May 27, 2017

2021年11月14日，举行第三届校董事会成立大会暨第一次全体会议，上海大学主要创办人李大钊之孙、"七一勋章"获得者李宏塔（第一排左7）和上海大学主要创办人瞿秋白之女、"七一勋章"获得者瞿独伊担任名誉董事

The first meeting of the 3rd SHU Board of Trustees, Mr. Li Hongta (seventh from left in the first row) and Ms. Qu Duyi serving as honorary directors, November 14, 2021

十、实施"五五战略"
Implementation of "Five-Five Strategy"

学校聚焦教育强国的国家战略和上海发展需求,不断优化学科布局,于2021年制定部署"五五战略",即以理工科的"五朵金花"和文科的"五大阵地"为主体,引领和推进学科专业调整,加强学科带头人队伍建设,推动学科深度交叉融合,对接新科技、新产业发展态势,实施学科建设协同推进计划,加速培养国家急需的拔尖创新人才。2023年7月,教育部推出高等教育综合改革试点战略工程。学校作为试点单位,围绕"大大提高高等教育人才创新能力""大大提高高等教育科技创新能力"这两个主要目标,结合学校"五五战略",积极探索实现目标的主要路径和方法。

SHU launched the "Five-Five Strategy" in 2021, comprising "Five Golden Flowers" in science and engineering disciplines and "Five Fronts" in humanities and social sciences. The strategy aimed to promote the adjustment of disciplines and majors, strengthen the construction of academic leaders, promote the deep cross-integration of disciplines, connect with the development trend of new technologies and industries, implement the collaborative promotion plan of discipline construction, and accelerate the cultivation of top-notch innovative talents urgently needed by the country. In July 2023, the Ministry of Education launched a pilot strategic project for comprehensive reform of higher education. SHU made active response, focusing on the two main goals of "improving the innovation ability of higher education talents" and "improving the scientific and technological innovation ability of higher education", and combining with the SHU "Five-Five Strategy", explored the main paths and methods to achieve the goals.

2021年11月26日,召开上海大学创新工作大会。校长刘昌胜作《紧抓机遇,追求卓越,推动创新工作跨越式发展》的大会报告,阐述"五五战略"

President Liu Changsheng reporting on the "Five-Five Strategy" at SHU Innovation Work Conference, November 26, 2021

Shanghai University

上海大学战略地图
SHU Strategies Map

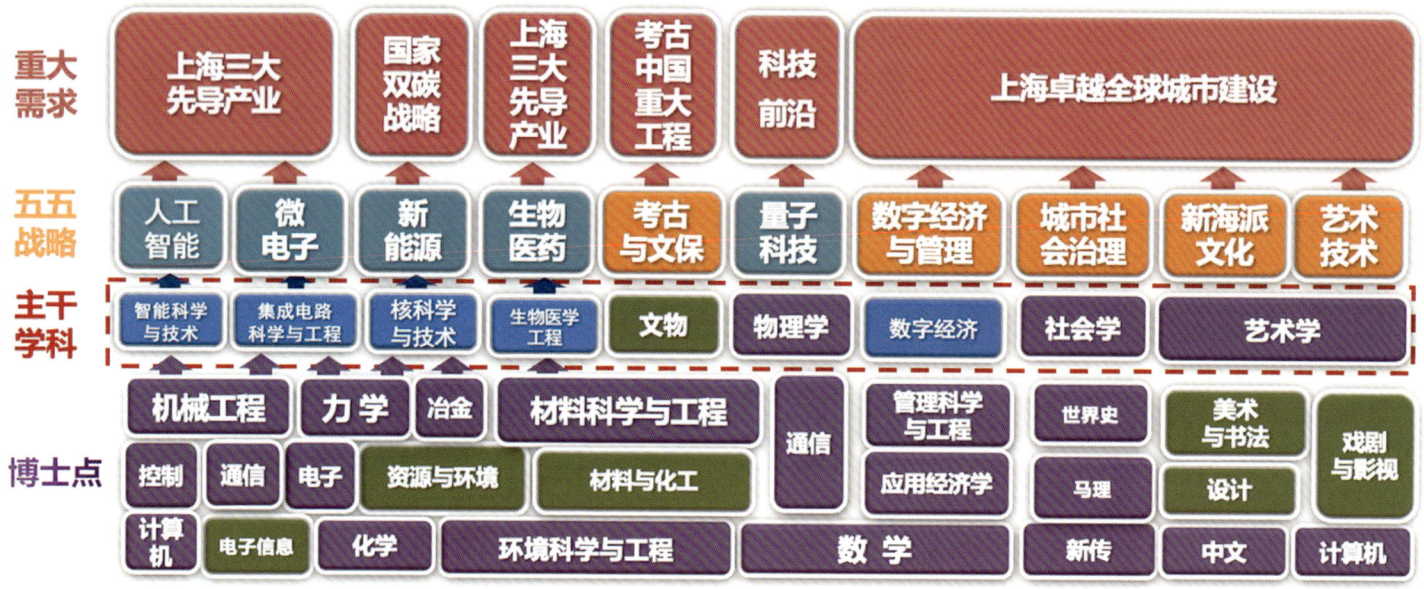

2020年6月6日，成立上海大学医工交叉研究院。上海市副市长陈群（左5）、市政府副秘书长虞丽娟（左6）、市教卫工作党委书记沈炜（左4）等为研究院揭牌
The founding ceremony of the SHU Medical-Engineering Cross Research Institute, June 6, 2020

2020年10月23日,成立上海大学人工智能研究院
The unveiling ceremony of SHU Artificial Intelligence Research Institute, October 23, 2020

2021年12月17日,上海大学与瑞士工程院院长贝努瓦·杜比团队联合组建中瑞先进技术研究院
SHU and the Benoit Dubi team jointly established the Sino Swiss Institute of Advanced Technology, December 17, 2021

2023年7月6日，成立上海大学卓越工程师学院，上海市教卫工作党委二级巡视员李蔚（左）和校党委书记成旦红为学院揭牌
The unveiling ceremony of SHU School of Elite Engineers, July 6, 2023

2024年1月29日，成立上海大学量子科技研究院
The unveiling ceremony of SHU Institute of Quantum Technology, January 29, 2024

2024年4月30日，成立上海大学材料生物学研究所
The SHU Institute of Materials Biology established, April 30, 2024

2024年5月21日，成立上海集成电路行业产教融合就业育人联盟
Employment and Education Alliance of Industry-Education Integration for Shanghai Integrated Circuit Industry established, May 21, 2024

第三部分 自强不息 复兴跨越

2021年,上海大学师生参与三星堆遗址考古发掘和文物保护工作
SHU faculty and students participating in the archaeological excavation and cultural relic protection of the Sanxingdui Ruins Site, 2021

2022年11月12日,成立上海大学海洋考古学研究中心,校党委书记成旦红(右)和校长刘昌胜为中心揭牌
SHU Research Center for Marine Archaeology established, November 12, 2022

2023年11月25日,成立上海大学上海城市更新与可持续发展研究院
Shanghai Institute of Urban Regeneration and Sustainability established, November 25, 2023

上海大学 Shanghai University

2024年10月10日，成立上海电影发展研究院
Shanghai Film Development Research Institute established, October 10, 2024

2024年11月2日，成立上海大学决策研究院
SHU Decision Research Institute established, November 2, 2024

第三部分　自强不息　复兴跨越

2024年6月28日，召开外国语言文学拔尖创新人才培养战略咨询会
The strategic consultation meeting for cultivating outstanding innovative talents in foreign languages and literature, June 28, 2024

2024年11月10日，举办"文理融通：AGI时代的数字人文"学术研讨会暨第六届中国数字人文年会
Conference on "Integration of Arts and Sciences: Digital Humanities in the AGI Era" and the 6th Digital Humanities Annual Meeting, November 10, 2024

十一、人才培养
Talent Cultivation

　　学校坚持社会主义办学方向，秉持"三全育人"（全员育人、全过程育人、全方位育人）理念，围绕立德树人根本任务，着眼于培养德智体美劳全面发展的社会主义建设者和接班人，回答好"培养什么人、怎样培养人、为谁培养人"这一教育的根本问题。

　　SHU steadfastly adheres to the socialist orientation of education, embracing the holistic education philosophy that encompasses education by all staff, throughout the entire process, and in all aspects. With a steadfast focus on the fundamental mission of fostering virtue and nurturing talent, SHU is dedicated to cultivating socialist builders and successors who are well-rounded in moral, intellectual, physical, aesthetic and labor development. This commitment is aimed at addressing the essential questions of education: "What kind of individuals to cultivate, how to cultivate them and for whom to cultivate them."

1997年10月13日，钱伟长校长到理学院指导基础强化班教学工作
President Qian Weichang instructing the Basic Intensive Class of College of Sciences, October 13, 1997

2024年12月9日，召开上海大学教育大会，校长刘昌胜作《锐意改革追卓越　倾心育人谋新篇》主旨报告
President Liu Changsheng addressing SHU Education Conference, December 9, 2024

（一）培养规模　Cultivation Scale

学校设有31个学院和1个MBA教育管理中心，涵盖哲学、经济学、法学、教育学、文学、历史学、理学、工学、医学、管理学、艺术学、交叉学科等学科门类。现有101个本科专业、26个一级学科博士学位授权点及9个自主设置交叉学科博士点、42个一级学科硕士学位授权点（含一级学科博士学位授权点）及1个二级学科硕士学位授权点（一级学科未覆盖），还有7个博士专业学位类别、30个硕士专业学位类别（含博士专业学位类别）、24个博士后科研流动站。另外，学校还建有一个专业涵盖面广、教育机制灵活、教学环境优良的继续教育学院。

SHU comprises 31 colleges and an MBA Education Management Center, offering a broad spectrum of disciplines including philosophy, economics, law, education, literature, history, science, engineering, medicine, management, art and interdisciplinary studies. It currently provides 101 undergraduate programs, 26 first-tier discipline doctoral degree authorization points, 9 independently established interdisciplinary doctoral programs, 42 first-tier discipline master's degree authorization points (which include first-tier discipline doctoral degree authorization points), and 1 second-tier discipline master's degree authorization point (not encompassed by first-tier disciplines). Additionally, SHU offers 7 doctoral degree categories, 30 master's degree categories (including doctoral degree categories), and hosts 24 postdoctoral research stations. Furthermore, the university is home to a continuing education college known for its extensive range of majors, adaptable educational frameworks and superior teaching environment.

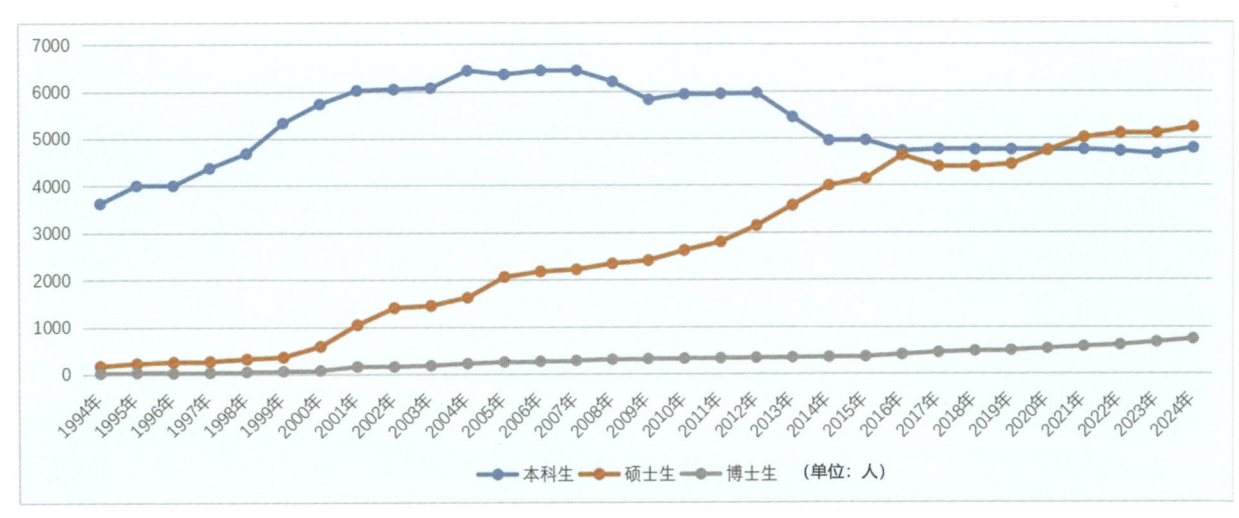

1994—2024年本、硕、博学生招生人数一览

Number of Enrolled Undergraduate, Master's and Doctoral Students (1994-2024)

1994 年学校本、硕、博学生招生人数占比示意图
Proportion of Enrolled Undergraduate, Master's and Doctoral Students in 1994

2024 年学校本、硕、博学生招生人数占比示意图
Proportion of Enrolled Undergraduate, Master's and Doctoral Students in 2024

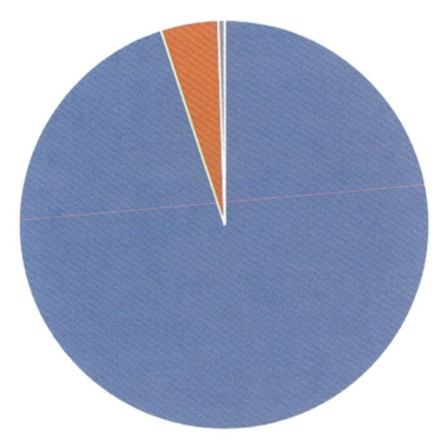

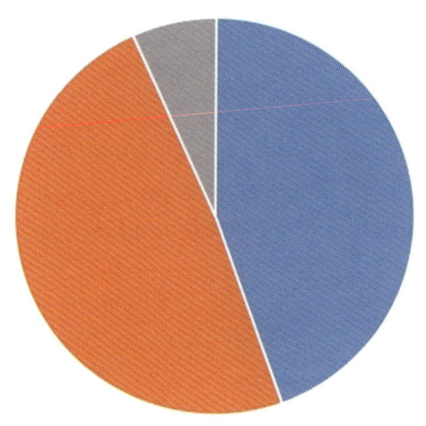

2024 年院系设置一览
Disciplines and Schools in 2024

学科门类	学院
理学	理学院、生命科学学院
工学	通信与信息工程学院、机电工程与自动化学院、材料科学与工程学院、计算机工程与科学学院、环境与化学工程学院、微电子学院、力学与工程科学学院、中欧工程技术学院、里斯本学院
文学、历史学、哲学、法学	马克思主义学院、文学院、新闻传播学院、外国语学院、文化遗产与信息管理学院、法学院、社会学院
经济学、管理学	经济学院、管理学院、悉尼工商学院
艺术学	音乐学院、上海美术学院、上海电影学院、上海温哥华电影学院
医学	医学院
教育学	体育学院
拔尖人才培养	钱伟长学院、未来技术学院
其他	国际教育学院、继续教育学院

2024 年硕士、博士学位授权点一览
Master's and Doctor's Granting Programs in 2024

类　别	名　称
一级学科博士学位授权点	社会学、中国语言文学、中国史、世界史、管理科学与工程、工商管理学、应用经济学、信息资源管理、数学、物理学、化学、土木工程、力学、冶金工程、材料科学与工程、电子科学与技术、信息与通信工程、计算机科学与技术、电气工程、控制科学与工程、机械工程、设计学、艺术学、新闻传播学、外国语言文学、化学工程与技术、环境科学与工程、马克思主义理论
交叉学科博士点	全球学、语言文化与世界文明、新药物与新材料、智能医学诊疗、人工智能、集成电路科学与工程、文物考古科学与技术、城市更新、材料信息学
一级学科硕士学位授权点	社会学、中国语言文学、中国史、世界史、政治学、工商管理学、管理科学与工程、理论经济学、应用经济学、信息资源管理、法学、数学、物理学、化学、土木工程、力学、冶金工程、材料科学与工程、电子科学与技术、信息与通信工程、软件工程、计算机科学与技术、仪器科学与技术、电气工程、控制科学与工程、机械工程、设计学、建筑学、艺术学、新闻传播学、生物学、生物医学工程、外国语言文学、化学工程与技术、核科学与技术、环境科学与工程、哲学、马克思主义理论、中共党史党建学、体育学、药学、集成电路科学与工程
二级学科硕士学位授权点	食品科学
博士专业学位类别	文物、电子信息、材料与化工、美术与书法、设计、戏剧与影视、资源与环境
硕士专业学位类别	社会工作、国际事务、国际中文教育、工程管理、会计、国际商务、数字经济、应用统计、金融、工商管理、博物馆、图书情报、法律、知识产权、土木水利、机械、能源动力、音乐、新闻与传播、生物与医药、翻译、体育、药学、文物、电子信息、材料与化工、美术与书法、设计、戏剧与影视、资源与环境
博士后科研流动站	力学、电子科学与技术、冶金工程、数学、材料科学与工程、信息与通信工程、机械工程、控制科学与工程、社会学、中国语言文学、电气工程、新闻传播学、环境科学与工程、中国史、世界史、物理学、管理科学与工程、美术学、戏剧与影视学、应用经济学、马克思主义理论、计算机科学与技术、化学工程与技术、艺术学

（二）学院与学科建设　College and Discipline Construction

2013年6月2日，成立上海大学音乐学院，第十届全国政协副主席徐匡迪为学院题写院名。图为徐匡迪（左）和教育部原副部长吴启迪为学院揭牌
The Music School of SHU unveiled, June 2, 2013

2015年7月5日，成立上海大学上海电影学院，校党委书记罗宏杰（左1）、院长陈凯歌（左2）、上海市教卫工作党委书记陈克宏（左3）、上海市文化广播影视管理局局长胡劲军共同为学院揭牌
The unveiling ceremony of SHU Shanghai Film Academy, July 5, 2015

第三部分　自强不息　复兴跨越

2016年12月11日，成立上海大学上海美术学院，上海市副市长翁铁慧（左）和院长冯远开启"上海美术学院之门"

The founding ceremony of SHU Shanghai Academy of Fine Arts, December 11, 2016

2018年10月20日，成立上海大学新闻传播学院，上海市委宣传部副部长朱咏雷（右）与校党委书记、校长金东寒为学院揭牌

The founding ceremony of the School of Journalism and Communication, October 20, 2018

2019年9月8日，成立上海大学力学与工程科学学院，校长刘昌胜院士（左2）、杨卫院士（右2）等为学院揭牌

The founding ceremony of the School of Mechanics and Engineering Science, September 8, 2019

2019年11月26日，成立上海大学微电子学院。图为2021年6月6日，上海市委副书记于绍良（首排左3）、副市长陈群（首排左4）、市委副秘书长燕爽（首排左1）、市政府副秘书长黄永平（首排右3）、市教卫工作党委书记沈炜（首排右2）等出席微电子学院第一届理事会聘任仪式
SHU School of Microelectronics established, November 26, 2019

2022年1月10日，成立上海大学文化遗产与信息管理学院，校党委书记成旦红（右3），校长刘昌胜（右4），校党委副书记、纪委书记段勇（右2）出席学院成立仪式
The founding ceremony of the School of Cultural Heritage and Information Management, January 10, 2022

2022年12月30日，成立上海大学未来技术学院。图为副校长汪小帆（中）和学院领导合影
The School of Future Technology established, December 30, 2022

（三）立德树人　Cultivating Talents

2001年8月，校党委副书记、副校长周鸿刚（右）向钱伟长校长汇报学生工作

Zhou Honggang (right), Deputy Secretary of SHU Party Committee and Vice President, reporting on student work to President Qian Weichang, August 2001

2002年5月，校党委副书记成旦红（左2）向钱伟长校长汇报学生工作

Cheng Danhong (second from left), Deputy Secretary of SHU Party Committee, reporting on student work to President Qian Weichang, May 2002

2005年8月4日，校党委副书记俞涛（左1）慰问军训学生

Yu Tao (first from left), Deputy Secretary of SHU Party Committee, talking with students during military training, August 4, 2005

2007年2月11日，校党委副书记滕建勇（左2）关心困难学生家庭

Teng Jianyong (second from left), Deputy Secretary of SHU Party Committee, visiting families of disadvantaged students, February 11, 2007

2013年10月，校党委副书记鲁雄刚（右1）到"挑战杯"（全国大学生科技学术竞赛）决赛现场慰问学生

Lu Xionggang (first from right), Deputy Secretary of SHU Party Committee, visiting the students at the finals of the "Challenge Cup", October 2013

2024年6月25日，校党委副书记、副校长胡大伟（右1）向"全国党建工作样板支部"、全国高校"百个研究生样板党支部"的结对代表赠书

Hu Dawei (first from right), Deputy Secretary of SHU Party Committee and Vice President, presenting books to paired representatives of the "National Model Party Branch" and the "100 Graduate Student Model Party Branches", June 25, 2024

1. 本科生教育教学改革
Reform on Undergraduate Education

2007年1月18日，举行上海大学人才学院第一期开学典礼（左起：校党委副书记滕建勇，校党委书记于信汇，校党委副书记、人才学院院长忻平）
The opening ceremony of the first class of the Talent Institute, January 18, 2007

2007年11月28日，成立上海大学社区学院（2019年学校入选教育部首批10所"一站式"学生社区综合管理模式建设试点高校）。图为常务副校长周哲玮为学院揭牌
SHU Community College unveiled, November 28, 2007

2009年，教育部正式批准上海大学进行自主招生选拔录取改革试点。从2011年起，学校全面推行以大类招生和通识教育培养为突破口的本科教育教学改革。图为2009年3月20日，副校长叶志明（中）主持自主招生新闻发布会
In 2009, the Ministry of Education officially approved SHU to carry out the pilot reform of independent enrollment. Since 2011, SHU has been carrying out the reform on undergraduate education and teaching with general education as the breakthrough point.

2011年10月9日，成立上海大学钱伟长学院（教育部首批17所"国家试点学院"之一，教育部首批"三全育人"综合改革试点院、系之一）。图为上海市教卫工作党委书记李宣海（右）和校党委书记于信汇为学院揭牌

The unveiling ceremony of the QianWeiChang College, attended by Li Xuanhai (right), Secretary of the CPC Committee of Shanghai Municipal Education and Health Work, and Yu Xinhui, Secretary of SHU Party Committee, October 9, 2011

2018年5月26日，副校长聂清（左1）参加2018年招生信息发布会暨本科招生咨询会

Vice President Nie Qing attending the 2018 enrollment information announcement meeting and undergraduate enrollment consultation meeting, May 26, 2018

2020年9月4日，举行上海大学"三全育人"工作推进会暨新学年本科生全程导师聘任仪式

Appointment Ceremony of Comprehensive Mentors for Undergraduates, September 4, 2020

第三部分　自强不息　复兴跨越

2020年10月26—30日，召开上海大学本科教育大会。学校15个单位获教育部首批"国家级一流本科专业建设点"
SHU Undergraduate Education Conference, October 26-30, 2020

2022年9月23日，成立伟长书院等12家书院
Twelve academies established, September 23, 2022

书院与相关学院一览
Academies and Affiliated Colleges

书 院	院 徽	相关学院
伟长书院		钱伟长学院
秋白书院		社会学院、法学院、马克思主义学院
宏嘉书院		通信与信息工程学院、计算机工程与科学学院
青云书院		文学院、外国语学院、文化遗产与信息管理学院
泮池书院		经济学院、管理学院、美术学院、音乐学院
文荟书院		悉尼工商学院
日新书院		生命科学学院、环境与化学工程学院、材料科学与工程学院
闳约书院		上海美术学院、上海电影学院、新闻传播学院
自强书院		机电工程与自动化学院
尚理书院		理学院、力学与工程科学学院
溯微书院		微电子学院
丝路书院		中欧工程技术学院、里斯本学院

2. 研究生教育教学改革
Reform on Postgraduate Education

1995年2月22日，举行上海社会科学院和上海大学联合办学培养研究生协议书签字仪式（右起：常务副校长杨德广、校党委书记吴程里、上海市教委副主任魏润柏、校长钱伟长、上海社会科学院院长张仲礼）
The agreement signing ceremony on joint postgraduate education between Shanghai Academy of Social Sciences and SHU, February 22, 1995

2009年10月12日，成为国家建设高水平大学公派研究生项目签约院校
SHU participating in the signing ceremony of Postgraduate Study Abroad Program for High-Level University Construction funded by China Scholarship Council, October 12, 2009

2003年11月10日，上海大学工商管理（MBA）教育管理中心正式挂牌。2022年1月，上海大学MBA荣获由美国工商管理硕士协会评选的"全球最佳创新战略奖"铜奖
SHU MBA program awarded the Bronze Award for "Best Global Innovation Strategy", January 2022

2013年10月25日，成立上海大学研究生院（右起：副校长吴明红，校长罗宏杰，校党委书记于信汇，副校长叶志明，校长助理、党委组织部部长徐旭）
SHU Graduate School established, October 25, 2013

上海大学
Shanghai University

2020年12月18日，举行上海大学研究生教育大会
SHU Graduate Education Conference, December 18, 2020

研究生三大节：学术节、体育节、艺术节
Annual Academic Festival, Sports Festival and Art Festival of Graduate Students

2019年10月1日，2005届宪法学与行政法学硕士生唐冰（右）少将在庆祝中华人民共和国成立70周年阅兵式上作为女将军领队，这是国庆阅兵首次在徒步方队安排女将军受阅
Major General Tang Bing (right), a 2005 graduate in constitutional and administrative law, one of the first female generals leading a marching unit on foot during the National Day parade marking the PRC's 70th anniversary, October 1, 2019

3. 继续教育
Continuing Education

1995—2024 年成人学历教育招生人数一览
Number of Enrolled Students for Adult Education (1995-2024)

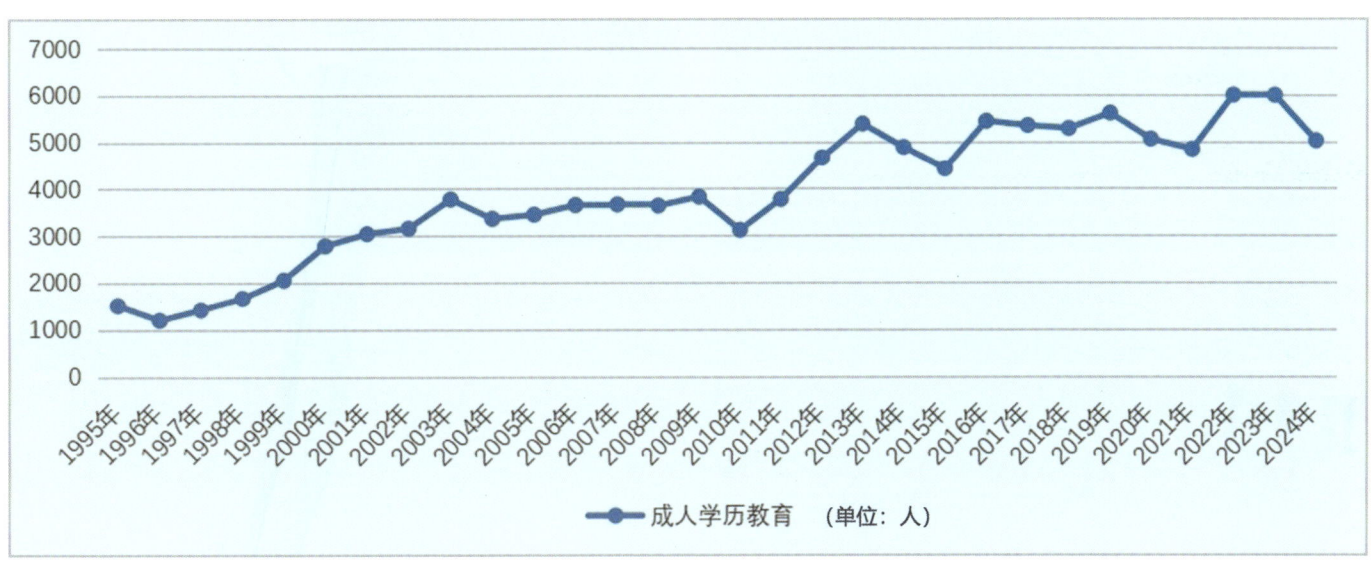

1995—2024 年自学考试毕业人数一览
Number of Graduates from Self-Taught Higher Education Examinations Exams (1995-2024)

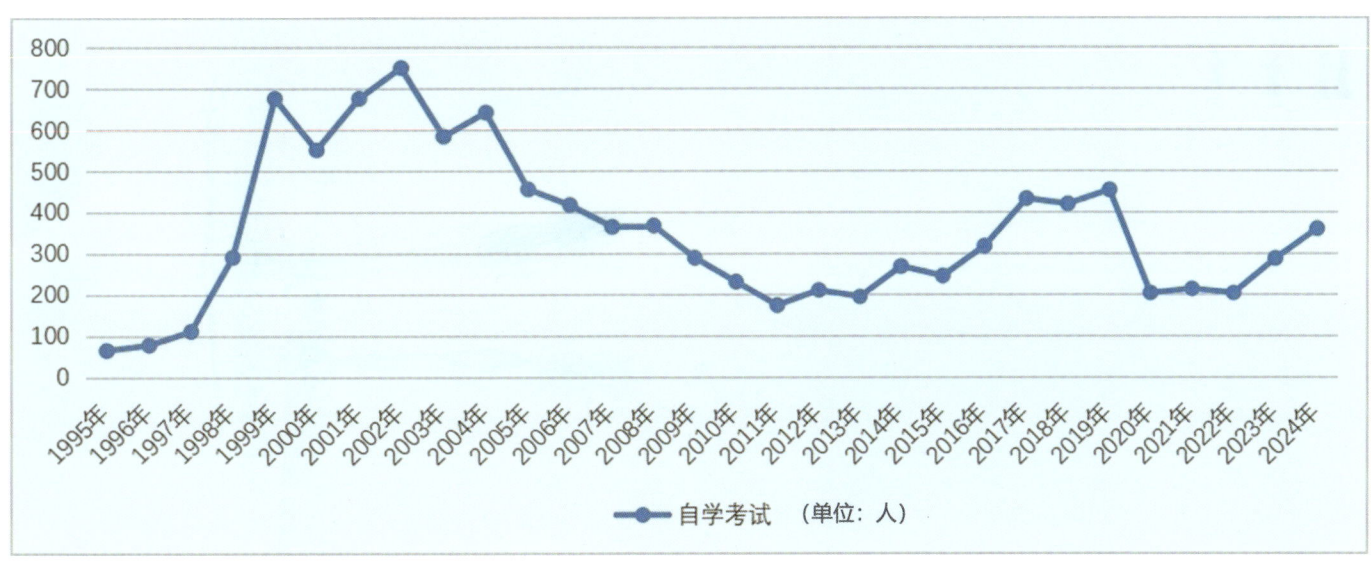

2003年11月24日，钱伟长校长视察成人教育学院，听取学院关于在嘉定安亭上海汽车城和浦东张江上海中芯国际等地增设办学点情况的汇报
President Qian Weichang inspecting the College of Continuing Education, November 24, 2003

2003年6月18日，学校与法国巴黎国际时装艺术学院（MOD'ART International）合作创办上海大学巴黎国际时装艺术学院。这是国内第一个引进奢侈品营销与管理专业的学院，国内第一个在上海创办中法合作的时装设计学院，法国外交部唯一指定的中法文化交流的时尚学院。图为学院举办的学生毕业秀
Students Fashion Show of SHU Paris International Fashion Art Institute established on June 18, 2003

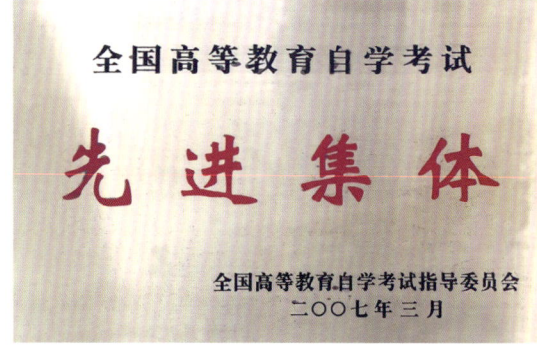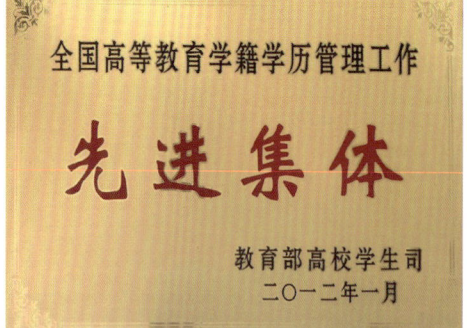

上海大学成人教育学院（2014年5月19日更名为上海大学继续教育学院）2002年、2007年被评为"全国高等教育自学考试先进集体"，2005年被评为"全国成人高等学校招生工作先进集体"，2012年被评为"全国高等教育学籍学历管理工作先进集体"，2019年被评为"全国优秀成人继续教育院校"
The College of Continuing Education SHU, winning the Award of National Outstanding Unit of Self-Taught Examination in 2002 and 2007, the Award of the National Outstanding Unit of Adult Higher Education Enrollment in 2005, and the Award of National Outstanding Unit for the Administration of Higher Education Student Status and Academic Credentials in 2012

（四）创新思政教学　Innovations in Ideological and Political Teaching

2014年12月11日，中宣部副部长王世明（前排左3）到校调研思政教育，在讲堂和学生一起听"大国方略"课
Wang Shiming (third from left), Vice Minister of the Publicity Department of the CPC Central Committee, inspecting the course "What Matters to Rising China?", December 11, 2014

2018年3月26日，创设育才大工科——"人工智能"公开课。图为学校计算机工程与科学学院、社会学院的两位教授正在联袂演讲
The open course of "Artificial Intelligence", March 26, 2018

2019年6月28日，校党委书记成旦红为应届本科毕业生上思想政治课
Cheng Danhong, Secretary of SHU Party Committee, giving a lecture on ideology and politics for the graduates, June 28, 2019

2021年4月27日,校长刘昌胜为学生上"赓续红色基因,传承上大精神"党课

President Liu Changsheng giving a lecture on "Inheriting the Red Spirit", April 27, 2021

2021年5月,"土木工程概论"获评"教育部课程思政示范课程",叶志明教授携团队获评"教育部课程思政教学名师和团队",学校获评"教育部课程思政教学研究示范中心"(全国15家本科院校之一)

SHU awarded the Demonstration Center for Ideological Research & Teaching by the Ministry of Education in May, 2021, together with other honors for "Introduction to Civil Engineering" course and course team

2024年8月30日,马克思主义学院青年教师张青子衿(右3)获第七届全国高校青年教师教学竞赛(思想政治课专项组)一等奖

Zhang Qingzijin (third from right), from the School of Marxism, winning the First Prize in the 7th National Teaching Competition for Young College Teachers (Group for Ideological and Political Courses), August 30, 2024

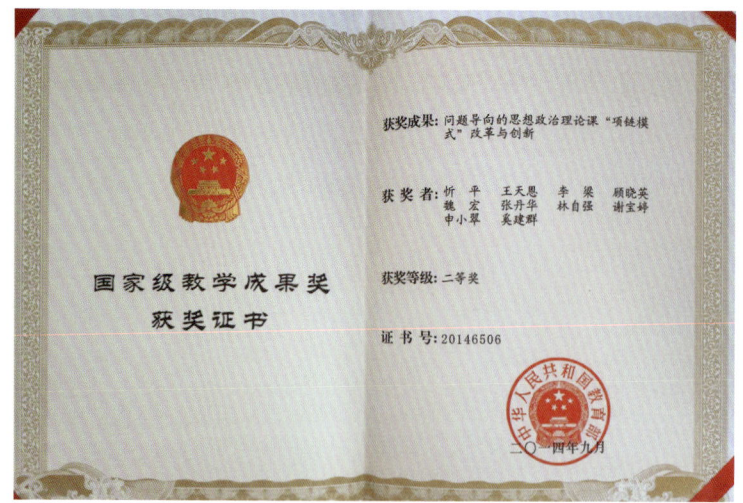

2014年9月,"问题导向的思想政治理论课程'项链模式'改革与创新"获国家级教学成果奖二等奖

"Reform and Innovation of the 'Necklace Mode' of Problem-Oriented Ideological and Political Theory Courses" winning the Second Prize of the National Teaching Achievement Award, September 2014

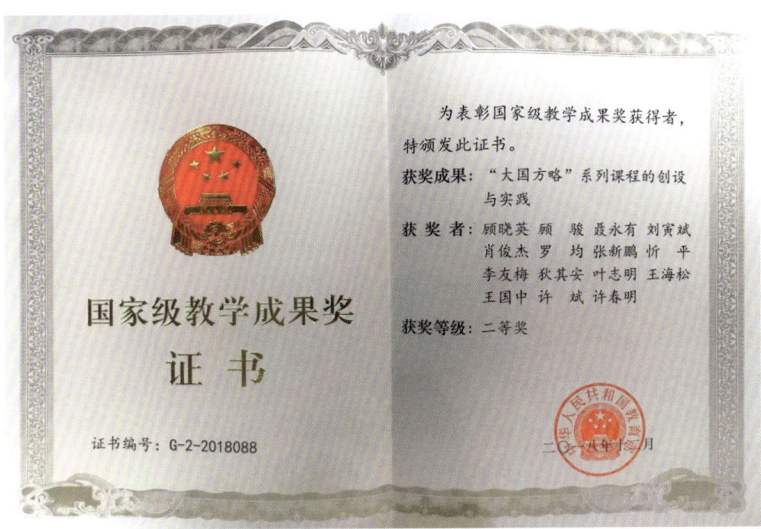

2018年12月,"'大国方略'系列课程的创设与实践"获国家级教学成果奖二等奖

The "What Matters to Rising China?" course series winning the Second Prize of National Teaching Achievement Award, December 2018

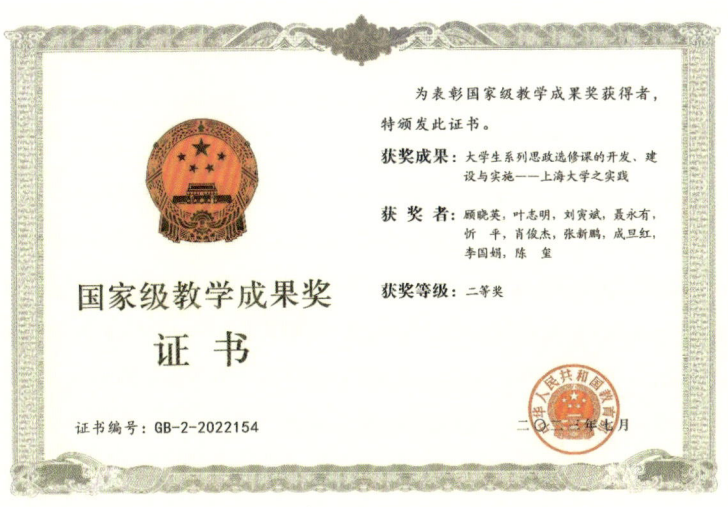

2023年7月,"大学生系列思政选修课的开发、建设与实践——上海大学之实践"获国家级教学成果奖二等奖

"SHU's Practice on Elective Ideological and Political Theory Course Construction" winning the Second Prize of the National Teaching Achievement Award, July 2023

2015年10月,"大国方略教学团队"获中央宣传部办公厅授予的"基层理论宣讲先进集体"称号

The teaching team of "What Matters to Rising China?" awarded "Outstanding Unit of Theory Teaching" by the General Office of the Publicity Department of the CPC Central Committee, October 2015

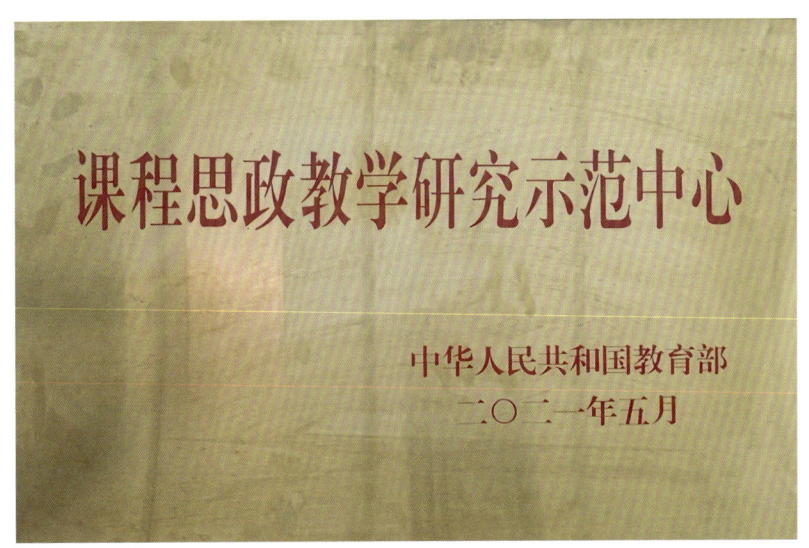

2021年5月,学校获"教育部课程思政教学研究示范中心"铜牌

Plague of Demonstration Center for Ideological Research & Teaching by the Ministry of Education, May 2021

（五）教学奖项　Awards in Teaching

国家级精品课程和一流本科课程一览

National Quality Courses and First-Class Undergraduate Courses

课程名称	课程负责人	获批年度	精品类别
土木工程概论	叶志明	2005	国家级精品课
档案学导论	金　波	2009	
工程力学	陈立群	2010	
商标纠纷矛与盾	陶鑫良	2014	国家精品视频公开课
品味物理	姜　颖	2014	
成为作家	葛红兵	2015	
创新中国	顾　骏 顾晓英	2017	国家精品在线开放课程
土木工程概论	叶志明	2018	
弹性力学	张俊乾	2020	首批国家级一流本科课程
线性代数	王卿文	2020	
心理学基础	许　科	2020	
数字信号处理 B	方　勇	2020	
国学与国学前沿	宁镇疆	2023	第二批国家级一流本科课程
汽车白车身成形制造全流程虚拟仿真实验	王武荣	2023	
经国济民	聂永有	2023	
创业人生	刘寅斌	2023	
运营管理	镇　璐	2023	
中国手语文化	倪　兰	2023	
基因工程原理	王　娇	2023	
金融系统工程	周　建	2023	
管理与组织	吕康娟	2023	
档案学导论	金　波	2023	
西方文论	曾　军	2023	
运动控制系统	汪　飞	2023	
高分子成型和加工	贺　英	2023	

国家级教学团队一览
National Teaching Teams

团队名称	负责人	获批年度
土木工程专业学科基础课程教学团队	叶志明	2008
社会学基础课程教学团队	李友梅	2009

国家奖教材一览
National Excellent Textbooks Awards

教材名称	编著者	奖 项	获奖年度
国际贸易理论与实务	陈 宪　韦金鸾　应诚敏　陈 晨	全国高校优秀教材奖二等奖	2002
土木工程概论 CAI	叶志明　汪德江　宋少沪　徐 旭	全国高校优秀教材奖二等奖	2002
传播学通论	戴元光　金冠军	全国高校优秀教材奖二等奖	2002
液压与气压传动	黄 谊（第三主编、第三单位）	全国高校优秀教材奖二等奖	2002
电力拖动自动控制系统——运动控制系统（第5版）	阮 毅　杨 影　陈伯时	全国教材建设奖高等教育类二等奖	2021
土木工程概论（第5版）	叶志明　姚文娟　汪德江	全国教材建设奖高等教育类二等奖	2021
企业管理概论（第六版）	卢 超　单蒙蒙（副主编、第二单位）	全国教材建设奖高等教育类二等奖	2021

国家级教学成果奖一览
National Teaching Achievements

成果名称	主要完成人	奖项	获奖年度	主要完成单位
入耳入脑入心 同向同行同频：以思政课为核心的课程思政教育教学改革与创新	许宁生　焦　扬　陈锡喜　沙　军　赵宪忠 褚君浩　姜智彬　刘淑慧　顾铮先　曹文泽 李　梁　张黎声　李　江　李国娟　吴　强 桂永浩　顾钰民　宗爱东	一等奖	2018	复旦大学、上海交通大学、上海市教育科学研究院、上海大学 等
土木工程类课程教学改革的研究与实践	叶志明　汪德江　徐　旭　宋少沪　张　凌	二等奖	2001	上海大学
问题导向的思想政治理论课"项链模式"改革与创新	忻　平　王天恩　李　梁　顾晓英　魏　宏 张丹华　林自强　谢宝婷　申小翠　奚建群	二等奖	2014	上海大学
构建基于大数据分析的常态化教育教学质量监控与保障体系	叶志明　宋少沪　辛明军　王光东　陈方泉 叶　红　郭长刚　田蔚文　楚丹琪　于海阳	二等奖	2014	上海大学
对照国际标准，强化工艺能力，培养高水平数控技术人才的创新与实践	鞠鲁粤　张　萍　陆建刚　刘　霞　林成辉 李　斌　姜锡鲁　傅丰伟　陈　觉　刘　涛	二等奖	2014	上海大学
"大国方略"系列课程的创设与实践	顾晓英　顾　骏　聂永有　刘寅斌　肖俊杰 罗　均　张新鹏　忻　平　李友梅　狄其安 叶志明　王海松　王国中　许　斌　许春明	二等奖	2018	上海大学
大学生系列思政选修课的开发、建设与实践——上海大学之实践	顾晓英　叶志明　刘寅斌　聂永有　忻　平 肖俊杰　张新鹏　成旦红　李国娟　陈　玺	二等奖	2023	上海大学
数据赋能：学位论文质量控制体系的构建与实践	汪小帆　田立君　魏峭巍　叶志明　刘文光 陈立群　张建华　张勇安　何小青　张文红 彭　艳　王　刚　盛万成　应时辉	二等奖	2023	上海大学
交叉融合、自主学创——面向冶金创新发展需求的研究生培养体系构建与实践	任忠鸣　王　江　鲁雄刚　董　瀚　邹星礼 邹秀晶　黄　健　尤静林　张捷宇　周　全 张登松　尚兴付　屠挺生	二等奖	2023	上海大学

（六）参加国际国内大学生竞赛　Awards in National and International Competitions

参加"挑战杯"（全国大学生课外学术科技作品竞赛）获奖一览
Awards in the "Challenge Cup"

获奖学院	作品名称	学生负责人	团队成员	指导老师	奖项	获奖年度	届别
材料学院	塑料模具钢表面抛光性能光学评定系统及应用	谢尘	/	汪宏斌	一等奖	2009	第十一届
悉尼工商学院	轨道交通车站施工安全监测与软件分析	包怡龄	包怡龄　赵莉　林璐璐	胡珉	一等奖	2011	第十二届
社会学院	上海市蒙维藏少数民族大学生族群认同研究	张广楚	张广楚　胡安琪　巴依尔　史心怡　姜晟	耿敬　张江华	一等奖	2011	第十二届
理学院	基于柱[5]芳烃和双咪唑盐的准轮烷型分子开关	赵浏	/	李春举	一等奖	2011	第十二届
社会学院	流浪儿童何以"流浪"——对新疆流浪儿童成因与对策研究	阿里木江·于山	周雨薇　章世园　帕提哈西·塔拉甫别克　夏兆强　曹诗婕	耿敬	特等奖	2013	第十三届
理学院	水溶性柱[5]芳烃对碱性氨基酸的选择性键合研究	马俊伟	/	李春举	一等奖	2013	第十三届
美术学院、法学院、文学院、社会学院	让非遗"活"在当下——黔东南地区苗绣艺人生活现况的调查研究	杨子爱	刘璐　闫利　高欣	陈青	一等奖	2015	第十四届
社会学院	从人生炼狱到圆梦天堂——以亚洲最大高考工厂毛坦厂中学为例	孙睿	程子杰　闵兰　徐玲枫　张梦笛	张江华	一等奖	2015	第十四届
通信与信息工程学院	多维视觉卒中后手功能康复定量评估平台	赵泽伟	王聪　陆雅婷　王桥元　张天	陆小锋	特等奖	2017	第十五届
生命科学学院、理学院、钱伟长学院	基于抗结直肠癌活性SGK1抑制剂的结构修饰、合成与活性研究	梁绪春	兰春岭　付文成　安玉　焦冠铭	肖俊杰	特等奖	2017	第十五届
材料科学与工程学院	一组适用于绿色建筑的智能调温调湿材料	窦维维	张志华　李小雨　方雅思　宋炳坷	高彦峰	一等奖	2017	第十五届

续表

学院	项目名称	负责人	成员		指导教师	奖项	年份	届次
悉尼工商学院	基于增强现实的狭窄通道自动巡检与安全诊断系统	周显威	林欣欣 潘惠婷	史礼华	胡珉	一等奖	2017	第十五届
社会学院	当代运河船民社会疏离治理模式研究——以民生为本的"嘉兴模式"	王雅婷	罗 雪 杨易文 汤景逸	陈艳楠 田文强 李金灿	耿 敬	一等奖	2017	第十五届
文学院	百年风华，劳工神圣有关"一战"华工文化记忆的调查研究	徐 嘉	郭艺颖 张若朴 梅其右 邹涵璐	高 昕 刘胤衡 杨智翔	杨位俭	特等奖	2019	第十六届
管理学院	基于供应链金融的"三维信用评价体系"助力中小微企业融资增信——对140家企业和40家金融机构的访谈调研	谢天豪	钱赛楠 闫娅男 杨佩芳 谢 冰	张尊力 李欣怡 艾浩然	储雪俭	特等奖	2019	第十六届
社会学院	公共服务资源供给与社区组织网络构建：以农村睦邻点为例的调查分析	蔡旻雯	文薇薇 严 俨 刘 畅	丁志文 陈 芳 马晓宇	金 桥	一等奖	2019	第十六届
社会学院	民族地区基层医疗服务改革的现状调查	李 鑫	於 阅 郭幕玚 张依芸 朱富强	陈 诚 管倩茹 李文涛	袁 浩 范明林 刘娇蕾	一等奖	2021	第十七届
上海美术学院	助力扶贫攻坚 筑梦红色青春——红色学府、非遗"联璧计划"	刁秋宇	吴柯颖 李可意 周 莹 吕宜峰	王一哲 李 凌 王 斌 谭 意	章莉莉 帅 萍	一等奖	2021	第十七届（红色专项）
新闻传播学院	讲好新四军老战士革命故事 在祖国大地上书写壮丽青春	刘 琦	张 玮 张新宁 王萌萌	汤晓洁 翟玉亭 汤诗韵	王晴川 余江如（客座教授）	一等奖	2021	第十七届（红色专项）
社会学院	"艺"呼百应，旧里焕新：艺术融入城市社区治理的实践探索与分析	周之叶	郑沅芷 罗苏妍 高彧萌 董 霄	张陈怡 曹 辰 赵晨阳	耿 敬 王南溟 李朔严	特等奖	2023	第十八届
未来技术学院	基于集群自我意识与智涌的"海灵"信息采集控制模型	宋子龙	陈 曦 石钊翔 赵晓鸣 吴建军	杜家辉 张嘉朝 惠文博	宋 锐 解杨敏 钟雨轩	特等奖	2023	第十八届（揭榜挂帅专项）
理学院	基于脉冲设计的CD-QAOA	王亚鹏	吴 羽	姚 航	陈 玺	一等奖	2023	第十八届（揭榜挂帅专项）

2013年10月17日，社会学院学生团队的参赛项目"流浪儿童何以"流浪"——对新疆流浪儿童成因与对策研究"获第十三届"挑战杯"全国大学生课外学术科技作品竞赛特等奖（学校首次获"挑战杯"竞赛特等奖）

SHU representative team winning the Grand Prize in the 13th "Challenge Cup" competition for the first time, October 17, 2013

2017年5月21日，机电工程与自动化学院学生课外实践社团"自强队"获2017中国服务机器人大赛仿真组赛冠军

SHU representative team winning the championship in the Simulation Category of the 2017 China Service Robot Contest, May 21, 2017

2017年7月21日，由悉尼工商学院和材料科学与工程学院学生组成的DreamHouse团队在第三届全球重大挑战论坛"学生日"活动（竞赛）中位列中国高校第一、全球第三

SHU representative DreamHouse ranking First among Chinese universities and Third globally during the "Student Day" event (competition) of the Third Global Grand Challenges Summit, July 21, 2017

2017年8月22日，学校研究生团队在第十二届中国研究生电子设计竞赛全国总决赛中获一等奖3个、二等奖2个，上海大学获优秀组织奖

SHU graduates team winning 3 First Prizes and 2 Second Prizes at the National Finals of the 12th China Graduate Electronic Design Contest, and SHU winning Excellent Organization Prize, August 22, 2017

2021年、2022年，学生团队参赛项目"宇树科技——引领全球四足机器人市场化""呼吸之检"分获第七、第八届中国国际"互联网+"大学生创新创业大赛国赛金奖。图为2021年10月15日，获第七届大赛金奖的机电工程与自动化学院学生团队

SHU projects "Unitree Technology—Leading the Global Marketization of Quadruped Robots" and "Breath Detection" winning gold medals at the national finals of the 7th and 8th China International "Internet Plus" College Student Innovation and Entrepreneurship Competitions, respectively, 2021 and 2022

2023年5月10日，计算机工程与科学学院学生团队获第十届ASC世界大学生超级计算机竞赛一等奖

SHU representative team winning the First Prize at the 10th ASC World University Supercomputer Competition, May 10, 2023

2024年11月2日，学校在第十四届"挑战杯"秦创原中国大学生创业计划竞赛决赛中首次夺得金奖，6支参赛学生团队以1金、3银、2铜的优异成绩首次捧得"优胜杯"

SHU winning Gold Prize and the "Winning Cup" for the first time in the 14th "Challenge Cup" QinChuangYuan Platform National College Students' Entrepreneurship Competition, November 2, 2024

（七）体育、文艺人才辈出　Achievements in Sports and Cultural Activities

校男子排球队在第六至第八届全国大学生运动会男子排球项目上实现了"三连冠"；2009年，校男子排球队运动员代表上海队参战，获第十一届全国运动会男子排球比赛冠军

SHU Men's Volleyball Team winning 3 consecutive championships in the National University Games; SHU athletes and other representatives from Shanghai Men's Volleyball Team winning the championship at the 11th National Games in 2009

2011年8月，校网球运动员参加第二十六届世界大学生夏季运动会，获网球项目女子双打亚军

The SHU tennis team, the winner of the Second Prize in tennis doubles in the 26th Summer Universiade, August 2011

工商管理专业本科生宋佳媛获2016年全国田径锦标赛女子铅球亚军、2017年亚洲田径大奖赛女子铅球冠军、2019年亚洲田径锦标赛女子铅球季军、2020年东京奥运会女子铅球比赛第五名、2021年第十四届全国运动会女子铅球比赛亚军，毕业后于2024年获巴黎奥运会女子铅球比赛铜牌

Song Jiayuan, SHU undergraduate majoring in Business Administration, won the silver medal in the women's shot put at the 2016 National Athletics Championships, the gold medal at the 2017 Asian Athletics Grand Prix, the bronze medal at the 2019 Asian Athletics Championships, and finished fifth at the 2020 Tokyo Olympics. In 2021, she secured the silver medal at the 14th National Games. After graduating, she won the bronze medal in the women's shot put at the 2024 Paris Olympics.

2005年7月,学校大学生艺术团获全国第一届大学生艺术展演活动声乐节目普通组一等奖,又在2009年、2015年、2018年、2021年、2024年屡获全国大学生艺术展演活动一等奖

The vocal music program winning the First Prize of the Nonprofessional Group in the First National Art Performances for College Students, July 2005, and another 5 First Prizes in 2009, 2015, 2018 and 2024

2024年9月17日,举行We爱·第八届海峡两岸青年短片大赛颁奖典礼

The 8th Cross Strait Youth Short Film Competition Award Ceremony, September 17, 2024

学生的美术、影视作品获奖一览
Students' Awards in Fine Arts, Film and Television Arts

作品名称	获奖年度	奖项	获奖人员
《云》(玻璃艺术)	2004	第十届全国美术作品展览铜奖	成乡(硕士生)
《群乡蔬谱图》(国画)	2014	第十二届全国美术作品展览"中国美术奖·创作奖"铜奖	陈福彬(博士生)
《上海轨道交通9号线醉白池站设计施工方案》(环境艺术设计)	2014	第十二届全国美术作品展览优秀奖	韩晓骏(硕士生)
《舍利》(电影)	2021	第二十六届釜山国际电影节善才奖(最佳短片奖)特别提及	李明洋(电影制作专业)
《舍利》(电影)	2022	第四十四届法国克莱蒙费朗国际短片电影节国际评审团特别奖	李明洋(电影制作专业)
《喀斯特》(电影)	2024	第八届平遥国际电影展"费穆荣誉·最佳影片"奖	杨穗益(博士生)

（八）毕业典礼　校长寄语　Graduation Ceremonies and Presidents' Addresses

1995 年 6 月，校长钱伟长出席毕业典礼
President Qian Weichang attending the graduation ceremony, June 1995

2012 年 6 月，校长罗宏杰出席毕业典礼
President Luo Hongjie attending the graduation ceremony, June 2012

2016 年 6 月，校长金东寒出席毕业典礼
President Jin Donghan attending the graduation ceremony, June 2016

2020 年 7 月，校长刘昌胜出席毕业典礼
President Liu Changsheng attending the graduation ceremony, July 2020

 上海大学　　Shanghai University

毕业季
The graduation season

十二、科学研究

Scientific Research

学校实施科研强校战略，积极对接国家和上海经济社会发展需求，不断强化顶层设计，完善科研管理体制机制，以创新思维推进科研高地建设，注重科研成果转化及应用，激发科技创新活力，学校科研竞争力和综合实力不断提升。

SHU implements the strategy of scientific research, actively aligning with the national and Shanghai's economic and social development needs. It continuously enhances top-level design, improves the management system and mechanisms for scientific research, and promotes the construction of research highlands with innovative thinking. SHU places emphasis on the transformation and application of research outcomes, stimulates the vitality of technological innovation, and steadily elevates its research competitiveness and comprehensive strength.

2000 年 6 月 2 日，召开上海大学科学研究与技术创新工作会议
Conference on Scientific Research and Technological Innovation at SHU, June 2, 2000

2020 年 11 月 20 日，召开上海大学首届文科大会
The first Conference on Humanities, November 20, 2020

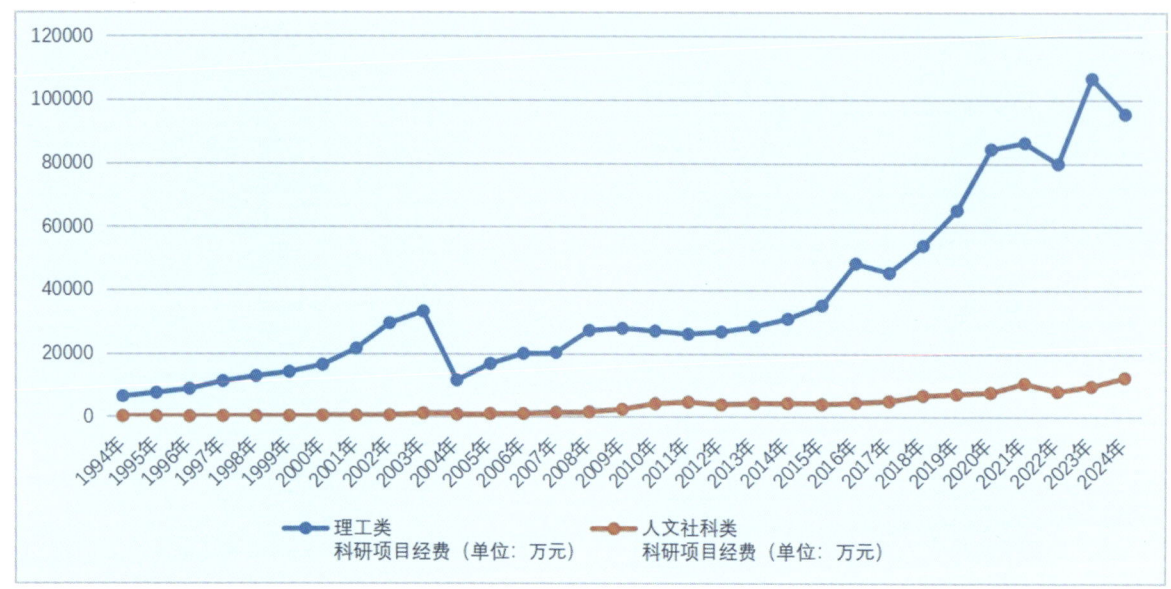

1994—2024 年科研经费一览
Research Funds (1994-2024)

（一）理工科重点研究基地　Key Research Centers in Science and Engineering

理工科重点研究基地一览
Key Research Centers in Science and Engineering

研究基地名称	承担单位	主管部门	获批年度
机电一体中心国家 863 计划智能机器人主题产业化基地	机电工程与自动化学院	国家科委	1999
上海市现代冶金材料制备实验室——省部共建国家实验室培育基地	材料科学与工程学院	国家科委	2003
先进钢铁材料技术国家工程研究中心（共建）、南方实验基地	材料科学与工程学院	国家发展改革委	2004
新型显示技术及应用集成教育部重点实验室	机电工程与自动化学院	教育部	2007
材料复合及先进分散技术教育部工程研究中心	理学院、材料科学与工程学院	教育部	2007
特种光纤与光接入网省部共建教育部重点实验室	通信与信息工程学院	教育部	2007
上海市特种光纤与光接入网重点实验室——省部共建国家重点实验室培育基地	通信与信息工程学院	科技部/上海市科委	2007
TFT-LCD 关键材料及技术国家工程实验室（共建）	机电工程与自动化学院	国家发展改革委	2008
纳米复合功能材料国际科技合作基地	理学院	科技部	2014

续表

创新人才培养示范基地	上海大学	科技部	2015
省部共建高品质特殊钢冶金与制备国家重点实验室	材料科学与工程学院	科技部	2015
特种光纤与先进通讯国际合作联合实验室	通信与信息工程学院	教育部	2016
有机复合污染控制工程教育部重点实验室	环境与化学工程学院	教育部	2018
海洋智能无人系统装备教育部工程研究中心	机电工程与自动化学院	教育部	2018
上海大学高等学校科技成果转化和技术转移基地	上海大学	教育部	2020
硅酸盐质文物保护教育部重点实验室	文化遗产与信息管理学院	教育部	2023
海洋智能无人集群技术与系统教育部重点实验室（B类）	人工智能研究院	教育部	2023
器官修复生物材料与技术国际合作联合实验室	生命科学学院	教育部	2023
转化医学国家科学中心（上海）上海大学分中心	转化医学研究院	国家发展改革委	2023
国家联合应用数学创新中心上大分中心	理学院	科技部	2023
上海市钢铁冶金新技术开发应用重点实验室	材料科学与工程学院	上海市科委	1995
上海市机械自动化及机器人重点实验室（2013年更名为"上海市智能制造及机器人重点实验室"）	机电工程与自动化学院	上海市科委	1997
上海市电站自动化技术重点实验室	机电工程与自动化学院	上海市科委	2004
上海市能源作物育种及应用重点实验室	生命科学学院	上海市科委	2005
上海市能源工程力学重点实验室	力学与工程学院	上海市科委	2007
上海资源环境新材料及应用工程技术研究中心	理学院	上海市科委	2009
上海市新型显示设计制造与系统集成专业技术服务平台	机电工程与自动化学院	上海市科委	2010
上海市先进复合材料设计与制造专业技术服务平台	理学院	上海市科委	2013
上海市高温超导重点实验室	理学院	上海市科委	2014
上海平板显示工程技术研究中心	机电工程与自动化学院	上海市科委	2014
上海材料基因组工程研究院	材料基因组工程研究院	上海市科委	2014
上海电影特效工程技术研究中心	上海电影学院	上海市科委	2016
上海市新能源汽车锂电池材料检测技术服务平台	环境与化学工程学院	上海市科委	2016
科学与工程计算专业技术服务平台	信息化工作办公室	上海市科委	2016
上海智能无人艇系统工程技术研究中心	机电工程与自动化学院	上海市科委	2017
上海市先进光波导智能制造与测试专业技术服务平台	通信与信息工程学院	上海市科委	2020

续表

名称	单位	主管部门	年份
上海金属零部件绿色再制造工程技术研究中心	材料科学与工程学院	上海市科委	2020
上海智能计算系统工程技术研究中心	计算机工程与科学学院	上海市科委	2020
上海多介质环境协同治理工程技术研究中心	环境与化学工程学院	上海市科委	2021
上海器官修复工程技术研究中心	医学院	上海市科委	2021
上海先进陶瓷结构设计与精密制造专业技术服务平台	理学院	上海市科委	2021
上海市高温材料及构件专业技术服务平台	材料科学与工程学院	上海市科委	2022
上海市智能汽车芯片及系统重点实验室（筹）	微电子学院	上海市科委	2022
上海新材料及应用协同创新中心（2012-2020）	理学院	上海市教委	2014
上海市无机质文物考古与保护利用协同创新中心	文化遗产保护基础科学研究院	上海市教委	2021
上海市公共艺术协同创新中心	上海美术学院	上海市教委	2021
上海市海洋人工智能协同创新中心	人工智能研究院	上海市教委	2021
上海市氨氢转化示范及应用协同创新中心	环境与化学工程学院	上海市教委	2021
上海市智能感知芯片技术协同创新中心	微电子学院	上海市教委	2021
上海市力学信息学前沿科学研究基地	力学与工程学院	上海市教委	2022
纺织行业碳纤维增强复合材料重点实验室	材料科学与工程学院	中国纺织工业联合会	2020
上海市智能网联汽车网络安全产业协同创新中心	计算机科学与工程学院	上海市经信委	2021
上海市集成电路与新型显示材料工程研究中心	微电子学院	上海市发展改革委	2022
上海市智能网联汽车网络安全重点实验室（筹）	计算机科学与工程学院	上海市经信委	2023
上海市海洋医学工程融合创新中心	医学院	上海市委军民融合办	2024

第三部分　自强不息　复兴跨越

2003年8月27日,成立"上海市现代冶金与材料制备重点实验室"培育基地,中国工程院院长、党组书记徐匡迪(左7)和上海市副市长严隽琪(发言者)出席揭牌仪式

The unveiling ceremony of the cultivation base of Shanghai Key Laboratory of Modern Metallurgy and Material Preparation, August 27, 2003

2007年3月17日,副校长汪敏(右3)在新型显示技术及应用集成实验室检查工作

Vice President Wang Min (third from right) inspecting Key Laboratory of Advanced Display and System Applications, March 17, 2007

2007年8月7日,举行材料复合及先进分散技术教育部工程研究中心建设论证会

The construction feasibility meeting of Engineering Research Center of Material Composition and Advanced Dispersion Technology under the Ministry of Education, August 7, 2007

2015年5月4日，第十届全国政协副主席徐匡迪（右）和中国工程院原副院长干勇为"省部共建高品质特殊钢冶金与制备国家重点实验室"揭牌

The unveiling ceremony of the State Key Laboratory of Advanced Special Steel (SHU), May 4, 2015

2022年12月8日，举行转化医学国家科学中心（上海）上海大学分中心成立揭牌仪式

The unveiling ceremony of SHU Branch of the National Center for Translational Medicine (Shanghai), December 8, 2022

（二）文科重点研究基地　Key Research Centers in Humanities and Social Sciences

文科重点研究基地一览

Key Research Centers in Humanities and Social Sciences

研究基地名称	承担单位	主管部门	获批年度
国家体育总局体育社会科学重点研究基地	体育学院	国家体育总局	2003
上海大学上海合作组织公共外交研究院	管理学院	外交部	2012
上海研究院	上海大学	中国社会科学院、上海市政府	2015
上海大学文化遗产保护基础科学研究院	文化遗产与信息管理学院	国家文物局、上海市政府	2017
上海大学土耳其研究中心	文学院	教育部	2017
中华古诗文吟诵和创作基地	文学院	教育部	2018
民政部政策理论研究基地	社会学院	民政部	2019
国家语言文字推广基地	文学院	国家语言文字工作委员会	2020
国家文物局中国海外文物研究中心（上海大学）	文化遗产与信息管理学院	国家文物局	2020
国际博物馆协会研究与交流中心	文学院	国际博物馆协会	2020
文化传播创新合作基地·上海中心	文学院	中国外文局	2023
中国共产党第一次全国代表大会纪念馆——上海大学国家革命文物协同研究中心	文化遗产与信息管理学院	教育部	2024
上海高校社会学E-研究院	社会学院	上海市教委	2003
上海大学中国社会转型与社会组织研究中心	社会学院	上海市教委	2007
上海市社会科学创新研究基地、上海发展战略研究所、上海市人民政府决策咨询研究基地领军人物工作室"吴信训工作室"	新闻传播学院	上海市人民政府发展研究中心	2010
全球问题研究院	文学院	上海市教委	2010
中国艺术产业研究院	上海美术学院	中国艺术科技研究所、中国民间文艺家协会	2011
上海会展研究院	新闻传播学院	上海市商务委员会	2011

续表

名称	单位	主管部门	年份
上海市社会科学创新研究基地、上海发展战略研究所、上海市人民政府决策咨询研究基地领军人物工作室"李友梅工作室"	社会学院	上海市人民政府发展研究中心	2013
上海市人民政府发展研究中心——上海大学"文化繁荣与社会发展"决策咨询研究基地	科研管理部人文社科处	上海市人民政府发展研究中心	2013
基层治理创新研究中心	社会学院	上海市教委	2013
上海高校人文社会科学研究基地"中国城市新移民问题研究中心"	社会学院	上海市教委	2014
上海高校人文社会科学研究基地"宗教与全球政治研究院"	文学院	上海市教委	2014
上海市公共艺术协同创新中心	上海美术学院	上海市教委	2014
上海高校人文艺术创新工作室"影视与新媒体创意制作"	上海电影学院	上海市教委	2015
"都市美术资源与公共文化研究"基地	上海美术学院	上海市哲社办	2016
"电影产业与中国故事创新研究"基地	上海电影学院	上海市哲社办	2016
上海电影特效工程技术研究中心	上海电影学院	上海市科委	2016
上海市朝鲜半岛研究会	文学院	上海市社联	2017
上海大学文化新经济研究院	文学院	中国文化新经济开发标准研究委员会	2018
上海红色文化研究院	文学院	上海市委宣传部	2019
上海学校习近平新时代中国特色社会主义思想研究中心	马克思主义学院	上海市教委	2019
上海大学基层治理创新研究中心	社会学院	上海市委宣传部	2020
"中国转型社会学"基地	社会学院	上海市哲社办	2020
上海大学国际禁毒政策研究中心	文学院	国家禁毒委员会办公室	2021
上海新的社会阶层研究中心	社会学院	上海市委统战部	2021
上海科技金融研究中心	经济学院	上海市科委	2022
上海企业创新与高质量发展研究中心	管理学院	上海市科委	2022
上海市人民政府决策咨询研究上海大学研究基地	科研管理部人文社科处	上海市人民政府发展研究中心	2023

第三部分 自强不息 复兴跨越

2013年3月24日，土耳其文化旅游部部长厄马尔·切利克（右2）和校长罗宏杰（右1）为教育部上海大学土耳其研究中心揭牌

The unveiling ceremony of the Center for Turkish Studies at SHU, attended by President Luo Hongjie and Urmar Celik, Minister of Culture and Tourism, Turkey, March 24, 2013

2015年6月5日，由中国社会科学院与上海市人民政府共同创建的新型智库——上海研究院成立，中共上海市委副书记、市长杨雄（后排右2）出席签约仪式，中国社科院副院长李培林（前排左）和上海市副市长翁铁慧签署协议

The unveiling ceremony of Shanghai Academy, a new-type think tank co-founded by the Chinese Academy of Social Sciences and the Shanghai Municipal People's Government, June 5, 2015

2017年4月12日，国家文物局局长刘玉珠（左）、上海市副市长翁铁慧签署战略合作协议；2017年10月19日，举行国家文物局与上海市人民政府共建的上海大学文化遗产保护基础科学研究院揭牌仪式

Liu Yuzhu (left), Director of the National Cultural Heritage Administration, and Weng Tiehui, Vice Mayor of Shanghai, signing an agreement on strategic cooperation, April 12, 2017; the unveiling ceremony of SHU Institute of Cultural Heritage Protection, October 19, 2017

 上海大学　　　　　　　　　　　　　　　　　　　　　　　　　　　　Shanghai University

2018年1月30日，聘请上海市委宣传部原副部长、上海市文化发展基金会理事长陈东（右）担任上海大学海派文化研究中心主任，校党委书记、校长金东寒颁发聘任书

Professor Chen Dong (right), appointed Director of the Center for Shanghai Culture Studies, January 30, 2018

2019年12月25日，成立上海大学新结构经济学研究院，聘请经济学家林毅夫（右2）为名誉院长，校党委书记成旦红、副校长聂清（右3）和林毅夫共同为研究院揭牌

Economist Lin Yifu (second from right), appointed honorary dean of Institute of New Structural Economics, December 25, 2019

2020年12月10日，成立国际博物馆协会研究与交流中心。国家文物局副局长关强（左4）出席成立仪式

The unveiling ceremony of International Museum Association Research and Exchange Center, December 10, 2020

第三部分　自强不息　复兴跨越

2021年5月14日，成立国家文物局中国海外文物研究中心。国家文物局副局长关强（左4），上海市副市长陈通（左3），校党委书记成旦红（左2），校党委副书记、纪委书记段勇（左1）出席成立仪式

The unveiling ceremony of the Research Center for Chinese Cultural Relics Overseas, National Cultural Heritage Administration, May 14, 2021

2022年10月13日，与中共一大纪念馆共建革命文物协同研究中心，市教卫工作党委副书记、市教委主任王平（左6），中共一大纪念馆党委书记、馆长薛峰（左5）出席揭牌仪式。2024年3月14日，该中心正式获批教育部、国家文物局"国家革命文物协同研究中心"

The unveiling ceremony of the Research Center for Revolutionary Cultural Relics co-constructed by SHU and the Memorial Hall of the First National Congress of CPC, October 13, 2022. National Collaborative Research Center for Revolutionary Cultural Relics by the Ministry of Education and National Cultural Heritage Administration established, March 14, 2024

（三）重大科研奖项　Key Awards in Scientific Research

理工科获国家级奖项一览
National Awards in Science and Engineering

科研项目	获奖年度	奖项等级	获奖人员	备注
非线性偏微分方程的差分方法和谱方法及应用	1995	国家自然科学奖　三等奖	郭本瑜	第一单位，第一完成人
三米激光丝杠动态测量仪	1995	国家科技进步奖　三等奖	陈明仪　孙麟治　程维明　刘继发　陆林海	第一单位，第一完成人
几种典型低温化学热处理渗层抗咬合、抗疲劳特性研究	1995	国家科技进步奖　三等奖	余忠荪 等	第四单位，第五完成人
金属间化合物的环境脆性研究	1997	国家自然科学奖　四等奖	万晓景　朱家红　经开良　张丙　金诚	第一单位，第一完成人
数字化制造关键技术研究及其在上海的工程应用	2003	国家科技进步奖　二等奖	陈云 等	第二单位
珠江三角洲环境中毒害有机污染物研究	2006	国家自然科学奖　二等奖	傅家谟　吴明红 等	第二单位，第一完成人
低维纳米功能材料与器件原理的物理力学研究	2012	国家自然科学奖　二等奖	张田忠 等	第二单位，第三完成人
碳/碳复合材料工艺技术装备及应用	2012	国家科技进步奖　二等奖	孙晋良　任慕苏　张家宝　李红　潘剑峰　陈来　周春节　沈建荣　凌宝民　杨敏	第一单位，第一完成人
军用先进核动力堆用锆合金关键基础研究	2012	国家科技进步奖　二等奖	周邦新　姚美意 等	第二单位，第一完成人
数字视频编解码技术国家标准AVS与产业化应用	2012	国家科技进步奖　二等奖	王国中　张爱东 等	第五单位
复杂岛礁水域无人自主测量关键技术及装备	2016	国家技术发明奖　二等奖	谢少荣　罗均　彭艳　蒲华燕 等	第一单位，第一完成人
高速运动刚柔相互作用系统非线性建模与振动分析	2017	国家自然科学奖　二等奖	陈立群　丁虎 等	第二单位，第二完成人
脉冲磁致振荡连铸方坯凝固均质化技术	2017	国家技术发明奖　二等奖	翟启杰　龚永勇　李仁兴　仲红刚　徐智帅 等	第一单位，第一完成人
石墨烯微结构调控及其表界面效应研究	2018	国家自然科学奖　二等奖	吴明红　潘登余　曹傲能　涂育松　王海芳	第一单位，第一完成人
海气界面环境弱目标特性高灵敏度微波探测关键技术及装备	2018	国家科技进步奖　二等奖	陈雪　杨毅　刘媛媛 等	第一单位，第三完成人

续表

基于M3组织调控的钢铁材料基础理论研究与高性能钢技术	2018	国家技术发明奖 二等奖	董 瀚 等	第一完成人
考古现场脆弱性文物临时固型提取及其保护技术	2019	国家科技进步奖 二等奖	罗宏杰 黄 晓 等	第三单位，第一完成人
复杂振动的宽域近零超稳抑制技术与装备	2019	国家技术发明奖 二等奖	蒲华燕 等	第二单位，第二完成人
海洋窄带环境复杂目标探测识别技术与装备	2020	国家科技进步奖 二等奖	罗 均　彭 艳 彭进霖　李常伟 陈 钧　沈礼权 张 泉　申万秋 邓红勇　张 丹	第一单位，第一完成人
京津冀地下水污染防治关键技术与应用	2023	国家技术发明奖 一等奖	吴明红 等	第三单位，第四完成人
土的统一硬化本构理论	2023	国家自然科学奖 二等奖	孙德安 等	第二单位，第二完成人

郭本瑜教授的"非线性偏微分方程的差分方法和谱方法及应用"项目获1995年度国家自然科学奖三等奖

Professor Guo Benyu winning the Third Prize of the State Natural Science Award in 1995

陈明仪教授领衔的"三米激光丝杠动态测量仪"项目获1995年度国家科技进步奖三等奖

Professor Chen Mingyi's team winning the Third Prize of the State Scientific and Technological Progress Award in 1995

余忠荪教授（右）参与完成的"几种典型低温化学热处理渗层抗咬合、抗疲劳特性研究"项目获1995年度国家科技进步奖三等奖

Professor Yu Zhongsun (right), together with other team members, winning the Third Prize of the State Scientific and Technological Progress Award in 1995

上海大学　　Shanghai University

万晓景教授（右1）领衔的"金属间化合物的环境脆性研究"项目获1997年度国家自然科学奖四等奖
Professor Wan Xiaojing's team (first from right) winning the Fourth Prize of the State Natural Science Award in 1997

傅家谟院士领衔的"珠江三角洲环境中毒害有机污染物研究"项目获2006年度国家自然科学奖二等奖
Academician Fu Jiamo's team winning the Second Prize of the State Natural Science Award in 2006

张田忠教授参与的"低维纳米功能材料与器件原理的物理力学研究"项目获2012年度国家自然科学奖二等奖
Professor Zhang Tianzhong, together with other team members, winning the Second Prize of the State Natural Science Award in 2012

孙晋良院士（左）领衔的"碳/碳复合材料工艺技术装备及应用"项目获2012年度国家科技进步奖二等奖；周邦新院士领衔的"军用先进核动力堆用锆合金关键基础研究"项目获2012年度国家科技进步奖二等奖
Academician Sun Jinliang's (left) team and Academician Zhou Bangxin's team winning the State Scientific and Technological Progress Award in 2012

第三部分　自强不息　复兴跨越

王国中教授参与的"数字视频编解码技术国家标准 AVS 与产业化应用"项目获 2012 年度国家科技进步奖二等奖

Professor Wang Guozhong, together with other team members, winning the Second Prize of the State Scientific and Technological Progress Award in 2012

谢少荣（左 2）教授领衔的"复杂岛礁水域无人自主测量关键技术及装备"项目获 2016 年度国家技术发明奖二等奖

Professor Xie Shaorong's (second from left) team winning the Second Prize of the State Technological Invention Award in 2016

陈立群教授（左）、丁虎教授参与的"高速运动刚柔相互作用系统非线性建模与振动分析"项目获 2017 年度国家自然科学奖二等奖

Professor Chen Liqun (left), Professor Ding Hu, together with other team members, winning the Second Prize of the State Natural Science Award in 2017

翟启杰教授（中）领衔的"脉冲磁致振荡连铸方坯凝固均质化技术"项目获 2017 年度国家技术发明奖二等奖

Professor Zhai Qijie's (center) team winning the Second Prize of the State Technological Invention Award in 2017

吴明红教授领衔的"石墨烯微结构调控及其表界面效应研究"项目获 2018 年度国家自然科学奖二等奖、"京津冀地下水污染防治关键技术与应用"项目获 2023 年度国家技术发明奖一等奖

Professor Wu Minghong's team winning the Second Prize of the State Natural Science Award in 2018 and the First Prize of the State Technological Invention Award in 2023

陈雪教授（中）参与的"海气界面环境弱目标特性高灵敏度微波探测关键技术及装备"项目获 2018 年度国家科技进步奖二等奖

Professor Chen Xue (center), together with other team members, winning the Second Prize of the State Scientific and Technological Progress Award in 2018

董瀚教授领衔的"基于 M3 组织调控的钢铁材料基础理论研究与高性能钢技术"项目获 2018 年度国家技术发明奖二等奖

Professor Dong Han's team winning the Second Prize of the State Technological Invention Award in 2018

罗宏杰教授（中）领衔的"考古现场脆弱性文物临时固型提取及其保护技术"项目获 2019 年度国家科技进步奖二等奖

Professor Luo Hongjie's team winning the Second Prize of the State Technological Invention Award in 2019

第三部分 自强不息 复兴跨越

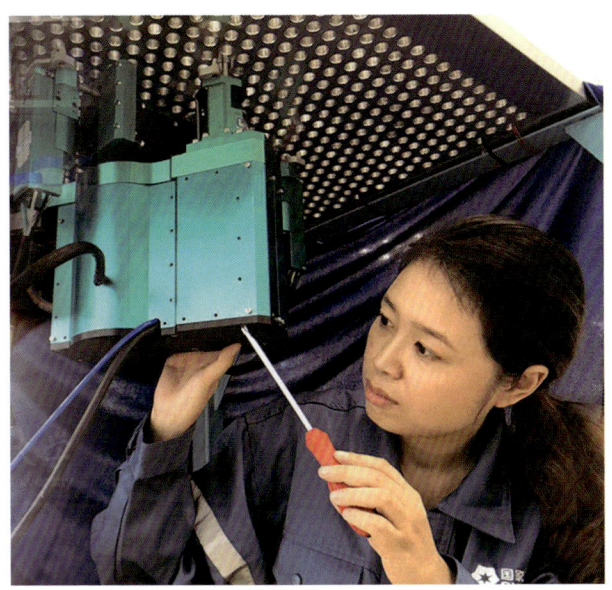

蒲华燕教授参与的"复杂振动的宽域近零超稳抑制技术与装置"项目获 2019 年度国家技术发明奖二等奖

Professor Pu Huayan, together with other team members, winning the Second Prize of the State Technological Invention Award in 2019

罗均教授（中）领衔的"海洋窄带环境复杂目标探测识别技术与装备"项目获 2020 年度国家科技进步奖二等奖

Professor Luo Jun's team winning the Second Prize of the State Scientific and Technological Progress Award in 2020

孙德安教授领衔的"土的统一硬化本构理论"项目获 2023 年度国家自然科学奖二等奖

Professor Sun De'an's team winning the Second Prize of the State Natural Science Award in 2023

教育部高等学校科学研究优秀成果奖（人文社会科学）获奖一览
Outstanding Achievement Awards for Scientific Research in Institutions of Higher Education (Humanities and Social Sciences)

项目类别	获奖项目名称	获奖年度	奖项	主要获奖人员
著作	中国社会总资金流量和结构监控	2002	三等奖	陈湛匀
	民众评价论	2006	三等奖	陈新汉
	我国流域跨界水污染纠纷协调机制研究：以淮河流域为例	2009	三等奖	赵来军
	权威评价论	2009	三等奖	陈新汉
	中国传播思想史（共四卷）	2009	三等奖	金冠军　戴元光
	当代西方传媒制度	2009	三等奖	郑涵　金冠军
	性别、语境与书写的政治	2015	二等奖	董丽敏
	春秋文学系年辑证（全四册）	2015	二等奖	邵炳军　甄洪永　刘挺颂　梁奇　王志芳　郝建杰　黄刚
	电影论——对电影学的总体思考（上、下册）	2015	三等奖	蓝凡
	新时期加强社会组织建设研究	2020	一等奖	李友梅
	数字档案馆生态系统研究	2020	一等奖	金波
	元末明初大转变时期东南文坛格局及文学走向研究	2020	二等奖	饶龙隼
	《永乐大典》小学书辑佚与研究	2020	二等奖	丁治民
	科学与政治之间：美国医学会与毒品管制源起（1847—1973）	2020	二等奖	张勇安
	古代埃及象形文字文献译注（上、中、下卷）	2020	二等奖	郭丹彤
	事实与价值——休谟问题及其解决尝试（修订本）	2020	二等奖	孙伟平
	十七世纪欧洲与晚明地图交流	2020	二等奖	郭亮
	集装箱港口运作管理优化问题研究	2020	二等奖	镇璐
	儒家的如何是好	2020	青年奖	朱承
	城市白领新移民研究	2020	三等奖	张文宏
	巴赫金对当代西方文学理论的影响研究	2024	二等奖	曾军
	大国发展道路：经验和理论	2024	二等奖	欧阳峣
	李白诗歌全集英译	2024	三等奖	赵彦春
	艺术与真理	2024	三等奖	刘旭光

续表

	论文标题	年份	奖项	作者
论文	中国的利率管制与利率市场化	2006	三等奖	王国松
	从财富分配到风险分配：中国社会结构重组的一种新路径	2012	三等奖	李友梅
	城市新移民社会融合的结构、现状与影响因素分析	2012	三等奖	张文宏
	传教士中医观的变迁	2012	三等奖	陶飞亚
	当代中国社会建设的公共性困境及其超越	2015	二等奖	李友梅 肖瑛 黄晓春
	文化资本与社会地位获得——基于上海市的实证研究	2015	二等奖	仇立平 肖日葵
	西方文论对中国经验的阐释及其相关问题	2020	二等奖	曾军
	从"国家与社会"到"制度与生活"：中国社会变迁研究的视角转换	2020	二等奖	肖瑛
	当代中国社会组织的制度环境与发展	2020	青年奖	黄晓春
	泛娱乐时代的影游产业互动融合	2020	三等奖	聂伟
	当代中国社会治理转型的经验逻辑	2024	二等奖	李友梅
	从档案管理走向档案治理	2024	二等奖	金波
	"家"作为方法：中国社会理论的一种尝试	2024	二等奖	肖瑛
	以毒品为武器：美国对华冷战宣传的新媒介（1950—1962）	2024	三等奖	张勇安
	融合生态、价值共创与深度赋能——未来媒体发展的核心逻辑	2024	三等奖	严三九
	Green Technology Adoption for Fleet Deployment in a Shipping Network	2024	三等奖	镇璐

李友梅教授等所著的《新时期加强社会组织建设研究》2020年获第八届高等学校科学研究优秀成果奖（人文社会科学）一等奖

Professor Li Youmei, one of the authors of *A Study on Strengthening the Construction of Social Organizations in the New Era*, winning the First Prize of the 2020 Outstanding Achievement Award for Scientific Research in Institutions of Higher Education (Humanities and Social Sciences)

李友梅教授等所著的《新时期加强社会组织建设研究》

A Study on Strengthening the Construction of Social Organizations in the New Era, by Professor Li Youmei, et al.

金波教授等所著的《数字档案馆生态系统研究》2020年获第八届高等学校科学研究优秀成果奖（人文社会科学）一等奖

Professor Jin Bo, one of the authors of *Ecosystem of Digital Archives*, winning the First Prize of the 2020 Outstanding Achievement Award for Scientific Research in Institutions of Higher Education (Humanities and Social Sciences)

金波教授等所著的《数字档案馆生态系统研究》

Ecosystem of Digital Archives, by Professor Jin Bo, et al.

美术作品与研究成果参加全国美术作品展览获奖一览

Awards for Artworks and Research Achievements in National Art Exhibitions

作品名称	获奖年度	奖　项	获奖人员
《静物系列——花》（油画）	1994	第八届全国美术作品展览优秀作品奖	黄阿忠
《畅想浦江》（油画）	1999	第九届全国美术作品展览银奖	邱瑞敏
《南京路下沉广场方案》（环境艺术设计）	2004	第十届全国美术作品展览金奖	秦一峰 岑沫石
《在另一个季节》（水墨画）	2004	第十届全国美术作品展览银奖	丁蓓莉
《上海地铁8号线设计方案》（环境艺术设计）	2004	第十届全国美术作品展览银奖	朱　宏 赵睿翔
《中国早期油画史》（著作）	2009	第一届"中国美术奖·理论评论奖"	李　超
《欢乐颂》（织绣）	2014	第十二届全国美术作品展览"中国美术奖·创作奖"铜奖	王　秦
《品鉴与经营——明末清初徽商艺术赞助研究》（著作）	2014	第二届"中国美术奖·理论评论奖"三等奖	张长虹

第三部分　自强不息　复兴跨越

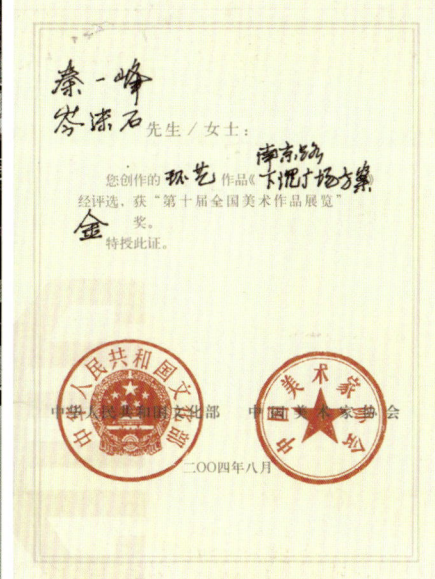

2004年8月，美术学院教师秦一峰、岑沫石的作品《南京路下沉广场方案》获"第十届全国美术作品展览"金奖
"Sinking Square Plan for Nanjing Road", by Qin Yifeng and Cen Moshi from Shanghai Academy of Fine Arts, winning the Gold Award of the "Tenth National Fine Arts Exhibition", August 2004

2004年12月，美术学院教师丁蓓莉的作品《在另一个季节》获"第十届全国美术作品展览"银奖
"In a Different Season", by Ding Beili from Shanghai Academy of Fine Arts, winning the Silver Award of the "Tenth National Fine Arts Exhibition", December 2004

2009年，美术学院教师李超所著的《中国早期油画史》获第一届"中国美术奖·理论评论奖"
A History of Early Period Oil Painting in China, by Professor Li Chao from Shanghai Academy of Fine Arts, winning the First "Theoretical Review Award of Chinese Fine Arts", 2009

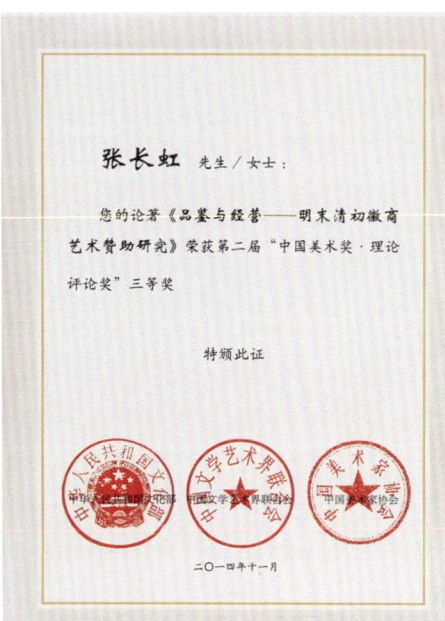

2014年11月，美术学院教师张长虹所著的《品鉴与经营——明末清初徽商艺术赞助研究》获第二届"中国美术奖·理论评论奖"三等奖

Appreciation and Management, by Professor Zhang Changhong from Shanghai Academy of Fine Arts, winning the Third Prize of the Second Theoretical Review Award of Chinese Fine Arts, 2014

2014年12月，美术学院教师王秦创作的《欢乐颂》在"第十二届全国美术作品展览"中获"中国美术奖·创作奖"铜奖

"Ode to Joy", by Wang Qin from Shanghai Academy of Fine Arts, winning the Bronze Prize of Creation Award of Chinese Fine Arts in the 12th National Fine Arts Exhibition, December 2014

影视作品获奖一览
Awards for Film and Television Products

作品名称	获奖年度	奖 项	获奖人员
《大闹天宫》（3D版）（动漫）	2012	第三十二届夏威夷国际电影节"最佳美术指导奖"，第八届中国国际动漫节"金猴奖"评选"中国动画电影优胜奖"	陈志宏
《山河故人》（电影）	2016	第十届亚洲电影大奖"最佳编剧奖"	贾樟柯
《犟驴小红军》（动漫）	2018	中国文化艺术政府奖第三届动漫奖"最佳动漫作品奖"	陈志宏
《妖猫传》（电影）	2018	第十二届亚洲电影大奖"最佳美术指导"	屠 楠 陆 苇
	2019	第三十二届中国电影金鸡奖"最佳美术提名"	
《江湖儿女》（电影）	2019	第十三届亚洲电影大奖"最佳编剧奖"，第十届中国电影导演协会"年度导演奖"	贾樟柯
《短梦记》（科幻短片）	2022	入选第七十八届威尼斯国际电影节展映	舒浩伦
《长津湖》（电影）	2022	第十八届中国电影华表奖"优秀故事片奖""优秀导演奖"	陈凯歌
《我和我的祖国》（电影）	2022	第十九届中国电影华表奖"优秀故事片奖""优秀导演奖"	
《志愿军：雄兵出击》（电影）	2024	第三十七届中国电影金鸡奖"最佳导演奖"	陆 苇
	2024	第三十七届中国电影金鸡奖"最佳美术提名"	

上海大学　　　　　　　　　　　　　　　　　　　　　　　　Shanghai University

2012年，电影学院教师陈志宏创作的《大闹天宫》（3D版）获第三十二届夏威夷国际电影节"最佳美术指导奖"、第八届中国国际动漫节"金猴奖"评选"中国动画电影优胜奖"

The Monkey King 3D: Uproar in Heaven, directed by Chen Zhihong, a teacher of Shanghai Film Academy, winning Outstanding Achievement in Animation at the Hawaii International Film Festival and The "Merit Award of 'Golden Monkey King Award' China Animated Feature" of the Eighth Chinese International Animation Festival, 2012

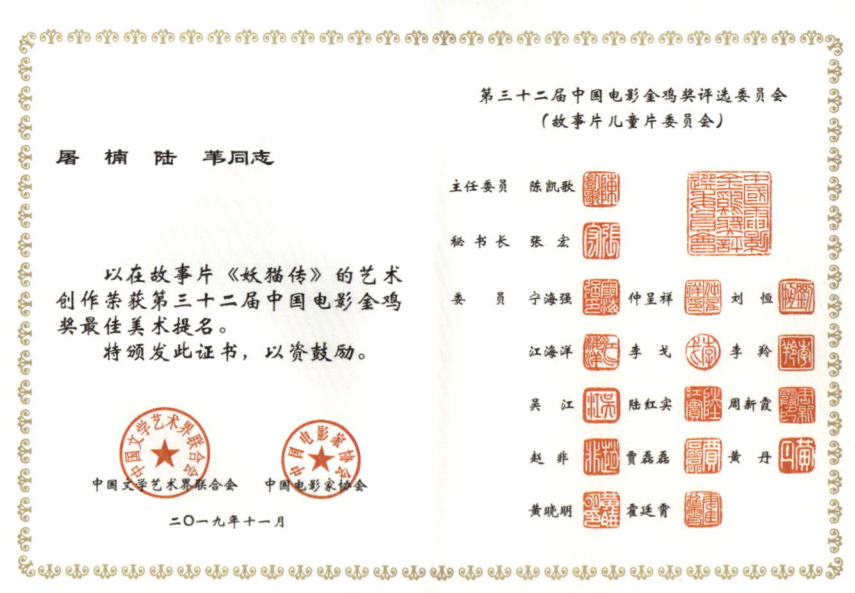

电影学院教师屠楠、陆苇创作的《妖猫传》获第十二届亚洲电影大奖"最佳美术指导"、第三十二届中国电影金鸡奖"最佳美术提名"

The movie Legend of the Demon Cat, with Tu Nan and Lu Wei as the design artists from Shanghai Film Academy, winning the "Best Production Design" prize at the 12th Asian Film Awards, and the "Best Art Direction" nomination prize at the 32nd China Golden Rooster Awards

（四）重大科研成果
Key Scientific Research Achievements

1. "自强 2000" 集群式高性能计算机系统
Ziqiang 2000 Cluster High Performance Computing System

由计算机工程与科学学院院长李三立院士领衔、于 2000 年研发成功的第一代集群式高性能计算机系统——"自强 2000"，是我国最早采用大规模并行集群式技术研制高性能计算系统的先例之一，是当时国内民口单位研制的峰值速度最高的高性能超级计算机。研究成果获 2001 年上海市科技进步一等奖。

The first-generation cluster-based high-performance computing system, Ziqiang 2000, was successfully developed in 2000 under the leadership of Academician Li Sanli. The achievement won the First Prize of the Shanghai Technological Invention Award in 2001.

2000 年 12 月 27 日，中共上海市委副书记、市长徐匡迪院士（前排左 2）到校视察，听取李三立院士（前排左 1）汇报"自强 2000"研究成果

Academician Xu Kuangdi (second from left in the front row) briefed on the Ziqiang 2000 research achievements by Academician Li Sanli (first from left in the front row) during his visit to SHU, December 27, 2000

2. 碳／碳复合材料工艺技术装备及应用
Carbon-Carbon Composites: Process Technology, Equipment and Applications

孙晋良院士是我国著名的产业用纺织材料及复合材料专家，由他领衔的上海大学复合材料研究中心是我国碳基复合材料及其预制体研制的重要基地，依靠自主研发形成了系列碳基复合材料关键技术，长期为我国多种固体火箭发动机配套关键材料，包括应用于神舟八号、神舟九号、神舟十号、神舟十一号、神舟十二号发射任务以及长征十一号固体运载火箭 1000 公里以上太阳同步轨道发射任务，为我国航天事业作出了重要贡献。研究成果获 2012 年国家科学技术进步奖二等奖。

Led by Academician Sun Jinliang, the SHU Composite Materials Research Center has made significant contributions to the development and application of carbon-carbon composites.

孙晋良院士在实验室
Academician Sun Jinliang in the laboratory

"碳／碳复合材料工艺技术装备及应用"项目获 2012 年国家科学技术进步奖二等奖证书
The certificate for the Second Prize of the State Scientific and Technological Progress Award, 2012

3. 堆用锆合金关键基础研究
Key Fundamental Research on Zirconium Alloys for Reactor Applications

周邦新院士是我国著名的核材料和核燃料元件领域的科学家和学科带头人之一，长期从事核材料的研发工作，由他领衔的上海大学核材料科研团队研发出多种耐腐蚀性能优良的锆合金，为我国核用锆合金国产化、自主化及核动力事业的发展作出了重要贡献。研究成果获 2011 年国防科学技术进步奖一等奖、2012 年国家科学技术进步奖二等奖。

Led by Academician Zhou Bangxin, the SHU nuclear material research team developed a range of zirconium alloys with exceptional corrosion resistance. These alloys have made significant contributions to the domestication and independent development of nuclear-grade zirconium alloys, as well as advancing nuclear power technologies in China.

周邦新院士在实验室
Academician Zhou Bangxin working in the laboratory

"军用先进核动力堆用锆合金关键基础研究"项目获 2012 年国家科学技术进步奖二等奖证书
The team winning the Second Prize of the State Scientific and Technological Progress Award, 2012

4. 创建材料信息学理论体系
The establishment of the theoretical framework of materials informatics

张统一院士是我国著名的材料科学、工程科学和固体力学专家，是推动国内材料基因组计划、材料信息学和机械信息学发展的重要学者。2014 年创设上海大学材料基因组工程研究院，2016 年申请获得国内首个以材料基因组工程为理念的"材料设计科学与工程"专业，在国内率先开设了"材料力学信息学"课程，依托钱伟长学院开展本科专业教育，以培养力学与材料科学相融合、专业知识学习和人工智能技术相融合的前沿交叉学科创新人才。

Academician Zhang Tongyi plays a pivotal role in advancing materials informatics, mechanical informatics and the materials genome initiative. Through his interdisciplinary approach, the "Materials Design Science and Engineering" program established by him fosters the development of innovative talent by combining expertise in materials science with cutting-edge AI techniques.

张统一院士为钱伟长学院师生讲授材料力学信息学
Academician Zhang Tongyi lecturing on Materials Mechanics Informatics to the faculty and students of QianWeichang College

5. 叶轮机械气动热力学变分原理和有限元法
The Variational Principle and Finite Element Method for Aerodynamic Thermodynamics of Turbomachinery

刘高联院士是我国工程热物理学家、流体力学家，长期从事叶轮机气动理论和流体力学的教学与研究工作，建立了以变分理论为骨干的新理论体系。他提出了流体力学变分原理的建立和变换的系统性途径，首次建立了叶轮机三维流动正命题、反命题及杂交命题的变分原理及广义变分原理族。同最优控制论结合，创立了三维叶栅和流道的优化设计理论，发展了可自动捕获各种未知界面的变域变分理论和广义有限元法。

Academician Liu Gaolian makes significant contributions to turbomachinery aerodynamics and fluid mechanics. He established a novel theoretical framework centered on variational principles, proposing systematic methods for their formulation and transformation in fluid mechanics. Liu is the first to develop variational principles and a family of generalized variational principles for three-dimensional flow, inverse and hybrid problems in turbomachinery.

刘高联院士在上海市应用数学和力学研究所资料室
Academician Liu Gaolian reading in the library of Shanghai Institute of Applied Mathematics and Mechanics

刘高联的《叶轮机械气动热力学变分原理和有限元法》手稿（部分）
Manuscript by Academician Liu Gaolian titled "The Variational Principle and Finite Element Method for Aerodynamic Thermodynamics of Turbomachinery" (partial)

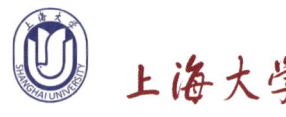

6. 自固化磷酸钙人工骨
Self-setting Calcium Phosphate Bone Cement

刘昌胜院士为我国著名生物材料学家，长期从事生物材料的基础与应用研究，所研制的自固化磷酸钙人工骨获产品注册证并已在临床上获得广泛应用。已申请发明专利 66 项，其中授权发明专利 40 项（美国授权专利 4 项）；发表 SCI 收录论文 260 余篇，包括生物材料领域著名期刊 *Biomaterials* 的 25 篇；出版中、英文专著（教材）4 种。

Academician Liu Changsheng has long been dedicated to fundamental and applied research in biomaterials. He developed a self-setting calcium phosphate bone cement, a groundbreaking biomaterial that has obtained product certification and is widely used in clinical applications. His work has led to the filing of 66 invention patents, with 40 granted, including 4 in the United States. He has published over 260 SCI-indexed papers, 25 of which appeared in the prominent journal *Biomaterials*. Additionally, he has authored 4 monographs and textbooks in both Chinese and English.

刘昌胜院士在实验室
Academician Liu Changsheng working in the laboratory

刘昌胜等著《纳米生物材料》
Nanobiomaterials by Liu Changsheng, et al.

7. 石墨烯微结构调控及其表界面效应研究
Iron Sieving in Graphene Oxide Membranes via Cationic Control of Interlayer Spacing

吴明红院士领衔的研究团队聚焦"石墨烯微结构的精准调控及其应用"并取得开创性研究成果，首次实现石墨烯单晶量子点和单层石墨烯微结构的精准控制，在国际顶级期刊 Nature 及其子刊上发表十余篇系列论文。相关研究成果获 2018 年国家自然科学奖二等奖。研究团队还依托有机复合污染控制工程教育部重点实验室，推动功能材料的基础科研成果向应用转化，在环境治理、绿色能源、生物医药等领域取得了重要应用性突破。

Academician Wu Minghong's research team has achieved pioneering results in the precise regulation of graphene microstructures and their applications. They are the first to control graphene single-crystal quantum dots and single layer graphene microstructures precisely, leading to over ten publications in top-tier journals such as Nature and its sub-journals. Her team has achieved significant breakthroughs in environmental remediation, green energy and biomedicine.

"石墨烯微结构调控及其表界面应用研究"项目获 2018 年国家自然科学奖二等奖证书
The certificate for the Second Prize of the State Natural Science Award, 2018

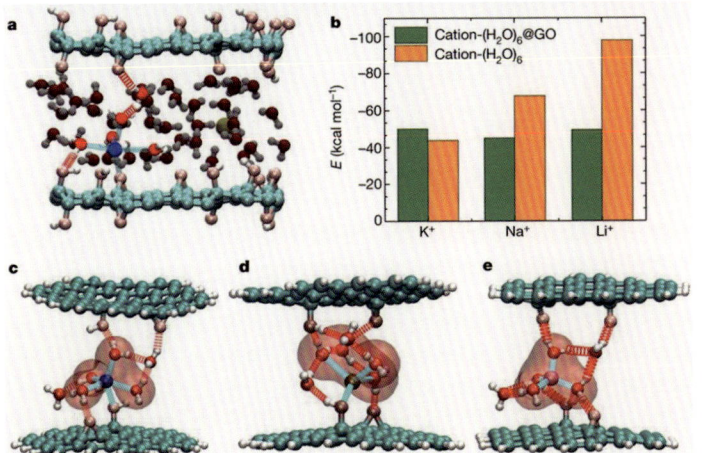

2017 年 10 月 9 日，石墨烯研究领域成果以"Ion Sieving in Graphene Oxide Membranes via Cationic Control of Interlayer Spacing"为题在 Nature 上以上海大学为第一单位发表，实现学校作为第一单位在顶尖科技期刊发文零的突破
SHU's first publication as the primary institution in Nature, with the article titled "Ion Sieving in Graphene Oxide Membranes via Cationic Control of Interlayer Spacing", October 9, 2017

Shanghai University

8. "精海"系列无人艇
Jinghai Series Unmanned Surface Vehicles (USV)

2013年以来，无人艇工程研究院研发的"精海"系列无人艇实现了多个海洋探索及关键领域应用，研究成果接连获得2016年国家技术发明奖二等奖、2018年国家科技进步奖二等奖、2019年国家技术发明奖二等奖、2020年国家科技进步奖二等奖，在该领域创下7项全国第一，包括我国第一艘在南海、第一艘在南极、第一艘在东海作业的无人艇等，为助力海洋强国战略贡献了"上大担当"。

Since 2013, the Jinghai series of USVs, developed by the USV Engineering Research Institute, have achieved significant milestones in ocean exploration and other key applications. The research outcomes have been recognized with multiple national awards. Notably, the Jinghai USVs accomplished seven national firsts, such as being China's first USVs to operate in the South China Sea, the Antarctic and the East China Sea. These achievements have significantly contributed to China's maritime power strategy, exemplifying SHU's commitment to national advancement.

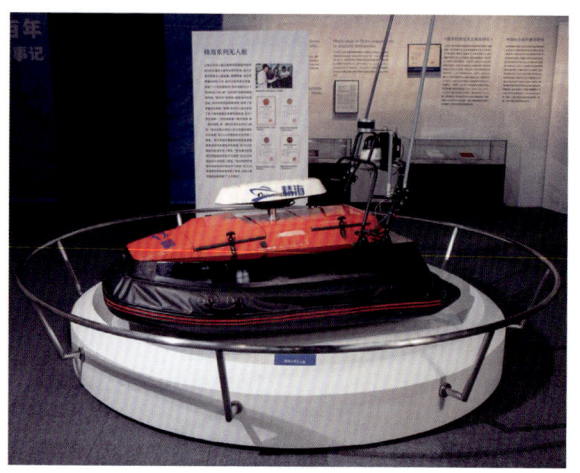

"精海"14号无人艇
The USV "Jinghai XIV"

"无人艇教师团队"的研究项目获国家级重大科研成果奖的证书
The certificates awarded to the "USV Teacher Team" for nationally recognized scientific achievements

2018年1月，"无人艇教师团队"获"全国高校黄大年式教师团队"称号的荣誉证书
The certificate of "National Huang Danian-Style Teacher Team in Higher Education Institutions" by the Ministry of Education, January 2018

9. 脉冲磁致振荡凝固均质化原创技术
The Original Technology of Pulsed Magneto-Oscillation (PMO) for Solidification Homogenization

翟启杰教授领衔的先进凝固技术中心，发明了脉冲磁致振荡凝固均质化原创技术，研究成果获 2017 年国家技术发明奖二等奖，并成功应用于苏钢、中天钢铁和新兴铸管等多家企业，为解决铸坯均匀性这一制约国际冶金界产品质量的瓶颈问题作出了原创性贡献。

Professor Zhai Qijie, leading the Advanced Solidification Technology Center, pioneered the original technology of PMO for Solidification Homogenization. This innovation was recognized with the Second Prize of the State Technological Invention Award in 2017. The PMO technology has been successfully implemented in several major enterprises, addressing the long-standing challenge of billet uniformity in the international metallurgical industry.

"脉冲磁致振荡连铸方坯凝固均质化技术"项目获 2017 年国家技术发明奖二等奖证书
The certificate for the Second Prize of the State Technological Invention Award, 2017

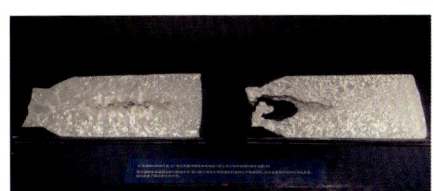

正常凝固的铝硅合金（左）与应用脉冲磁致振荡凝固均质化原创技术凝固的铝硅合金（右）（应用脉冲磁致振荡凝固均质化技术，可以有效改善铸坯成分均匀性）
Aluminum-silicon alloy solidified under conventional conditions (left) compared to aluminum-silicon alloy solidified using the original PMO Solidification Homogenization technology (right). Applying PMO technology can effectively improve the compositional uniformity of casting billets.

10. 基于 M3 组织调控的钢铁材料基础理论研究与高性能钢技术
Fundamental Theoretical Research and High-Performance Steel Technology Under M3 Microstructure Control

董瀚教授领衔的"基于 M3 组织调控的钢铁材料基础理论研究与高性能钢技术"项目获 2018 年国家技术发明奖二等奖，该项目针对钢铁材料强度与塑韧性倒置的难题，首次提出"多相（Multiphase）、亚稳（Metastable）和多尺度（Multiscale）" M3 组织和性能调控理论，解决了钢铁材料强度与塑韧性倒置问题，发明了高强度高塑性第三代汽车钢技术、低成本高性能温成形技术、高强高塑低合金钢技术、高强高韧低合金钢技术，实现量大面广的汽车钢和低合金钢塑韧性大幅度提高，使我国钢铁材料基础研究从跟跑变成领跑。

Professor Dong Han's team introduced the M3 (Multiphase, Metastable and Multiscale) microstructure and property control theoryto overcome the traditional strength-toughness trade-off in steel materials. The innovations have significantly enhanced the toughness and ductility of commonly used automotive and low-alloy steels, elevating China's steel material research to a leading position globally.

"基于 M3 组织调控的钢铁材料基础理论研究与高性能钢技术"项目获 2018 年国家技术发明奖二等奖证书
The certificate for the Second Prize of the State Technological Invention Award, 2018

Shanghai University

11. 考古现场脆弱性文物临时固型提取及其保护技术
Technology of Temporary Consolidation for Fragile Cultural Relics during Archaeological Excavation

罗宏杰教授领衔的研究团队所开展的考古现场脆弱性文物临时固型提取及其保护技术，具有广泛的应用领域。该项技术结合预加固及雾化加固的工艺，能成功实现极脆弱文物的临时固型提取。研究成果获2019年国家科学技术进步奖二等奖。

Professor Luo Hongjie's team has developed a groundbreaking technology for the temporary consolidation and protection of fragile cultural relics during archaeological excavations. The team's work was recognized with the Second Prize of the State Scientific and Technological Progress Award in 2019.

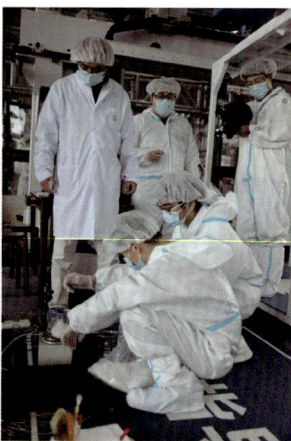
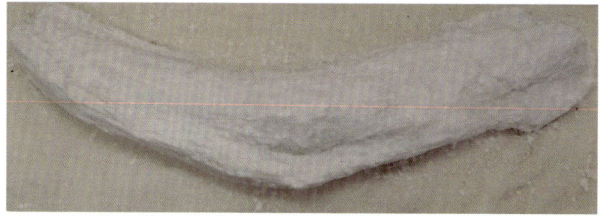

该技术应用在三星堆遗址祭祀坑发掘现场提取象牙
This technology has been applied at the Sanxingdui site to extract ivory from sacrificial pits

12. 高分辨半导体显示制造关键技术
Key Technologies for High-Resolution Semiconductor Display Manufacturing

新型显示技术及应用集成教育部重点实验室成立于2007年，是上海市属高校第一个教育部重点实验室。在实验室主任张建华教授的带领下，在柔性显示关键材料和面向新冠肺炎快速安全诊断的DR影像系统医用平板探测器关键技术研发方面取得了重大突破。

Under the leadership of Professor Zhang Jianhua, the Key Laboratory of Advanced Display and System Applications of SHU has achieved significant breakthroughs in key materials for flexible displays and in developing critical technologies for medical flat panel detectors in DR imaging systems, aiming at rapid and safe diagnosis of pneumonia. Established in 2007, this laboratory is the first key laboratory of the Ministry of Education among Shanghai's municipal universities.

DR 影像系统医用平板探测器
A medical flat panel detector for DR imaging systems

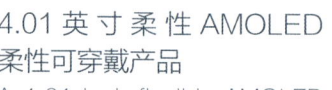

4.01英寸柔性AMOLED柔性可穿戴产品
A 4.01-inch flexible AMOLED wearable device

13. 在国际刊物 CNS 发表研究成果
Papers Published in *Cell*, *Nature* and *Science*

在国际刊物 CNS 发表研究成果一览
Papers Published in *Cell*, *Nature* and *Science*

发表时间	作　者	论文标题	刊物名称
2017 年 10 月	吴明红	Ion Sieving in Graphene Oxide Membranes via Cationic Control of Interlayer Spacing	*Nature*
2018 年 3 月	Mark Waller（马克·沃勒）	Planning Chemical Syntheses with Deep Neural Networks and Symbolic AI	*Nature*
2018 年 8 月	曹世勋	Observation of Dicke Cooperativity in Magnetic Interactions	*Science*
2021 年 8 月	钟云波	Hierarchical Crack Buffering Triples Ductility in Eutectic Herringbone High-entropy Alloys	*Science*
2023 年 3 月	陈亮	Cysteine Carboxyethylation Generates Neoantigens to Induce HLA-Restricted Autoimmunity	*Science*
2023 年 8 月	杨绪勇	Tautomeric Mixture Coordination Enables Efficient Lead-Free Perovskite LEDs	*Nature*
2024 年 6 月	杨绪勇	Fabrication of Red-Emitting Perovskite LEDs by Stabilizing Their Octahedral Structure	*Nature*
2024 年 8 月	卞月珉	Viral DNA Polymerase Structures Reveal Mechanisms of Antiviral Drug Resistance	*Cell*

Shanghai University

（五）优秀学术期刊　Excellent Academic Journals

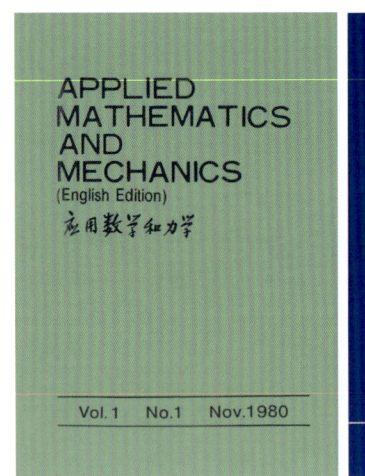 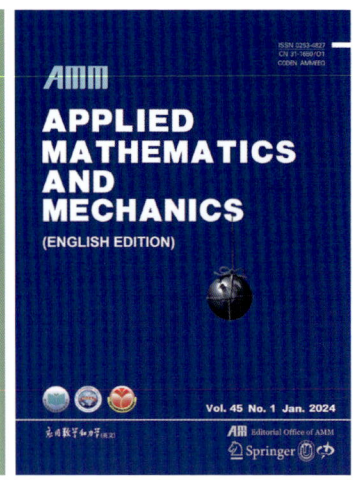 

《应用数学和力学（英文）》（*Applied Mathematics and Mechanics（English Edition）*）创办于 1980 年，创刊人为钱伟长院士，现任主编是郭兴明教授，是国内最早被 SCI 和 EI 收录的应用数学和力学类期刊，曾获第五届"中国出版政府奖"（提名奖）、连续十三届荣获"中国最具国际影响力学术期刊"，入选中国科技期刊卓越行动计划一期（重点）、二期（领军）项目

Applied Mathematics and Mechanics (English Edition), founded by Academician Qian Weichang in 1980 and currently led by Professor Guo Xingming, is one of China's earliest SCI- and EI-indexed journals in applied mathematics and mechanics. It has won the "Nomination Award for China Government Prize for Publishing", listed among the "Most Influential International Academic Journals in China" for thirteen consecutive sessions, and selected into both Phase I (Key) and Phase II (Leading) of the China STEM Journal Excellence Action Plan

《社会》创刊于 1981 年，现任主编是李友梅教授，曾获第二届"中国出版政府奖"（提名奖）、第三届"中国出版政府奖""中国最具国际影响力学术期刊""中国百强报刊"，国家哲学社会科学基金资助期刊、教育部高校哲学社会科学名刊工程入选期刊

Chinese Journal of Sociology, founded in 1981 and currently led by Professor Li Youmei, has been nominated for the Second and Third China Publishing Government Award and listed among the "Academic Journals with the Highest International Impact in China" and "Top 100 Newspapers and Journals". The journal is supported by the National Fund for Philosophy and Social Sciences of China and selected into the Project for Promoting Leading Journals in Philosophy and Social Sciences by the Ministry of Education

《中国运筹学会会刊（英文）》（*Journal of the Operations Research Society of China*）的现任主编是袁亚湘院士，曾获中国科技期刊国际影响力提升计划一期 D 类项目、二期 C 类项目，高质量期刊分级目录跨学科应用数学类 T1 期刊

Journal of the Operations Research Society of China, currently led by Academician Yuan Yaxiang, selected into the Project for Enhancing International Impact of China STM Journals (Phase I, Class D; Phase II, Class C), the first-class journal in High-Quality STM Journals Grading Directory on Interdisciplinary Applied Mathematics approved by China Association for Science and Technology

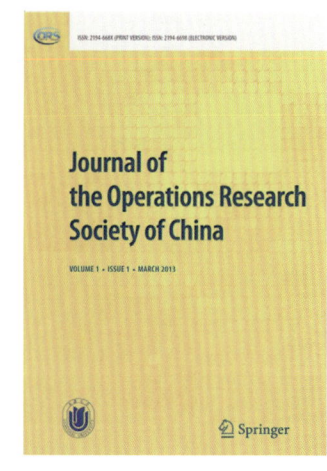

《先进制造进展（英文）》（*Advances in Manufacturing*）的创刊主编是罗宏杰教授，现任主编是张建华教授，曾获"中国最具国际影响力学术期刊"

Advances in Manufacturing, founded by Professor Luo Hongjie, currently led by Professor Zhang Jianhua, listed among the "Academic Journals with the Highest International Impact in China"

《电化学能源评论（英文）》（*Electrochemical Energy Reviews*）的创刊主编和现任主编是张久俊院士和孙学良院士，曾获中国科技期刊国际影响力提升计划D类项目、"中国最具国际影响力学术期刊"

Electrochemical Energy Reviews, founded and currently led by Academician Zhang Jiujun and Sun Xueliang, selected into the Project for Enhancing International Impact of China STM Journals (Class D) and listed among the "Academic Journals with the Highest International Impact in China"

重要数据库收录期刊
Journals Indexed in Major Databases

类　别	期刊名称
SCI	《电化学能源评论（英文）》《应用数学和力学（英文）》《先进制造进展（英文）》
SSCI	《中国社会学评论》
ESCI	《应用数学与计算数学学报（英文）》《中国运筹学会会刊（英文）》《社会（英文）》
EI	《电化学能源评论（英文）》《应用数学和力学（英文）》《先进制造进展（英文）》《应用数学与计算数学学报（英文）》《中国运筹学会会刊（英文）》
PubMed	《生物材料转化电子杂志（英文）》
Scopus	《电化学能源评论（英文）》《应用数学和力学（英文）》《先进制造进展（英文）》《应用数学与计算数学学报（英文）》《中国运筹学会会刊（英文）》《生物材料转化电子杂志（英文）》《应用科学学报》《中国社会学评论》《社会（英文）》
CSCD	《先进制造进展（英文）》《应用数学和力学（英文）》《电化学能源评论（英文）》《中国运筹学会会刊（英文）》《上海大学学报（自然科学版）》《应用科学学报》《运筹学学报（中英文）》
CSSCI	《社会》《上海大学学报（社会科学版）》
北大核心	《社会》《上海大学学报（社会科学版）》《上海大学学报（自然科学版）》《应用科学学报》《运筹学学报（中英文）》

十三、社会服务
Social Services

学校在人才培养、科学研究、中华优秀传统文化传承等方面服务于国家科技发展战略，服务于我国"一带一路"倡议，服务于上海地区建设。

SHU contributes to the national science and technology development strategy, the Belt and Road Initiative, and the development of the Shanghai region through talent cultivation, scientific research and the preservation of outstanding traditional Chinese culture.

（一）科技园区　Science and Technology Parks

2001年5月14日，成立产学研结合的国家级上海大学科技园区"四通纳米港"。中国科学院纳米项目首席科学家张立德（左1），上海大学党委书记、常务副校长方明伦（右1）出席揭牌仪式

The unveiling ceremony of national-level SHU Science and Technology Park, Sitong Nanotechnology Port, May 14, 2001

2003年7月23日，上海大学科技园区通过国家科技部和教育部的验收，认定为国家级大学科技园

The SHU Science and Technology Park passing the acceptance inspection by the Ministry of Science and Technology and the Ministry of Education, July 23, 2003

2020年6月22日，举行环上大科技园揭牌，上海大学与宝山区携手打造示范性创新创业集聚区

The unveiling ceremony of SHU Rim Science and Technology Park, June 22, 2020

（二）产学研融合　Integration of Industry, Academia and Research

2001年7月28日，举行中国航天机电集团与上海大学、复旦大学、上海交通大学联合研究中心签约仪式（左2起：上海大学副校长王奇，上海大学原党委书记吴程里，上海市副市长周慕尧，中国航天机电集团公司副总经理殷兴良，上海市科委副主任丁薛祥，复旦大学党委书记秦绍德，上海大学党委书记、常务副校长方明伦）

The signing ceremony of the Joint Research Center between China Aerospace Science and Industry Corporation (CASIC) and SHU, Fudan University and Shanghai Jiao Tong University, July 28, 2001

2015年6月16日，学校承办"中国非遗传承人群研培计划"试点工作现场协调会议；2017年11月16日，召开"2017年中国非遗传承人群培计划经验交流会"及作品交流展，集中呈现全国78所研培高校的教学成果和工作经验，文化部副部长项兆伦（右2）、文化部非遗司司长陈通（右3）出席

The coordination meeting of the pilot work of Research and Training Program for Talents of Chinese Intangible Cultural Heritage at SHU, June 16, 2015; the Art Exhibition and the Experience Exchange Meeting of Talents Training for Intangible Cultural Heritage at SHU, November 16, 2017, attended by Xiang Zhaolun, Vice Minister of Culture (second from right), and Chen Tong, Director of the Intangible Cultural Heritage Department of Ministry of Culture (third from right)

第三部分　自强不息　复兴跨越

2023年12月21日，上海大学"精海"无人艇研制团队的两位教师携"极测1号""极测2号"无人艇出征南极科考，校长刘昌胜（中）为他们授旗送行
Two members from the SHU Jinghai USV team departing for Antarctica with two USVs for a scientific expedition, December 21, 2023

2024年7月26日，学校与宝山区人民政府、杭州宇树科技签署战略合作协议，共同建设通用智能机器人产业制高点（前排左起：校友、宇树科技CEO王兴兴，宝山区区委常委、副区长王鼐，副校长张建华；后排左起：宝山区区委书记李晨昊，校党委书记成旦红）
The signing ceremony of the strategic cooperation agreement among SHU, Baoshan District People's Government and Hangzhou Unitree Technology, July 26, 2024

2024年11月20日，举行人形机器人联合创新中心签约及揭牌仪式，校长刘昌胜（后排右2）、副校长张建华（前排右）出席
The signing and unveiling ceremony of the Humanoid Robot Joint Innovation Center, November 20, 2024

2025年2月17日，中共中央总书记、国家主席、中央军委主席习近平在北京出席民营企业座谈会，校友王兴兴作为民营企业负责人代表参会并发言
On February 17, 2025, Xi Jinping, General Secretary of the CPC Central Committee, President of the PRC and Chairman of the Central Military Commission, attended Chinese private enterprises symposium in Beijing. SHU alumnus Wang Xingxing, founder and CEO of Unitree Robotics, gave a talk as a representative.

（三）基础教育合作办学 Joint Education in Basic Education

2016年1月12日，举行上海大学基础教育发展集团成立签约仪式，校党委书记罗宏杰（后排右5）、宝山区区委书记汪泓（后排右6）出席

The signing ceremony for the establishment of SHU Basic Education Group, January 12, 2016

2021年5月28日，举行学校和嘉定区教育局共建上海大学嘉定基础教育集团签约仪式，嘉定区副区长王浩（左）和校党委副书记、副校长龚思怡为集团揭牌

The unveiling ceremony of Jiading Basic Education Group, SHU, jointly established by SHU and Jiading District Education Bureau, May 28, 2021

2024年9月1日，举行上海大学附属嘉定实验学校新校舍启用仪式（左起：上海大学副校长王从春、嘉定区区长高香、嘉定区区委书记陆方舟、市教卫工作党委书记沈炜、上海大学党委书记成旦红、上海大学校长刘昌胜、市教委副主任王浩、嘉定区副区长汤东英）

The inauguration ceremony of the new campus of SHU Affiliated Jiading Experimental School, September 1, 2024

（四）志愿者服务　Volunteering Services

2003年开始，学校每年选派志愿者参加大学生志愿服务西部计划。图为2007年7月20日举行的上海市大学生志愿服务西部计划出征仪式暨表彰大会

Students of SHU attending the departure and award ceremony for "Go West" Volunteer Program (Shanghai), July 20, 2007

2010年12月，学校团委被中共中央、国务院授予"上海世博会先进集体"。图为2010年6月21日，学校举行世博会志愿者誓师动员大会

The SHU World Expo Volunteer Mobilization Meeting, June 21, 2010. In December, the Youth League Committee of SHU was awarded the Excellent Unit of Shanghai World Expo by the Central Committee of the CPC and the State Council, December 2010.

2018年开始，学校每年选派志愿者赴中国国际进口博览会开展志愿服务。图为2018年11月，参加首届中国国际进口博览会的志愿者合影

SHU volunteers at the 1st China International Import Expo, November 2018. Since then, the university has sent volunteers annually to provide services for the event.

十四、国际交流与合作
International Exchanges and Cooperations

学校坚持高水平教育对外开放，2010年起，首次提出国际化战略；2016年，全面实施国际化战略；2021年，在上海大学首届教育对外开放大会上提出建构"国际化的上海大学"；2024年，学校第四次党代会将国际化战略作为学校发展三大战略之一。

学校以国家重大需求为导向，强化与世界一流大学的实质性合作，迄今已与全球55个国家和地区的263所高校及科研机构建立了交流与合作关系。学校被教育部评为来华留学示范基地单位、首批高层次国际化人才培养创新实践基地，拥有5个"高等学校学科创新引智计划"基地、4个中外合作办学学院和5所孔子学院。目前在校就读的国际学生3144人，来自全球159个国家和地区，其中国际学历生2320人。

SHU is committed to the opening-up of high-level education. It launched the internationalization strategy in 2010, started to fully implement the strategy in 2016 and unveiled the vision of building "Internationalized Shanghai University" in 2021. The strategy was reaffirmed as one of the university's three core development strategies at the Fourth SHU Party Congress in 2024.

Guided by national strategic needs, SHU fosters substantive partnerships with world-class institutions, building ties with 263 universities and research institutes across 55 countries and regions. It has been recognized by the Ministry of Education as Model Base for International Studies in China and among the first cohort of Innovative Practice Bases for Cultivating High-Level Internationalized Talents. The university hosts 5 "111 Plan" Discipline Innovation and Talent Introduction Bases, 4 Chinese-foreign cooperative education institutes, and 5 Confucius Institutes. Currently, 3,144 international students from 159 countries and regions study at SHU, including 2,320 degree-pursuing ones.

建立校际交流与合作关系的海外高校及科研机构情况
国家和地区数（63）学校数（359）
Overseas Universities and Research Institutions Partnering with SHU

欧洲 (101)

英国（UK）（20）
- 拉夫堡大学
- 萨塞克斯大学
- 贝尔法斯特女王大学
- 利物浦约翰莫尔斯大学
- 爱丁堡大学
- 牛津大学
- 伦敦玛丽女王大学
- 剑桥大学
- 利兹大学
- 皇家艺术学院
- 埃塞克斯大学
- 曼彻斯特大学
- 肯特大学
- 思克莱德大学
- 布鲁内尔大学
- 利物浦大学
- 兰卡斯特大学
- 伦敦大学学院
- 伦敦政治经济学院

爱尔兰（Ireland）（4）
- 科克大学
- 梅努斯大学
- 都柏林城市大学
- 科克理工学院

比利时（Belgium）（2）
- 根特大学
- 布鲁塞尔自由大学

葡萄牙（Portugal）（3）
- 里斯本大学
- 米尼奥大学
- 里斯本澳门科学文化中心

西班牙（Spain）（5）
- 西班牙巴塞罗那自治大学
- 西班牙马拉加大学
- 西班牙胡安卡洛斯国王大学商学院
- 巴斯克大学
- 瓦伦西亚理工大学

第三部分　自强不息　复兴跨越

法国（France）（16）
法国工程技术大学
巴黎第二大学
格勒诺布尔阿尔卑斯大学
里尔大学
让·姆兰里昂第三大学
勃艮第-弗朗什孔泰大学
勃艮第大学
雷恩商学院
诺曼底管理学院
法国巴黎高等对外贸易学院
洛林大学
蔚蓝海岸大学
ECAM Lyon 工程师学校
蒙彼利埃第三大学
欧洲研究国际中心 CIFE
国际档案理事会
联合国教科文组织

荷兰（Netherlands）（2）
海牙大学
埃因霍芬理工大学

德国（Germany）（11）
奥尔登堡大学
慕尼黑工业大学
德累斯顿应用科技大学
开姆尼茨工业大学
莱茵-瓦尔应用科技大学
不来梅大学
卡尔斯鲁厄合作大学
卡塞尔大学
德国 FAIR 数据基础设施联盟
马克斯·普朗克固体化学物理学研究所
亚琛工业大学

意大利（Italy）（10）
特伦托大学
罗马大学
罗马第二大学
罗马第三大学
那不勒斯东方大学
萨勒诺大学
米兰圣心天主教大学
都灵大学
墨西拿大学
国际劳工组织国际培训中心

圣马力诺共和国（The Republic of San Marino）（1）
圣马力诺大学

丹麦（Denmark）（1）
南丹麦大学

瑞典（Sweden）（5）
延雪平大学
瑞典西部大学
乌普萨拉大学
舍夫德大学
查尔姆斯理工大学

波兰（Poland）（3）
华沙大学
波兹南工业大学
洛兹电影学院

芬兰（Finland）（2）
奥卢大学
瓦萨大学

斯洛伐克共和国（Slovakia）（1）
布拉迪斯拉发经济与公共管理学院

白俄罗斯（Belarus）（2）
白俄罗斯国立大学
白俄罗斯国立信息技术无线电电子大学

立陶宛（Lithuania）（1）
考纳斯理工大学

爱沙尼亚（Estonia）（2）
塔尔图大学
塔林理工大学

拉脱维亚（Latvia）（2）
里加理工大学

里斯巴商业、艺术和技术大学

奥地利（Austria）（1）
库夫斯坦因应用科技大学

塞尔维亚（Srbija）（1）
贝尔格莱德大学

希腊（Greece）（2）
塞萨洛尼基亚里士多德大学
欧洲公法组织

匈牙利（Hungary）（1）
赛格德大学

俄罗斯（Russia）（4）
俄罗斯国家研究型高等经济大学
莫斯科国立大学
乌拉尔国立经济大学
伊尔库茨克国立理工大学

亚洲 (96)

吉尔吉斯斯坦(Kyrgyzstan)（1）
吉尔吉斯斯坦国立大学

哈萨克斯坦(Kazakhstan)（3）
哈萨克斯坦共和国欧亚大学
哈萨克斯坦国立大学
苏莱曼-德米雷尔大学

乌兹别克斯坦(Uzbekistan)（4）
世界经济外交大学
国家美术设计学院
公共管理学院
塔什干国立经济大学

巴基斯坦（Pakistan）（1）
卡拉奇工商管理学院

伊朗（Iran）（1）
谢里夫理工大学

阿塞拜疆（Azerbaijan）（3）
阿塞拜疆国立经济大学
巴库国立大学
阿塞拜疆国立石油大学

亚美尼亚（Armenia）（1）
叶里温国立大学

土耳其（Türkey）（2）
海峡大学
萨班哲大学

以色列（Israel）（2）
海法大学
特拉维夫大学

巴林（Bahrain）（1）
巴林大学

印度（India）（1）
韦洛尔理工大学

马来西亚（Malaysia）（2）
拉曼大学
马来西亚国立大学

泰国（Thailand）（4）
宋卡王子大学
西那瓦国际大学
清迈大学
玛希隆大学

印度尼西亚（Indonesia）（1）
泗水大学

越南（Vietnam）（1）
胡志明市国家大学

韩国（Republic Korea）（12）
成均馆大学
梨花女子大学
庆熙大学
建国大学
国立釜山大学
中央大学
东国大学
全北国立大学

湖南大学
首尔市立大学
加图立大学
湖南大学

日本（Japan）(21)
早稻田大学
京都大学
东北大学
千叶大学
近畿大学
关西学院大学
大阪市立大学
广岛市立大学
芝浦工业大学
大阪艺术大学
富山大学
大正大学
香川大学
创价大学
武藏野大学
神田外语大学
专修大学
东洋大学
神户大学
日本医科大学
冈山大学

新加坡（Singapore）(1)
新加坡国立大学

中国（港澳台地区）China (Hong Kong, Macau, Taiwan) (34)
香港大学
香港浸会大学
香港城市大学
香港岭南大学
澳门大学
澳门科技大学
澳门城市大学
台湾铭传大学
高雄大学

东海大学
台湾师范大学
台湾大学
台湾清华大学
成功大学
中正大学
宜兰大学
台湾科技大学
东吴大学
中原大学
中国文化大学
中央大学
静宜大学
台湾交通大学
辅仁大学
台北市立大学
台湾政治大学
台北商业大学
佛光大学
台湾东华大学
彰化师范大学
逢甲大学
世新大学
元智大学
淡江大学

大洋洲 (16)

澳大利亚（Australia）(14)
悉尼科技大学
莫纳什大学
皇家墨尔本理工
麦考瑞大学
昆士兰大学
昆士兰科技大学
新南威尔士大学
斯威本科技大学
迪肯大学
拉筹伯大学
科廷大学
伍伦贡大学
西澳大利亚大学
格里菲斯大学

新西兰（New Zealand）(2)
奥克兰大学
奥塔哥大学

北美洲 (32)

加拿大（Canada）(7)
多伦多大学
不列颠哥伦比亚大学
温哥华电影学院
西安大略大学
瑞尔森大学
阿卡迪亚大学
滑铁卢大学

美国（United States）(24)
加州大学伯克利分校
史蒂文森理工
宾夕法尼亚大学沃顿商学院
德克萨斯大学奥斯汀分校
德克萨斯大学里奥格兰德河谷分校
西北大学
莱斯大学
罗格斯大学
纽约州立大学石溪分校
纽约州立大学布法罗分校
纽约市立大学
明尼苏达大学双城分校
明尼苏达大学莫里斯分校
普渡大学
康奈尔大学
肯塔基大学
怀俄明大学
北卡罗莱纳州立大学
天普大学
内华达大学里诺分校
佛罗里达州立大学
乔治亚州立大学
卫斯理安学院
韦恩州立大学
巴德学院

拉丁美洲 (15)

古巴（Cuba）(1)
古巴圣地亚哥东方大学

巴西（Brazil）(4)
坎皮纳斯州立大学
圣保罗大学
巴西利亚大学
巴伊亚联邦大学

墨西哥（Mexico）(3)
蒙特雷科技大学
墨西哥国立自治
普埃布拉美洲大学

阿根廷（Argentina）(3)
阿根廷国家科学技术研究委员会
布宜诺斯艾利斯大学
阿根廷国立艺术大学

秘鲁（Peru）(1)
秘鲁天主教大学

多米尼加（The Dominican Republic）(1)
圣多明各理工大学

乌拉圭（Uruguay）(1)
乌拉圭共和国大学

智利（Chile）(1)
智利大学

非洲 (3)

南非（South Africa）(3)
约翰内斯堡大学
内罗毕大学
赞比亚大学

第三部分 自强不息 复兴跨越

（一）合作办学　Joint Education and Partnerships

1994年7月20日，上海市高教局批复同意上海大学和澳大利亚悉尼科技大学合作创办"上海大学悉尼工商学院"。图为当年9月7日举行学院成立揭牌仪式（右：上海大学副校长兼悉尼工商学院院长黄黔）。这是国内首家通过国家认证的中外合作商学院

The unveiling ceremony of Sydney Institute of Language and Commerce (SILC) Business School on September 7, 1994, which was co-founded by SHU and University of Technology Sydney (UTS) on July 20 the same year

上海大学中外合作创办的学院一览
Sino-Foreign Jointly Established College at SHU

成立时间	学院名称
1994年7月20日	悉尼工商学院
2005年2月14日	中欧工程技术学院
2014年6月15日	上海温哥华电影学院
2022年4月18日	里斯本学院

2020年2月，上海大学悉尼工商学院成为全国首家本科层次通过AACSB认证的中外合作办学机构

The SILC Business School, becoming the first Sino-foreign cooperative educational institution at the undergraduate level in China to receive AACSB accreditation, February 2020

2008年7月8日，举行上海大学与悉尼科技大学双学位新一轮合作协议签字仪式，常务副校长周哲玮（左2）、副校长唐豪（左1）出席

The new agreement signing ceremony for the dual-degree program between SHU and UTS, July 8, 2008

2005年2月14日,学校与法国技术大学集团签订关于合作创办上海大学中欧工程技术学院,这是国内第一个中国与欧盟合作办学项目。图为2006年11月5日,第十届全国政协副主席徐匡迪(右)和法国工程院院长弗朗索瓦·吉诺为学院揭牌

Sino-European School of Technology, SHU, unveiled by Xu Kuangdi (right), Vice Chairman of the CPPCC, and Francois Guinot, President of the French Academy of Engineering, November 5, 2006

2014年6月15日,学校与温哥华电影学院召开新闻发布会,上海市文化广播影视管理局党委副书记、局长胡劲军(右4),上海大学校长罗宏杰(右5),温哥华电影学院创始人兼院长James Grfin(右6)共同宣布上海温哥华电影学院成立

The press conference announcing the establishment of Shanghai Vancouver Film School, June 15, 2014

2022年4月18日,教育部批准学校与葡萄牙里斯本大学合作共建上海大学里斯本学院。图为当年9月23日举行学院成立揭牌仪式

The unveiling ceremony of the Ulisboa School of SHU, a joint initiative between SHU and the University of Lisbon, September 23, 2022

（二）校际交流　Intercollegiate Exchanges

1998年8月17—18日，学校主办第三届国际非线性力学会议，上海市副市长周慕尧（右4）出席开幕式

The Third International Conference on Nonlinear Mechanics hosted by SHU, August 17-18, 1998

2001年4月15日，学校主办先进机器人发展战略国际研讨会，校党委书记、常务副校长方明伦（右3），副校长龚振邦（右1）出席

IARP Workshop on Advanced Robotics hosted by SHU, April 15, 2001

2010年10月28日，举行上海大学与泰国王子大学签署合作框架协议仪式，校党委书记于信汇（后排右5）、副校长吴松（后排右3）出席

The signing ceremony for memorandum of understanding between Prince of Songkla University and SHU, October 28, 2010

2016年3月9日，与德国卡尔斯鲁厄应用技术大学签署校际合作协议，副校长丛玉豪（前排右）代表学校签字

The signing ceremony for memorandum of cooperation between Karlsruhe University of Applied Sciences and SHU, March 9, 2016

Shanghai University

2023年3月20日，学校和国际博物馆协会（ICOM）共同主办，国际博物馆协会研究与交流中心（ICOM-IMREC）和中国海外文物研究中心两个专业智库承办"博物馆、去殖民化、文物返还：全球对话"专家研讨会

The ICOM-IMREC's seminar on "Museums, Decolonization, and Restitution: A Global Conversation", co-hosted by SHU and the International Council of Museums (ICOM), March 20, 2023

2013年8月23—26日，由中国社会科学院和上海市人民政府联合主办的首届"世界考古·上海论坛"在上海中华艺术宫召开。从第二届开始，上海大学参与承办，会场在上海大学图书馆报告厅，目前已承办至第五届。图为2023年12月15日，上海大学承办第五届"世界考古论坛·上海"，中国社会科学院院长、中国历史研究院院长高翔（右7），上海市市长龚正（右8），文化和旅游部副部长、国家文物局局长李群（右4）共同颁发世界考古论坛重要考古研究成果

The Fifth Shanghai Archaeology Forum was held at SHU, December 15, 2023. Gao Xiang (seventh from right), President of the Chinese Academy of Social Sciences and the Chinese History Research Institute, Shanghai Mayor Gong Zheng (eighth from right), and Li Qun (fourth from right), Vice Minister of Culture and Tourism and Director of the National Cultural Heritage Administration, jointly presented important archaeological research achievements.

2024年4月23日，与西班牙瓦伦西亚理工大学签署校际交流框架协议和学生交流协议，副校长于雪梅（右）代表学校签字

The signing ceremony of inter-university exchange framework agreement and student exchange agreement between SHU and Valencia Polytechnic University (Universitat Politčcnica de Valčncia, UPV), Spain, April 23, 2024

2024年7月15日,学校举办"2024国际档案研修班"。中央档案馆副馆长、国家档案局副局长林振义(前排左11)、国际档案理事会主席、卢森堡国家档案馆馆长Josée Kirps(前排左12),中国人民大学原常务副校长冯惠玲(前排左13)、上海市档案局(馆)长徐未晚(前排左9)出席开幕式
The 2024 International Archives Training Program, July 15, 2024

2024年11月4日,校长刘昌胜(坐者左)率团出席第十二届世界城市论坛,代表学校与联合国人居署签署合作协议
President Liu Changsheng (left in sitting) signing a cooperation agreement with the United Nations Human Settlements Programme (UN-Habitat) during the 12th World Urban Forum, November 4, 2024

2024年12月11日,校党委书记成旦红(左)代表学校与巴伊亚联邦大学签订协议,合作成立"中国—拉丁美洲发展研究中心"
Cheng Danhong (left), Secretary of SHU Party Committee, signing an agreement with Federal University of Bahia (UFBA) to jointly establish the China-Latin America Development Research Center, December 11, 2024

（三）师生海外交流　Overseas Exchanges

2017年10—11月，材料科学与工程学院教师在美国罗格斯大学电子和计算机工程系进行访学

Faculty of the School of Materials Science and Engineering attending a program at the Department of Electrical and Computer Engineering of Rutgers University, from October to November in 2017

2018年7月15—27日，学校派出30名商科教师在美国沃顿商学院接受项目培训。2023年4月22日，学校启动"沃顿－上大全球青年领导力项目"，至2024年12月共派出54名学生

Faculty of SHU business programs attended a training program at the Wharton School of the University of Pennsylvania from July 15 to 27, 2018. The "Wharton-SHU Global Youth Leadership Program" was launched in SHU on April 22, 2023.

2018年7—8月，人文社会科学类7个学院的20名学生参加英国牛津大学和剑桥大学人文课程暑期项目。至2024年12月，牛津大学短期项目共派出173名学生

Students of SHU humanities and social sciences programs attending a summer program at Oxford University and Cambridge University, July to August, 2018

2024年11月11—18日，材料基因组工程研究院、通信学院、上海城市更新与可持续发展研究院的5名教师参加在比利时布鲁塞尔自由大学和葡萄牙新里斯本大学举办的上海大学首期LEAD青年学术领导力和数字领导力培训工作坊

Five teachers attending the first LEAD Youth Academic Leadership and Digital Leadership Training Workshop, organized by SHU at the University of Brussels in Belgium and NOVA University Lisbon in Portugal, November 11-18, 2024

（四）孔子学院　Confucius Institutes

上海大学为中方合作院校的孔子学院一览

Confucius Institutes Co-founded by SHU and Overseas Universities

成立时间	孔子学院名称
2006 年 12 月 24 日	泰国宋卡王子大学普吉孔子学院
2007 年 10 月 24 日	爱尔兰科克大学孔子学院
2010 年 4 月 14 日	土耳其海峡大学孔子学院
2010 年 11 月 6 日	美国肯塔基大学孔子学院（已停办）
2014 年 4 月 15 日	巴林王国巴林大学孔子学院
2023 年 9 月 11 日	巴西巴伊亚联邦大学孔子学院

2008 年 10 月 21 日，上海市教委副主任王奇（右）与爱尔兰教育部部长为爱尔兰科克大学孔子学院揭牌

Deputy Director Wang Qi (right) of Shanghai Municipal Education Commission and the Irish Minister for Education unveiling the Confucius Institute at University College Cork, October 21, 2008

2013 年 12 月 7 日，国家汉办授予上海大学"孔子学院先进中方合作院校"称号，中共中央政治局委员、国务院副总理刘延东（左）为上海大学授牌

Liu Yandong (left), Vice Premier of the State Council, presenting the medal to SHU, winner of the "Outstanding Chinese Partner of Confucius Institute", December 7, 2013

上海大学　Shanghai University

2014年4月15日，上海市副市长翁铁慧（左3）出席巴林王国巴林大学孔子学院揭牌仪式
The unveiling ceremony of the Confucius Institute at Bahrain University, attended by Weng Tiehui, Vice Mayor of Shanghai (third from left), April 15, 2014

2023年9月11日，校党委副书记欧阳华（左2）与巴伊亚联邦大学校长为巴西巴伊亚联邦大学孔子学院揭牌
Deputy Secretary of SHU Party Committee Ouyang Hua (second from left) and the President of the Federal University of Bahia unveiling the Confucius Institute at the Federal University of Bahia in Brazil, September 11, 2023

（五）国际学生培养　Cultivation of International Students

2002年11月15日，举行"爱汉语、爱中国、爱上大——上海大学外国留学生汉语竞赛"

A Chinese Language Competition for International Students at SHU, November 15, 2002

2024年1月19日，举行上海大学国际学生颁奖典礼暨2024新春晚会

International Student Awards Ceremony and Spring Festival Gala at SHU, January 19, 2024

1994—2024年国际学生在校人数一览

Number of International Students at SHU (1994–2024)

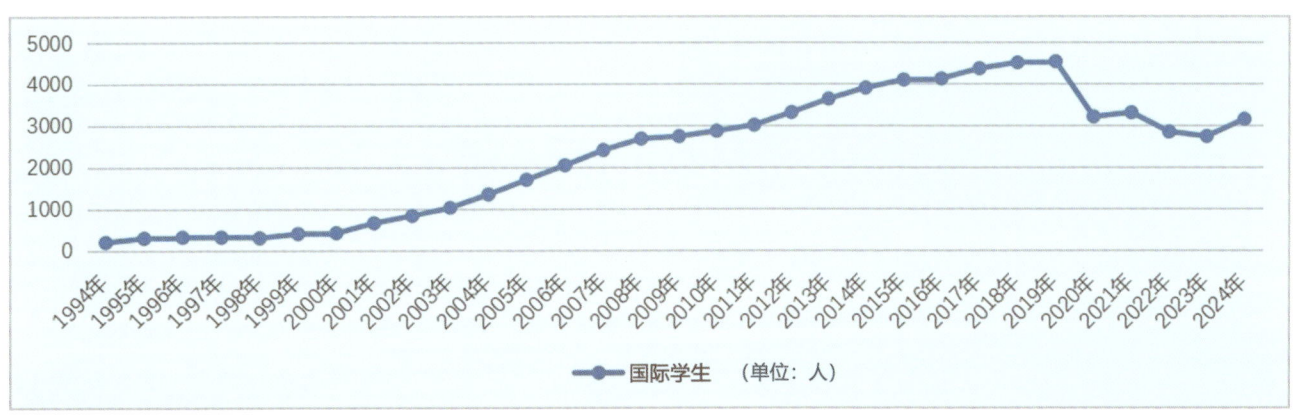

十五、校园文化
Campus Culture

学校持续推进以精神文明建设为核心内容的校园文化建设，营造美丽的校园景观和丰富的人文环境，用好数字化资源，挖掘学校红色基因。通过文化育人，文化铸魂，形成良好的校风、教风、学风。

SHU promotes campus culture cefeaturing on spiritual civilization, creating a beautiful campus environment and a rich cultural atmosphere, utilizing digital resources, and exploring the school's red heritage. Through cultural education, it fosters a positive campus spirit, teaching philosophy and academic atmosphere.

1999年5月31日，召开上海大学精神文明建设工作会议（左起：校纪委书记廖由雄，校党委副书记、副校长周鸿刚，校党委书记、常务副校长方明伦，校党委副书记杨慧如；右2：副校长沈学超；右1：副校长夏玲英）
A meeting on the construction of spiritual civilization at SHU, May 31, 1999

自1994年起，学校一直是上海市文明单位。2017年11月，获首届"全国文明校园"称号（上海仅两所高校获此奖项）
SHU awarded the inaugural "National Civilized Campus" title (one of the only two universities in Shanghai to receive this honor), November 2017

第三部分　自强不息　复兴跨越

2010年12月，中共中央、国务院授予校团委"上海世博会先进集体"
The Youth League Committee of SHU was awarded the Excellent Unit of Shanghai World Expo by the Central Committee of the CPC and the State Council, December 2010.

2010年4月，学校获教育部授予"2009年度全国毕业生就业典型经验高校"称号
SHU awarded the title of "National Model Institution for Graduate Employment Experience in 2009" by the Ministry of Education, April 2010

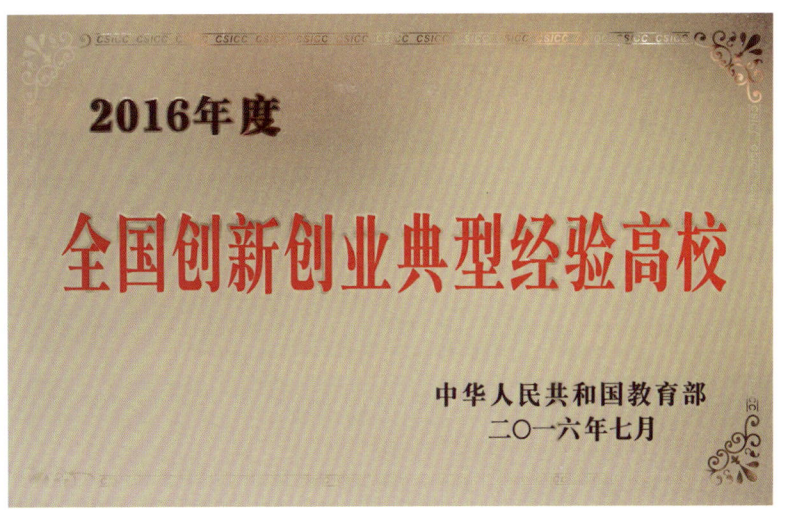

2016年7月，学校获教育部授予"2016年度全国创新创业典型经验高校"称号
SHU awarded the title of "National Model Institution for Innovation and Entrepreneurship Experience in 2016" by the Ministry of Education, July 2016

（一）校园文化品牌　Established Campus Cultural Programs

菊文化节——始于 2003 年，至 2024 年已举办二十二届
SHU Chrysanthemum Culture Festival, first held in 2003, had been held 22 times by 2024.

"泮池之声"新年音乐会——始于 2005 年，至 2024 年已举办十九届
SHU New Year Concert, first held in 2005, had been held 19 times by 2024.

第三部分　自强不息　复兴跨越

国际文化节——始于2013年，至2024年已举办十一届
SHU International Culture Festival, first held in 2013, had been held 11 times by 2024.

（二）智慧校园　Smart Campus

学校一站式服务中心监测平台
The monitoring platform of the One-Stop Service Center at SHU

智慧教室
A smart classroom

图书馆"24小时智慧共享空间"
The library's 24/7 Smart Learning Commons

（三）纪念场馆　Memorial Venues

2014年10月23日，红色文化教育基地——"溯园·上海大学（1922—1927）"正式开放；2019年，挂牌上海市爱国主义教育基地

Suyuan, the SHU (1922-1927) Memorial Garden, officially opened on October 23, 2014.

2019年5月27日，钱伟长纪念馆正式开放；2020年10月9日，挂牌民盟中央传统教育基地

The Qian Weichang Memorial Hall officially opened on May 27, 2019.

2022年5月30日，钱伟长图书馆入选全国首批科学家精神教育基地

The Qian Weichang Library listed in the First Batch of National Scientist Spirit Education Bases on May 30, 2022

Shanghai University

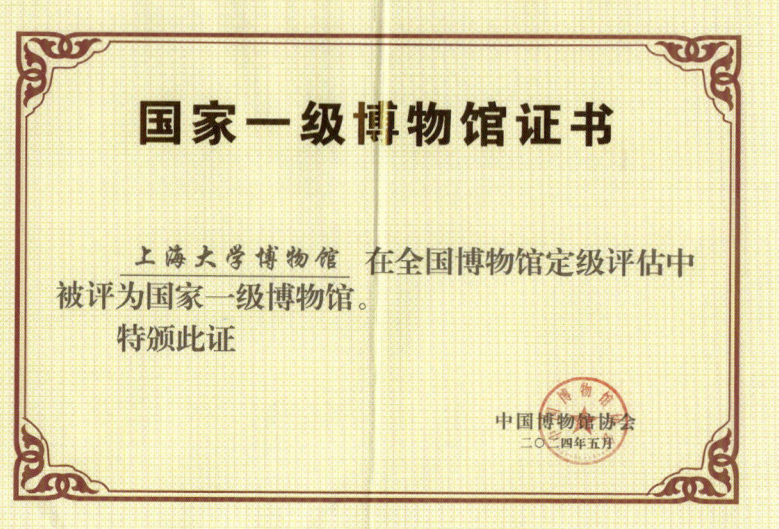

2024年5月18日，上海大学博物馆获评第五批国家一级博物馆
The SHU Museum recognized as a National First-Class Museum on May 18, 2024

2024年6月19日，上海大学新校史馆（一期）建成开放
The new SHU History Museum (Phase I) officially opened to the public on June 19, 2024.

第三部分　自强不息　复兴跨越

（四）校友情结　Alumni Ties

在校友的支持下，自2016年起，学校举行毕业典礼当晚，上海中心大厦专门运用彩光及动态光，开启为上海大学毕业生送上祝福的景观照明

On the evenings of graduation ceremony, SHU marks the occasion by illuminating the Shanghai Tower with colorful, dynamic lighting, symbolizing its blessings and hopes for the graduates. This tradition, supported by the alumni since 2016, serves as a shining tribute to the graduating classes.

2018年，校友周忻（左）、朱旭东（右）代表企业"易居"，向学校捐赠5000万元，设立"上海大学易居校长基金"；还向机电工程与自动化学院捐赠1000万元，设立"方周自强奖"

Donation ceremony of Zhou Xin (left) and Zhu Xudong (right), SHU E-House President's Fund and "FangZhou Ziqiang Award" established, 2018

2018年1月，校党委书记、校长金东寒（右），党委副书记徐旭（左）为校董、校友会副会长、上海新航星投资集团有限公司董事长何志明颁发捐赠证书

President Jin Donghan (right) and Deputy Secretary of SHU Party Committee Xu Xu (left) presenting the donation certificate to He Zhiming (center), Chairman of the Board of Shanghai New Sail Star Group, January 2018

2018年1月，校党委书记、校长金东寒为校友彭宏陵（右）颁发卓越贡献奖

President Jin Donghan presenting Outstanding Contribution Award to Peng Hongling for his consistent supports for the development of SHU, January 2018

2018年7月19日，机电工程与自动化学院离休教授陈伯时（右）捐出个人积蓄50万元，在学院设立"陈伯时教育基金"，校党委副书记徐旭代表学校接受捐赠

Donation ceremony of Chen Boshi, a retired professor from the School of Mechatronic Engineering and Automation (right), and the "Chen Boshi Education Fund" established, July 19, 2018

2019年，上海大学终身教授邓伟志捐资在学院设立"邓伟志教育基金"，2024年又捐出个人所获的上海市第十五届哲学社会科学优秀成果奖学术贡献奖奖金。图为2024年5月25日，校党委书记成旦红为邓伟志（左）颁发捐赠证书

Cheng Danhong, Party Secretary of SHU Party Committee, presenting a donation certificate to Deng Weizhi (left), May 25, 2024. In 2019, Deng, a lifetime professor of SHU, established the "Deng Weizhi Education Fund".

第三部分　自强不息　复兴跨越

2019年10月11日，校长刘昌胜（前排右7）、校党委副书记欧阳华（前排右10）接待参加"上海工业大学1979级研究生入学40周年纪念会"的校友
The former graduate students of SHU (formerly SUT) coming back to celebrate the 40th anniversary of the admission in 1979, October 11, 2019

2023年9月23日，上海大学爱尔兰校友会在爱尔兰科克大学成立
The founding ceremony of Ireland Branch of Alumni Association at University College Cork, September 23, 2023

十六、师资队伍
Faculty

学校实施人才强校战略，健全优秀人才引育体系，打造高素质、专业化、创新型的教师人才队伍。

SHU implements a talent-driven strategy to strengthen the university, improve the system for attracting and nurturing outstanding talents, and build a high-quality, professional and innovative faculty team.

1999年，学校举办新进教师岗前培训班，校党委副书记毛杏云（右）主持，钱伟长校长出席并讲话，校长助理刘晓明（左）出席
An orientation training session for new faculty members, with President Qian Weichang (center) attending and delivering a speech, 1999

2001年11月，钱伟长校长和青年教师在一起
President Qian Weichang with young faculty members, November 2001

第三部分　自强不息　复兴跨越

2015年9月10日，召开上海大学庆祝第三十一个教师节暨表彰大会，校党委书记、纪委书记夏小和（左1），总会计师宋彬（右1）为获奖教师颁奖
A celebration for the 31st Teachers' Day and awards ceremony, September 10, 2015

（一）专任教师基本情况　Overview of Full-Time Faculty

1994—2024年专任教师人数一览
Number of Full-Time Faculty (1994–2024)

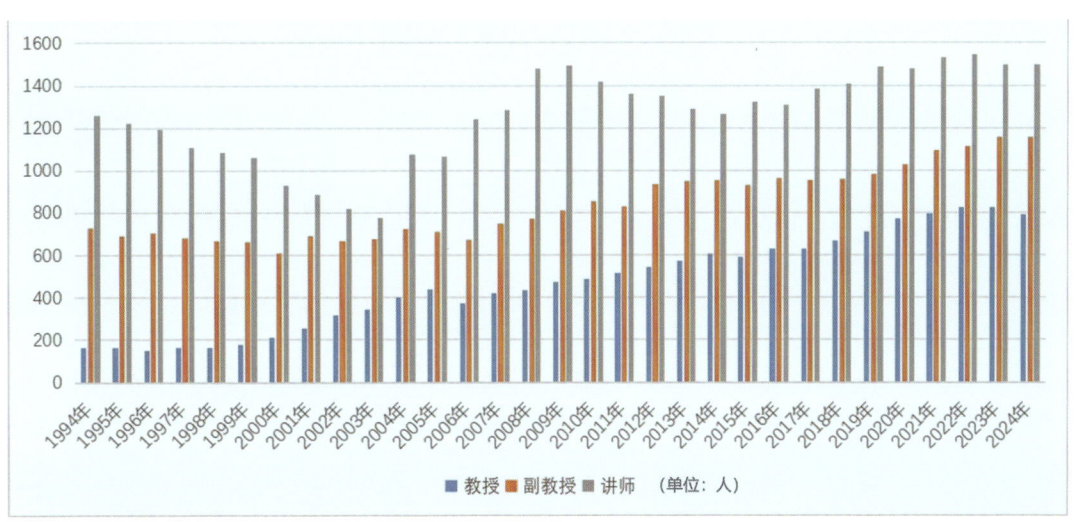

1994 年合并初专任教师中教授、副教授占比示意图
Proportion of Professors and Associate Professors in 1994

2024 年专任教师中教授、副教授占比示意图
Proportion of Professors and Associate Professors in 2024

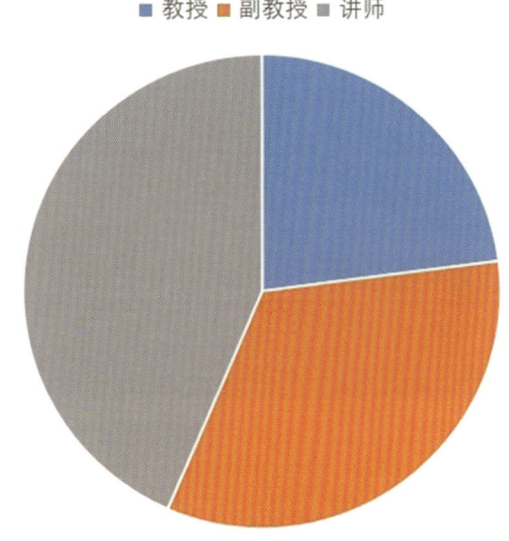

1994 年合并初专任教师中具有博士学位占比示意图
Proportion of Full-Time Faculty with Doctoral Degrees in 1994

2024 年专任教师中具有博士学位占比示意图
Proportion of Full-Time Faculty with Doctoral Degrees in 2024

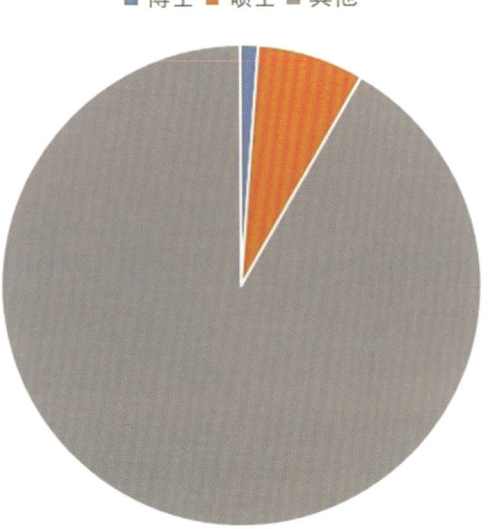

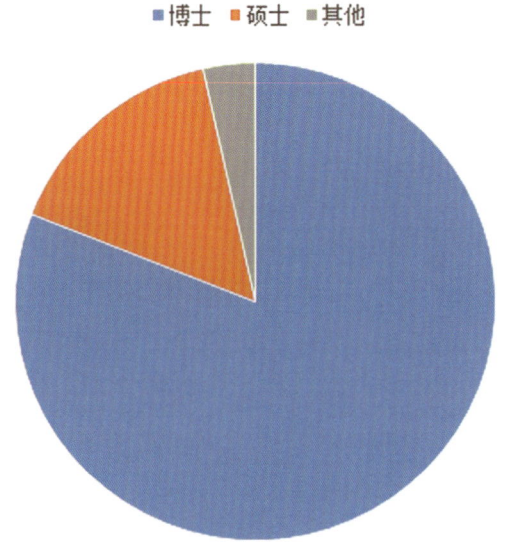

（二）高层次人才　High-level Talents

各类高层次人才
High-level Talents

人才类型	人数（人）
中国科学院院士、中国工程院院士	10
海外院士	24
国家级海外高层次人才	22
国家级海外青年高层次人才（含优青海外）	26
国家杰出青年科学基金项目	37
国家国防科技卓越青年科学基金项目	1
国家优秀青年科学基金	29
"长江学者"特聘教授	20
"长江学者"讲座教授	5
青年长江学者	11
国家"万人计划"领军人才	17
国家百千万人才工程国家级人选	20
中宣部文化名家暨"四个一批"人才	7
科技部创新领军人才	3
万人计划青年拔尖人才	11
中国科学院百人计划	15
中宣部宣传思想青年英才	2

1. 中国科学院院士、中国工程院院士（全职）
Academicians of the Chinese Academy of Sciences and the Chinese Academy of Engineering (Full-Time)

在学校建设和发展过程中，有 10 位院士怀揣热情和理想，在教书育人的道路上，践行科学家精神和教育家精神，成为师生追求真理勇攀高峰的表率。他们中，有些由上海大学培养，攀上科学高峰；有些自带华冠奔赴而来，再创科研佳绩；有些在上海大学一直坚守，大师风范永驻。

During the development of SHU, ten academicians, with the spirit of scientists and educators, have dedicated themselves to teaching and mentoring with passion and ideals. They have set powerful examples for students and faculty in the pursuit of truth and excellence. They reached the pinnacle of their fields, and left their lasting legacy.

钱伟长（1955 年当选学部委员）
Qian Weichang (Elected Member of the Chinese Academy of Sciences in 1955)

黄宏嘉（1980 年当选学部委员）
Huang Hongjia (Elected Memberof the Chinese Academy of Sciences in 1980)

徐匡迪（1995 年当选中国工程院院士）
Xu Kuangdi (Elected Academician of the Chinese Academy of Engineering in 1995)

周邦新（1995 年当选中国工程院院士）
Zhou Bangxin (Elected Academician of the Chinese Academy of Engineering in 1995)

第三部分　自强不息　复兴跨越

孙晋良（1997年当选中国工程院院士）
Sun Jinliang (Elected Academician of the Chinese Academy of Engineering in 1997)

刘高联（1999年当选中国科学院院士）
Liu Gaolian (Elected Academician of the Chinese Academy of Sciences in 1999)

金东寒（2009年当选中国工程院院士）
Jin Donghan (Elected Academician of the Chinese Academy of Engineering in 2009)

张统一（2011年当选中国科学院院士）
Zhang Tongyi (Elected Academician of the Chinese Academy of Sciences in 2011)

刘昌胜（2017年当选中国科学院院士）
Liu Changsheng (Elected Academician of the Chinese Academy of Sciences in 2017)

吴明红（2021年当选中国工程院院士）
Wu Minghong (Elected Academician of the Chinese Academy of Engineering in 2021)

2. 上海大学终身教授
Lifetime Professors at SHU

方明伦（2005 年聘任）
Fang Minglun (Appointed in 2005)

刘高联（2006 年聘任）
Liu Gaolian (Appointed in 2006)

周邦新（2006 年聘任）
Zhou Bangxin (Appointed in 2006)

徐匡迪（2006 年聘任）
Xu Kuangdi (Appointed in 2006)

黄宏嘉（2006 年聘任）
Huang Hongjia (Appointed in 2006)

孙晋良（2009 年聘任）
Sun Jinliang (Appointed in 2009)

董乃斌（2009年聘任）
Dong Naibin (Appointed in 2009)

戴世强（2009年聘任）
Dai Shiqiang (Appointed in 2009)

邓伟志（2011年聘任）
Deng Weizhi (Appointed in 2011)

龚振邦（2011年聘任）
Gong Zhenbang (Appointed in 2011)

董远达（2011年聘任）
Dong Yuanda (Appointed in 2011)

周哲玮（2015年聘任）
Zhou Zhewei (Appointed in 2015)

（三）重点学科及其科研团队　Key Disciplines and Research Teams

教育部国家重点学科"钢铁冶金"团队
Members of the Iron and Steel Metallurgy team, a National Key Discipline under the Ministry of Education

教育部国家重点学科"流体力学"团队
Members of the Fluid Mechanics team, a National Key Discipline under the Ministry of Education

第三部分 自强不息 复兴跨越

教育部国家重点学科"机械电子工程"团队
Members of the Mechatronic Engineering team, a National Key Discipline under the Ministry of Education

教育部国家重点学科"社会学"团队
Members of the Sociology team, a National Key Discipline under the Ministry of Education

省部共建高品质特殊钢冶金与制备国家重点实验室高温叶片科研团队（先进钢铁材料技术国家工程研究中心、南方实验基地科研团队）
Members of Superalloy Turbine Blade research team, the State Key Laboratory of Advanced Special Steel, Shanghai City and the Ministry of Education, also research group of Southern Experimental Base, National Engineering and Research Center for Advanced Steel Technology

省部共建高品质特殊钢冶金与制备国家重点实验室模具钢科研团队
Members of the Mold Steel research team, the State Key Laboratory of Advanced Special Steel, Shanghai City and the Ministry of Education

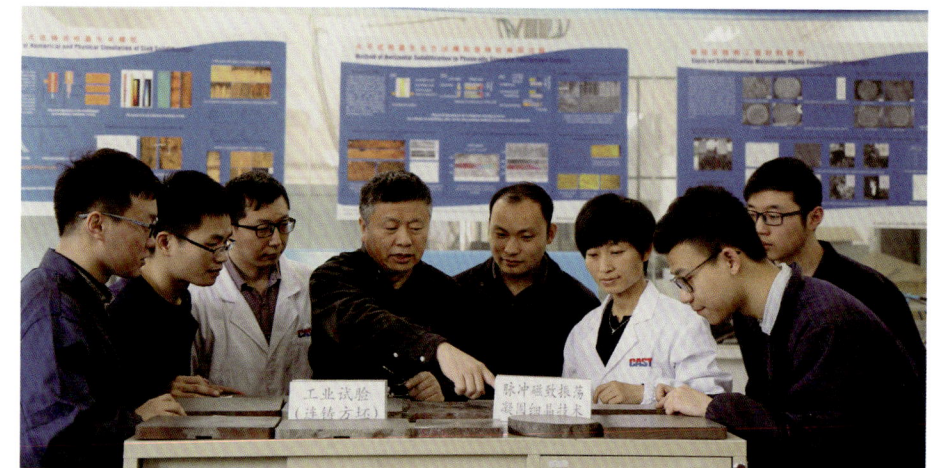

省部共建高品质特殊钢冶金与制备国家重点实验室凝固中心科研团队
Members of the Advanced Solidification Technology team, the State Key Laboratory of Advanced Special Steel, Shanghai City and the Ministry of Education

新型显示技术及应用集成教育部重点实验室科研团队
Members of the research team of the Key Laboratory of Advanced Display and System Applications, the Ministry of Education

第三部分　自强不息　复兴跨越

材料复合与先进分散技术教育部工程研究中心科研团队
Members of the Engineering Research Center of Material Composition and Advanced Dispersion Technology, the Ministry of Education

特种光纤与光接入网省部共建教育部重点实验室科研团队
Members of the Key Laboratory of Specialty Fiber Optics and Optical Access Networks, Shanghai City and the Ministry of Education

有机复合污染控制工程教育部重点实验室科研团队
Members of the Key Laboratory of Organic Compound Pollution Control Engineering, the Ministry of Education

海洋智能无人系统装备教育部工程研究中心科研团队（海洋智能无人集群技术与系统教育部重点实验室科研团队）
Members of the Engineering Research Center of Marine Intelligent Unmanned Systems and Equipment, the Ministry of Education

TFT-LCD 关键材料及技术国家发展改革委国家工程实验室科研团队
International Symposium on Advanced Display Materials and Devices, State Engineering Laboratory of TFTLCD, 2016

纳米复合功能材料国际科技合作基地科研团队
Members of the research team of the International Science and Technology Cooperation Base for Nanocomposite Functional Materials

第三部分　自强不息　复兴跨越

硅酸盐质文物保护教育部重点实验室科研团队（上海大学文化遗产保护基础科学研究院科研团队）
Members of the research team of the Key Laboratory of Silicate Cultural Relics Conservation, the Ministry of Education (the Institute of Cultural Heritage Conservation Science, SHU)

器官修复生物材料与技术国际合作联合实验室科研团队
Members of the research team of Joint International Research Laboratory of Biomaterials and Biotechnology in Organ Repair

国家联合应用数学创新中心上海大学分中心科研团队
Members of the research team of National Joint Innovation Center for Applied Mathematics (SHU center)

Shanghai University

教育部上海大学土耳其研究中心科研团队
Members of the Center for Türkiye Studies at SHU, the Ministry of Education

国家自然科学基金"人工智能驱动的多物理耦合力学"创新研究团队
Members of the innovative research team on "Artificial Intelligence-Driven Multi-Physics Coupling Mechanics", National Natural Science Foundation of China

国家自然科学基金"海洋自主智能无人艇系统理论、技术及应用"创新研究团队
Members of the innovative research team on "Theory, Technology, and Application of Autonomous Intelligent Unmanned Surface Vehicles", National Natural Science Foundation of China

教育部哲学社会科学数字社会治理创新团队
Members of the innovative research team on "Digital Social Governance in Philosophy and Social Sciences", the Ministry of Education

（四）国家荣誉称号获得者　Faculty Winning National Honors

国家荣誉称号获得者一览
Faculty Winning National Honors

荣誉称号	姓　名	年　份
全国先进工作者	曹家麟	2000
全国先进工作者	孙晋良	2015
全国先进工作者	陈立群	2020
全国五一劳动奖章	孙晋良	2012
全国五一劳动奖章	尹默林	2021
全国五一劳动奖章	张建华	2024
全国教育系统劳动模范	吴程里	1995
全国教育系统劳动模范	陈明仪	1995
全国教育系统劳动模范	曹家麟	1998
全国模范教师	吴明红	2004
全国模范教师	戴世强	2007
全国模范教师	陈立群	2009
全国模范教师	陈立群	2019
全国模范教师	任忠鸣	2024
全国优秀教师	曹家麟	1995
全国优秀教师	吴锡龙	1995
全国优秀教师	李　梁	2009
全国优秀教育工作者	林振汉	2001

Shanghai University

曹家麟
Cao Jialin

孙晋良
Sun Jinliang

陈立群
Chen Liqun

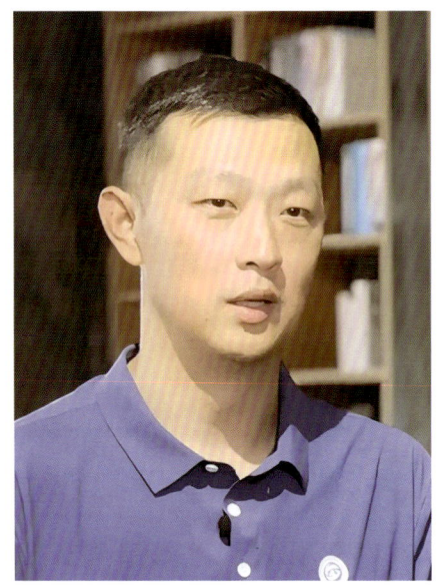

尹默林
Yin Molin

张建华
Zhang Jianhua

十七、党的建设
Party Building

学校党委始终把牢正确政治方向，坚持和加强党对学校的全面领导，加强党的思想、组织、作风建设，压紧压实各级党组织管党治党责任，充分发挥党支部的战斗堡垒作用和党员的先锋模范作用，依靠全体教职员工，推进学校的发展和改革。

The SHU Party Committee has consistently reinforced the Party's leadership, ensuring Party organizations at all levels take responsibility and play an active role. Party branches have been central to the university's development, with Party members leading by example and inspiring faculty and staff to work together toward the university's ongoing reforms and growth.

1995年1月18日，学校召开第一次党的建设工作会议，首次提出"围绕中心抓党建、抓好党建促中心、检验党建看中心"的党建工作理念。从这一年开始，学校每年初都要召开一次党建工作会议，秉持理念，统一思想，动员全校党员为完成学校的中心工作而努力。2007年召开的学校第一次党员代表大会进一步明确，党建工作理念为"围绕中心抓党建、抓好党建促中心、检验党建看发展"

The first Party building conference of SHU, January 18, 1995

（一）党员代表大会和校领导班子建设　SHU's CPC Congresses and Leadership Construction

1994年5月27日，中共上海市委副书记陈至立、市教委主任郑令德与校领导集体合影
前排左起：巡视员李明忠、巡视员余忠荪、常务副校长杨德广、党委副书记毛杏云、郑令德、校长钱伟长、陈至立、党委书记吴程里、党委副书记杨慧如、常务副校长方明伦；后排左起：副校长沈学超、纪委书记廖由雄、副校长壮云乾、副校长龚振邦、副校长陈大森、巡视员汪国铎、巡视员徐得名、副校长黄黔
Group photo of Chen Zhili, Deputy Secretary of the Shanghai Municipal Committee of the CPC, Zheng Lingde, Director of the Shanghai Municipal Education Commission, and SHU leaders, May 27, 1994

1999年，校领导集体合影
前排左起：党委副书记、副校长周鸿刚，党委副书记毛杏云，校长钱伟长，党委书记、常务副校长方明伦，党委副书记杨慧如；后排左起：校长助理刘晓明，副校长周哲玮，副校长王奇，副校长沈学超，副校长壮云乾，巡视员刘德重，副校长龚振邦，副校长夏玲英
Group photo of SHU leaders, 1999

第三部分　自强不息　复兴跨越

2004年5月，校领导集体合影
前排左起：副校长叶志明，副校长曹家麟，党委副书记沈学超，党委书记、常务副校长方明伦，校长钱伟长，党委副书记、副校长周鸿刚，副校长周哲玮，副校长李友梅，副校长金国华；后排左起：校秘书长曾文彪，校长助理汪敏，巡视员薛志良，工会主席壮云乾，巡视员唐豪，校长助理刘宇陆，校长助理俞涛，总经济师张平伟
Group photo of SHU leaders, May 2004

2007年4月，校领导与钱伟长校长合影
左起：副校长吴松，副校长唐豪，副校长汪敏，外校挂职干部，副校长叶志明，巡视员薛志良，党委副书记、纪委书记忻平，常务副校长周哲玮，总经济师张平伟，党委副书记、副校长李友梅，党委副书记滕建勇
Group photo of President Qian Weichang and other SHU leaders, April 2007

上海大学
Shanghai University

2007年1月12日，中国共产党上海大学第一次代表大会召开。党委书记于信汇向大会作题为《落实科学发展观 加强内涵建设 构建和谐校园 为推进学校持续健康快速发展而奋斗》的工作报告
The First CPC Congress of SHU, January 12, 2007

中国共产党上海大学第一届委员会全体委员合影
前排左起：副校长汪敏，党委副书记滕建勇，党委副书记、副校长李友梅，党委书记于信汇，党委副书记、常务副校长周哲玮，党委副书记、纪委书记忻平，副校长叶志明，副校长吴松；第三排左5：工会主席薛志良
Group photo of the members of the First CPC Committee of SHU

第三部分　自强不息　复兴跨越

2013年6月26日，中国共产党上海大学第二次代表大会召开。党委书记于信汇向大会作题为《解放思想 抓住机遇 锐意改革 开创建设高水平大学新局面》的工作报告（主席台首排左起：副校长吴松，副校长叶志明，校党委副书记、纪委书记忻平，校长罗宏杰，上海市教卫工作党委书记薛明扬，校党委书记于信汇，校党委副书记、副校长李友梅，校党委副书记鲁雄刚，副校长汪敏，校工会主席薛志良）
The Second CPC Congress of SHU, June 26, 2013

Shanghai University

2018年6月29日,中国共产党上海大学第三次代表大会召开。党委书记金东寒向大会作题为《牢记使命 自强不息 追求卓越 努力建设世界一流、特色鲜明的高水平大学》的工作报告
The Third CPC Congress of SHU, June 29, 2018

中国共产党上海大学第三届委员会全体委员合影
前排左起:党委宣传部部长胡大伟,党委教师工作部副部长张洁,副校长欧阳华,副校长吴明红,党委副书记、纪委书记段勇,党委书记、校长金东寒,党委副书记徐旭,党委副书记、副校长龚思怡,副校长聂清,副校长汪小帆(列席代表),党委统战部部长兼党委教师工作部部长曹为民
Group photo of the members of the Third CPC Committee of SHU

第三部分　自强不息　复兴跨越

2024年7月4日，中国共产党上海大学第四次代表大会召开。党委书记成旦红向大会作题为《赓续红色血脉　勇于担当作为　服务国家战略　为建设中国特色、世界一流大学不懈奋斗》的工作报告

The Fourth CPC Congress of SHU, July 4, 2024

中国共产党上海大学第四届委员会全体委员合影
前排左起：党委宣传部部长曾军，党委统战部部长兼党委教师工作部部长曹为民，副校长王从春，党委副书记、副校长胡大伟，党委副书记段勇，党委书记成旦红，党委副书记、校长刘昌胜，党委副书记、纪委书记周建军，副校长聂清，总会计师苟燕楠，组织人事部常务副部长沈艺

Group photo of the members of the Fourth CPC Committee of SHU

1994—2024 年校党政负责人更迭一览
SHU Leaders (1994–2024)

职　务	姓　名	任职年月	职　务	姓　名	任职年月
党委书记	吴程里 方明伦 于信汇 罗宏杰 金东寒 成旦红	1994.5—1998.10 1998.10—2005.6 2005.6—2014.11 2014.11—2017.9 2017.9—2019.5 2019.5—	党委副书记 纪委书记	毛杏云 杨慧如 孙路一 周鸿刚 沈学超 成旦红 周哲玮 俞　涛 忻　平 李友梅 滕建勇 鲁雄刚 夏小和 徐　旭 龚思怡 金东寒 段　勇 刘昌胜 欧阳华 胡大伟 周建军 廖由雄 周鸿刚（兼） 忻　平（兼） 夏小和（兼） 段　勇（兼） 周建军（兼）	1994.5—2001.2 1994.5—2001.2 1994.5—1996.1 1996.11—2005.6 2001.2—2007.1 2001.2—2005.6 2005.6—2011.12 2005.6—2006.8 2006.6—2014.10 2006.8—2016.5 2007.1—2009.7 2009.8—2014.5 2014.10—2018.1 2014.10—2019.7 2016.5—2022.1 2017.4—2017.9 2018.1— 2019.6— 2019.8—2024.4 2023.11— 2024.4— 1994.5—2000.4 2001.2—2005.6 2006.6—2014.10 2014.10—2018.1 2018.1—2024.4 2024.4—

续表

校　长	钱伟长	1994.5—2010.7	常务副校长	方明伦	1994.5—2005.7
	罗宏杰	2012.1—2015.6		杨德广	1994.5—1996.6
	金东寒	2015.6—2019.5		郭本瑜	1994.5—1995.8
	刘昌胜	2019.6—		周哲玮	2005.7—2012.1
名誉校长	严东生	1994.5—2016.9	副校长	沈学超	1994.5—2001.2
	黄宏嘉	1994.5—2021.9		龚振邦	1994.5—2002.2
				壮云乾	1994.5—2003.6
				黄　黔	1994.5—1996.5
				陈大森	1994.5—1995.5
				周哲玮	1996.5—2005.6
				周鸿刚	1996.11—2005.7
				夏玲英	1996.11—2002.2
				王　奇	1998.10—2000.12
				曹家麟	2001.2—2004.5
				金国华	2003.1—2005.7
				李友梅	2003.6—2016.6
				叶志明	2003.6—2014.9
				汪　敏	2005.7—2017.5
				唐　豪	2006.9—2016.6
				吴　松	2006.9—2013.7
				吴明红	2013.10—2024.1
				丛玉豪	2014.11—2017.5
				徐　旭	2014.11—2018.2
				龚思怡	2016.6—2022.1
				欧阳华	2016.6—2019.8
				段　勇	2017.5—2018.2
				聂　清	2017.8—
				汪小帆	2018.2—2023.9
				王从春	2022.1—
				胡大伟	2023.11—
				于雪梅	2023.11—
				张建华	2024.5—
			正局级巡视员	郭本瑜	1995.8—1999.8
			副局级巡视员	徐得名	1994.5—1995.12
				李明忠	1994.5—1995.12
				余忠荪	1994.5—1999.5
				汪国铎	1994.5—1996.11
				刘德重	1998.4—2002.2
				薛志良	2001.2—2014.1
				唐　豪	2001.2—2006.9
			总会计师	宋　彬	2015.6—2017.10
				苟燕楠	2019.4—

（二）思想建设　Ideological Construction

1999年4月1日，校党委召开全校中层干部会议，正局级巡视员、全国政协委员郭本瑜（右2）和全国人大代表江建中（右1）、全国政协常务委员邓伟志（右4）、全国政协委员陈明仪（右5）向大家传达全国人大九届二次会议和全国政协九届二次会议精神

A meeting of all mid-level cadres, focusing on the spirit of the second session of the Ninth National People's Congress and the second session of the Ninth National Committee of the Chinese People's Political Consultative Conference, April 1, 1999

2005年11月14日，召开党员先进性教育活动总结大会
The Concluding Conference of the Educational Campaign to Preserve the Vanguard Nature of CPC Members, November 14, 2005

第三部分　自强不息　复兴跨越

2008年10月20日，召开开展深入学习实践科学发展观活动动员大会
The campaign for Implementation of the Scientific Outlook on Development, October 20, 2008

2019年9月10日，召开"不忘初心、牢记使命"主题教育动员部署会
The launch meeting of the campaign themed "Staying True to Our Original Aspiration and Founding Mission", September 10, 2019

Shanghai University

2019年12月19日，上海大学发起成立全国红色文化战略联盟
The establishment of the National Red Culture Strategic Alliance initiated by SHU, December 19, 2019

2023年2月25日，上海大学中共党史党建研究院成立，校党委书记成旦红和中共上海市委党史研究室主任严爱云（左）为研究院揭牌
The unveiling ceremony of the Institute of CPC History and Party Building at SHU, February 25, 2023

第三部分　自强不息　复兴跨越

2023年4月14日，举办上海大学党委学习贯彻习近平新时代中国特色社会主义思想主题教育读书班

A thematic study session organized by the Party Committee of SHU, focusing on Xi Jinping Thought on Socialism with Chinese Characteristics for a New Era, April 14, 2023

2024年9月19日，召开党纪学习教育总结会

The Concluding Conference of the Party Discipline Education Campaign, September 19, 2024

（三）组织建设　Organizational Building

2021年5月，上海大学工会、妇委、组织人事部、党政办公室、对外联络处（校友办公室）、图书馆、博物馆、档案馆共同发起"上大师生心向党 同心接力绣党旗"活动。从5月12日到6月28日，先后有98个党支部1312名党员师生参与手绣。党旗以"国家级非物质文化遗产——上海绒绣"为载体，旗面共36500针，寓意100个365天，象征着中国共产党领导中国人民走过的100年光辉历程，彰显着上大师生永远跟党走的决心

The Party flag, featuring 36,500 stitches, was embroidered over 100 days using the technique of Shanghai velvet embroidery, a national intangible cultural heritage, showcasing the Party's glorious century of leadership and highlighting the cultural significance of traditional craftsmanship, lasting from May 12 to June 28, 2021 by 1, 312 SHU faculty and student Party members

2022年8月26日，举行上海市教委财务处党支部、上海大学财务处党支部、上海大学微电子学院党委结对共建签约仪式（右2：校总会计师苟燕楠）

The signing ceremony for the joint development partnership held among three Party branches, August 26, 2022

基层党组织和党员数量一览
Number of Party Organizations and Party Members

	1994 年 5 月	2024 年 12 月
二级单位党委	13	36
党总支	56	31
党支部	312	583
党员	3663	13025

党建工作荣誉一览
Party Building Achievements

荣誉名称	获得部门	授予单位	年度
1993—1998 党的建设和思想政治工作先进普通高等学校	上海大学	中共中央组织部、宣传部、国家教委	1998
全国党建工作标杆院系	上海大学理学院党委	教育部	2018
全国党建工作样板支部	上海大学通信与信息工程学院特种光纤与光接入网党支部	教育部	2018
全国党建工作样板支部	上海大学机电工程与自动化学院智能制造及机器人中心党支部	教育部	2019
全国党建工作样板支部	上海大学新闻传播学院本科生党支部	教育部	2022
全国党建工作样板支部	上海大学材料科学与工程学院特殊钢精炼教工党支部	教育部	2022
全国党建工作样板支部	上海大学机关财务处党支部	教育部	2022
全国党建工作样板支部	上海大学悉尼工商学院研究生经金党支部	教育部	2024
全国党建工作样板支部	上海大学力学与工程科学学院固体力学研究所党支部	教育部	2024
全国党建工作样板支部	上海大学国际部国际合作处党支部	教育部	2024
全国高校"双带头人"教师党支部书记工作室	上海大学思想政治教育教研部党支部书记工作室	教育部	2018
全国高校"百个研究生样板党支部"	上海大学社会科学学部2016级硕士研究生党支部	教育部	2019
全国高校"百个研究生样板党支部"	上海大学文化遗产与信息管理学院研究生第一党支部	教育部	2024
全国高校"双带头人"教师党支部书记"强国行"专项行动团队	上海大学通信与信息工程学院特种光纤与光接入网党支部	教育部	2024
全国高校"双带头人"教师党支部书记"强国行"专项行动团队	上海大学机电工程与自动化学院智能制造及机器人中心党支部	教育部	2024

（四）纪检工作　Discipline Inspection Work

2019年8月，上海大学被上海市纪委、监察委确定为监察职能向市管高校延伸试点单位。2020—2024年，校纪委（监察专员办公室）连续五年获评上海市管高校纪检监察机构考核"优秀"等次，校党委副书记、纪委书记、监察专员段勇、周建军连续五年获评上海市管高校纪检监察机构主要负责人履职专项考核"优秀"等次。2022年，校纪委副书记滕云获上海市纪检监察系统先进工作者、中央纪委国家监委嘉奖（上海高校唯一）。

In August 2019, SHU was selected as a pilot institution for extending supervisory functions to municipal-level universities. From 2020 to 2024, SHU's Discipline Inspection Commission was rated "Excellent" for five consecutive years. During this period, Duan Yong, Deputy Secretary of SHU Party Committee and Secretary of SHU Discipline Inspection Commission, and Zhou Jianjun, were also rated "Excellent" for five consecutive years in the performance evaluations for principal officials of municipal university discipline inspection and supervision agencies. In 2022, Teng Yun, Deputy Secretary of the Discipline Inspection Commission, received a commendation from the Central Commission for Discipline Inspection and the National Supervisory Commission, making her the only university official from Shanghai that won this honor.

2023年12月6日，校党委副书记、纪委书记、监察专员段勇在上海市廉洁文化建设工作会议上作交流发言

Duan Yong, Deputy Secretary of SHU Party Committee and Secretary of SHU Discipline Inspection Commission, delivering a speech at the Shanghai Municipal Conference on the Construction of a Clean Culture, December 6, 2023

2024年11月28日，校党委副书记、纪委书记、监察专员周建军（右2）为新任处级干部作专题廉政党课，并开展集体廉政谈话

Zhou Jianjun (second from right), Deputy Secretary of SHU Party Committee and Secretary of SHU Discipline Inspection Commission, delivering a theme lecture on integrity for newly appointed cadres, November 28, 2024

（五）统战工作 United Front Work

上海大学统战系统荟萃学术论坛是学校统战工作品牌，自2010年至今已举办十五届。图为2010年11月25日，校党委副书记、副校长李友梅（右）和致公党上海市委副主委、上海大学教授任忠鸣主持首次论坛

The inaugural SHU United Front System Academic Forum, November 25, 2010

2013年10月8日，全国人大常务委员会副委员长、民盟中央主席张宝文（左）与校党委书记于信汇为民盟上海市委、上海大学合作组建的费孝通学术思想研究中心揭牌

The unveiling ceremony of the Fei Xiaotong Academic Thought Research Center, October 8, 2013

2023年3月30日，学校获批上海市委统战部首批9个上海新时代党的统一战线研究基地之一。研究基地下设3个中心：中国共产党统一战线史研究中心、上海新的社会阶层研究中心、筑牢中华民族共同体意识理论研究中心（左3：校党委副书记、纪委书记段勇）

On March 30, 2023, SHU was enlisted as one of the first nine research bases for the Party's united front work in the new era in Shanghai by the United Front Work Department of the Shanghai Municipal Committee of the CPC. (Third from left is Duan Yong, Deputy Secretary of the Party Committee and Secretary of the Discipline Inspection Commission of SHU)

学校民主党派基层组织和统战团体
SHU's Organizations of Democratic Parties and United Front

民主党派基层组织	统战团体
民革上海大学委员会	上海大学归国华侨联合会
民盟上海大学委员会	上海大学少数民族联合会
民建上海大学委员会	欧美同学会上海大学分会
民进上海大学委员会	上海大学党外知识分子联谊会
农工党上海大学支部	
致公党上海大学委员会	
九三学社上海大学委员会	

百年上大　薪火相传

　　溯源奋进恰风华，百年传承再出发。上海大学精神给予上大人勇毅前行的信心和决心，以及追求卓越的智慧和力量。百年只是序章，未来必定可期，更将大有可为。

A Century of SHU: Passing the Torch

Rooted in our heritage, we stride forward with renewed vigor, embarking on a new century of progress. The SHU spirit instills in its members unyielding confidence, steadfast determination and the intellectual fortitude to pursue excellence. A century is merely the prologue—a future of boundless potential awaits, where greater accomplishments shall surely unfold.

一、百年奋进恰风华
A Century of Progress, a Flourishing Era

百年恰是风华正茂，百年初心历久弥坚。全体上大人汇聚在中国共产党的旗帜下，用奋斗和拼搏谱写一曲曲动人的乐章。

Over the past century, the faculty and students of SHU have united in dedication and perseverance, composing inspiring chapters through relentless efforts. Today, as we celebrate this milestone, our original aspirations remain steadfast, guiding us toward a future filled with promise and vitality.

2022年5月27日，举行纪念上海大学建校100周年暨庆祝上海大学新合并组建28周年升旗仪式

The flag-raising ceremony commemorating the 100th anniversary of SHU and the 28th anniversary of its merger, May 27, 2022

上海大学
Shanghai University

2022年7月1日,《纪念上海大学建校100周年活动公告(第一号)》在《光明日报》发布

"Announcement (No.1) of the 100th Anniversary Celebration of SHU" published in *Guangming Daily*, July 1, 2022

纪念上海大学建校100周年活动一览
Events for SHU's 100th Anniversary

时间	活动名称
2021年12月18日	"茶叙共话校友情·凝心聚力贺百年"——上海大学校友会"临泮茶会"暨校友座谈交流会
2021年12月19日	校党委书记成旦红接受《新华日报》专访:《一种为理想献身的精神》
2021年12月24日	纪念建校百年楹联征集
2021年12月29日	《溯源初心恰风华 百年传承再出发》在《光明日报》专版刊登
2021年9月—2022年6月	跨越百年的青春回眸——《他们从上海大学(1922-1927)走进新中国》读后感征文比赛
2022年1—11月	"弘扬创新精神,纪念建校百年"第五届本科生学术论坛
2022年2月22日	上海大学建校100周年IP形象和文创产品设计大赛
2022年2—10月	"百年伟业源流长,赤子之心耀前路"系列采访活动
2022年3月21日	纪录片《琼崖纵队》在央视《国家记忆》栏目播出
2022年5月27日	百年恰青春 奋斗正当时——直属单位系统纪念上海大学建校100周年红色咏诵
	纪念上海大学建校100周年暨庆祝上海大学新合并组建28周年升旗仪式
2022年6月25—26日	纪录片《惊涛》在安徽卫视播出
2022年7月1日	《纪念上海大学建校100周年活动公告(第一号)》在《光明日报》发布
2022年7月2日	纪念上海大学建校100周年活动标识发布
2022年8月5日	电影《孤星计划》(初名《星辰大海》)开机
2022年8月8日	天安门国旗受赠仪式(2021年10月23日上海大学成立纪念日在天安门广场升起的国旗)

时间	活动名称
2022年8月18日	百年统战——百年上大与党的统一战线政策的伟大实践研讨会
2022年8月21—23日	纪念上海大学建校100周年化学前沿论坛
2022年9月16日—2023年2月17日	大任于斯 伟业流长——纪念上海大学建校100周年成果展
2022年9月18日	红色学府·百年上大——上海大学粤港澳大湾区校友纪念母校建校百年座谈会暨上海大学深圳校友组织成立仪式
2022年9月20日、9月27日、10月11日	纪录片《红色学府——20世纪20年代的上海大学》在东方卫视播出
2022年9月22日—2023年8月	百年上大正青春——纪念上海大学建校100周年沉浸式艺术展
2022年9月23日	纪念上海大学建校100周年·全球大学校长论坛暨教育国际化高峰论坛
2022年9月23日—11月23日	肯登攀——纪念上海大学建校100周年陈家泠艺术邀请特展
2022年10月8日	百年党史 百年教育——中国共产党创办高等教育100年学术研讨会
2022年10月16日	《红色学府 百年初心》在《解放日报》整版刊登
2022年10月23日	久久溯源 百年传承——红色场馆与新时代高校协同育人工作创新论坛
	纪念上海大学建校100周年暨高质量发展论坛
2022年11月12日	"临泮书话·百年记忆"百年上大系列纪念活动
2022年11月12日—12月9日	书文雅墨——纪念上海大学建校100周年主题书法展

百年上大　薪火相传

2022年7月2日，发布纪念上海大学建校100周年活动标识
The logo for the 100th anniversary celebration of SHU released on July 2, 2022

2022年8月5日，以1922—1927年上海大学师生投身革命为历史背景的电影《孤星计划》（初名《星辰大海》）在上海大学开机，2024年12月7日电影正式在全国上映
Burning Stars (originally titled *Sea of Stars*), a film about SHU's revolutionary history (1922-1927), starting shooting at SHU on August 5, 2022 and released on December 7, 2024

2022年8月8日,天安门管委会向上海大学赠送2021年10月23日(上海大学成立纪念日)在天安门广场升起的国旗

The Administration of Tian'anmen Area presenting SHU with the national flag that was raised at Tian'anmen Square on October 23, 2021 (the anniversary of SHU's founding), August 8, 2022

2022年8月18日,举办"百年统战——百年上大与党的统一战线政策的伟大实践研讨会"

The academic seminar on "A Century of United Front Efforts: The Great Practice of the Party's United Front Policy at SHU", August 18, 2022

百年上大　薪火相传

2022年9月16日，"大任于斯　伟业流长——纪念上海大学建校100周年成果展"开幕

The opening of "Deepen Fine Tradition, Poised for New Start—Exhibition to Commemorate the 100th Anniversary of SHU", September 16, 2022

2022年9月20日、9月27日、10月11日，纪录片《红色学府——20世纪20年代的上海大学》在东方卫视播出

The documentary Red University: SHU in the 1920 saired on Shanghai Dragon TV on September 20, 27 and October 11 in 2022, highlighting SHU's role in revolutionary activities during the era

2022年9月23日，举办"纪念上海大学建校100周年·全球大学校长论坛暨教育国际化高峰论坛"

The Global University Presidents' Forum and Education Internationalization Summit in commemoration of the 100th anniversary of SHU, September 23, 2022

2022年9月23日，举行"肯登攀——纪念上海大学建校100周年陈家泠艺术邀请特展"开幕仪式，校长刘昌胜（右）代表学校接受上海大学教授陈家泠捐赠作品《和美》

The opening ceremony of "Daring to Climb—The Art Exhibition of Chen Jialing for SHU's 100th Anniversary", with President Liu Changsheng (right) accepting the donated artwork Harmonyand Beauty from Chen, former professor at SHU Shanghai Academy of Fine Arts, September 23, 2022

2022年10月8日,举办"百年党史·百年教育——中国共产党创办高等教育100年学术研讨会"

The academic seminar on the 100th anniversary of higher education founded by the CPC, October 8, 2022

2022年10月16日,《红色学府 百年初心》在《解放日报》整版刊登

A full-page feature titled "Red University: A Century of Original Aspirations", published in *Jiefang Daily* on October 16, 2022

2022年10月23日，举行上海大学学生创新创业实践基地启用仪式

The inauguration ceremony of the SHU Students' Innovation and Entrepreneurship Practice Base, October 23, 2022

2022年10月23日，承办"久久溯源 百年传承——红色场馆与新时代高校协同育人工作创新论坛"

The innovative forum on collaborative education between red memorial sites and universities in the new era, commemorating the 100th anniversary of SHU, October 23, 2022

百年上大　薪火相传

2022年10月23日，举办"纪念上海大学建校100周年暨高质量发展论坛"
The forum commemorating the 100th Anniversary of SHU and Focusing on High-Quality Development, October 23, 2022

2022年10月18日，北京大学为学校建校100周年发来贺信
A congratulatory letter from PKU to SHU for its 100th anniversary

2022年10月18日，清华大学为学校建校100周年发来贺信
A congratulatory letter from Tsinghua University to SHU for its 100th anniversary

百年上大　薪火相传

贺 信

值此上海大学建校 100 周年之际，谨向全体师生和广大校友致以热烈祝贺和诚挚的问候！

百年风雨历程，上海大学自强不息，海纳百川，形成了独具特色的办学机制和人才培养模式，为国家和社会培养了大批的人才，为祖国科教事业的发展做出了积极的贡献。

我由衷地相信，上海大学在党和国家的关怀下，在社会各界人士和广大校友的支持下，贯彻党的教育方针，坚持社会主义办学方向，励精图治，拼搏进取，建成世界一流、特色鲜明的综合性研究型大学的目标一定会早日实现。

祝愿上海大学的明天更加美好！

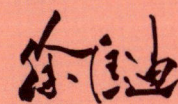

2022 年 10 月 18 日

2022 年 10 月 18 日，徐匡迪院士为学校建校 100 周年发来贺信

A congratulatory letter to SHU for its 100th anniversary from Academician Xu Kuangdi, former Mayor of Shanghai, President of the Chinese Academy of Engineering and lifetime professor of SHU

贺 信

秋光绚丽，金风送爽，在这美好的季节，我们共同纪念上海大学建校 100 周年。我谨代表中国人民解放军军事科学院，向上海大学全体领导、师生及海内外校友致以热烈祝贺和诚挚问候！

上海大学是我们党主导创办的第一所正规大学，也是一所有着悠久的历史文化和光荣的革命传统的红色学府。一百年来，上海大学始终坚持为党育人、为国育才，在中国革命、建设和改革的各个时期，都培养了一大批杰出人才，为国家的各项事业发展作出了卓越贡献。

展望未来，任重道远。衷心祝愿上海大学在未来的征程中，高举习近平新时代中国特色社会主义思想伟大旗帜，培养更多能够堪当民族复兴重任的时代新人，早日把学校建设成为与上海城市地位相匹配、世界一流、特色鲜明的综合性研究型大学。

期盼军事科学院与上大加强相关领域的交流合作，一同为实现中华民族伟大复兴的中国梦作出新的更大贡献！

军事科学院院长

2022 年 10 月，中国人民解放军军事科学院院长杨学军上将为学校建校 100 周年发来贺信

A congratulatory letter to SHU for its 100th anniversary from General Yang Xuejun, President of the Academy of Military Sciences of the People's Liberation Army of China

二、寻根溯源传薪火
Tracing the Roots, Igniting the Future

上海大学创办至今已逾百年。校友杨尚昆、阳翰笙、匡亚明、俞平伯、谭其骧，以及李硕勋与赵君陶之子李鹏，都曾为上海大学题词、发来贺电。校友李大钊、于右任、邵力子、邓中夏、瞿秋白、蔡和森、沈泽民、张太雷、恽代英、任弼时、杨贤江、李硕勋、赵君陶、秦邦宪、杨之华、林钧、张治中、张景曾、张庆孚、孔另境、周大根、糜文浩、沙文求、陈赓、江锦维、陶新畲、丁嘉树、杨秀涛、盛世铎等的后人纷纷来上海大学，追寻先人足迹，激励上大师生继承先辈遗志。

Since its founding over a century ago, SHU has received congratulations and inscriptions from notable alumni. The descendants of many distinguished figures, including revolutionary leaders and scholars, have since formed ties with the university. These individuals have traced the footsteps of their ancestors, recalled revolutionary history, and inspired the university's faculty and students to uphold the legacy of their forebears.

2014年10月23日，上海大学校长罗宏杰（左1）与于右任之子于中令（左3）、邵力子之孙邵美成（左2）、秦邦宪之女秦新华为"溯园·上海大学（1922—1927）"落成仪式揭幕

Luo Hongjie, President of SHU (first from left), along with Yu Zhongling (son of Yu Youren, third from left), Shao Meicheng (grandson of Shao Lizi, second from left), and Qin Xinhua (daughter of Qin Bangxian) at the inauguration ceremony of Suyuan, the SHU (1922-1927) Memorial Garden, October 23, 2014

2014年10月29日，丁嘉树之子丁勇（左）向上海大学博物馆捐赠父亲的毕业证书

Ding Yong (son of Ding Jiashu, left) donating his father's diploma to the SHU Museum, October 29, 2014

2020年10月13日，恽代英的孙女恽梅（右1）、穆为夫妇，孙女恽清（左1）、查文端夫妇，侄孙女恽凡青，侄孙恽铭庆（右2）、孟文慧夫妇，内侄恽甫铭、许士英夫妇向上海大学捐赠描述恽代英烈士生平事迹的书画。上海大学校长刘昌胜（左2）接受捐赠

Descendants of Yun Daiying donating books and paintings depicting his life to SHU, October 13, 2020

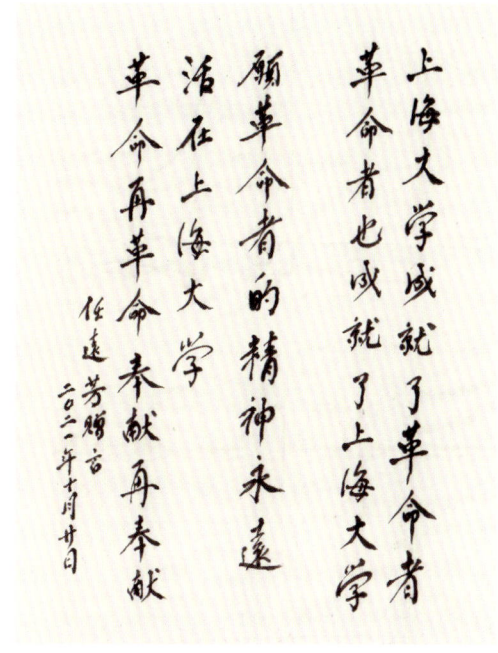

2021年10月23日，任弼时之女任远芳为上海大学题词

An inscription for SHU by Ren Yuanfang, daughter of Ren Bishi, October 23, 2021

2021年10月23日，中国共产党早期领导人研究中心成立。聘请任弼时之女任远芳，邵力子曾孙女邵巧云，恽代英孙女恽梅，秦邦宪孙女秦红（右1），瞿秋白、杨之华外甥女吴幼英（右3），张太雷外孙冯海龙（左3），陈赓之子陈知涯（左1）等校友后人，以及陈独秀孙女陈长璞（右2）、周恩来侄孙女周蓉（左2）为首批特约研究员，上海大学党委书记成旦红（左4）颁发聘书

The Research Center for Early Leaders of the CPC established, with Cheng Danhong (fourth from left), Secretary of SHU Party Committee, presenting appointment letters to the first group of special researchers, October 23, 2021

上海大学　Shanghai University

2021年11月14日，李大钊之孙、"七一勋章"获得者李宏塔（左图中）和瞿秋白与杨之华之女、"七一勋章"获得者瞿独伊（右图）被聘为上海大学名誉校董。上海大学党委书记成旦红（左图右）、校长刘昌胜（左图左）颁发聘书

Li Hongta (center), grandson of Li Dazhao and "July 1st Medal" recipient in the left photo, and Qu Duyi, daughter of Qu Qiubai and Yang Zhihua, also a "July 1st Medal" recipient, appointed honorary trustees of SHU, November 14, 2021

2022年10月23日，李大钊之孙、"七一勋章"获得者、上海大学名誉校董李宏塔，于右任侄孙女于媛，蔡和森与向警予孙女蔡予，恽代英孙女恽梅，孔另境之女孔海珠，邓果白之子邓伟志（左3），郭毅之子郭也平（左2），周大根之孙周亚南（右2），江锦维之子江兆平（右1）、江企平（左1），盛世铎之子盛昌旦（右3），陶新畲之女陶静等人出席纪念上海大学建校100周年系列活动

Descendants of notable alumni attending events commemorating the 100th anniversary of SHU, October 23, 2022

百年上大　薪火相传

2022年11月12日，举办"临泮书话·百年记忆"百年上大系列纪念活动，李大钊之孙李宏塔（第二排左6），蔡和森、向警予孙女蔡予（第二排右3），恽代英孙女恽梅（第二排右6），瞿秋白、杨之华外甥女吴幼英（第二排右4），孔另境长女孔海珠（第二排右5），盛世铎之子盛昌旦（第二排左2），周大根之孙周亚南（第二排左8），糜文浩侄孙糜强（第二排右2）等校友后人齐聚

Group photo of descendants of notable alumni gathering for the "Linpan Talk: Centennial Memories of Shanghai University" event to celebrate SHU's rich history, November 12, 2022

2023年10月22日，李硕勋与赵君陶的孙女李小琳参观上海大学校史馆和"李硕勋与赵君陶在上海大学期间的文献资料展"

Li Xiaolin, granddaughter of Li Shuoxun and Zhao Juntao, visiting the exhibition on their documentary materials at the SHU History Museum, October 22, 2023

上海大学的先辈和后辈跨越世纪的薪火相传
The Century-Spanning Torch Passing in SHU: From Predecessors to Successors

（一）邓果白和后人在上海大学　Deng Guobai and His Descendants at SHU

邓果白（1907—1967），1925 年秋进入上海大学社会学系学习
Deng Guobai (1907-1967) enrolled in Sociology Department of SHU in 1925.

邓伟志（1938— ），邓果白之子，上海大学终身教授、社会学系教授，第九届、第十届全国政协常委
Deng Weizhi (1938-), Deng Guobai's son, a lifetime professor of SHU and member of the Standing Committee of the Ninth and Tenth CPPCC National Committee

邓瞳瞳（1969— ），邓伟志之女，1987—1991 年在上海大学社会学系学习
Deng Tongtong (1969-), Deng Weizhi's daughter, studied at the Sociology Department of SHU from 1987 to 1991.

（二）郭毅和后人在上海大学　Guo Yi and His Descendants at SHU

郭毅（1905—1942），1924年进入上海大学社会学系学习

Guo Yi (1905-1942) enrolled in Sociology Department of SHU in 1924.

郭健（1931—2025），郭毅之侄，1988年2月—1989年7月在上海大学文学院学习

Guo Jian (1931-2025), Guo Yi's nephew, studied at the College of Liberal Arts of SHU from February 1988 to July 1989.

郭亮（1963— ），郭健之女，1985—2023年在上海大学工作

Guo Liang (1963–), daughter of Guo Jian, worked at SHU from 1985 to 2023.

郭唯博（1982— ），郭毅曾孙，2001—2005年在上海大学材料科学与工程学院学习

Guo Weibo (1982-), great-grandson of Guo Yi, studied at School of Materials Science and Engineering of SHU from 2001 to 2005.

（三）周颂西和后人在上海大学　Zhou Songxi and His Descendants at SHU

周颂西（1883—1965），1923年任上海大学中国文学系教授

Zhou Songxi (1883-1965), professor of the Chinese Literature Department at SHU, 1923

周正（1956— ），周颂西之孙，1978—1982年在上海工业大学冶金系学习

Zhou Zheng (1956-), grandson of Zhou Songxi, studied at the Department of Metallurgy at SUT from 1978 to 1982.

周力（1963— ），周颂西之孙，1981—1986年在上海工业大学电机系学习

Zhou Li (1963–), grandson of Zhou Songxi, studied at the Department of Electrical Engineering at SUT from 1981 to 1986.

（四）陶光潮和后人在上海大学　Tao Guangchao and His Descendants at SHU

陶光潮（1904—1975），1924年进入上海大学社会学系学习

Tao Guangchao (1904-1975) enrolled in the Department of Sociology of SHU in 1924.

孙语（2000— ），陶光潮曾外孙女，2019—2023年在上海大学经济学院学习

Sun Yu (2000-), great-granddaughter of Tao Guangchao, studied at the School of Economics of SHU from 2019 to 2023.

上海大学赋
Ode to Shanghai University

　　维以公元二〇二二年十月二十三日，岁在壬寅，时届上海大学百年华诞。泮池映日，丛菊临秋，四海师生咸感校泽，共庆嘉会。越明年，乃修《章程》，定校训，又新筑校史馆。以黉舍之经营，系国运之复兴，宜配文以颂之。乃述校史，并申其志，作《上海大学赋》，辞曰：

　　控江潮以望海兮，揽大洋于东方。垂云间之盛名兮，溯英灵于晋唐。变世局与声教兮，图新命于浦江。怀国运与民生兮，开吾校之滥觞。

　　惟以精诚交引，意气铿锵。允文允武，日就月将。齐北大之陈李兮，继五四之轩昂。输黄埔之将士兮，振统战之宏纲。峻哉右老，允承扶匡。董理青云，擘画谆详。悬羽纛以相招兮，会雄杰于一堂。延高士以执掌兮，更辅弼乎栋梁。立章程与宗旨兮，崇文化与贤良。燎工运之星火兮，举夜校于微茫。施化育于平民兮，觉精神于里坊。普权利于妇女兮，成勋绩于共襄。发革命之洪钟兮，铸五卅之辉煌。先瞿邓之向导兮，继何刘之慨慷。筹河山以重整兮，担群族之兴亡。

　　若夫蹈时代之先路兮，沐改革之初阳。幸徽名之有继兮，辟素域以复彰。乃合四校而为一，鼎三足而堂皇。先生子竞，肇建黌序，潜龙启蛰，早梅凌霜。钱公令德，识途知远，徐子佑佐，集梧鸣凰。凿泮池以敬师兮，临桃浦以徜徉。醉杨柳之依婉兮，品玉兰之馨香。思朱陆于鹅湖兮，辩庄惠于濠梁。筑群馆以储宝兮，聚册府之琳琅。有乐乎以迎宾兮，昭诗礼以呈祥。历四时之甘苦兮，纳五洲之棣棠。谋尽心以报效兮，毕此生而不忘。

　　况夫诸科兼备，名师荟萃，新知旧学，传习流芳。以数理为基础，施力学于国防。研新材以造物，觅上古之遗藏。赋智能于万器，运化电以游缰。筑广厦于九州，驰迅艇于汪洋。探生命之奥衍，疗痼疾而复康。察社会而明法，裕经济以通商。美光影与绘事，奏雅乐而绕梁。诵华章于盛世，著青史于上庠。迎晨曦以奋发，砺新锐之锋芒。继往圣之绝学，入文明之殿堂。振江海之强音，腾寰宇以翱翔。循乾坤之大道，共日月其永昌。

　　赞曰：巍巍吾校，弘毅自强。大任于斯，伟业流长。开物成务，厥志丕扬。风华超迈，鸣盛万邦。

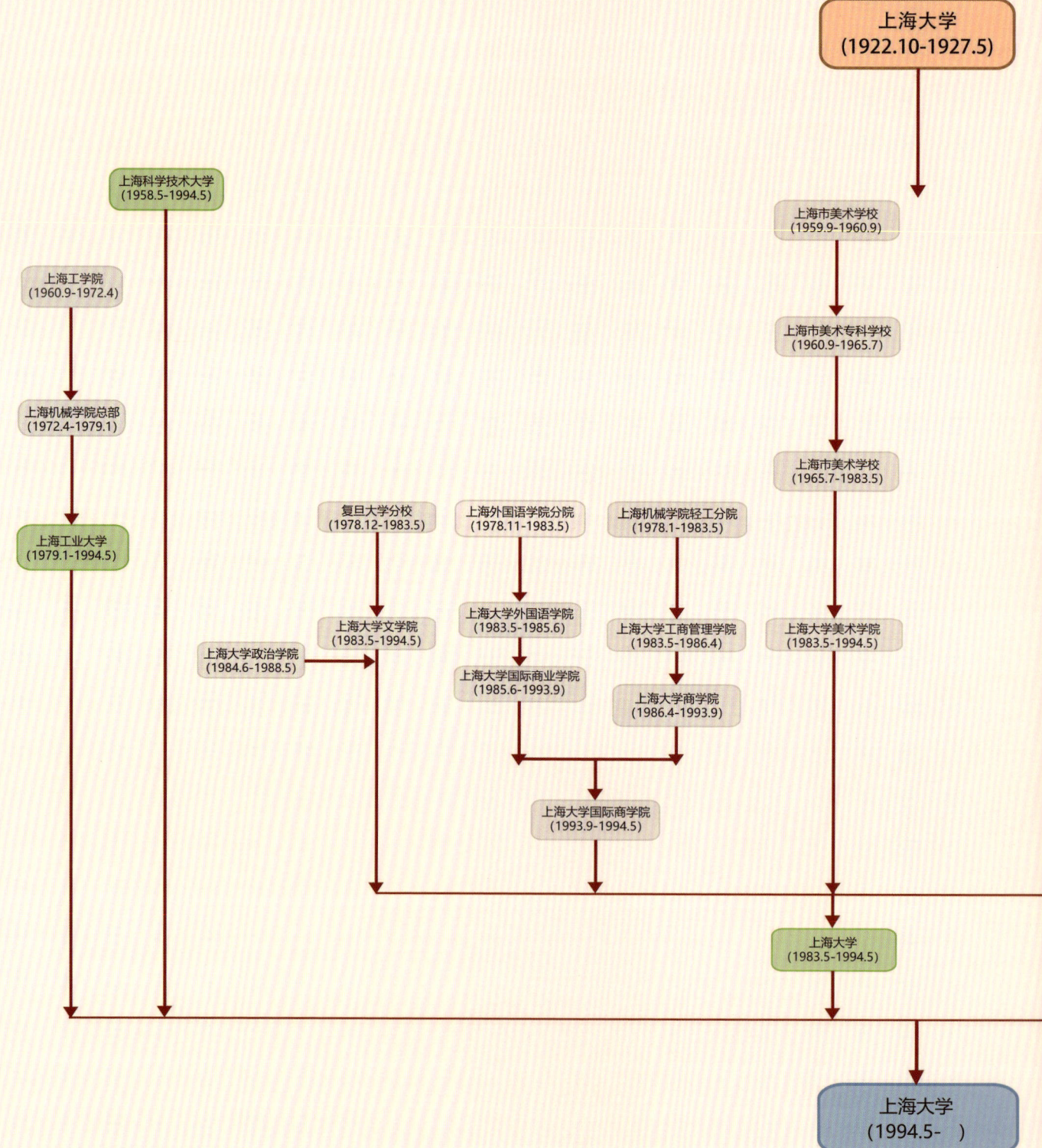

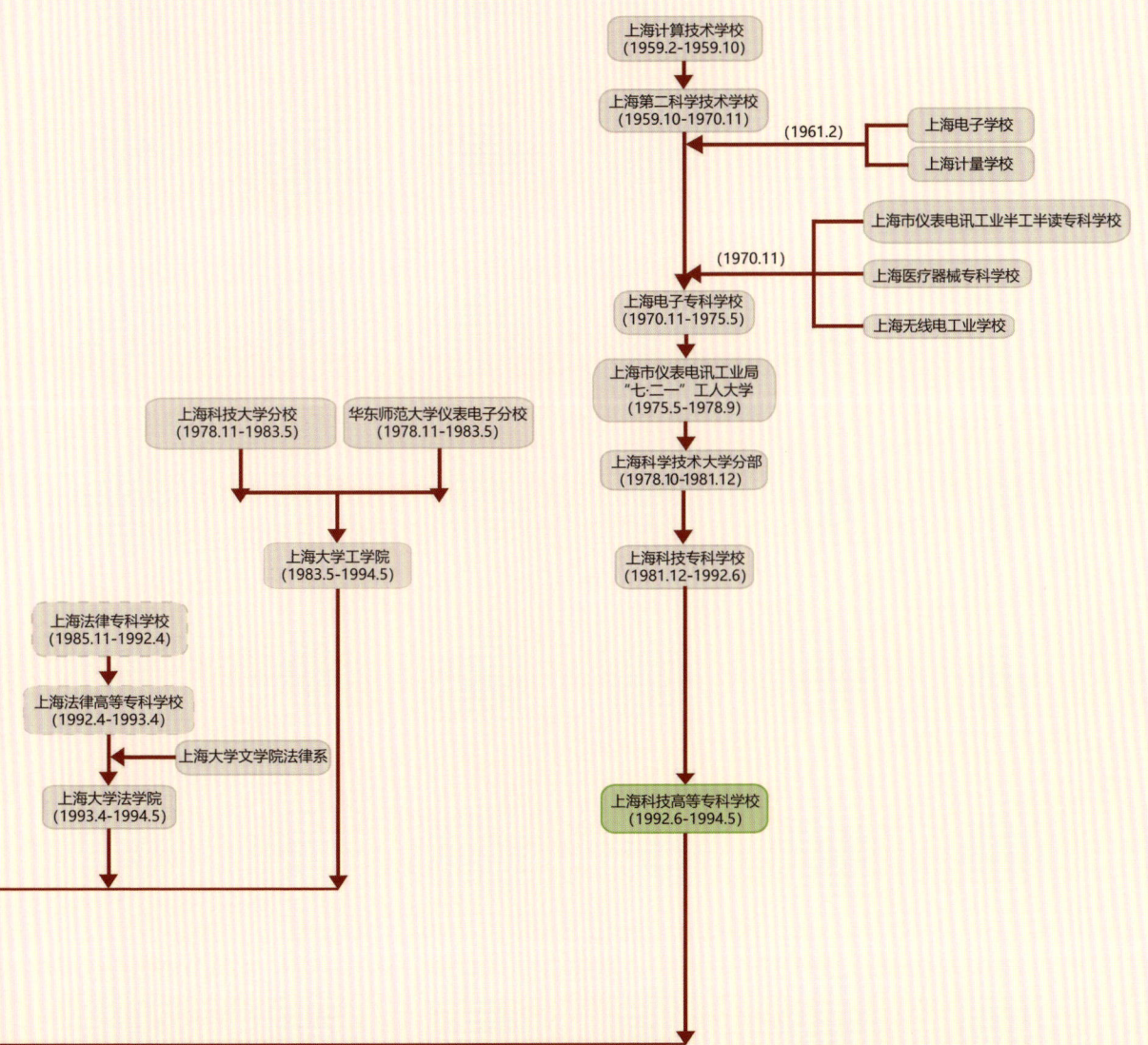

图书在版编目（CIP）数据

上海大学 / 本书编委会编． -- 上海：上海大学出版社，2025.4．--ISBN 978-7-5671-5210-6

Ⅰ．G649.285.1

中国国家版本馆 CIP 数据核字第 2025GE9664 号

责任编辑　傅玉芳　石伟丽
　　　　　刘　强　庄际虹
技术编辑　金　鑫　钱宇坤
装帧设计　柯国富

上海大学

本书编委会　编

出版发行	上海大学出版社
社　　址	上海市上大路99号
邮政编码	200444
网　　址	https://www.shupress.cn
发行热线	021-66135112
出 版 人	余　洋
印　　刷	上海颛辉印刷厂有限公司
经　　销	各地新华书店
开　　本	889mm×1194mm　1/12
印　　张	38
字　　数	760千字
版　　次	2025年4月第1版
印　　次	2025年4月第1次
书　　号	ISBN 978-7-5671-5210-6/G·3681
定　　价	380.00元

版权所有　侵权必究
如发现本书有印装质量问题请与印刷厂质量科联系
联系电话：021-57602918